# ROLES AND RELATIONS IN BIBLICAL LAW

# Roles and Relations in Biblical Law

## A Study of Participant Tracking, Semantic Roles, and Social Networks in Leviticus 17-26

*Christian Canu Højgaard*

https://www.openbookpublishers.com

©2024 Christian Canu Højgaard

This work is licensed under an Attribution-NonCommercial 4.0 International (CC BY-NC 4.0). This license allows you to share, copy, distribute, and transmit the text; to adapt the text for non-commercial purposes of the text providing attribution is made to the authors (but not in any way that suggests that they endorse you or your use of the work). Attribution should include the following information:

Christian Canu Højgaard, *Roles and Relations in Biblical Law: A Study of Participant Tracking, Semantic Roles, and Social Networks in Leviticus 17-26*. Cambridge, UK: Open Book Publishers, 2024, https://doi.org/10.11647/OBP.0376

Further details about CC BY-NC licenses are available at http://creativecommons.org/licenses/by-nc/4.0/

All external links were active at the time of publication unless otherwise stated and have been archived via the Internet Archive Wayback Machine at https://archive.org/web

Any digital material and resources associated with this volume will be available at https://doi.org/10.11647/OBP.0376#resources

Semitic Languages and Cultures 25

ISSN (print): 2632-6906
ISSN (digital): 2632-6914

ISBN Paperback: 978-1-80511-149-8
ISBN Hardback: 978-1-80511-150-4
ISBN Digital (PDF): 978-1-80511-151-1

DOI: 10.11647/OBP.0376

Cover image: A fragment of a Hebrew Bible manuscript (Leviticus 18.15-19.3) from the Cairo Genizah (Cambridge University Library, T-S A3.30). Courtesy of the Syndics of Cambridge University Library.
Cover design: Jeevanjot Kaur Nagpal

The main fonts used in this volume are Charis SIL, SBL Hebrew, and SBL Greek.

# CONTENTS

Acknowledgements .................................................... vii

Abbreviations ............................................................ ix

1. Introduction: Law as Literature—Literature as Social Network ...................................................... 1

2. Towards a Social Network Analysis of the Holiness Code .................................................. 9

3. Tracking the Participants .................................... 71

4. Semantic Roles and Decomposition of Agency ............................................................. 131

5. Dynamicity: A Collostructional Approach ......... 155

6. Causation: Instigation, Volition, Affectedness, and a Hierarchy of Agency ................................... 193

7. Participants in Social Networks ......................... 273

8. Conclusion: The Social Network of Leviticus 17–26 ............................................... 361

Bibliography .......................................................... 377

Indices .................................................................. 431

# ACKNOWLEDGEMENTS

This work would not have been completed without the help and support of many people. It was Nicolai Winther-Nielsen who first introduced me to Biblical Hebrew and the Hebrew Bible. He did so with a dedication that left a lasting impression, and his passion for the language and literature of the Bible keeps stimulating my own work. Later he came to co-supervise my doctoral dissertation, on the basis of which this book is written. I cannot thank him enough.

I am highly indebted to Eep Talstra, who kindly produced a participant-tracking dataset for Leviticus for the purposes of my research. He has left a lasting stamp on Biblical scholarship, and I hope the present book honours his legacy.

Thank you to the staff and researchers at the Eep Talstra Centre for Bible and Computer. A special thank you to Willem van Peursen for making my research possible, and to Dirk Roorda and Martijn Naaijer for their tireless assistance in programming.

Thank you to Margaretha Folmer, Eveline van Staalduine-Sulman, Jan Kleinnijenhuis, Laura Kallmeyer, and Benjamin Suchard for their insightful comments on an earlier version of this book.

Thank you to my colleagues at Fjellhaug International University College for their support in many different ways.

It has been a profound pleasure to work with the people of Open Book Publishers. Thank you to Anne Burberry for her diligent assistance in reading, revising, and copyediting the manuscript, Jeevanjot Kaur Nagpal for the cover design, and Alessandra Tosi for managing the publication process. A special thank you to the editor, Geoffrey Khan, who is not only a brilliant scholar whose insights and comments have stimulated my research and improved the quality of this book; he is also generous and caring, and it has been my great pleasure to get to know him.

My deepest thanks are to my wife, Miriam, for her enduring love and support during this research.

*Soli Deo Gloria*

# ABBREVIATIONS

## Abbreviations Related to the Hebrew Bible

| | |
|---|---|
| BH | Biblical Hebrew |
| CBH | Classic Biblical Hebrew |
| HB | Hebrew Bible |
| H | Holiness Code |
| HS | Holiness School |
| LBH | Late Biblical Hebrew |
| P | Priestly Code |
| TBH | Transitional Biblical Hebrew |

## Abbreviations Related to Grammar and Linguistics

| | |
|---|---|
| * | ungrammatical sentence |
| 1/2/3 | grammatical number |
| AFF | affectedness |
| D | *piʿʿel* |
| Dp | *puʿʿal* |
| F | feminine |
| G | *qal* |
| H | *hifʿil* |
| HtD | *hitpaʿʿel* |
| Hp | *hofʿal* |
| HsT | *hištafʿal* |
| INST | instigation |
| LOC | locative |
| M | masculine |
| N | *nifʿal* |

| | |
|---|---|
| NP | nominal phrase |
| PAct | participant actor |
| Pl | plural |
| PP | prepostional phrase |
| Pred | predicate |
| PRef | participant reference |
| PROC | processive |
| PSet | participant set |
| PTC | participle |
| Subj | subject |
| SEML | semelfactive |
| Sg | singular |
| UVF | univalent final |
| VOL | volition |

## Abbreviations Related to Statistics

| | |
|---|---|
| ¬ | negation |
| Σ | summation |
| MDS | multidimensional scaling |
| PCA | principal component analysis |

## Other Abbreviations

| | |
|---|---|
| BHSA | Biblia Hebraica Stuttgartensia Amstelodamensis |
| ETCBC | Eep Talstra Centre of the Hebrew Bible |
| RRG | Role and Reference Grammar |
| SNA | social network analysis |
| TF | Text-Fabric |
| WIVU | Werkgroep Informatica Vrije Universiteit |

# 1. INTRODUCTION: LAW AS LITERATURE—LITERATURE AS SOCIAL NETWORK

For most contemporary readers of Leviticus, the terse language, the strange treatment of impurities, the bloody sacrifices, and the harsh executions appear odd if not directly offensive. The poetic and prophetic portions of the Hebrew Bible may seem more appealing, perhaps more 'inspired'. Many scholars have the same impression of Leviticus and the other priestly sections of the Pentateuch (e.g., Exod. 25–40; Numbers). To mention but one classical example, Julius Wellhausen (1927; originally published 1883) regarded the priestly literature as a decay away from the heartfelt and authentic prophetic experiences of the early prophets of the Hebrew Bible. By contrast, in the later, priestly literature, the cult was merely "a pedagogic instrument for discipline."[1] Within the last three or four decades, however, new readings of priestly law and cult have emerged. Narrative, rhetorical, and anthropological studies of the book have uncovered a richness and rationality within the priestly worldview. It has been shown that Leviticus, far from being an arbitrary collection of

---

[1] "in der mosaischen Theokratie ist der Kultus zu einem pädagogischen Zuchtmittel geworden" (Wellhausen 1927, 423). For a recent, critical evaluation of the Wellhausenian 'axiom' of P as a decay from the "lively Deuteronomic religion," see Weinfeld (2004).

primitive laws, is in fact a literary composition in its own right that reflects a system of thought and values.[2]

Nevertheless, it has proven difficult to conceptualise the world view of Leviticus. For one thing, this world view is hardly ever explicated in the book itself. World views and values are often implicit and unconscious, and the priestly literature of the Hebrew Bible offers no exception in this regard. Motivational clauses are occasionally used with the laws, but most of them are never explained. The only recurring elements in any law are the *people* spoken to or referred to and the *actions* prescribed or prohibited. People and events are thus the most generic building blocks of the laws. Or, put differently, at the heart of the laws is a concern for people and their actions. It is a striking feature of the laws of Leviticus that they are often not general but situational, that is, they refer to specific people in specific situations. For example, the command "Every one of you shall fear his mother and his father" (Lev. 19.3) is not a general prescription of fear or reverence but specifically concerns how the intended audience of the law were supposed to treat their parents—not the other way round, as far as this law is concerned. The law is neither motivated nor reasoned, so how much can actually be deduced from it? Probably not that much. However, the mother and father of Lev. 19.3 are mentioned elsewhere in the law text, as are the audience ('you'), and they appear in a variety of relationships and interactions. Accordingly, it is possible to map the people and their interactions and begin scrutinising the roles of each

---

[2] I shall return to this development within Biblical scholarship (see chapter 2, §2.0).

person within the resulting network of people in interaction. The position of each person in the network reflects his or her status, power, and social capital. And since ethics is about the exercise of power, a mapping like the one imagined here opens the way for scrutinising the ethics of the text. This kind of analysis is known as social network analysis (SNA), and it is the purpose of this book to investigate the social network of Lev. 17–26, also known as the Holiness Code (H),[3] and survey the potential of this approach for analysing the ethics and values of an ancient law text.

The kind of social network analysis envisioned in this study represents a novelty within Biblical Studies, and it is far from the traditional source- and redaction-critical approaches that dominated the field for more than a century. Nevertheless, SNA is not completely unrelated to other approaches to Biblical law. Recent decades' narrative, rhetorical, and social readings of Biblical law form the backdrop of this study, with a common focus on making sense of the extant text. In the context of these approaches, SNA offers yet another strategy for reading the text, by paying special attention to participants and events. So, in chapter 2, I shall present the place of social network analysis among traditional and recent approaches to Biblical law. Within this context, the theoretical underpinnings of SNA will be presented and related to the study of ancient law texts. Chapter 2 will also relate the present

---

[3] When I use the label 'Holiness Code', I do not use it to refer to a documentary source or a redactional layer, but simply as a convenient designation for the extant text of Lev. 17–26. The scholarly debate on the origins of H will be summarised in chapter 2, §1.0.

work to previous attempts at analysing the people of H. Whereas most previous research on the participants of H has been aimed towards understanding the 'real', historical persons and towards dating the text or layers of the text, the social network characterisation of the participants proposed here is restricted to the text itself. While the participants may certainly refer to historical persons, I am primarily interested in how the participants are characterised by the author of the text and what role they play in the implied social community of the text. How, and to what extent, the implied social community refers to a historical setting is a secondary question in this respect and not addressed in this book. More interesting are the methodological challenges of creating a social network model of an ancient law text like H, and the remainder of this book is dedicated towards this goal. Chapters 3–6 address the fundamental methodological questions in turn, before chapter 7 presents the social network of H and fleshes out its implications.

Basically, a (social) network consists of nodes connected by edges. The resulting network forms a graph to be explored and analysed statistically for the purpose of deriving the properties of the network at large as well as the structural roles of the nodes. In previous applications of SNA to literature, it has been common to treat participants as the nodes and interactions as edges. Most commonly, participants and interactions have been tagged manually. While a similar procedure could be carried out for H, it would be problematic for several reasons. For one thing, H contains 4,092 individual linguistic references which need to be connected and linked to the textual participants in order to retrieve the nodes for the network analysis (Talstra 2018b). This task is known as participant tracking or participant resolution and is a complicated task, since BH—like any other natural language—has its own conventions with respect to participant references. Thus, a detailed study of the participant references and their linking to textual participants will be presented in chapter 3.

Secondly, the participants are connected by interactions, grammatically realised as predicates, e.g., speak, sanctify, kill, etc. H contains 936 predicates, corresponding to 181 different verbs. In SNA, edges are normally conceptualised as one particular form of connection, in order to reduce the complexity of the network to binary connections (e.g., who speaks to whom, or who is married to whom). In the SNA of H, all types of interactions are included, in order to be able to construe the role of a participant in light of all its interactions. Chapter 4 addresses the question of how one can compare two types of events. How should a speech interaction between two participants be interpreted *vis-à-vis* a cultic, economic, or emotional transaction between two other participants? The starting point of this inquiry is the linguistic theory of Role and Reference Grammar (RRG), which offers a framework for deriving semantic roles from the lexical aspect of verbs, also known as *Aktionsart*. In particular, two verbal features will be argued to be critical for quantifying events, namely, dynamicity and causation. Each of these will be explored in depth in order to identify correlations with the morphology and syntax of Biblical Hebrew: dynamicity in chapter 5, and causation in chapter 6. Finally, a hierarchy of semantic roles collects the insights yielded in chapters 4–6 and concludes the chapter.

Chapter 7 combines the efforts of chapters 4–6 to create a social network model of H. The social network will be explored using a variety of statistical measures in order to understand the structure of the community at large. In fact, two networks will be discussed and correlated: 1) an ordinary social network modelling participant tracking data and semantic roles (agency), and 2) a so-called control network that takes into account the roles of the participants with respect to their place in the syntactic structure of the text. The last section of the chapter zooms in on a selection of participants to demonstrate the method and to consider their roles in light of the network and their concrete interactions with other participants. Finally, it will be discussed how the social network relates to and sheds further light upon the ethical and theological values embodied in the text.

Chapter 8 concludes the book with an overall summary and a detailed evaluation of each of the methods applied, including participant tracking, event structure analysis, and social network analysis. Finally, new trajectories for research emerging from this study will be outlined.

The research carried out relies on the ETCBC database of the Hebrew Bible, formerly known as the WIVU database. The ETCBC database contains the Hebrew text of the scholarly edition of the HB, *Biblia Hebraica Stuttgartensia*, published by the German Bible Society. The text is richly augmented with linguistic features, most importantly, full morphological parsing of all constituents, part-of-speech tagging, phrase type and function, and clause type and function. A representation of the ETCBC database is publicly accessible as the *Biblia Hebraica Stuttgartensia Amstelodamensis* (BHSA; Roorda et al. 2019). The BHSA is available with Text-Fabric (Roorda et al. 2020), a Python package for processing ancient corpora, including, at the time of writing, the Hebrew Bible, the Samaritan Pentateuch, the Syriac Peshitta, the Dead Sea Scrolls, the Quran, transcriptions of Neo-Aramaic recordings, and archives of cuneiform tablets, among others. All datasets and programming scripts referred to throughout this book are available online (https://github.com/ch-jensen/Roles-and-Relations).

# 2. TOWARDS A SOCIAL NETWORK ANALYSIS OF THE HOLINESS CODE

## 1.0. The Holiness Code in Modern Scholarship

There is no question that Lev. 17–26 stands out from the rest of Leviticus. It is full of exhortations and motivations which distinguish this part of the book from the first half of Leviticus (and Exod. 25–40 for that matter). Most distinctive are the so-called divine *Selbstvorstellungsformeln* (אֲנִי יהוה 'I am YHWH'; e.g., Lev. 18.2), a term originally coined by Walther Zimmerli (1963), which occur 47 times in this text.[1] By contrast, this phrase occurs only twice in Lev. 1–16 (11.44, 45). The *Selbstvorstellungsformeln* function as strong, theological motivations for adhering to the law (Preuß 1985). Another distinct feature of Lev. 17–26 is the collation of groups of legislation in paraenetic frames in which the divine *Selbstvorstellungsformeln* are often placed, most evidently in Lev. 18.1–5, 24–30.[2] This part of Leviticus certainly has

---

[1] The *Selbstvorstellungsformeln* are formulated in varied ways, sometimes in connection with reference to the exodus: "I am YHWH your God, who brought you out of the land of Egypt" (19.36; 22.33; 23.43; 25.38, 42, 55; 26.13, 45); see also Müller (2015).

[2] Apart from the paraeneses in 20.7–8, 22–27, which seemingly mirror those in Lev. 18, the paraenetic frames in H are not undisputed. Otto (2009, 140) suggests 19.1–4, 36b–37; 22.8, 31–33; 25.18–19, 38, 42a, 55; 26.1–2. Grünwaldt (1999, 132), however, does not regard 19.3–4 and 20.27 as part of the paraenetic framework (see also Blum 1990, 319–22).

a particular flavour, or "besondere Farbe," in the words of Erhard Blum (1990, 319).[3] Structurally, moreover, the text resembles other legal collections in the Pentateuch: the Covenant Code in Exod. 20.22–23.33 and the Deuteronomic Code in Deut. 12–26 (Jürgens 2001, 126). All of these texts are characterised by introductory altar legislation concerning sacrifices, the place for sacrifices, and blood (Exod. 20.22–26; Deut. 12.1–14.21; cf. Lev. 17), and by concluding exhortations (Exod. 23.20–33; Deut. 27–28; cf. Lev. 26). In between, these texts contain various social and cultic legislation. Apart from its structure and *Farbe*, Lev. 17–26 is distinguished from the rest of the priestly material by its vocabulary, content, and style (see Joosten 1996, 6–7). Moreover, whereas the first half of Leviticus is concerned with the cult, "Lev. 17–27 offers another look at cultic procedures from the larger perspective of the community and nation as a whole" (Averbeck 1996, 914).

It was Graf (1866) who first argued for the original independence of these chapters.[4] According to him, Lev. 18–26 was originally an independent document authored by the prophet

---

[3] Unlike most previous scholars, however, Blum (1990, 319–22) was not led by this phenomenon to consider Lev. 17–26 an originally independent document or a later expansion of the priestly document (P). Rather, according to Blum, the high frequency of paraenetic material in Lev. 17–26 does not point to a qualitative difference from P, only a quantitative one. Blum argues that the paraenetic tone of Lev. 17–26 crucially depends on the content matter of these chapters. The paraeneses are not arbitrarily distributed but correlate with specific legislation.

[4] For an extensive review of previous research on the Holiness Code, see Sun (1990, 1–43; see also Tucker 2017, 10–28).

Ezekiel, an argument made on the grounds of linguistic similarities between H and the book of Ezekiel (1866, 81–83).[5] Graf was soon supported by August Kayser (1874, 64–79), who added Lev. 17 to the corpus, and by Wellhausen (1927; originally published 1883) who popularised the view as part of his new documentary hypothesis of the history and religion of ancient Israel. For Wellhausen, H marked a transition between early Deuteronomy and the later priestly document.[6] The name 'Holiness Code' (*Heiligkeitsgesetz*) itself was first coined by August Klostermann (1893).[7] Whereas Klostermann merely used the label as a convenient way to refer to Lev. 18–26, later generations of scholars willingly used

---

[5] To be sure, even before Graf, scholars had noted the distinctiveness of Lev. 17/18–26 (e.g., Ewald 1864, I:131–32, 140).

[6] "Jedoch die Sammlung Lev. 17–26 ist bekanntlich von diesem [i.e., the priestly redactor] nur überarbeitet und recipirt [*sic*], ursprünglich aber ein selbständiges Korpus, welches auf dem Übergange vom Deuteronomium zum Priesterkodex steht, bald diesem, bald jenem sich nährend" (Wellhausen 1927, 83 n. 1).

[7] Ironically, although the name 'Holiness Code' suggests otherwise, Klostermann (1893, 376–77) did not regard H as anything but a 'colourful mix of fabrics': "Daraus erklärt sich mir die unvergleichlich fragmentarische Natur, die bunte Mischung der Stoffe, der sonderbare Kontrast zwischen der in den identischen Formeln zu Tage tretenden Absicht, alles zu erschöpfen, und zwischen der wirklichen Lückenhaftigkeit, Unordnung und Unvollständigkeit des mit jener Tendenz Gegebenen, welche dem ausmerksamen Beobachter als charakterische Merkmale von Lev. 18–26 entgegentreten."

the name as designating a coherent, pre-existing law code.[8] For more than a century, the independence and integrity of the Holiness Code as a pre-priestly document remained almost undisputed.[9] The scholarly consensus, however, was shaken when Karl Elliger (1966) contended that H should rather be seen as a series of expansions (*Ergänzungen*) to the Priestly Code (P).[10]

In 1987, Israel Knohl published his article 'The Priestly Torah versus the Holiness School', which was soon to become very influential. Knohl argued that the differences between P and H were not merely distinctions or variations, but discrepancies requiring the conjecture that there existed a Holiness School (HS) with a polemical agenda against P. Thus, H now became the product of post-priestly Holiness redactors. Knohl's thesis was later substantially supported by Jacob Milgrom (1991; 2000; 2001; 2003) and marked a turning point within the scholarly debate on Leviticus. A group of scholars including Robert A. Kugler (1997), David P. Wright (1999; 2012), Christophe Nihan (2007),

---

[8] Early scholars include Wurster (1884), Kornfeld (1952), Elliot-Binns (1955), Reventlow (1961), Kilian (1963), Feucht (1964), and Thiel (1969). Most recently, Grünwaldt (1999) has revived the hypothesis.

[9] Not all scholars accepted the Graf-Wellhausen hypothesis. Hoffmann (1906, II:380–90) contended that there was no substantive difference between P and H. Also, Eerdmans (1912, 83–87) argued that Lev. 17 was not a fitting introduction to an independent law code and that the youngest parts of Lev. 17–26 did not constitute a coherent whole. Küchler (1929) objected that there was no internal structure justifying the notion of an independent code.

[10] Elliger's thesis was later supported by Cholewiński (1976), who noticed in H a general polemic against the so-called priestly *Grundschrift*.

Jeffrey Stackert (2007; 2009), and Reinhard Achenbach (2008) adopted and further developed the Knohl-Milgrom hypothesis. Most recently, Thomas King (2009), Megan Warner (2012; 2015; 2018), and Paavo N. Tucker (2017) have argued for a HS redaction in Genesis and/or Exodus.[11]

Although the contributions of King, Warner, and Tucker indicate a growing consensus assuming the existence of a late Holiness School, the Knohl-Milgrom hypothesis has not gone unchallenged. To begin with, others attribute the redaction of H to the final redaction of the Pentateuch rather than to HS (e.g., Otto 1994a; 1994b, 233–42; 2009; 1999; 2015). Furthermore, Baruch J. Schwartz (2009) has warned against assigning all redactional activity to HS, because it undermines the identification of H in the first place.[12] The most radical critique was raised by scholars

---

[11] King (2009) argues that the priestly narratives in Gen. 1–Exod. 6 were compiled by HS alongside the priestly legal material. Similarly, Warner (2012; 2015; 2018), with her focus on the ancestral narratives in Genesis, proposes that the redactional material in these texts, thought by some to be Deuteronomistic, could be attributed to HS. Tucker (2017, 29), relying on the assertion of Milgrom, Knohl, and King, among others, that Exod. 6.2–8; 29.43–46; 31.12–17 should be attributed to the H-redactor due to affinities with the Holiness Code, considers all the priestly material in Gen. 1–Lev. 26 a so-called 'H-composition'. In addition, in his commentary on Genesis, Arnold (2009) proposes HS as the final editor of Genesis.

[12] According to Schwartz (2009, 9), "if all redactional activity is automatically attributed to HS, the catalogue of features associated with HS will soon come to include a number of those having no connection with

who rejected the notion of a Holiness Code altogether. Henry T. C. Sun (1990), in an extensive redaction-critical study of H, concluded that the theory of an originally independent law code in Lev. 17–26 cannot be justified, due to the chapters' lack of internal coherence, the different dating of various sections, and, most importantly, the fact that no pervasive compositional layer throughout the entire text can be identified.[13] Erhard S. Gerstenberger (1996, 18) also denied the existence of H as a distinct source or redactional layer and dubbed the notion of an independent Holiness Code nothing more than a "wishful phantom of scholarly literature."[14]

---

H whatsoever and whose only qualification for inclusion among the literary features of the Holiness School is that they appear in redactional passages in the Pentateuch."

[13] A similar critique was already raised by Noth (1977, 12), who claimed that "Chapters 17 and following do not admit of division under major themes into sections classed according to content, as in the first half of the book. Here in general each chapter contains in itself more or less coherent groups of instructions relating to widely differing subjects" (see also Blenkinsopp 1992, 224).

[14] According to Gerstenberger, Lev. 1–10 follows logically after the construction of the sanctuary narrated in Exod. 35–40. The remainder of the book, however, seems to be arbitrarily ordered. For example, Gerstenberger (1996, 17) argues that one would expect the legislation on impurities (Lev. 11–15; 21–22) to be placed prior to the inauguration account (Lev. 8–9) rather than being interspersed around the book. Gerstenberger explains the "disparate structure" of Leviticus and other Pentateuchal material as the result of an extensive scribal process of composing the text from various sources. According to Gerstenberger (1996,

Similar conclusions were reached by a series of other scholars, although on a quite different basis. These scholars did not consider Lev. 17–26 a mere blend of laws, nor an independent law code or a post-priestly redaction. Rather, according to Blum (1990), the unit should be considered an integral part of the priestly composition of Gen. 1–Lev. 26, the so-called *priesterliche Komposition*.[15] Frank Crüsemann (1992) also rejected the traditional notion of an independent H, as well as Knohl's argument for a radical discrepancy between P and H. On the contrary, according to Crüsemann (1992, 323–25), Lev. 17–26 is closely connected to the priestly compositional layer and the overall Sinai legislation.[16] These objections echo the early critique by Volker Wagner (1974), who proposed an alternative structure of Leviti-

---

18), Lev. 16–26 "thus seems to derive from an extended process of collection and interpretation that is no longer transparent and probably took place quite independently of the composition of the first fifteen chapters."

[15] According to Blum (1990, 318–29), the occurrences of *Selbstvorstellungsformeln* ("I am Yhwh") and related statements outside H (e.g., Exod. 6.2–8; 12.12; Lev. 11.44–45) imply that these characteristic features cannot be used to identify H as a distinct source. Blum, therefore, concluded that the distinctiveness of Lev. 17–26 is not due to its exclusive use of exhortations and *Selbstvorstellungsformeln*, but rather to the concentration of these expressions within this text. Remarkably, the same observations led Knohl (1987) to argue for a Holiness School being responsible for redactions outside H.

[16] Nevertheless, Crüsemann (1992, 325) considers Lev. 17–26 "in der Priesterschrift ein relativ selbständiger Teil."

cus, treating parts of H as a subunit of previous priestly material.[17] In subsequent contributions, Blum and Crüsemann have been followed by Rainer Albertz (1994; 2012; 2015) and Andreas Ruwe (1999).

The 1990s witnessed a boom of novel, synchronic readings of Leviticus. Despite their obvious differences, a common denominator of these studies was the quest to grasp the rhetorical intent of the final form of the text. In other words, far from seeing the ritual and social laws as arbitrarily scattered throughout the book, scholars began to consider these laws to have been purposefully employed and structured by an author or editor. Mary Douglas (1993; 1995; 1999) pioneered a new way of reading Leviticus. Since her work also relates more specifically to new literary trends, a more detailed account of her work is provided below (§2.0). Erich Zenger (1996a) suggested a seven-fold chiastic structure of Leviticus, based on linguistic similarities and differences in the speech-introducers in Leviticus, as well as the subscriptions of the passages.[18] Since he subsumes chapters 16–17

---

[17] Wagner (1974, 314) divided Exod. 25–Lev. 25 into four major sections: Blueprint and inventory of the sanctuary (Exod. 25–31); rituals (Lev. 1–7); cultic impurities (Lev. 11–22); calendar (Lev. 23–25). Somewhat similar is Ska's (2001, 346–49) macrostructure of Leviticus, dividing it into two major units: inauguration of the cult (Lev. 1–10) and ethical prescriptions (Lev. 11–27). The latter unit can be divided into four blocks: Lev. 11–15; 16; 17–24; 25–27.

[18] The seven-fold structure proposed by Zenger (1996b, 37; 1999) consists of concentric rings around Lev. 16–17: A: Sacrifices (Lev. 1–7); B:

## 2. Towards a Social Network Analysis of the Holiness Code

into one coherent unit marked by "starke sprachliche, vorstellungsmäßige und strukturelle Querverbindungen" (Zenger 1999, 64), his argument brings into question whether Lev. 17 can reasonably be regarded as an introduction to H as a distinct unit.[19] Christopher R. Smith (1996) likewise proposed a seven-fold structure of Leviticus, in this case from the viewpoint of genre. Apart from noting that the legal material of the book is clustered into collections of related material, signalled by conclusions, final exhortations, summaries, compliance reports, and speech-introductions, he claimed that the material was organised at an even higher level, genre. Accordingly, Smith proposed a seven-fold structure of Leviticus based on alternations between law and narrative.[20] A rather different approach to reading Leviticus is found in the work of Wilfried Warning (1999), who investigated patterns of word repetitions. In addition to identifying lexical patterns within smaller textual units, he also found lexical patterns spanning larger segments of the book, even crossing the tradi-

---

Priests (8–10); C: Everyday life (11–15); D: Atonement (16–17); C': Everyday life (18–20); B': Priests (21–22); A': Sacrifices and festivals (23–26; 27).

[19] Along similar lines, Britt and Creehan (2000) argued for considering Lev. 16 and 17 to be a compositional unit. They supported their claim by suggesting that 16.30–17.11 forms a chiasm, thus effectively bridging the two chapters.

[20] Smith's (1996) suggested structure is as follows: Lev. 1–7 (law); Lev. 8–10 (narrative); Lev. 11–15 (law); Lev. 16 (narrative); Lev. 17.1–24.9 (law); Lev. 24.10–23 (narrative); Lev. 25–27 (law). His proposal, however, requires Lev. 16 to be a narrative, which is questionable.

tional boundaries between P and H. One example is the distribution of the lexeme יצק 'pour', which occurs eight times in Leviticus and, according to Warning (1999, 136–38), forms a chiastic structure.[21] Whereas the three first and the three last occurrences deal with the pouring out of oil, the two middle attestations concern the pouring out of blood. According to Warning, this chiastic structure, centred around the pouring out of blood, suggests that the distribution of יצק 'pour' is no mere accident. The first seven instances of יצק are found in P, and the eighth is found in H; hence, if the distribution of יצק is indeed evidence of a creative author/redactor, a clear-cut distinction between P and H is compromised. Finally, in his identification of a sabbatical calendar constituting the backbone of the priestly *Grundschrift*, Philippe Guillaume (2009) breaks down the traditional distinction between P and H, because Lev. 23 and 25 are added to this calendar.[22] According to Guillaume, the sabbatical calendar ranges from the creation week (Gen. 1) to the Passover celebration in Canaan (Josh. 5), and, while the non-sabbatical elements of the Pentateuch do not comprise a coherent narrative, the priestly sabbatical calendar—including Lev. 23 and 25—does.[23] According to

---

[21] יצק 'pour' occurs in Lev. 2.1, 6; 8.12, 15; 9.9; 14.15, 26; 21.10.

[22] Guillaume argues for a priestly *Grundschrift* underlying the extant text from Gen. 1–Josh. 18.

[23] It should be noted, however, that in reconstructing the basic priestly *Grundschrift*, Guillaume (2009, 12) disregards intervening, non-priestly material. Thus, while the claimed 'coherent narrative' is argued to be a once independent source, it now appears as a redactional layer in the extant text.

Guillaume (2009, 168), this suggests that the sabbatical calendar is not a secondary addition to the *Grundschrift* but its *"raison d'être."*

To summarise, then, the history of research on the composition and origins of Lev. 17–26 displays a trajectory not unusual for Biblical scholarship. While the vast majority of critical scholars maintained and supported the idea of an originally independent, pre-priestly Holiness Code for more than a century, the first major objections to this idea in the 1960s eventually led to a lack of any consensus whatsoever. Today, scholars could hardly be more divided over this question, ranging from those who assume the Knohl-Milgrom hypothesis almost as an axiom, and who further the hypothesis of a Holiness School responsible for editing most parts of Genesis–Leviticus, to scholars who propose novel suggestions for structuring Leviticus irrespective of the traditional boundary between P and H. Finally, one group of scholars has rejected both the idea of a redactional layer associated with H and the notion of coherence in Lev. 17–26, and in the entire book for that matter. Thus, while probably no one would question that Lev. 17–26 distinguishes itself by its paraenetic style, emphasis on holiness for the entire people, and resemblance to other legal collections of the Pentateuch, there is no consensus about what to make of these features.

## 2.0. Leviticus as Literature

Biblical scholarship has seen another development during the last three or four decades. As a consequence of the disappointing results of classical source- and redaction-critical approaches and an increasing interest in the authors of the received text, Biblical scholars began turning to synchronic readings of the extant text.

There was a growing awareness that the Biblical text as we now have it is not just a compilation of disparate sources, but the creative product of an author or authors. With respect to Biblical law, historical-critical scholarship had (and has) a tendency to distinguish narrative and law, often considering the narratives of the Pentateuch to be the earliest layers and the laws later expansions. Rhetorical criticism, on the other hand, is occupied with the extant text and aims to investigate the meaning of the text at large.[24]

From a literary point of view, then, Leviticus is a book in a five-book collection, the Pentateuch.[25] Even more than that, Leviticus is commonly seen as the central book around which the

---

[24] "The techniques of literary criticism are necessary to appreciate the organisation of a piece of literature, the ideas it embodies, and the standpoint of the writer. Rhetorical criticism links the concerns of literary and historical criticism. It attempts to show how an author writing in a particular context organised his work to try to persuade his readers to respond in the way he wanted" (Wenham 2000, 3).

[25] Whether Leviticus is a book in its own right or the result of a somewhat arbitrary division of the Pentateuch into five pieces is the topic of much scholarly debate. For one thing, the narrative of Leviticus is part of the Sinai story (Exod. 19.1–Num. 10.10; see Ruwe 2003), as indicated by the opening sentence of Leviticus, וַיִּקְרָא אֶל־מֹשֶׁה 'and he called upon Moses', a narrative form without explicit subject—a rather unusual introduction to a book. This train of thought has led to the argument that the five books of Moses do not form a Pentateuch but a Triptych, and that Exodus–Leviticus–Numbers is just one book (Koorevaar 2008). On the other hand, it has been argued that Num. 1–10 is related more

storyline of the Pentateuch evolves (Zenger 1996b, 36). The book is framed by wilderness accounts, describing the exodus and arrival at Sinai (Exodus), and the departure from Sinai (Numbers). An outer frame depicts the creation and promises of the land (Genesis) and instructions for living in the promised land (Deuteronomy). These frames set the Sinai revelation in Leviticus at the centre of the entire Pentateuch. Numerous proposals as to the structure of Leviticus have been made. Some consider the inauguration of the cult to be the climax of Leviticus (Watts 1999; 2013; Ruwe 2003), others the Day of Atonement (Smith 1996; Zenger 1996b; 1999; Warning 1999; Jürgens 2001; Morales 2015), and others the 'holiness chapter', chapter 19 (Douglas 1993; 1995; 1999; Kline 2005; 2015). Nihan (2007, 109) sees a linear development of "Israel's gradual initiation (by Yahweh himself) into the requirements of the divine presence" in three successive stages: 1) the public theophany as a divine response to the inauguration of the priesthood (Lev. 9.23–24); 2) the theophany inside the inner sanctum (Lev. 16.2); and 3) the promise that YHWH will walk in the midst of his people (Lev. 26.12). Thus, the debate on the structure of Leviticus and its role within the composition of the Pentateuch is far from settled.

---

closely to Exod. 19–40 than to Leviticus, and that the division of the Pentateuch into five books bears on thematic and conceptual differences (Nihan 2007, 69–74; Blum 1990). Moreover, a number of studies have proposed separate structures for Leviticus, assuming the book to form a cohesive whole (Douglas 1993; 1995; 1999; Smith 1996; Zenger 1996a).

More generally, literary and narrative approaches tend to struggle with the fact that laws comprise the vast majority of the text in Leviticus. In his commentary on the Pentateuch, John H. Sailhamer (1992) exposited the five books of the Pentateuch as a narrative by emphasising narratological devices, such as parallel structures, narrative plot, and recurrent *Leitwörter*.[26] This approach works well in Genesis and Exodus, which are predominantly formed by narratives. As for Leviticus, Sailhamer demonstrated a number of significant parallels between the primeval history (Gen. 1–11) and Leviticus. Thus, according to Sailhamer, the narrative of Leviticus is purposefully crafted as a continuation of the story begun in Genesis. Nevertheless, Leviticus is not lent much space in the commentary in comparison to Genesis and Exodus, probably due to the fact that Leviticus is considerably more difficult to interpret with traditional narratological tools.[27]

The deficiencies of narratological readings acknowledged, other strategies were applied to capture the structure and message of Leviticus. The pioneer of this trend was Douglas (1993; 1995; 1999), who advanced the idea of analogical reading. According to Douglas (1999, 15–20), Leviticus has been completely misunderstood, because the structure and the rationale of the book were investigated from a Western point of view. While

---

[26] As an example of Sailhamer's (1992, 143) narratological hermeneutics, repetitions are interpreted as rhetorical means by which it is emphasised that "the matter has been firmly decided by God and that God will act quickly to bring about his promise."

[27] The same critique can be levelled against the narratological readings by Clines (1978) and Mann (1988); see Watts (2013, 48).

Westerners are used to reasoning in terms of causality, logical entailments, and abstractions, analogical reasoning works through correlations, that is, one phenomenon is given meaning by its correlation to another phenomenon. By implication, meaning evolves gradually and circularly and not according to a linear, narrative plot. According to Douglas, the most significant analogy with which to capture the deeper meaning of Leviticus is the analogy of the Tabernacle. In particular, she argued for structuring Leviticus according to three concentric rings correlating to the tripartite division of the tabernacle. In light of this analogy, it is not surprising that the theme of holiness, normally attributed to the Holiness Code, is far more explicit in the latter half of the book. By analogy, in chapters 18–20, the reader has now entered the Sanctum from the courtyard of the sanctuary and, in 25–27, proceeds to the Holy of Holies.

Douglas' proposal has not gone unchallenged, but she certainly became a great inspiration for interpreters of Leviticus.[28] A decade later, Moshe Kline (2008; 2015) likewise proposed structuring Leviticus according to three conceptual rings, seeing chapter 19 as the centrepiece—the 'fulcrum'—of Leviticus. According to Kline (2015, 243), the 'fulcrum' is surrounded by three concentric rings: an inner ring (Lev. 16–18; 20.1–22.25), a middle ring (8–12; 22.26–24.23), and an outer ring (1–7; 25–27). This structure is analogous to that of the Taberacle, such that, by delving into Leviticus, the reader gradually approaches the Holy

---

[28] Douglas' novel ideas occasioned the anthology *Reading Leviticus: A Conversation with Mary Douglas* (1996). For critical evaluations of Douglas' approach, see Watts (2007, 15–27) and Nihan (2007, 84–85).

of Holies. Thus, like Douglas, Kline argued that the book should be read not linearly but rather according to its conceptual rings and the textual 'weave' they constitute. The intriguing structures proposed by Douglas and Kline have not met widespread acceptance. One reason might be that Douglas' three proposals were all different, indicating that an analogical reading is somewhat subjective and lacks linguistic evidence. Moreover, it is curious that, in contrast to other ancient literature, Leviticus never explicates the analogies (see Watts 2013, 49).

Nevertheless, narratological and analogical readings of Leviticus paved the way for a new appreciation of Leviticus as literature. Although none of the paradigms reviewed above have gained widespread recognition, they signal the beginning of paying more attention to narratological and rhetorical features and of appreciating the entire text with its curious mix of rituals, social laws, speeches, narratives, and exhortations.

## 3.0. Law as Rhetoric

Rhetorical analysis of Biblical law is another strategy for reading the extant text and grasping its meaning and intention. However, whereas narrative approaches tend to prioritise the narrative storyline of the text, rhetorical analysis does not necessarily prioritise one genre over the other. Indeed, one strength of rhetorical analysis is its potential for revealing how different genres work together rhetorically in the final form of the text. In his *Reading Law* (1999), James W. Watts explored the rhetoric of the Pentateuch, in particular with respect to the rhetorical effects of combining narrative, laws, and exhortations. According to Watts, the combination of narrative (story) and law (list) is one of the strongest features in the persuasiveness of the Pentateuch. Drawing upon the work of John D. O'Banion (1992), Watts (1999, 38–39) argued that laws and narratives are interdependent in order to achieve the highest possible level of persuasion. While lists are powerful tools for systematic expressions of any kind, including laws, they need the justification and explanation provided by narratives. Narratives, although not void of ethics, cannot stand alone if they are to persuade because they do not directly dictate or prohibit any action.[29] Thus, "The story alone may inspire, but to no explicit end. The list alone specifies the desired actions or beliefs, but may not inspire them" (Watts 1999, 45). Besides these two elements, Watts (1999, 45) points to divine sanction as a third component of Pentateuchal rhetoric. The Pentateuch appeals to YHWH and his blessings and curses as rhetorical means of impressing the audience. This phenomenon is especially apparent in Deuteronomy, but also in H, which concludes with an appeal to the audience to obey the law, enacted by means of invoking divine sanctions (Lev. 26). The priestly legislation (Exod. 25–Num. 9) at large makes use of all three rhetorical components, although it is dominated by lists (Watts 1999, 52–55). While the lists describe the ideal priesthood and ideal community in blessed

---

[29] Wenham's *Story as Torah* (2000) is a similar account of the relationship between law and narrative, yet from the opposite perspective. In his book, Wenham explores the books of Genesis and Judges with an eye to their ethical implications. His work also illustrates that narratives require more (and a different kind of) interpretation in order to grasp their underlying ethical messages than do law texts.

coexistence with YHWH, the narratives intruding the lists illustrate the dangers of disobedience. The only exception is Lev. 8–9, which, according to Watts (1999, 54), is the climax of the entire Pentateuch and "narrates the fulfilment of the priestly ideal in the Tabernacle worship." The idealism and the warnings come together in Lev. 26, although the warnings occupy most of the space. However, through reference to YHWH's promises to the ancestors (Lev. 26.42–45), the entire discourse "becomes more than a statement of obligations enforced by threats; it unveils a vision of hope grounded in YHWH's covenant commitment to Israel" (Watts 1999, 55). The same three components can explain the structuring of the Pentateuch as a whole, beginning with the long stretches of narratives in Genesis and Exodus, followed by the priestly legislation, and concluded by the divine sanctions in Deuteronomy. The "intent and effect" of this composition, along with other rhetorical devices, are to "persuade readers to accept it as *The Torah* and use its norms to define themselves as Israel" (Watts 1999, 156; italics original).[30] According to Watts (1999, 88), then, although the composition of the Pentateuch is complex and its origins even more so, the narratives, laws, and exhortations together "create the rhetorical force of Torah."

---

[30] As for Leviticus, Watts (2013, 98) argues that its rhetorical intent is "the authority of Torah and the legitimacy of the Aaronide priests' monopoly." It has been questioned, however, whether the Pentateuch (and Leviticus in particular) was indeed composed by Aaronide priests to legitimate their monopoly (Gane 2015). After all, the priests do not play the most significant role in the social network implied by Lev. 17–26 (a point to be discussed in chapter 7, §5.1.4).

The rhetoric of law and narrative has also been explored from the perspective of ritual theory, in particular by Bryan D. Bibb in his *Ritual Words and Narrative Worlds in the Book of Leviticus* (2009). While synchronic approaches to Biblical literature have sometimes—if not often—been aimed at smoothing out the 'knots' of the texts, it is safe to say that Bibb goes in another direction. According to Bibb, the literary quality of Leviticus as it now stands is in fact due to the very internal tensions that have so often tempted modern critics to drive fissures into the book. One of the most striking features of Leviticus is its blend of narrative and ritual. That is, Leviticus contains narrative descriptions of rituals but also seemingly timeless prescriptions of ritual performance. Thus, Leviticus cannot be reduced to either descriptive or prescriptive, narrative or law. As Bibb (2009, 34) puts it, "Leviticus is not a priestly manual, a descriptive account of ritual behaviour, or a fictional narrative with literary purposes. Actually, to some degree it is all of these things, but none of them define the book. These various generic elements interact in the final mix of the book to form a genre called here 'narrativized ritual'." The blend of narrative and (ritual) law is not supposed to negate either element. As Bibb (2009, 37) describes, the implied reader of Leviticus, the later Israelite, reads a description of rituals to be performed by his ancestors; however, the laws are not merely descriptive but "normative descriptions of the past." Put differently, "historic instructions to the ancestors function as ongoing requirements for the descendants." Thus, by means of its narrative style, the text creates a gap between past and present, but at the same time it also bridges the gap by connecting the reader with the glorious past of the ancestors. In the words of Bibb (2009, 57), "The interplay between ritual and narrative construct a ritual world in the past that the present reader can inhabit, creating a literary world in which temporal distinctions are meaningless." Bibb also addresses the visible tension between the two halves of Leviticus. Whereas chapters 1–16 predominantly restrict holiness to the priestly domain, chapters 17–27 broaden holiness to a quality to be strived for by the entire community, most explicitly stated in 19.2: "You shall be holy, because I, YHWH your God, am holy," addressing the whole congregation. While the borders of holiness are thus transcended, the old borders nevertheless still remain. On the one hand, the entire community is to be holy, and all of the Israelites are responsible for adhering to the law, for example, to distinguish clean and unclean animals. On the other hand, even in H, the special requirements for priests still remain.[31] This tension suggests that the cultic holiness established in the first half of Leviticus is maintained in the latter half alongside an apparent expansion of the concept. Thus, holiness is a dynamic concept that creates a tangible tension in the text. According to Bibb (2009, 164), far from undermining the literary quality of Leviticus, the tension rather adds to it:

---

[31] There are precise regulations for when the priests can access the altar (Lev. 22.1–9), and lay people are certainly not allowed. There are strict rules as to whom the priests can marry (21.7), and even stricter rules for the high priest (21.13–15). For a general account of the priestly conception of holiness, see Jenson (1992).

> The temptation has been to draw the contrast between these two sections (P and H) too sharply, and to see each as part of its own theological and social world. Rather, the second half of the [sic] Leviticus addresses different topics while using much of the same language, giving rise to a dynamic tension through which each half of the book transforms and interprets the other.

Thus, in a ritual reading of Leviticus, the gaps, tensions, and inconsistencies of the text do not negate the book as a piece of literature. Rather, according to Bibb (2009, 165), "the text consciously presents itself as complete, rational, and reliable."

Another important study of law and narrative is Assnat Bartor's dissertation *Reading Law as Narrative* (2010). By combining narrative theory and cognitive psychology, Bartor analyses the narrative features of Pentateuchal casuistic laws.[32] According to her, these laws are well suited to a narratological interpretation in that they contain conflict and resolution, events and participants. As such, these laws are in fact "miniature stories" (Bartor 2010, 7). By recording within the individual case laws the inner

---

[32] Casuistic laws, or case laws, are laws that are conditional in nature and contain a protasis (the condition) and an apodosis (the legal consequence). By contrast, the so-called apodictic laws are unconditional and simply command or prohibit a particular act. The terms 'casuistic law' and 'apodictic law' were originally coined by Alt (1967). In her definition of case laws, apart from laws following a strict casuistic pattern, Bartor also includes laws which present legal cases in an atypical manner, e.g., by referring to the addressees directly in the second person instead of the regular third person address, or by introducing the case with a relative clause instead of the regular prefatory conjunctions כִּי 'when/if' or אִם 'when/if'.

thoughts and emotions of the participants, direct speeches, and the attitudes of the lawgiver, an illusion of reality is created "by means of imitation (i.e., *mimesis*)" (Bartor 2010, 85; italics original).[33] The reader or hearer of these laws can sympathise with the involved participants and be persuaded by the justice of the lawgiver, for the purpose of bringing about obedience (Bartor 2010, 184). Bartor (2010, 25) surveys the "participation" of the lawgiver and the addressees in the laws; fundamentally, "The delivery of the laws is an event involving an encounter between the lawgiver and the law's addressees." Most commonly, the encounter is established by a speech act by which the addressees are addressed by the lawgiver. However, other types of interaction occur as well. In her brief account of the Holiness Code, Bartor notes that one characteristic feature of H is the permanent presence of the lawgiver. The addressees are constantly reminded of the lawgiver (e.g., "I am YHWH your God"), and the lawgiver (YHWH) frequently promises to personally punish transgressors of the law (e.g., Lev. 17.10; 20.3, 5–6; 23.30), as well as laying claim to actions carried out for the benefit of the addressees, for example the exodus (19.36; 22.33; 23.43; 25.38, 42, 55; 26.13,

---

[33] "The ability to create an illusion of reality by means of imitation (i.e., *mimesis*) is one of the signal characteristics of narrative. A vivid and dramatic description of the events in which the characters participate affords readers the illusion that they are seeing things with their own eyes, and direct transmission of the characters' conversation produces the (false) sense that they are hearing their voices. Reducing the narrator's role, as it were, to showing or voicing, gives the written text the ability to mimic the verbal and nonverbal events that make up reality" (Bartor 2010, 85).

45). Importantly, the 'presence' of the lawgiver and the interactions between the lawgiver and the addressees establish, or strengthen, a relationship between the two parties: "The participation of the lawgiver and of the addressees is the concrete embodiment of their relationship, for which the law (among other means) is a vehicle" (Bartor 2010, 57).

Bartor's narrative reading of Biblical law reflects a view of law where legal texts are treated as social literature. In other words, law is "a way of speaking about people and about the relationships between them" (Bartor 2010, 2). Thus, while laws often employ formal and abstract language, they have implications for concrete people in specific situations. As Bartor (2010, 5) explains, "All laws deal directly or indirectly with human affairs. They deal with realistic events that occur in time and in space and use true-to-life characters to establish norms and formulate policy. Laws present and represent stories about people, about their property and their ties to their communities, and about interpersonal relationships and the relationships between communities." Although this view of law does not exhaust the concept of law, it allows for the exploring of legal texts as something more than mere lists of rules. The laws are related to a metanarrative and convey experiences and values.[34]

---

[34] As Morrow (2017, 43) phrases it, "Law always has a narrative function, in that it 'tells a story' about what a particular society values, about who is an insider and who is an outsider, how the society is organized, and what it does when faced with certain forms of social disruption. By the same token, stories can be 'law' in that they have a prescriptive function: they can inculcate values and norms of behaviour that are as

To some extent, the social network model proposed in this study builds on Bartor's sociological approach. Bartor's strategy, however, was limited to the consideration of casuistic laws, because they exhibit the most narratological traits attested in Biblical law. Meanwhile, the apodictic laws are equally concerned with human affairs and are embedded in the same narrative contexts as the casuistic laws. Therefore, to represent a fuller scope of Biblical law and its social implications, we need to employ a less genre-centred framework. In what follows, I shall introduce the sociological framework required for capturing the social dimension of Lev. 17–26, not only as a collection of laws but as a structured document with narratives, laws, and exhortations.

## 4.0. Leviticus and Relational Sociology

The reading strategy adopted for this study is to conceive of Leviticus as a book that employs laws as well as narratives and exhortations to tell a story. The most important 'building blocks' of any story are its participants and the events happening among the participants. It is the participants with whom we identify and sympathise (or whom we despise) as we delve into the narrative world. Over the course of the story, the participants might undergo changes as a result of their experiences and involvements in various relationships. The participants are described in specific contexts and involved in interactions which affect their internal relationships and their community. Conflicts are the results of

---

binding as any set of rules. Both functions come together in the first five books of Moses."

interactions gone wrong, whereas resolutions are new interactions restoring the community. In other words, the participants of a story, including those of Leviticus, form a network where the behaviour of one participant, or an alliance or conflict between two participants, affects the entire network. In order to analyse the 'story' of the Holiness Code, I shall analyse its participants and their interactions by applying social network analysis (SNA). While a technical introduction to SNA is postponed to chapter 7 (§2.0), at this point it is relevant to consider how SNA generates meaning from a network of participants, and how SNA applies to legal texts.

By itself, SNA is not an apt candidate for literary analysis. SNA offers a wide range of visual and statistical tools to describe interactions, clusters, and patterns of social networks. In this regard, SNA can be considered a toolbox, but it relies on a theoretical framework in order to generate meaning from numbers and graphs (see Scott 2017, 8). By 'meaning', I refer to *why* people interact as they do in some relationships and differently in other relationships. Or, put differently, *why* participants fulfil specific roles. The answers to these questions do not arise simply from statistical analysis but from a sociological framework that can explain the numbers or graphs in a meaningful way. One such theoretical framework is that of relational sociology (e.g., Groenewegen et al. 2017).[35] In essence, relational sociology aims towards a description of individual persons (or communities) that

---

[35] For general introductions to relational sociology, see Dépelteau (2018) and Donati (2011). Relational sociology is typically attributed to Harrison C. White (2008; originally published 1992).

balances both individual and community. Accordingly, relational sociology does not emphasise the community so much that the community would predetermine the role of a person. For example, poverty and wealth certainly have social aspects, but they are not systemic or predetermined. Nor are they solely individual qualities that exist prior to social interaction, as so-called substantialists would tend to argue. Substantialists treat individuals (and systems) as self-contained, independent substances and think of social roles in terms of innate, personal qualities. For example, power is viewed in terms of persons with or without certain inner qualities or proclivity towards power. Within Western philosophy, substantialist thinking can be traced back to Aristotle, who thought of entities in terms of discrete categories. A similar way of thinking is found in the publication *Individualität und Selbstreflexion* (Wagner and Oorschot 2017), which shows an interest in the literary construction and conception of individuals in the Hebrew Bible. Although perhaps not representative of the opinion of all contributors to the anthology, Bernd Janowski (2017, 339) argues that the social role of a person can be deduced from the correlation between the inner person (the self) and its outer expressions (name, tattoos, clothes, and personal objects).[36]

Thus, relational sociology rejects both substantialist and systemic descriptions of individuals. Poverty is neither the result of a system or an innate quality. Rather, poverty arises as the

---

[36] In another contribution, however, Schellenberg (2017, 382) argues that the focus of Biblical law is not on individuality (in the sense of self-reflection) but on conformity to the demands of the social group and the legislator. This approach aligns better with relational sociology.

result of often complex social interactions and involves both individual and community. Essential to this view is the idea that "Individual persons are inseparable from the transactional contexts within which they are embedded" (Emirbayer 1997, 287). By using the term 'transactional', Mustafa Emirbayer seeks to convey the notion of a dynamic situation involving persons who derive their identity and meaning from the roles they play in that situation. A transaction need not be a transfer of physical goods, but can be any exchange between two entities, be it conversations or non-verbal gestures (Gibson 2005). During these transactions, the identity and meaning of the participants are constantly negotiated in the ever-changing contexts of interaction. In short, therefore, relational sociology seeks to balance individual and community without putting excessive emphasis on either of these extremes. Or, put differently, it takes a middle path between a methodological *holism* (the social as an expression of a system) and a methodological *individualism* (the social as the product of individual conduct), as formulated by Pierpaolo Donati (2017). As a result, the smallest object under investigation is therefore not the individual but two individuals in some kind of interaction. In this light, power is not a quality possessed by some person but rather the product of at least two persons in interaction. What follows is that concepts such as power, equality, and agency are not something to be held by an individual and brought into concrete social settings. Neither are individuals predetermined by the structure of the community to be powerful or equal. On the contrary, equality is the outcome of social interaction; that is, "Inequality comes largely from the solutions that elite and nonelite actors improvise in the face of recurrent organizational problems" (Emirbayer 1997, 292).

Interactions do not occur arbitrarily or in a void. Rather, they are guided by expectations. This fact is most clearly illustrated in trade transactions. These transactions are guided either by expectations formulated in concrete contracts or expectations based on previous experiences, for example, the cost of goods in previous transactions (Fuhse 2009, 52). The same principles essentially apply to all other social relationships. Expectations generally exist on two levels: 1) "interpersonally established expectations and cultural forms;" and 2) "individual perception and expectations" (Fuhse 2009, 53).[37] That is, the reason why individuals act in a particular way is a complex interplay of interpersonal (cultural) expectations and individual expectations. Adding to the complexity, the ever-changing network and fluid structural roles of the participants entail the addition of yet another component to the relationalists' understanding of networks, namely, time. The pioneer of relational sociology, Harrison C. White (1992, 67; quoted in Mische 2014, 82), advanced the idea of a "narrative of ties" in order to capture the phenomenon of ties being constructed and reconstructed over time.

Within a relational approach to the description of individual and society, then, interactions are the main component of

---

[37] McLean (2017, 1) explains culture as follows: "The term culture is one of the most complex terms in the social sciences to define, but we can understand it broadly to refer to the knowledge, beliefs, expectations, values, practices, and material objects by means of which we craft meaningful experiences for ourselves and with each other."

analysis. They have often been ignored as researchers have focused primarily on structure and whether participants are related or not. To counter this structuralist bent, Jan A. Fuhse (2009) has called for increased focus on the content of relational ties, as well as on the personal expectations involved in transactions. However, Fuhse also claimed that the inner processes of the individuals involved are less important than what is actually transferred within the social network.

To summarise, then, relational sociology demands that meaning and social roles are not seen as predicated by the society at large or as something to be seized by the individual. Rather, the roles of individuals are attained through transactions. For a relationalist, the keyword is interaction or transaction. The transactions themselves are guided by personal and interpersonal (cultural) expectations, and the roles of the participants are thus open to (re)negotiation.

A relational approach poses particular challenges for analysing social structures and social roles based on an ancient text like Leviticus. One can hardly investigate the psychological expectations of the participants involved, nor fully apprehend the cultural forms of the relational ties. Deriving meaning from a text is thus more complicated than regular sociological fieldwork where quantitative data can be enriched with qualitative interviews. Moreover, the interactions and internal relationships between the participants are fixed in the text; hence, in this particular sense, in contrast to real-world networks, the text is static. In the next section, therefore, we need to ask how meaning can be derived from the social network of a text.

## 5.0. Social Network Analysis of Law Texts

A written text is fixed and comprehensive. The text is comprehensive in the sense that it provides a natural boundary for analysis. A finite number of individuals and interactions are recorded, and it would normally be meaningless to look for additional interactions. The present study focuses on Lev. 17–26, which attests 59 participants and 479 interactions (see chapter 7, §3.1). Obviously, more participants and more interactions could be added to the network, had the object of inquiry been expanded to include the rest of Leviticus or the Sinai-story (Exod. 19.1–Num. 10.10) or other parts of the Pentateuch. In any case, one has to make an informed choice as to the extent of the object. For this study, a case can be made for the literary distinctiveness of Lev. 17–26, given its focus on holiness and the community and its higher frequency of exhortations in comparison to the surrounding material of Leviticus. Thus, although the classical distinction between P and H has been challenged in recent times, no other structuring of the book has gained widespread recognition.

Like any other text, H presents a certain perspective on the social community implied by the text, and the interactions recorded naturally represent the author's view of the relationships.[38] If the text does indeed represent a real social setting, the participants would certainly have been involved in other interactions

---

[38] Even if one regards Leviticus as a compilation of different sources, the viewpoint of the extant text is that of the final redactor. The redactor may depend on the viewpoints of his or her text's sources, but the choice of which sources to collect and how to shape the text is essentially a creative choice made by the redactor.

not recorded in the text, and they might have viewed the other participants differently to the author. These constraints do not negate the value of the text. As a historical text, Leviticus provides a glimpse of social life in the ancient Near East. Obviously, like any other text, Leviticus presents a subjective view of history, and other historical documents may present alternative views. However, this situation of inescapable subjectivity is not so different from the typical domains of interest for social network analysts, who typically begin their analysis by recording the viewpoints of individuals. A historical, written text is extraordinary only because it ultimately presents one viewpoint, namely the author's viewpoint. This fact has an important implication. Due to the fact that Leviticus is a law text, it necessarily expresses the *expectations* of the lawgiver. Here is an important connection to relational sociology, which emphasises that expectations guide transactions and that expectations are moulded by culture. Simply put, the law text is an expression of the lawgiver's expectations, that is, his value system and the 'meaning' he ascribes to his social world. More concretely, we must distinguish between the implied social community and the author's expectations. On the one hand, it is clear that H is not a prescription of how the implied community should be organised. Rather, it assumes the existence of a priestly class, laypeople, and foreigners, among many other participants. In addition, the legislation also assumes various interactions. For example, it is entirely reasonable to assume that the blasphemer's cursing runs counter to the values and expectations of the author (Lev. 24.10–23). On the other hand, the author of H clearly has certain expectations as to how the participants must behave in particular situations. With regard to the blasphemer, the author clearly expects and applauds capital punishment for blasphemy, at least within this concrete context. Thus, we must distinguish between the implied social network and the theological and ethical expectations of the author. Put differently, the author does not present an ideal community but prescribes certain interactions within the implied less-than ideal society. With this distinction in mind, we can scrutinise the author's expectations in light of the implied social network.

In an early essay, Lon L. Fuller (1969) explored the relationship between law and human interaction. According to Fuller, there are essentially two kinds of law. On the one hand, there is declarative law, which is probably the kind of law most people would intuitively think of as law, namely, an official, written decree. On the other hand, there is customary law, which is not the product of legislators but rather a subtle code of conduct that governs our behaviour towards one another. It is the latter type of law to which Fuller's essay directs most of its attention. Customary law, then, is an unwritten code of conduct, enforced through interaction. Indeed, it is "a language of interaction" (Fuller 1969, 2). As a code of conduct, customary law regulates the behaviour of individuals, often in an unconscious manner. The code is unwritten and implicit, but everyone knows when the code has been violated. The name of the law may be ill-chosen, as 'customary' may seem to imply an obligation that has arisen through mere repetition or tradition. Fuller (1969, 9–10) proposes the definition "a system of stabilized interactional expectancy," which refers to a situation where the participants act according to a sense of obligation based upon certain expectancies for right behaviour. The expectancies need not be explicit. In fact, they typically only become explicit when they are violated. Another way of putting it is that customary law is "a program for living together" (Fuller 1969, 11), and customary law achieves this program by interlocking the individuals of the society into fixed roles of right behaviour. Fuller's view of law as based upon expectations is important, because it aligns well with relational sociology. Recall the relational view of the meaning of social networks as expressed through personal and interpersonal expectations. The implicit purpose of customary law is to facilitate interaction by leveraging personal and interpersonal expectations in order to fix individuals into social roles according to the value system of a particular culture. Now, Leviticus is not a customary law, but the interactional principles still hold. The genre of Leviticus is best described as common law, that is, a collection of laws comprised of real-life cases (Berman 2017).[39] In essence, the

---

[39] Berman (2017) argues that Biblical law is common law, that is, Biblical law is not a fixed and exhaustive 'code' like modern codes to which judges have to refer when deciding on concrete cases. According to Berman (2017, 109–10), "Within common-law systems, the law is not found in a written code which serves as the judges' point of reference and which delimits what they may decide. Adjudication is a process whereby the judge concludes the correct judgment based on the mores and spirit of the community and its customs. Law gradually develops through the distillation and continual restatement of legal doctrine through the decisions of courts. When a judge decides a particular case, he or she is empowered to reconstruct the general thrust of the law in

legal cases are interactional insofar as they prescribe the behaviour of individuals in specific contexts. Therefore, as Fuller (1969, 26) argues, common law is more deeply rooted in human interaction than modern law. A reading of Lev. 17–26 confirms this view. In fact, the text is composed of divine speeches to Moses, who mediates the speeches to the Israelites and the priests. As for the laws themselves, they are concerned with relationships among the Israelites, as well as the relationship between the Israelite community and outsiders. From a modern point of view, it may seem odd to analyse the social network of a law text. However, given the interactional nature of common law, it makes perfect sense.

---

consultation with previous judicial formulations. Critically, the judicial decision itself does not create binding law; no particular formulation of the law is final. As a system of legal thought, the common law is consciously and inherently incomplete, fluid and vague." The characterisation of Biblical law as common law implies that Israelite judges would not consider the laws a "source" to be explicitly referred to, but rather a "resource" to consult (Berman 2017, 210). Thus, the purpose of Biblical law is not to provide an exhaustive compendium of laws to be applied in real cases, but rather to inform the ethical values of the judges. Bergland's (2020) characterisation of Torah (understood here as a genre) as "covenantal instruction" is important in this respect. By 'covenantal instruction', what is meant is that the Torah is not legislative in the modern sense, but that it certainly remains normative. According to Bergland (2020, 99), the normative dimension explains why there are so many literary parallels between the legal corpora of the Pentateuch.

## 6.0. The Participants of the Holiness Code and Their Roles

The Holiness Code contains 59 human/divine participants (see chapter 7, §3.1). A few of these are named, but most are anonymous, or hypothetical, indefinite 'persons' (e.g., the recurrent reference to אִישׁ 'anyone'). This study is certainly not the first one to explore the roles of these participants, but it has been common to explain the role of a participant with respect to one or two other participants (most frequently YHWH and the addressees of the text, the sons of Israel) or to a concept (e.g., holiness or purity). This is at least one of the reasons why scholarly work on the participants of H has reached diverging conclusions. In this section, previous work on the participants will be reviewed in order to qualify the research questions to be pursued by the SNA. Much scholarly work has focused on historical questions or more general portrayals of the participants, not necessarily restricted to the Holiness Code.[40] Those studies will not concern us here, as

---

[40] Hence, although much work has been dedicated to the study of YHWH and Moses in the Pentateuch, their roles have rarely been discussed with respect to H. One exception is Bibb (2009, 159–63) who offers a brief discussion of the triangular relationship between the Israelites, the priests, and YHWH. YHWH is characterised as representing "the sacred principle at the heart of society" on which the coherence of the society depends (Bibb 2009, 163). J. W. Watts (1999) presents a short examination of the characterisation of YHWH in H as part of a larger exposition of the "rhetorical characterization" of YHWH in the Pentateuch. According to Watts (1999, 102), at this point in the Pentateuch, the "divine name [...] has become richly evocative of the layers of characterization provided by preceding texts," including the depiction of YHWH as the

the present study is concerned with the literary roles of the participants within the Holiness Code.

## 6.1. The Addressees

The speeches that comprise H are addressed to the בְּנֵי יִשְׂרָאֵל 'sons of Israel', as well as the priests, Aaron and his sons (e.g., 17.2). To be sure, some speeches are addressed exclusively to Aaron and/or Aaron's sons (21.1, 17; 22.2), other speeches solely to the sons of Israel (e.g., 18.2; 19.2; 20.2). The role of the priests will be discussed later (see §6.5); hence, by 'addressees', I refer here to the sons of Israel. Within the speeches, the sons of Israel are commonly addressed by both 2MPl and 2MSg references. This *Numeruswechsel* has received much attention in scholarly research on H. The question is whether the *Numeruswechsel* should be seen as indicative of sources and redactional activity during the composition of the text, as has been the traditional understanding,[41] or whether participant shifts are intentional, rhetorical devices with specific meanings attached to them. Today, the

---

saviour of Israel, cult-founder, holy God, and protective overlord. More generally, Watts focuses his discussion on how the Pentateuchal laws inform the image of God, in relation and contrast to the narrative sections of the Pentateuch.

[41] *Numeruswechsel* became a fundamental interpretative key in the form-critical approach advanced by Von Rad (1953), who identified a number of forms in Lev. 19 based on grammatical person and number, e.g., vv. 9–10 (2MSg) and 11–12a (2MPl). Apparently, these forms were collected by a redactor, the so-called *Prediger*, who also sometimes added paraeneses to address the community. Kilian (1963, 57–63), although

tendency to propose sources or redactions on the basis of *Numeruswechsel* is decreasing. For one thing, archaeologists have uncovered inscriptions with unexpected number shifts, a fact that challenges the dating of textual strata based solely on *Numeruswechsel* (Greenberg 1984, 187; Berman 2017, 4). Moreover, scholars have increasingly tended to investigate the overall structure of texts and, hence, do not attribute much compositional significance to small linguistic discrepancies. Moshe Weinfeld (1991, 15), in his commentary on Deuteronomy, argues that the number shifts in Deuteronomy "may simply be a didactic device to impress the individual or collective listener, or it may reflect the urge for literary variation." In some cases, according to

---

not basing his source- and redaction-critical analysis of Lev. 17–26 entirely on number shifts, distinguished between a series (*Reihe*) of singular apodictic laws and a series of plural apodictic laws in Lev. 19 (see also Elliger 1966; Cholewiński 1976; Reventlow 1961). In his important study of apodictic laws in the HB, Gerstenberger (2009; originally published 1965) claimed that apodictic laws in the 2MPl could almost always be considered paraenetic additions by later redactors. More contemporary scholarly works likewise consider *Numeruswechsel* as a diagnostic clue for identifying redactional activity, e.g., Sun (1990), Hartley (1992), Bultmann (1992), and Grünwaldt (1999). To be sure, Sun (1990, 187) is hesitant to use participant shifts as signs of redactional activity, because, according to him, Lev. 19 cannot be reconstructed on the basis of *Numeruswechsel*. Nevertheless, in his discussion of Lev. 25, he asserts that the plural references in vv. 2–7 provide "a clue to the relative date of this unit" in relation to the parallel text in Exod. 23.10–11, which is entirely in the singular (Sun 1990, 503).

Weinfeld (1991, 15), number shifts may be due to quotation,[42] or may be rhetorical devices used to heighten the suspense of a discourse.

This scholarly trend is also reflected in the study of Leviticus. One example is Milgrom in his commentary on Lev. 25. Even though he generally admits the possibility of identifying different textual strata, with respect to Lev. 25, he calls this search "meaningless," because "The chapter, as is, flows logically and coherently" (Milgrom 2001, 2150). Ruwe (1999) also reads the number shifts in light of the overall structure of the text and the presumed functions of those shifts. For instance, according to Ruwe (1999, 132), the shifts between plural references in Lev. 18.1–5, 24–30 and singular in vv. 7–23 have a rhetorical function, namely, emphasising the difference between the introductory and concluding exhortations (Pl) and the legal core (Sg).[43] Finally, Nihan (2007, 522) rejects the ambitious reconstructions of Lev. 25 attempted by Elliger (1966, 335–49) and Alfred Cholewiński (1976, 101–18), among others, because, as he argues, "The resulting texts are too fragmentary to be coherent and in many cases the systematic alternation between singular and plural address (see, e.g., v. 13–17!) or between personal and impersonal formulation requires the text of Lev. 25 to be significantly

---

[42] Indeed, Milgrom (2001, 2155) suggests that the seemingly abrupt number shifts in Lev. 25.2–7 are due to the incorporation and expansion of Exod. 23.10–11 in Lev. 25. See also Stackert (2007, 126–27).

[43] In cases where rhetorical functions cannot be deduced from the participant reference shifts, Ruwe would not deny a source- or redaction-critical reason for those shifts (e.g., Lev. 19.27b).

emended to fit the theory." Therefore, most scholars today, while not denying a compositional growth of the text, would refrain from reconstructing the text on the basis of participant reference shifts.[44] Indeed, it is more common to see the participant reference shifts as rhetorical and structural devices.[45] The rhetorical function of the participant reference shifts in H will be discussed further in chapter 3 (§3.7).

Among the participants of the text, the addressees of the divine and Mosaic speeches in Lev. 17–26 have attracted the most attention. As one of the major participants, the sons of Israel engage in multiple relationships, and most of the remaining participants are identified with reference to them (e.g., 'your father' and 'the sojourner who sojourns among you'). Since the addressees are connected with so many different participants, they most

---

[44] Recently, however, Arnold (2017) has revived the classical quest to trace the origins of Deuteronomy 12–26 on the basis of *Numeruswechsel*. In fact, he claims that the rhetorical and stylistic readings of grammatical number are "overcorrections" which have missed the diachronic significance of those shifts (Arnold 2017, 165). Although he accepts the now common view that *Numeruswechsel* also has rhetorical functions, he argues that pericopes with a dominance of 2MSg references are older than pericopes with a mix of 2MSg and 2MPl references.

[45] To be sure, traditional historical-critical scholars also appreciated the rhetorical or communicative function of participant reference shifts. Reventlow (1961, 163), for instance, attributed the plural references in H to a so-called *Prediger* who used plural references to give his preaching a deep, personal address. One wonders, however, why a redactor would appreciate the dynamics caused by participant shifts, while the author of an original source would not.

likely fulfil different roles in different relationships. Social network analysis can shed more light on these roles and provide a clearer picture of the overall role of the addressees within the community implied by the author. Moreover, in this particular study, the addressees will be differentiated with respect to the specific ways in which they are referred to: the 'sons of Israel' (and other collective designations), the directly addressed individual (2MSg), and the indirectly addressed individual (3MSg), the latter of which makes frequent appearances in the casuistic laws. With this distinction recognised, it can be investigated whether certain relationships and events pertain to one or other of these subcategories of the addressees.

## 6.2. The Women

Judith R. Wegner (1998, 42–43) has claimed that "the largest and most important subgroup in Leviticus is the entire class of women." As concerns Lev. 17–26, women occur frequently in the anti-incest laws in chapters 18 and 20, and there are several references to women as members of the priestly family in chapters 21–22. Moreover, female handmaids are mentioned (19.20–22; 25.6, 44), as well as Shelomith, the mother of the blasphemer (24.10–11), and the women in the curses of Lev. 26 (vv. 26 and 29). In total, there are 20 distinct women in this part of Leviticus (see chapter 7, §5.3.1). Women are predominantly referred to by role (what they do), or by relationship (most commonly family relationships; Dupont 1989, 202). Only once is a woman referred to by her name.⁴⁶ It has been a topic of debate whether the women are included in the designation בְּנֵי יִשְׂרָאֵל 'the sons of Israel'—the addressees of the text—or perhaps in its parallel expression בֵּית יִשְׂרָאֵל 'the house of Israel'.⁴⁷ It is clear that the women generally constitute a peripheral group within H. It is not so clear, however, what exact role they fulfil and what purpose they serve in the text. Some claim that the text pictures the women as the property of male Israelites, hence the anti-incest laws would amount to anti-theft laws (Wegner 1998, 45; 1988, 13; Noth 1977, 135).⁴⁸ More common is the viewpoint that the anti-incest laws in Lev. 18 and 20 should be interpreted in light

---

⁴⁶ Interestingly, participants are rarely named in H. Apart from the mother of the blasphemer, Shelomith, only YHWH, Moses, and Aaron are named. Unlike these divine/male participants, Shelomith is never active and is only included to provide a subtle, polemical (?) identification of the blasphemer.

⁴⁷ The discussion is crucial because the overall picture of the women in Lev. 17–26 would significantly change if they were included among the addressees on a par with males. Joosten (1996, 34) suggests that בֵּית יִשְׂרָאֵל 'the house of Israel' may indeed include women, but this idea has been rejected by Milgrom (2000, 1412).

⁴⁸ Quite the opposite viewpoint is advanced by McClenney-Sadler (2007) in her investigation of the structure of Lev. 18. McClenney-Sadler (2007, 90) argues for a "hierarchy of duty" beginning with YHWH's legal rights (v. 6), then the mother's rights (v. 7a), and the father's rights (v. 7b–11), etc.. If this hierarchy is indeed true, it implies that "the importance of wives and mothers in ancient Israelite culture is emphasized literarily, thus balancing gender asymmetry in these laws" (McClenney-Sadler 2007, 91).

of the present holiness context, irrespective of whether the individual laws ever existed independently. According to Joanne M. Dupont (1989, 164–65), the incest prohibitions express a multifaceted picture of the women. The text depicts the women as potential threats to male holiness, but it also protects their legal rights and even regards them as legally responsible persons (see Lev. 20.10–21).[49] The women of Lev. 17–26 have also been considered free agents, because "the primary concern is for the woman and the man to protect a *third entity*—the boundaries constituting the classificatory system which constitutes their world. This is an ontological concern" (Ellens 2008, 296; italics original).[50] Finally, the role of the women has been considered "instrumental" for "Israel's access to and continued relationship with its God" (Harrington 2012, 78).

In sum, although there is no dispute that the women in the Holiness Code are peripheral in that they are only referred to indirectly, there is still some doubt as to their role in the text. That they are peripheral within the outlook of the text does not necessarily correlate with social marginalisation. To my knowledge, no one has claimed that the father is marginalised, even though he is never focalised as an agent and is only referred to indirectly (e.g., 'your father'; Lev. 18.7). The role of the women (and the

---

[49] Dupont (1989, 164) accounts for this tension by suggesting that Lev. 20.10–21 reflects a later time "in which women, not only men, were considered legal persons with legal responsibilities."

[50] This classification only pertains to the so-called 'sex texts' of Leviticus (15.18, 24, 33b; 18; 19.20–22, 29; 20.10–21; 21.9).

## 2. Towards a Social Network Analysis of the Holiness Code    51

father) will be reconsidered in chapter 7 (§5.3) with respect to the social network of Leviticus.

### 6.3. The Brother/Fellow

The so-called golden rule ("Love your fellow as yourself;" Lev. 19.18) has been a central topic for Jewish and Christian interpreters (Mathys 1986; Schenker 2012; Barbiero 1991, esp. 319–24).[51] It is commonly accepted that the fellow is an ethnic member of the Israelite community (Milgrom 2000, 1654; Mathys 1986, 38–39; Moenikes 2012, §2.2.1; Crüsemann 1992, 377; Noth 1977, 141–42). Firstly, רֵעֲךָ 'your fellow' occurs in the immediate context of אָחִיךָ 'your brother', עֲמִיתֶךָ 'your fellow countryman', and בְּנֵי עַמֶּךָ 'sons of your people', all terms that indicate members of the community.[52] Secondly, the similar command to love the sojourner as oneself (19.34) suggests that the term 'fellow' is limited to ethnic members of the society. Thus, the fellow is a member of the society who has certain rights to be respected by the addressees of the text. If, however, רֵעֲךָ is synonymous to אָחִיךָ, עֲמִיתֶךָ, and בְּנֵי עַמֶּךָ, another important passage adds to the picture of the fellow, namely chapter 25, with its recurrent references to אָחִיךָ 'your brother' who has fallen into severe poverty. Moreover, in Lev. 25, the brother/fellow is not only related to 'you' (Sg) but also to the sojourner to whom he reaches out for help (25.47–54), as well as his family members by whom he is

---

[51] For references to early Jewish interpretations of the רֵעַ 'fellow', see Neudecker (1992, 499–503).

[52] "Clearly, all these synonyms refer solely to Israelites" (Milgrom 2000, 1632).

allowed to be redeemed from debt (25.25, 48–49). Thus, although the fellow/brother is certainly not one of the most central figures in the speeches of H, he is engaged in a variety of interactions with different participants. Thus, the fellow/brother is an important character for understanding the social dynamics of the community implied by the text, and deserves closer attention.

## 6.4. The Foreigners

H refers to a number of non-Israelite persons, most frequently גֵּר 'sojourner', but also בֶּן־נֵכָר 'son of a foreigner', עֶבֶד 'slave', and בְּנֵי הַתּוֹשָׁבִים 'sons of resident (sojourners)'. Most scholarly debate has been focused on the identity of the גֵּר. The traditional understanding of the גֵּר was developed by Alfred Bertholet (1896), who argued that the characterisation of the גֵּר underwent a change from a *persona misera* in Deuteronomy to a proselyte in post-priestly literature. Thus, according to Bertholet, in P, including H, the גֵּר is a non-Israelite who has assumed most of the religious stipulations of the Israelite. In H, then, "Ger ist ganz und gar ein religiöser Begriff geworden" (Bertholet 1896, 174).[53] This tradi-

---

[53] This understanding remained the consensus until recently (Baentsch 1893, 137; Kellermann 1977, 446; Mathys 1986). Mathys (1986, 45) concludes that some of the references to the גֵּר (Lev. 17.8; 22.18) probably refer to a proselyte, but admits that there is not an unequivocal example in H. A number of recent scholars have retained Bertholet's construal of the גֵּר as a religious entity, although it has become more common to envisage a Northern Israelite identity for the גֵּר (Cohen 1990; Douglas 1994). Thus, according to these historical reconstructions, the גֵּרִים are not gentiles who have converted to Judaism, but

tional notion has been challenged by scholars who see a religious/cultic distinction between the גֵר and the ordinary Israelites and emphasise the social and ethnic aspects of the characterisation of the גֵר.⁵⁴ Finally, it has also been argued that H does not present a coherent picture of the גֵר; hence, the גֵר is a compositional entity in the text.⁵⁵

---

"half-brothers, not-quite-kin, fellow-worshippers of the same God" (Douglas 1994, 286). Achenbach (2011, 41), although not considering the גֵרִים to be "proselytes," argues that H assumes them to be "fully integrated members of the religious community, despite their ethnic, political and economic status, where their position is different from the native-born Israelite citizen."

⁵⁴ Milgrom (2001, 2236) posits that the term גֵר consistently refers to a social—and not a cultic/religious—category, a "resident non-Israelite," landless by definition, although a few of these resident non-Israelites could acquire wealth and "presumably unarable" land (for his general discussion of the role and identity of the גֵר, see Milgrom 2000, 1493–1501). The opposite stance is taken by Nihan (2011, 117), who argues that the גֵר is predominantly "economically independent" in H and that Lev. 19.9–10 is an exception to this portrayal. Like Milgrom, however, Nihan rejects the traditional understanding of the גֵר as a proselyte or 'half-brother' (see also Albertz 2011, 57–58; Vieweger 1995, 274–75). Rendtorff (1996) analyses the גֵר in relation to other participants of H, namely the עָנִי 'poor', תּוֹשָׁב 'alien/resident', שָׂכִיר 'labourer', עֶבֶד 'slave', אָח 'brother', and אֶזְרָח 'native'. According to Rendtorff, in light of these various participants, the term גֵר appears to refer to a social and ethnic category on the margins of society.

⁵⁵ So Bultmann (1992, esp. 175–96), who argued for a mixed picture of the גֵר in H due to the compositional growth of the text. According to Bultmann, Lev. 19 shows a mixed picture of the גֵר, with the term referring partly to the same Israelite minority as in Deuteronomy, and partly

Construal of the גֵר is complicated by the rather different contexts in which the participant appears. In Lev. 17, the גֵר is portrayed as a person engaged in Israelite cultic activities, indicating that the גֵר is somewhat integrated into the religious community. This impression is furthered by the claims in 18.26 and 24.22 that the laws listed in these respective pericopes pertain to both the native Israelite and the גֵר. On the other hand, the mentioning of the גֵר along with the poor in 19.10 suggests that גֵר is not only an ethnic category but also a social one. The command to love the גֵר as oneself (19.34) is paralleled by the command to love one's neighbour (19.18), supporting an ethnic interpretation of the גֵר. Finally, in chapter 25, the גֵר is apparently a rich person to whom even an Israelite can become a debt slave (25.47). However, just a few verses earlier, the Israelites are allowed to purchase slaves from the בְּנֵי הַתּוֹשָׁבִים הַגָּרִים עִמָּכֶם 'sons of the resident (aliens) sojourning among you' (25.45).[56] The suggestion that this last designation is semantically identical to גֵר is generally

---

to a religious category equal to the native of the land. In Lev. 17, the term גֵר refers exclusively to members of a wing of the Judaic community, while Lev. 25 provides a unique case where גֵר refers to a non-Israelite. Van Houten (1991), although reaching a quite different conclusion as to the identity of the גֵר, argues that the complex characterisation of the גֵר is due to the efforts of an editor to integrate different conceptions into H. In the resulting text, according to Van Houten (1991, 151–55), the גֵּרִים are those Israelites who stayed behind during the exile.

[56] This translation largely follows Milgrom (2001, 2229).

rejected.⁵⁷ Milgrom (2001, 2187), however, argues that the complex phrase גֵּר וְתוֹשָׁב 'resident (and) sojourner' (see 25.23, 35) is a hendiadys denoting that the גֵּר has settled down in a community. Although תוֹשָׁבִים occurs independently in 25.45, the hendiadys is implied (Milgrom 2001, 2229). Thus, in these cases, the term תּוֹשָׁב does not represent an additional participant, but a specification of the residential status of the sojourner. Two other complications arise from chapter 25. Firstly, the addressees of Moses' speech, the sons of Israel, are called גֵּרִים וְתוֹשָׁבִים 'resident sojourners' in YHWH's land (25.23). Secondly, the singular addressee is commanded to help his poverty-stricken brother by

---

⁵⁷ Most scholars would differentiate between גֵּר and תּוֹשָׁב. Joosten (1996, 74) argues that, in contrast to the term גֵּר, which denotes a juridical status, תּוֹשָׁב refers to a social condition, a person "who immigrated from another locality and who must typically attach himself to a free citizen in order to assure his livelihood." Zehnder (2005, 346) adds that, in some cases at least, תּוֹשָׁב can refer to ethnicity (25.44–45). Following Joosten, Nihan (2011) sees a social distinction between גֵּר and תּוֹשָׁב. A resident alien with the juridical status of גֵּר can lose this status and become תּוֹשָׁב. In this situation, he is not protected by the law and "he may legitimately be forced to sell his children as debt slaves (Lev. 25.45–46)" (Nihan 2011, 123; see also McConville 2007, 30). In contrast, Achenbach (2011) sees the difference between גֵּר and תּוֹשָׁב as one of belonging. The תּוֹשָׁב and the גֵּר have equal juridical rights, but the גֵּר is a full member of religious society (Achenbach 2011, 41, 46). According to Achenbach (2011, 47–48), then, the lexeme תּוֹשָׁב, presumably belonging to the late strata of the priestly law, has taken over the former meaning of גֵּר as found in Deuteronomy, namely the *persona misera*.

treating him as a גֵּר וְתוֹשָׁב 'resident sojourner' (25.35). These overlapping terms are curious, because they appear to break down the distinction between the גֵּרִים and the Israelites.

In sum, the construal of the role of the גֵּר is complicated by the various religious and social contexts in which the גֵּר is mentioned, as well as the characterisation of other participants as גֵּרִים and תוֹשָׁבִים. In general, however, the גֵּר is interpreted as a person on the margins of society. As José E. Ramírez Kidd (1999, 62) argues, the גֵּר seems to take a middle position between the foreign nations, which are certainly outside the bounds of the law and Israelite society, and the Israelite community. The question is how proximate the גֵּר is to the Israelite community. To capture the status of the גֵּר, Milgrom (2000, 1496) distinguishes between the civil law, where the גֵּר enjoys full equal status, and the religious law, where the גֵּר "is bound by the prohibitive commandments, but not by the performative ones."[58] Nihan stresses the dissymmetry between the גֵּר and the native Israelites even more. Firstly, since only the native Israelites can own land, "the land

---

[58] Similarly, Joosten (1996, 55) argued that גֵּר is a technical term for "a person (possibly a family or group) conceded a certain juridical status because of the fact that he has settled among a foreign tribe or people." Although the גֵּר is generally a free agent and is not obliged to live like an Israelite in all aspects of life, he is nevertheless bound by "prohibitions, such as those prohibiting sacrifices to other gods or the eating of blood" (Joosten 1996, 66; see also Ramírez Kidd 1999, 63). It has, however, been objected that the distinction between prohibitions and performative commandments is not so sharp, and that Lev. 16.29, albeit not in H, undermines the distinction (Zehnder 2005, 349 n. 1).

remains in H the central foundation for the legal distinction between Israelites and resident aliens" (Nihan 2011, 124). Secondly, Nihan (2011, 124–29) argues that the dissymmetry is even bigger within the cultic domain, because some cultic laws are only addressed to the Israelites (e.g., Lev. 17.3–7) and because the requirement of holiness only applies to Israelites. However, although only the Israelites are directly commanded to be holy (19.2), holiness plays into the characterisation of the גֵּר as well. As Weinfeld (1972, 232) explained, "The author of the Priestly Code, to whom sacral-ritual matters are of primary importance, is concerned with preserving the sanctity and purity of the congregation inhabiting the *holy land* and therefore takes steps to ensure that this sanctity be not profaned by the *ger*" (italics original; see also Barbiero 2002, 240). Ramírez Kidd (1999, 48–71) added that the matter of the role of the גֵּר in P and H is secondary to that of holiness.[59] Thus, the laws of the Holiness Code are not so much concerned with the legal status of the גֵּר, but rather "show a particular concern […] to adjust the conduct of the גֵּר to the rules of cultic purity which preserve the holiness of land and people" (Ramírez Kidd 1999, 62; see also Jenson 1992, 116).

Although much research has been focused on the legal status of the גֵּר *vis-à-vis* the Israelites, some studies have also turned

---

[59] It should be noted, however, that Ramírez Kidd's argument rests upon a redaction-critical reconstruction of the text in which the statements that include the גֵּר are often regarded as late additions (e.g., Lev. 17.15; 18.26). It seems that Ramírez Kidd attributes less value to these late additions—and thus to the role of the גֵּר—because the laws are thought of as originally pertaining exclusively to the Israelites.

to the relationship between the גֵּר and other presumably socially marginalised participants (Achenbach 2011; Rendtorff 1996; Joosten 1996, 73–76). In particular, Rolf Rendtorff (1996, 79) proposed a social hierarchy of the minority groups in Lev. 25: גֵּר 'sojourner' > תּוֹשָׁב 'resident/alien' > שָׂכִיר 'hired labourer' > slave. Rendtorff cautions, however, that the three first participants can be ordered in various ways. Only 'slave' unambiguously belongs to the lowest layer of society. The שָׂכִיר 'hired labourer' is a "laborer resident on the person's land" (Milgrom 2001, 2161). The Holiness Code also mentions the בֶּן־נֵכָר 'son of a foreigner'[60] and זָר 'stranger'.[61] The challenge of capturing the roles of these minor participants is the scarcity of references to

---

[60] According to Joosten (1996, 75), בֶּן־נֵכָר means "one who is ethnically not a member of the people of Israel" (see Gen. 17.12). The term occurs only once in H (Lev. 22.25), and that verse has typically been interpreted as a prohibition against acquiring blemished animals from foreigners (Elliger 1966, 300; Noth 1977, 163; Wenham 1979, 295–96). In fact, Gerstenberger (1996, 330) simply describes the בֶּן־נֵכָר as an "animal merchant." Achenbach (2011, 44) remarks that the בֶּן־נֵכָר, a "non-resident alien," is completely absent from H (except, of course, for Lev. 22.25) because he is considered "excluded from the cultic and religious community."

[61] The זָר occurs in H only in Lev. 22.10–13 and relates to a prohibition against eating sacred food. According to Wuench (2014, 1137–39), this term is the most general term for 'stranger' and does not typically imply a value judgment of the person. In other words, the זָר is an outsider, sometimes also ethnically (see also Milgrom 2000, 1861; Wenham 1979, 294). Achenbach (2011, 45) makes a sharper judgment of the זָר in H when he describes the זָרִים as people "who are not willingly integrated as *gerîm* into the social-religious community of Israel."

them and, importantly, the fact that they occur even less frequently as independent participants. The שָׂכִיר 'hired labourer', for example, occurs twice in a dependent construction (19.13; 25.6), three times as a predicate (25.40, 50, 53), and only once as an independent participant (22.10), if its juxtaposition with תּוֹשָׁב should not be interpreted as a hendiadys, thus signifying a resident labourer (see Milgrom 2000, 1861).

To conclude, the scholarly discussion of the identity, social and legal status, and role of the גֵּר 'sojourner' in the Holiness Code reveals the complex characterisation of this participant. Irrespective of whether the text is compiled of different sources and thus (unintentionally?) combines rival notions of the גֵּר, a social network analysis will analyse the participant as it is presented in the extant text. Moreover, social network tools allow for a controlled analysis of the sojourner with respect to all its relationships (e.g., the Israelites, the fellow/brother, YHWH, the women, the father, among others), as well as providing a quantifiable basis on which the participant can be compared to other participants of the social network, even if the participants are not directly connected. Social network analysis does not directly reveal the ethnicity or historical identity of the sojourner, but it provides a framework for analysing where the sojourner is socially situated with respect to the implied community of the text.

## 6.5. The Priests

Although the Holiness Code involves a shift of focus from cult to community, the priests remain central figures. They are referred to as 'Aaron', 'the sons of Aaron',[62] or simply הַכֹּהֵן 'the priest' (e.g., 17.5; 23.11). Specific regulations pertain to the sons of Aaron (21.1–9) and to Aaron (21.10–23). Most of the time, Aaron and his sons are addressed together (e.g., 17.2; 22.2). As has already been noted with reference to Bibb, there is a marked tension between the conceptions of holiness found in the first and second parts of Leviticus (see §3.0). While in P, holiness is associated with the cult and the priests, H calls for communal holiness. This tension has led to two very different understandings of the origins and writers of H. While Klaus Grünwaldt (2003) suggested that laypeople were responsible for H, given its democratisation of holiness and the limited role of the priests, Knohl (1988, ix; quoted in Milgrom 1991, 27) argued that H was an "attempt by priestly circles in Jerusalem to contend with the prophet's criticism" of the rituals and temple institutions (see also Knohl 2007). These different theories illustrate the difficulties in conceptualising the role of the priests within the text. On the one hand, the priests continue to serve an important role in H, as illustrated by Lev. 17 and 23, where sacrifices are handled by the priests. Moreover, according to Nihan (2007, 485), "Contrary to the community, priests are no longer exhorted to become holy by keeping Yahweh's laws, they are *innately* holy *because* they have been set aside (consecrated) to present Yahweh's 'food'" (italics original). This role entails greater responsibility, which explains the prohibitions against priestly blemishes in Lev. 21.16–24 (Schipper and

---

[62] The sons of Aaron are also called הַכֹּהֲנִים 'the priests' (21.1).

Stackert 2013, 477; Bibb 2009, 161).[63] At the same time, the conception of holiness and the privileged cultic role of the priests seemingly undergo a change in H. In fact, in most of the speeches, all of Israel is addressed, even in cultic matters, and Milgrom (2000, 1451) ascribes an "egalitarian thrust" to H.[64] Lev. 21.8 is a key verse in this respect.[65] If the 2MSg 'you' in וְקִדַּשְׁתּוֹ D 'you shall sanctify him' does indeed refer to the addressees, it may be that the people are to 'transfer' the priest into a status of holiness, which would imply that priestly holiness is not so different from that of the people (so Grünwaldt 2003, 239; Christian 2011, 368–69). Another, more common interpretation assumes a declarative meaning of the verb, hence, 'treat as holy' (Milgrom 2000, 1809; see also Müller 2015, 83).[66] Nevertheless, even Milgrom (2000, 1410) argues that the people "is charged with the responsibility of overseeing the priests," since the priestly legislation is addressed to the entire people in 21.24. More radically, according to Mark A. Christian (2011, esp. 352–96), the role of the priests has effectively been reduced to a matter of handling blood rituals,

---

[63] Schipper and Stackert (2013, 466–68) do not relate blemishes directly to holiness. According to them, the problem of blemished priests is not that they are not holy, but that YHWH will not accept them in his proximity because they would threaten the holiness of the sanctuary. In other words, sacrificial and priestly blemishes pertain to holiness only indirectly.

[64] See also Knohl (2007, 192), who argued that the Holiness School strove "to create a deep affiliation between the congregation of Israel and the Tabernacle-Temple and its worship."

[65] See chapter 3, §3.5 for a detailed discussion.

[66] See the discussion of קדשׁ 'holy' in chapter 6, §3.2.1.

while the people has become a nation of "lay quasi-priests" (Christian 2011, 380). For one thing, it is not priestly activity which effected the sanctification of the people in the first place, but rather YHWH's unmediated salvation of his people from Egyptian bondage (22.32b–33). Secondly, according to Christian, the people has received direct revelation from YHWH concerning the distinction between clean and unclean animals, an otherwise priestly task.[67] Christian (2011, 388–89), therefore, views "the difference between priests and laity" as "pragmatic rather than theological."

In sum, the role of the priests in the Holiness Code remains unresolved. Have the priests lost their privileged role in favour of the people, who are now their overseers? Or do the priests still play a cultic role in Israelite society? In my network analysis of the text, I shall consider the role of the priests by looking at the interactions between the priestly participants and their third parties (i.e., participants interacting with the priests), and also by considering the interactions between the third parties themselves,

---

[67] Christian, however, overlooks the fact that the instruction to distinguish between clean and unclean animals is *not* unmediated. As a matter of fact, Moses is the mediator of all divine speeches in Leviticus (except for the divine speech to Aaron in 10.8–11). The phrase וָאֹמַר לָכֶם 'and I said to you' in 20.24 is embedded in Moses' speech. It likely refers back to the instructions in 11.44 (see Christian 2011, 381 n. 1703), but those instructions are themselves embedded in a speech by Moses and Aaron. Thus, the instructions in Leviticus are not direct, unmediated revelation to the people, but mediated by Moses, and sometimes also Aaron, the high priest.

in order to determine how embedded the priests are in the community.

## 6.6. The Blasphemer

In the only narrative in the Holiness Code (Lev. 24.10–23), a man who is half-Israelite and half-Egyptian holds a curious role. The man has often been called 'the blasphemer', for want of a real name, and due to his cursing of the divine Name for which he received capital punishment. It has been taken for granted that the blasphemer is a גֵּר 'sojourner' (Hutton 1999; Meyer 2005).[68] Curiously, however, the blasphemer is never explicitly called a גֵּר, but repeatedly הַמְקַלֵּל 'the curser' (24.14, 23). As the narrative goes, the congregation does not know what to do with the blasphemer, apparently because he is not a 'pure' native Israelite. In other words, is the blasphemer exempt from punishment since only his mother is an Israelite? The legal principle *lex talionis*, put forward as a response to the blasphemy, is said to apply to both the native and the sojourner. By implication, then, if even non-

---

[68] Meyer (2005, 202) dubs the blasphemer a "half-caste [...] who by implication should be regarded as a גֵּר." This designation apparently stems from his interpretation of Lev. 24.10–23 as a whole, which, he argues, functions "to remind the returned Elite that those that were not regarded as belonging to their group were a threat to them. This opened the way for exploitation"—an exploitation that did indeed happen in chapter 25, according to Meyer (2005, 252). Thus, according to Meyer, chapter 24 represents a transition towards a more negative view of the גֵּר. Meyer's interpretation requires the blasphemer to be a גֵּר despite the fact that he is never called one in the text.

Israelite sojourners must be punished for blasphemy, the blasphemer must too, since he falls in between native Israelites and non-Israelite sojourners.

The blasphemer has been characterised as the stereotypical outsider of the society (Rooke 2015; Holguín 2015). Recent deconstructionist approaches have emphasised an outsider perspective by pointing to the fact that the blasphemer is only introduced by his mother's name and is identified as a half-Egyptian (Rooke 2015, 167).[69] The blasphemer has also been likened to a *mestizo* (Spanish for a person of mixed racial origin) who has become the "victim of impossible demands that a closed community places upon the marginalized individuals who live on its fringes" (Holguín 2015, 99). In agreement with Deborah W. Rooke, Julián A. G. Holguín presents the *mestizo* as the paradigmatic outsider, in contrast to his opponent, אִישׁ הַיִּשְׂרְאֵלִי 'an Israelite man', who is the paradigmatic insider.

The characterisation of the blasphemer as a paradigmatic outsider, however, does not seem to do full justice to the role of the blasphemer in H. Unlike many other participants, the blasphemer does in fact instigate an event and is generally more

---

[69] In addition, Rooke (2015, 161–62) argues that, while the identity of the community of H is constructed in masculine terms, e.g., addressing the community as 'the sons of Israel', the blasphemer is introduced as the son of an Israelite woman, Shelomith, and his act of cursing the divine name (נקב 'curse') is expressed by the same root from which the word that P uses for 'feminine' (נְקֵבָה) is formed. According to Rooke (2015, 165), then, by using gendered language, the author of Lev. 24.10–23 draws a picture of "the innermost heart and the outermost boundary of the community."

agentive than many other participants (e.g., most of the women). Moreover, the blasphemer's curse occasions a speech by YHWH to Moses in which the important legal principle, the *lex talionis*, is unfolded. Thus, as will be argued, the blasphemer has a rather significant structural role within the discourse of H (see chapter 7, §5.2.3). In sum, therefore, characterisation of the blasphemer must account for the fact that the blasphemer is both quite agentive *and* becomes the subject of imprisonment and capital punishment.

## 6.7. The Land

Perhaps surprisingly, some scholars have considered אֶרֶץ 'land' as a participant almost on a par with human participants. Indeed, as several commentators have noted, the land occasionally occurs as an agent and is seemingly personified in H (Hieke 2014, 1095; Barbiero 2002, 240).[70] Esias E. Meyer (2015b) discusses all cases in H in which the land occurs as the syntactic subject of a proposition. The land can be defiled (18.25, 27), spit out (18.25, 28), prostitute herself (19.29), rest (25.2; 26.34, 35), give her crops (25.19; 26.4, 20), take pleasure (26.34, 43), and eat (26.38). Notable in Meyer's contribution is his exploration of the triangular relationship between YHWH, the people, and the land. According to Meyer (2015b, 442), the strongest relationship is between YHWH and the land, because the land is said to belong to YHWH,

---

[70] Nihan (2007, 560) explains the relationship between the land and its inhabitants as "almost organic."

while the people are only tenants of Yhwh (25.23).⁷¹ The land has an intermediary role, since Yhwh's blessings and curses are mediated by the land (e.g., 18.24–30; 26.4; Meyer 2015b, 443–45). In an extensive treatment of the land in H, Jan Joosten (1996, 152–54) dedicates a few pages to remarks on the so-called personification of the land in H. He describes the land as an "independent agent" and "an animate being far more powerful than its inhabitants" (Joosten 1996, 152–53). Joosten notes that there is a tension in H because the land belongs to both Yhwh and the Israelites at the same time. The tension can be explained in terms of the cultic conception of H: "the land is Yhwh's because he dwells there, it is Israel's because of their relationship to Yhwh and his temple" (Joosten 1996, 181).⁷² More recently, Joosten (2010) has explored the conception of the land in H from a rhetorical point of view. In particular, he argues that the land has a rhetorical role as "the significant third" (*le tiers significative*; Joosten 2010, 392–94). The land is frequently referred to as 'your land', but occasionally also as 'my land'. The rhetorical implication of this "play on pronominal possessive suffixes" (*jeu de pronoms possessifs*) is to enhance the relationship between the divine speaker and his audience by means of relating the discourse to a

---

⁷¹ Milgrom (2000, 1404–5) remarks that H never describes the land as the נַחֲלָה 'possession' of Israel but only as their אֲחֻזָּה 'holding', thus eschewing the notion of permanent possession.

⁷² Cf., however, Milgrom (2000, 1404), who rejects the idea that Yhwh's ownership of the land is due to his dwelling in the land. In many other respects, Milgrom agrees with Joosten's understanding of the role of the land.

third, concrete entity to which the audience can readily refer.[73] Stackert (2011) emphasises the agency of the land in H in his article on land and sabbath. According to Stackert (2011, 240), the land is personified and idealised as a "holy servant of the Israelite god." In particular, the land has an active role and "is required" to observe the sabbatical year (Stackert 2011, 247 n. 22). Indeed, the land is depicted as an "idealized Israelite" in parallel to the people itself (Stackert 2011, 246).

While the role of the land is certainly interesting, the present study will restrict itself to the human/divine participants and leave the role of the land open for further research.

## 6.8. Summary and Implications

Most accounts of the participants in the Holiness Code are limited to the study of individuals or small sets of participants. The strengths of these traditional approaches are readily apparent in that they often combine literary and historical considerations. A significant limitation, on the other hand, is that they do not take the entire network of participants into account, at least not in any structured way. Consequently, although a number of participants are often claimed to be marginalised—for example, the women, the blasphemer, and the sojourner—such conclusions would be more valid if these participants were compared to one another, in order to account for their respective roles in light of the remaining participants and their impact on the community. In

---

[73] Christian (2011, 363) adds to Joosten's rhetorical analysis that the people seems to have a mediating role in Lev. 25.5 in allowing for the land to rest.

other words, the role of a participant cannot satisfactorily be measured independently of the network of participants, because roles are dynamic and interdependent.

The aim of the present study is to classify the participants and their roles based on their interactions and relationships with other participants and in light of their position within the social network. The advantage is that all participants and interactions are included in the calculation, so that the characterisation of one participant is always seen in light of the entire network of participants. By applying SNA, statistical methods can be employed to measure the structural roles of the participants, and interactions and relationships can be quantified. It is thus possible to compare the roles of all participants in the network despite differences in frequency and distribution across the text. In other words, the roles of the women can be compared to that of the blasphemer, although they never interact. Given its emphasis on the participants and verbal interactions of the extant text, a social network analysis of the Holiness Code has its own limitations. Firstly, it is not concerned with historical questions, for example, the 'real-world' identity of the גֵּר 'sojourner'. Secondly, it only includes clauses with a minimum of two participants and a verbal event, at least in the method applied here. Thus, if the text characterises the participants by other linguistic means, these will not be included in this analysis (see chapter 7, §3.1 for further discussion).

More concretely, the review of previous research has revealed a number of inconsistencies in the profiling of the participants. Several important questions can more readily be addressed with SNA:

## 2. Towards a Social Network Analysis of the Holiness Code    69

- The addressees: Does the subcategorisation of the addressees (Pl vs Sg) entail different roles in the social network of the text? (chapter 3, §3.7 and chapter 7, §5.1.2)
- The women: What is the role of the women? Are they profiled as free agents, patients, or instruments? (chapter 7, §5.3.1)
- The brother/fellow: How should we understand the role of the brother/fellow within the dynamics of clan, society, and foreigners? (chapter 7, §5.2.2)
- The sojourner: Where is the גֵּר 'sojourner' situated with respect to the Israelite community? Is he situated on the fringes of society, or is he closer to the core of the community than other presumably marginalised participants? (chapter 7, §5.1.3)
- The priests: What is the role of the priests *vis-à-vis* the roles of the people and YHWH? (chapter 7, §5.1.4)
- The blasphemer: How should the role of the blasphemer be accounted for in light of his active involvement in the unique narrative event in H on the one hand, and his miserable fate at the hands of the Israelite congregation on the other hand? (chapter 7, §5.2.3)

# 3. TRACKING THE PARTICIPANTS

## 1.0. Introduction

For a social network analysis of the Holiness Code, participant tracking is the obvious first step.[1] The people of the Holiness Code are members of an implied social network, and in order to investigate their interactions, it is necessary that they first be consistently delineated. This is the task of participant tracking. In everyday reading or conversation, participant tracking may seem like a trivial task. After all, readers hardly spend much time pondering 'who is who' when reading a text or engaging in dialogue. They intuitively rely on grammatical understanding, semantic knowledge, and cultural conventions to subconsciously organise the participants in their minds. The subtle interaction of grammatical cohesion and cultural or literary convention is a challenge, however, to the study of participants from ancient texts like the Holiness Code, because we cannot be sure whether our cultural and literary awareness is aligned with the text or imposed by the modern reader. In relying on intuition, there is an inherent risk of misreading the text or perhaps harmonising complexities in it which could otherwise reveal interesting rhetorical or ideological concerns.

---

[1] This may even be true for exegesis: "To a large extent one could even call exegesis a kind of participant analysis: who is who in a text and how do the various participants, the writer and the reader included, interact?" (Talstra 2016a, 245).

An instructive example is found in Lev. 25.17: "You shall not cheat one another, but you shall fear your God; for I am Yhwh your God." At first glance, the sentence seems straightforward. A cursory reading will associate the "I" with Yhwh. After all, the "I" is explicitly identified with Yhwh. The sentence is perplexing, however, for at least two reasons. Firstly, "you shall fear your God" puts God in the third person, as if this "God" is different from the "Yhwh your God" identified with the first-person reference. Are the addressees simply commanded to fear whatever god(s) they observe? Or is the same God referred to in both the first and third person in the same verse? Secondly, the verse is part of a speech which Moses is commanded to speak on behalf of Yhwh (25.1–2). V. 17 is thus part of Moses' speech. This observation would explain why the first instance of "God" is put in the third person in v. 17, since Moses would logically refer to God in the third person. A disturbing thought emerges, because if this interpretation is indeed true, is Moses then the "I"? Does he refer to himself as "Yhwh your God"? Why would Moses not simply say "You shall fear God, for *he* is Yhwh your God"? Is the complexity evidence of a rhetorical device purposefully employed by the author to put Yhwh in the first person for some communicative reason? Or are Moses and Yhwh deliberately conflated or associated for theological purposes? This issue will be discussed further below (§3.6), but it illustrates well the complexities of texts—Biblical texts included—which too often evade the eyes of the reader. The procedure of participant tracking proposed in this chapter, then, is all about formalising the otherwise intuitive process of identifying participants. The purpose of doing this is to reveal the complexities of the text by suspending the tendency for human readers to harmonise discrepancies. To assist participant tracking, a computational approach will be presented and discussed. The benefit of computational approaches is that computers excel at tracking formal grammatical connections, e.g., the links between subjects and predicates based on morphological agreement, but they cannot normally identify connections between participant references on the basis of semantics. For example, they cannot usually track down synonyms, because synonyms are not formally connected, but rely on the meaning evoked in the mind of the hearer/reader. For this reason, a computational approach can help the researcher to be aware of the border between syntax and semantics.

The participant-reference analysis undertaken in this study stands on the shoulders of Eep Talstra, who pioneered the study of participant tracking in the Hebrew Bible. He is the creator of several computer programs that can track and systematise the participants of a text, from the smallest linguistic entities to text-level participants. Talstra kindly created a state-of-the-art dataset for the purposes of the present study—a dataset now freely accessible online (2018b). The dataset reveals important issues pertaining to participant tracking, and the aim of this chapter is twofold. On the one hand, the complexities seen in the dataset will be reviewed, and resolutions will be suggested whenever possible. On the other hand, abnormalities may not be resolved by strict linguistic and structural analysis, but may rather point to pragmatic functions, which will be discussed accordingly.

## 2.0. Methodology and Data

### 2.1. Methodology

Despite the fact that the 'who is who' question must be fundamental to exegesis and translation, only a minority of studies have been dedicated to a systematic analysis of participant references in the Hebrew Bible. Here I will briefly mention the most important ones, before presenting Talstra's procedure in more detail. In his study of the Joseph story (Gen. 37; 39–48), Robert E. Longacre (2003; originally published 1989) proposed an "apparatus" for participant references (including nouns, proper names, pronominal elements, and null references, among others) as well as a ranking of participants with respect to their roles in the narrative. Informed by social linguistics, Longacre showed how linguistic entities were consciously employed to introduce or track a participant with a certain role.[2] Lénart J. de Regt (1999a) documented both usual patterns and special patterns of participant-reference shifts throughout the Hebrew Bible, with reference to the marking of major and minor participants and their (re)introductions in the text (see also De Regt 2001; 2019). Steven E. Runge (2006) investigated the encoding of participants in Gen. 12–25 and Exod. 1–12. In particular, his study provided a discourse-functional description of the encoding of participants based on semantic and cognitive constraints. Oliver Glanz (2013)

---

[2] Longacre (2003, 141) lists seven "operations" that can be performed in Biblical narratives using the "apparatus" of participant references: 1) introduction; 2) integration; 3) tracking; 4) reinstatement; 5) confrontation; 6) contrastive status; and 7) evaluation.

studied the participant-reference shifts in Jeremiah with respect to unexpected changes of grammatical person, number, and gender. De Regt's and Glanz's insights are relevant for the discussion of divine communication patterns in Leviticus (see §3.6). Most recently, Christiaan M. Erwich (2020) has created an algorithm for parsing Biblical texts to detect all sorts of referring entities, called mentions (i.e., all entities with marking of person, gender, and/or number), and to resolve co-referring entities. Although his research focused on the Psalter, the algorithm is applicable to all books of the Hebrew Bible. The algorithm certainly does not solve all exegetical problems pertaining to participant references, but it clearly shows the scope of formal participant tracking and where literary analysis should rightly begin. In contrast to De Regt and Glanz (and Talstra; see below), however, Erwich does not discuss the patterns of reference shifts. Moreover, most probably for practical reasons, he does not consider the complexities of synonyms and part-whole relationships, as is done in Talstra's research and the present study (see §§3.8–3.9). Regrettably, due to the time constraints of the present project, I have not had the opportunity to relate Erwich's findings more specifically to my own participant data from Leviticus.

The most important contributions to the systematic study of participant tracking in the Hebrew Bible were made by Talstra. Because Talstra's dataset of participants in Lev. 17–26 will form the backbone of the present participant analysis, his methodology deserves an introduction. Talstra has always opted for a bottom-up methodology for the grammatical description of linguistic structures. This procedure was implemented at the very beginning of the creation of the WIVU database of the Hebrew Bible at the Werkgroep Informatica at Vrije Universiteit in Amsterdam.³ According to this methodology, text parsing begins with a structural analysis of the distributional entities of the text, words and morphemes. At later stages, the objects are parsed into word groups (phrases), clauses, and sentences. The distributional approach is followed by linguistic analysis to calculate the functions of words, phrases, and clauses by means of identifying patterns of linguistic behaviour. Thus, the methodology can be termed a form-to-function methodology.⁴ The form-to-function approach has also been the basis for Talstra's manifold experiments in participant tracking, which include works on Zechariah (2018a), Exod. 16 (2014), and Exod. 19 (2016a; 2016b). Talstra has described his procedure in one of his articles on Exod. 19 (2016b). The procedure follows eight steps, as briefly outlined here:

1. **Identification:** All possible participant-reference candidates (PRef) are selected on the basis of grammatical features marking person, gender, and/or number. Clear

---

³ For a detailed account of the methodology, see Talstra and Sikkel (2000; see also Talstra 2004). For a technical description of the data creation process, see Kingham (2018).

⁴ "I decided not to try to begin with the design of a set of grammatical rules, to be applied by a computer programme in performing the morphological and syntactic parsing. But from that very start and continually so in the group of the colleagues that joined me in the project, we have tried to use the Biblical texts as an area of testing proposals of syntactic parsing" (Talstra 2003, 8)—a draft kindly shared with me by Eep Talstra. For the published, shortened version, see Talstra (2004).

cases are finite verbs, personal pronouns, and pronominal suffixes. Cases with gender and number information only are also included, that is, demonstrative pronouns, nouns, and NPs. Some phrases, called 'compound phrases' or 'complex phrases' (the latter designation employed in this study), contain multiple subunits and require further analysis, since the components of the phrase may themselves be referring to entities apart from the phrase itself. This issue is discussed further below (§3.1).

2. **Testing:** It is tested how the PRefs can be matched to one another. There are generally three mechanisms: Firstly, suffixes may refer back to another suffix or a noun phrase. Secondly, subjects co-refer with their verbal predicates. And thirdly, lexemes co-refer with identical lexemes in the text. While identical lexemes can easily be mapped across the entire text, the two former linking procedures normally apply only within the same textual domain.[5] Nominal clauses offer a separate challenge, since the subject and the non-verbal predicate need not be co-referring. Thus, additional analysis is required for nominal clauses (see §3.2).

---

[5] A textual domain is formed by one or more sentences and comprises an entire stretch of discourse (narrative or direct speech). A text is formed by one or more textual domains which form a textual hierarchy. Direct speech domains are often embedded in narrative speech introductions, and direct speeches may even contain portions of narrative or embedded direct speech. The recognition of textual domains is imperative for a successful participant-tracking analysis, because participant references usually change across domain boundaries (see step 4 below).

3. **Participant sets:** Sets of PRefs matched by any of the linking mechanisms described in step 2 are combined into so-called participant sets (PSet). By implication, PRefs with no matches are skipped (see further discussion in §3.3). However, first-person and second-person references are always accepted as PSets. In most cases, they refer back to references in other domains. The linking procedure sometimes encounters different referents with identical references. Further analysis is needed to disambiguate these references (see §3.4). Finally, each PSet is given a relevant label derived from the text (most commonly, proper name, NP, or pronoun).
4. **Communication patterns:** PSets are linked across domains by introducing new linking rules. While third-person references can easily be mapped onto identical lexemes in other textual domains, first- and second-person references require a different set of rules. In particular, when the border between a narrative domain and a direct speech domain is crossed, the participant references normally change. Firstly, the speaker of a quotation is normally introduced in the third person in a narrative domain and referred to in the first person within the quotation itself. Secondly, the audience is introduced in the narrative domain in the third person and normally addressed in the second person in the quotation domain. Therefore, speaker and audience must be linked across domains by taking these participant-reference shifts into account.

## 3. Tracking the Participants

5. **Lexical identity:** The remaining PSets that are not part of any communication patterns are linked beyond domain level. Typically, third-person references are linked across domains based on lexical identity.

6. **Participant actors:** The connected PSets are connected at a higher linguistic level using the label 'participant actor' (PAct). This step subsumes the linking mechanisms of steps 4 and 5 (communication patterns and lexical identity). At this stage of participant tracking, a number of linguistic phenomena require additional analysis, most significantly because of divergences from normal communication patterns. In Lev. 17–26, abnormalities have been encountered with respect to both sender/speaker (§3.6) and addressee/audience (§3.7). The crucial question is whether these phenomena represent syntactic patterns to be handled in a formal participant tracking algorithm or can only be resolved by recourse to semantics or literary analysis.

7. **Synonyms:** Some PActs are likely to be co-referring despite their different labels. The most frequent issue is probably יהוה 'YHWH' and אֱלֹהִים 'God', which cannot be combined on the basis of lexical identity but nevertheless refer to the same participant. The collocation of synonymous PActs enters a domain where linguistic and literary analysis meet, since a purely formal analysis can hardly account for all relevant cases. Moreover, the collocation of synonymous PActs evokes literary and rhetorical con-

siderations, because different references to the same participant may serve pragmatic purposes (e.g., the references יהוה 'YHWH' and אֱלֹהִים 'God' may not simply be employed for the sake of variation; rather, each reference may carry its own theological import). A number of such phenomena are encountered in Leviticus (see §3.8).

8. **Participant clusters:** Some PActs are similar but not entirely synonymous. Rather, they constitute part-whole relationships (e.g., רֹאשׁ הָהָר 'top of the mountain' is part of הָהָר 'the mountain'). These references denote a specific part or member of a participant and thus form clusters of related participants. The clustering of related participants allows for a distinction between main actors (e.g., 'the mountain') and dependent actors ('top of the mountain'). The implications of this for Lev. 17–26 are discussed in §3.9.

## 2.2. The Dataset

The Talstra dataset of Lev. 17–26 consists of 4,092 rows and 370 different participant actors (PActs). A sample of the dataset is found in Table 1 (excluding book, chapter, and verse references for the sake of space). The second column, 'surface text', contains the surface text of the Hebrew text. 'Line' refers to the so-called clause atom, but relative to the chapter; that is, the first clause atom of a chapter is the first line.[6] 'Pred' contains the verbal predicate of the clause, while 'lexeme' supplies the lexemes of the

---

[6] The clause atom annotation is the result of the distributional analysis of the Hebrew text represented in the ETCBC database. The numbering

surface text. 'PSet' contains the participant sets calculated in step 3 (see Talstra's eight-step methodology above). 'PAct' refers to the participant actors calculated in step 6. In many cases, apart from the sample below, a reference is not given, because only references with co-referring matches are included in the analysis. The two last columns provide the first and last slot of the participant reference relative to the line.

Table 1: The first five rows of the participant tracking dataset (Lev. 17.1–2a)

| Ref | Surface Text | Line | Pred | Lexeme | PSet | PAct | First Slot | Last Slot |
|---|---|---|---|---|---|---|---|---|
| 1 | יְדַבֵּר '[he] said' | 1 | דבר | דבר | 3sm = יהוה 'YHWH' | יהוה 'YHWH' | 2 | 2 |
| 2 | יהוה 'YHWH' | 1 | דבר | יהוה | 3sm = יהוה 'YHWH' | יהוה 'YHWH' | 3 | 3 |
| 3 | אֶל־מֹשֶׁה 'to Moses' | 1 | דבר | אל משה | 0sm = מֹשֶׁה 'Moses' | מֹשֶׁה 'Moses' | 4 | 5 |
| 4 | לֵאמֹר 'saying' | 2 | אמר | לאמר | 3sm = יהוה 'YHWH' | יהוה 'YHWH' | 1 | 2 |
| 5 | דַּבֵּר 'speak' | 3 | דבר | דבר | 2sm = | מֹשֶׁה 'Moses' | 1 | 1 |

# 3.0. Participant-Tracking Phenomena in Lev. 17–26

In what follows below, important linguistic phenomena concerning the participant tracking of Lev. 17–26 will be discussed and related to Talstra's eight-step procedure outlined above. I have not had access to Talstra's computer programs, so the present

---

of clause atoms thus follows the distributional order of the text. Each clause fragment is considered a clause atom, and one or more clause atoms form a complete clause (see Talstra and Sikkel 2000).

analysis relies on a systematic cross-validation of the dataset to detect patterns of participant tracking. The cross-validation involves both computational detection of general patterns and manual inspection of the annotations.

## 3.1. Complex Phrases

Complex phrases are phrases with multiple constituents, which pose a fundamental challenge to participant tracking. Talstra (2016b, 13) hints at the issue in his consideration of the prepositional phrase לְזִקְנֵי הָעָם 'to the elders of the people' (Exod. 19.7), which is a complex phrase comprised of two nouns in a construct chain.[7] The question is whether both nouns should be considered participants. In Exod. 19, which is the text under consideration in Talstra's study, עַם 'people' occurs in other constructions, suggesting that the noun is a referring entity and not merely modifying the elders. זָקֵן 'elder' is not an independent reference and does not occur elsewhere in Exod. 19, so it is not treated as a referring entity. Thus, the complex phrase לְזִקְנֵי הָעָם consists of two referring entities, 'people' and 'elders of the people'. It is clear, then, that complex phrases can be operating at various levels of grammar, in this case the phrase level and the word level.

---

[7] A construct chain is formed by two or more nouns juxtaposed. In its simplest form, the chain consists of a noun in the construct state followed by a noun in the absolute state, e.g., בְּנֵי יִשְׂרָאֵל 'sons of Israel'. The absolute state is the base form of the word, whereas the construct state is a derived form that signals a constructional relationship with the subsequent word. Here, the first member of the construct chain will be called the *nomen regens* and the last member the *nomen rectum*. For further explanation, see Van der Merwe et al. (2017, §25).

In addition, complex phrases can be operating on the subphrase and morpheme levels. An example from Lev. 17.2 shows the complexity:

Figure 1: Text-Fabric screenshot of phrase- and subphrase structure (Lev 17.2a)

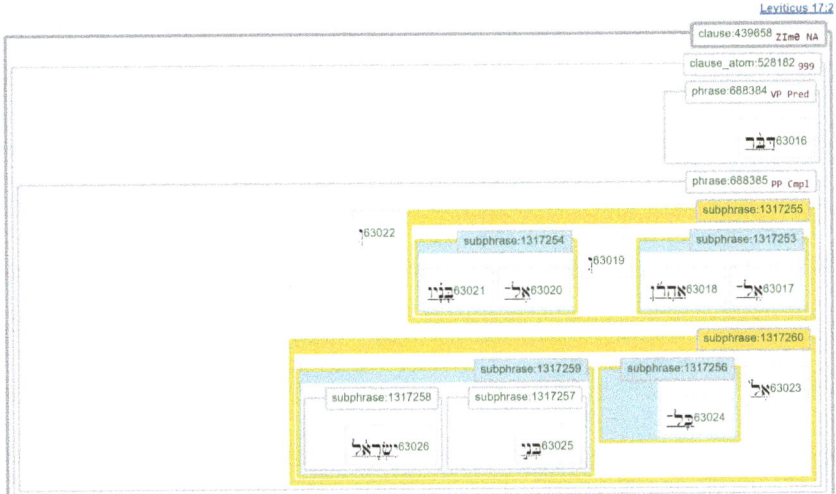

The complement phrase of the clause in Figure 1 is a complex phrase. The yellow fields represent the two primary embedded subphrases: 'to Aaron and to his sons' and 'to all the sons of Israel'. In addition, both subphrases contain two additional subphrases (marked by blue), and the last of these subphrases 'sons of Israel' is itself composed of two subphrases. Finally, the suffix of בָּנָיו 'his sons' contains another participant reference, the suffix referring to 'Aaron'. Thus, this phrase is complex and contains nine constituents.[8] Any of the subphrases, as well as the suffix,

---

[8] The nine constituents are: אֶל־אַהֲרֹן וְאֶל־בָּנָיו 'to Aaron and to his sons', אֶל־אַהֲרֹן 'to Aaron', אֶל־בָּנָיו 'to his sons', ו (suffix) 'his', אֶל כָּל־בְּנֵי יִשְׂרָאֵל 'to

may indeed refer to participants of the text, but this is not necessarily so. Semantically, the phrase is curious, because it appears that Aaron, Aaron's sons, and the Israelites are three distinct entities. One might actually, on the other hand, expect Aaron and his sons to be members of 'all the sons of Israel'. In fact, when a new participant, בֵּית יִשְׂרָאֵל 'the house of Israel', is introduced in the following verse (v. 3), does that participant refer merely to 'all the sons of Israel', or does it include Aaron and his sons? In other words, the semantic delineation of these participants is anything but clear. With respect to participant tracking, the question is whether the complex phrase concerns three distinct participants, or perhaps one major participant ('all the sons of Israel') with two specified subspecies. Although curious, the phenomenon is not rare in literature and speech. Indeed, it is a common feature of speech to vary between the use of group-references of which the participant is a member, and individual references to the participant in question. In light of the present project, the three participants are considered distinct. This choice allows for the analysis of the roles of Aaron, his sons, and the Israelites (excluding Aaron and his sons) over against one another (see chapter 7, §5.1.2). One implication of this choice is that the laws of Lev. 18–20 are treated as addressed solely to the lay Israelites, excluding the priests. Obviously, the laws apply to all members of the society, including the priestly class. On the other hand, the sons of Israel and the priests (Aaron and his sons) sometimes refer explicitly to two different entities (e.g., 22.2–3). In

---

all the sons of Israel', ־כָּל 'all', בְּנֵי יִשְׂרָאֵל 'the sons of Israel', בְּנֵי 'the sons', and יִשְׂרָאֵל 'Israel'.

short, therefore, participants are not always distinct and may even overlap. In some cases, a semantic overlap may be dealt with by specifying part-whole relationships (see §3.9). In any case, since the present project relies on a clear delineation of participants, the resulting list of participants bears evidence of compromise (see §3.10).

Returning to the complex phrase of Lev. 17.2, one wonders whether 'Israel' is a real, independent participant or whether it merely qualifies 'the sons'. In fact, the lexeme 'Israel' occurs eight times in Lev. 17 and only in genitival constructions, including 'sons of Israel' (17.2, 5, 12, 13, 14) and 'house of Israel' (17.3, 8, 10). Furthermore, is כֹּל 'all/anyone' a participant reference, or does it rather modify 'sons of Israel'? That is, should the phrase be translated 'the entirety of the sons of Israel' or 'all the sons of Israel'? Strictly speaking, since כֹּל is a noun and part of a noun chain, it could be considered a member of 'sons of Israel'; hence, 'the entirety of the sons of Israel'. Logically, however, כֹּל does not denote a participant other than 'sons of Israel', but simply signifies that the entire people is addressed. In this case, therefore, we should treat כֹּל as a modifier rather than a participant reference on its own. The policy implemented by Talstra (2016b, 13) is to treat כֹּל as a modifier except in cases where the word is used as an independent noun phrase. More generally, the solution to dealing with complex phrases lies with the matter of formal dependency. A formally independent participant is a participant that occurs either as an independent noun phrase or as the last noun of a construct chain, the so-called *nomen rectum*. Formally dependent participants, by contrast, never occur in these constructional slots. For this reason, 'Israel' is in fact considered an independent participant in Lev. 17, because it is always the last word of the construct chains. By contrast, 'sons' never occurs independently in that chapter. There are no בָּנִים 'sons' apart from 'his sons' (17.2) and 'sons of Israel'. Therefore, 'sons' is not considered a participant on its own. Neither is כֹּל 'all/anyone', which is also formally dependent in Lev. 17.2a. Although the lexeme occurs eight times in the chapter, it occurs only in construct chains, including כָּל־בְּנֵי יִשְׂרָאֵל 'all the sons of Israel' (17.2), כָּל־דָּם 'any blood' (17.10), כָּל־נֶפֶשׁ 'any soul' (17.12, 15), כָּל־בָּשָׂר 'any/all flesh' (17.14 [×3]), and כָּל־אֹכְלָיו 'anyone eating it' (17.14).

In sum, the use of independency as a criterion allows for the automatic disregarding of nouns that are not independently referring to a textual participant. Thus, rather than all four subphrases of 'all the sons of Israel' being considered participants, only two are: בְּנֵי יִשְׂרָאֵל 'sons of Israel' and יִשְׂרָאֵל 'Israel'.

## 3.2. Nominal Clauses

The second step of the participant-tracking procedure is to test linking mechanisms for matching co-referring entities within the same domain, including subjects and predicates. Not surprisingly, in the dataset, subjects and their verbal predicates normally refer to the same referent (95.57% of the cases). For nominal clauses, the picture is different.[9] In nominal clauses with explicit subject and predicate, only 56.47% of the predicates refer

---

[9] Scholars disagree as to the precise definition of nominal clauses. While it is generally acknowledged that a nominal clause distinguishes itself

to the referent of the subject. In the remaining nominal clauses, predicate and subject are annotated differently.[10] The difference is striking and points to an important issue. In many cases, it is reasonable to consider the subject and its non-verbal predicate to refer to the same referent, for example the common declaration אֲנִי יהוה 'I am YHWH' (1). In this case, both references refer to the same participant. In other cases, however, the relationship between the subject and the predicate is less identical (2):[11]

(1)  אֲנִי יְהוָה

   'I am YHWH.' (Lev. 18.6)

---

from verbal clauses by containing a non-verbal predicate, the non-verbal predicate has been defined in various ways. While Richter (1980, 12) argues that the term 'nominal clause' should be reserved for clauses without any verbal morpheme, it has been common to at least include the copula היה 'be' (Joüon and Muraoka 1993, §154; Dyk and Talstra 1999). De Regt (1999a) excludes participles from his definition of nominal clauses (see also Gross 1980), while Niccacci (1999, 243) treats clauses with verbal predicates in the second position as nominal clauses, because, according to him, the verb "plays the role of a noun." Baasten (2006) argues that what is normally called a 'nominal clause' should rightly be called a 'non-verbal clause', because the predicate of a non-verbal clause can be a nominal, a prepositional, or an adverbial phrase, among other things. An introduction by Miller (1999) summarises the "pivotal issues" in the analysis of the nominal clause ('verbless clause' in her terminology). In the present discussion, a nominal clause is defined as a clause with a subject and a non-verbal predicate, though this includes participles and the copula היה 'be'.

[10] The calculation does not take into account those clauses where the subject is not annotated.

[11] The predicate is highlighted in red.

(2) כְּאֶזְרָח מִכֶּם יִהְיֶה לָכֶם הַגֵּר ׀ הַגָּר אִתְּכֶם

'Like a native of you shall the sojourner sojourning among you be to you.' (Lev. 19.34)

The meaning of the nominal clause in (2) is not that the sojourner and the native Israelite are the same—quite the opposite. The distinction is maintained, but the sojourner is to be treated as if he were a native. Thus, in this case, the subject and the predicate refer to two different participants. More precisely, the predicate *qualifies* the subject by relating the subject to the group expressed by the predicate. The difference between the two examples just given can be captured as the distinction between *identifying* predicates and *classifying*—or *descriptive*—predicates that has been noted by several linguists (Waltke and O'Connor 1990, §8.4; Joüon and Muraoka 1993, §154ea; Andersen 1970, 31–34).[12] Francis I. Andersen, who introduced the terms to explain the semantic relationship between subjects and predicates in nominal clauses, explained that an identifying predicate supplies the identity of the subject and has a total semantic overlap with the subject. A classifying predicate, on the other hand, only has a partial

---

[12] Joüon and Muraoka (1993, §154ea) use the term 'descriptive' for classifying predicates because, according to them, this designation accounts better for existential and locative sentences. Moreover, their use of 'identification' differs significantly from other accounts in that, for the clause to be identifying, the predicate needs to *uniquely* indicate and identify the subject. They offer 'I am Joseph' as an example of a sentence that would normally be interpreted as an identification clause but, according to their definition, could also be a descriptive clause, if the subject were construed as belonging to the class of men called Joseph.

semantic overlap with the subject and "refers to the general class of which the subject is a member" (Andersen 1970, 32). Bruce K. Waltke and Michael P. O'Connor (1990, §8.4) provide examples to show the difference:

(3)     הִיא־צֹעַר

'It is Zoar.' (Gen. 14.2)

(4)     טָמֵא הוּא

'He is unclean.' (Lev. 13.36)

In (3) the proper noun identifies the pronoun, that is, the referent of the pronoun is identified as the town Zoar.[13] In (4), the predicate (טָמֵא) classifies the subject (הוּא) as a member of a larger group defined as unclean. However, the two examples also raise a more fundamental question: How are the phrase functions, subject and predicate, to be determined in the first place? Andersen (1970) answered the question with respect to the notions of 'old' and 'new' information. Accordingly, the subject expresses the old or known information to which new information is added (the predicate). Old and new information relate to definiteness, because already known information is likely to be more definite than new information. However, as objected by J. Hoftijzer (1973), definiteness is not a purely formal category for Andersen, but also requires logic and semantics. Hoftijzer himself abandons

---

[13] Apparently, in contrast to Waltke and O'Connor, Hoftijzer (1973, 492) interprets this example (Gen. 14.2) as classifying.

the traditional notions of subject and predicate in favour of entirely formal ones.[14] More recently, Janet W. Dyk and Eep Talstra (1999) presented a paradigm for identifying subject and predicate in nominal clauses on the basis of purely formal criteria: phrase type and definiteness. Their proposal involves a basic hierarchy of definiteness based on phrase types, with 10 levels ranked from the most definite: suffix[15] > demonstrative pronoun > personal pronoun > definite NP > proper noun > indefinite NP > interrogative pronoun > adjective > PP > locative. According to Dyk and Talstra, in relation to the choice between subject and predicate, suffixes are always the subject, while prepositional phrases and locatives are normally only the predicate.[16] The remaining forms can be either subject or predicate depending on the other referring phrase in the clause. That is, the phrase with the highest level of determination will be the subject. For clauses with two phrases of identical type, more analysis is required. As a rule, the entity that is most deictic is determined to

---

[14] The notion of 'subject' and 'predicate' for distinguishing the constituents of nominal clauses has also been critiqued by Van Wolde (1999) who favours the cognitive categories 'given' and 'new'.

[15] More specifically, suffixes attached to the particles יֵשׁ '[particle of existence]', אַיִן '[particle of non-existence]', הִנֵּה 'behold', עוֹד 'still', and locatives.

[16] According to Janet W. Dyk (personal conversation), the term 'locatives' refers to anything that can indicate a location, including toponyms and nouns like אֶרֶץ 'earth/land'. Until now, however, this particular information has not been sufficiently encoded in the database. Hence, further research is needed to validate the decision tree for choosing between subject and predicate.

be the subject. For example, for a clause with two personal pronouns, a first person pronoun ranks higher than a second person pronoun, which ranks higher than a third person pronoun (Dyk and Talstra 1999, 179). The benefit of this paradigm is that it effectively separates the subject-predicate determination from the semantics of the clause (classifying vs identifying).[17] Moreover, the paradigm does not rely on the word order of the clause, which has often been the case in other paradigms (e.g., Andersen 1970; Joüon and Muraoka 1993, §154; Waltke and O'Connor 1990, §8.4). In fact, word order more likely correlates with information structure and, in particular, the marking of topic and focus (Lambrecht 1994).[18]

---

[17] It should be noted that Dyk and Talstra's paradigm is not reflected perfectly in the version of the database used in the present project (BHSAc). Even the corpus treated in Dyk and Talstra's paper was either not completely parsed with the suggested algorithm or was later overwritten with new annotations. For example, Dyk and Talstra (1999, 153) determined the demonstrative pronoun in הַאַתָּה זֶה 'is this you?' (1 Kgs 18.7) to be the subject, due to its relatively higher degree of definiteness. However, in the current version of the database (accessed 6 June 2023), the personal pronoun is annotated as the subject.

[18] Information structure is the component of sentence grammar that conceptualises the pairing of mental propositions (or states of affairs) with the lexicogrammatical structures of the sentence. The term was first coined by Halliday (1967), but the theory received its most profound treatment in Lambrecht (1994). According to this theory, syntax is not autonomous, but rather a vehicle for expressing mental ideas. That is, the speaker employs word order, among other lexicogrammatical tools, to utter a proposition in accordance with what he assumes the

I suggest, then, that the participant-tracking analysis of nominal clauses must proceed in two steps. Firstly, subject and predicate are determined on the basis of relative definiteness. Secondly, the meaning of the clause can be determined according to the definiteness of the predicate. If the predicate is an indefinite NP, or less definite according to Dyk and Talstra's hierarchy, then the predicate is classifying. If the predicate is a proper name or more definite, the predicate is identifying. This paradigm helps to sort out some difficult nominal clauses in Lev. 23:

(5) מוֹעֲדֵי יְהוָה אֲשֶׁר־תִּקְרְאוּ אֹתָם מִקְרָאֵי קֹדֶשׁ

'The appointed times of YHWH, which you shall proclaim, are holy convocations.' (Lev. 23.2)

(6) וּמִנְחָתוֹ שְׁנֵי עֶשְׂרֹנִים סֹלֶת בְּלוּלָה בַשֶּׁמֶן

'Its grain offering is two-tenths of choice flour mixed with oil.' (Lev. 23.13)

(7) אַךְ בֶּעָשׂוֹר לַחֹדֶשׁ הַשְּׁבִיעִי הַזֶּה יוֹם הַכִּפֻּרִים הוּא

'Now, on the tenth [day] of this seventh month, the day of atonement it is.' (Lev. 23.27)

In (5), the subject is identified as מוֹעֲדֵי יהוה 'appointed times of YHWH' because its *nomen rectum*, יהוה 'YHWH', is more definite

---

hearer to already be cognitively aware of or not. Among the key components of information structure are topic and focus, the former referring to the information presupposed to be known by the hearer and the latter to the new assertion. The concept of information structure was adopted in RRG, where it was proposed that languages have specific inventories of syntactic structures available for the speaker to communicate a particular proposition (Van Valin 2005, 13).

than the *nomen rectum* of the second constituent, קֹדֶשׁ 'holy', which is an undetermined noun. Since the predicate is indefinite, it is reasonable to interpret the appointed times of YHWH as belonging to the class of 'holy convocations', hence a *classifying* clause. In (6), the first constituent, מִנְחָתוֹ 'its grain offering', is definite, in contrast to the second constituent, which is an indefinite noun phrase. Therefore, the first constituent is the subject, and the predicate *classifies* or describes the grain-offering, that is, the grain offering is one of choice flour. The sentence in (7) consists of three constituents: a complex time phrase, a definite noun phrase, and a personal pronoun. The main challenge is to identify the antecedent of the personal pronoun (הוּא 'he/it'). Probably, the antecedent must be inferred from the time phrase which presupposes the noun יוֹם 'day', marked by the square brackets in the translation. If this interpretation is true, the time phrase is a *casus pendens* that reactivates the time frame (notice the demonstrative pronoun הַזֶּה 'this') first introduced in v. 24.[19] According to the paradigm, then, the personal pronoun is the subject, and the

---

[19] The *casus pendens* is a dislocated constituent preceding the clause, and is commonly accepted as a means for a speaker/writer to reactivate a topic (Khan 1988; Westbury 2014; Jensen 2017). According to Givón (2001, II:265), the *casus pendens* (or 'left dislocation') is a referent-encoding device with one of the highest anaphoric distances. This means that the left dislocation can pick up a topic over a long distance in the discourse. With respect to the HB, instances of *casus pendens* occur "particularly frequently" in the legal material (Khan 1988, 98; see in particular his appendix on extraposition in legal formulae, pp. 98–104).

noun phrase the predicate. Given the definiteness of the predicate, the predicate is *identifying*; hence, the specific day referred to by the pronoun is identified as the day of atonement.

In sum, the two-step procedure proposed here on the basis of Dyk and Talstra's paradigm for determining subject and predicate proves useful for interpreting the nominal clauses of Lev. 17–26. This task is useful not only for exegesis but also for participant tracking, because it provides the means by which to discern whether the clause contains two participants (classifying) or only one (identifying).

## 3.3. One-Time Participants

The participant-tracking methodology proposed by Talstra is essentially about clustering participant references according to co-reference. By implication, any participant must have at least two references; otherwise, no clusters will be formed, and no textual participant will be derived. The advantage of this procedure is that many non-referential nouns are left out of the analysis simply due to their infrequency. The dataset contains 370 unique PActs, and that number would probably have been much higher if all references were included. The downside of the approach is the neglect of participants which are indeed referential but only occur once in a chapter. In the analysis of Lev. 17.2a above, (§3.1) the reference 'his sons' was only briefly considered. The subphrase refers to Aaron's sons, who are members of the group of addressees in the clause 'speak to Aaron, and to his sons, and to all the sons of Israel'. While 'Aaron' occurs twice in the chapter and 'sons of Israel' multiple times, 'his sons' only occurs once. As a consequence of the participant-tracking methodology, 'Aaron's sons' is not considered a participant in the analysis, because of its single attestation. Other participants are also ruled out on this account, including אֶזְרָח 'native' (18.26), עָנִי 'poor' (19.10), כַּלָּתוֹ 'his daughter-in-law' (20.12), אֱלֹהִים 'God' (22.33), and שְׁלֹמִית 'Shelomith' (24.11), none of which occurs more than once in their respective chapters. As for the last example, it is particularly interesting. While most participants in H are anonymous, a few are named, including Moses, Aaron, and YHWH. To this narrow group belongs Shelomith, the mother of the blasphemer in the narrative of Lev. 24.10–23. However, although she is named, she is only named with respect to her relationship with the blasphemer, so she does not have an independent role in the text. Therefore, the program may do well in skipping this reference. As for the second example in the list above, 'the poor', it is skipped, even though it is grammatically definite and, hence, referential. Moreover, 'the poor' occurs in parallel to גֵּר 'sojourner', which is in fact tracked because it reappears in 19.33. Thus, the neglect of referents with only one occurrence sometimes leads to the omission of a participant. A solution to this issue may therefore be to consider the definiteness of one-time, independent participant references, since definiteness signals referentiality. In the present study, the relevant participants have been included manually in the pile of human/divine participants under consideration.

A slightly different phenomenon is found in Lev. 23. In this chapter, the noun קָצִיר 'harvest' occurs four times, but always with different genitival modifiers: קְצִירָהּ 'its harvest', that is, the harvest of the land (23.10), קְצִירְכֶם 'your (Pl) harvest' (23.10), אֶת־ קְצִיר אַרְצְכֶם 'the harvest of your (Pl) land' (23.22), and קְצִירְךָ 'your (Sg) harvest' (23.22). Thus, although קָצִיר occurs multiple times, it is always modified by different nouns or suffixes and is therefore not considered a participant.

Another problem arising from the 'one-time reference issue' is that actors that only occur once in a chapter may actually have co-referents in other chapters of the text. For instance, while אֶזְרָח 'native' only occurs once in Lev. 18, it also occurs in 17.15; 19.34; 23.42; 24.16, 22. Because the computer programs only work at chapter level, they will not map co-referring entities from different chapters in the larger context. The speech in Lev. 25–26 is another example of this issue. Despite the fact that the speech in Lev. 25 is continued and concluded in chapter 26, the two chapters are treated separately in the dataset. As a consequence, the audience is labelled differently in Lev. 25 and 26. In the first chapter, the audience is labelled בְּנֵי יִשְׂרָאֵל 'sons of Israel' because of the speech introduction in v. 2, whereas in the second chapter, the audience is only implied and is therefore labelled אַתֶּם 'you', probably based on the 2MPl suffixes in 26.1. This issue points to the intrinsic relationship between participant tracking and discourse structure. A discourse may cover multiple chapters, such as Lev. 25–26, or may even be reduced to a few verses, such as the three speeches in Lev. 22 (vv. 1–16, 17–25, 26–33). In the latter case, the participants are reintroduced, and identical participant references cannot automatically be mapped across the borders of the speeches. Therefore, when conducting participant tracking for multiple chapters (or multiple discourses within the same chapter), one will need to consider whether the participants of one chapter are the same as similar-looking participants in another chapter. For the participant analysis of Lev. 17–26, this is a crucial step, since it can be reasonably hypothesised that these chapters form a literary unit within the book of Leviticus and that the participants recur throughout the chapters. It is therefore necessary to introduce a new step of participant tracking where actors are fetched from each chapter of a longer discourse and mapped onto identical actors in other chapters.

## 3.4. Identical References

The genre of H poses a specific challenge for participant tracking. As a law text, the text involves numerous abstract participants in order to present legal cases. Commonly, an abstract participant is introduced by an indefinite NP, e.g., אִישׁ 'a man/anyone'. Other options are the indefinite כֹּל 'anyone' (17.14), נֶפֶשׁ 'soul' (17.15), אָדָם 'human being' (18.5), or אִישׁ אוֹ־אִשָּׁה 'a man or a woman' (20.27). In contrast to individuals such as Moses or Aaron, these entities do not refer to a person in the 'real' world. It is questionable whether these words should be considered participants at all, because when they claim to refer to 'anyone', they operate on a different level to real participants like Moses and Aaron, ontologically speaking. They cannot be delineated as participants, because 'anyone'—in fact, 'everyone'—is included in them. On the other hand, it is interesting to observe how the text itself carefully distinguishes these vague references. 'Anyone' is not always 'anyone'. Indeed, the text introduces delineations which have legal value and social implications and thus contribute to the analysis of the social network implied by the text. With these caveats in mind, indefinite, pronominal NPs are included in the analysis.

Lev. 17 offers the first example where 'anyone' is not simply 'anyone'. The chapter contains four case laws, each introduced by אִישׁ 'anyone' (vv. 3, 8, 10, 13). A fifth case is given in 17.15, now introduced in a more generalised way by referring to כָּל־נֶפֶשׁ 'any soul'. The case laws all deal with cultic regulations on animal slaughter, each one dealing with different aspects: slaughtering of animals outside the Tent of Meeting (vv. 3–7), burnt offerings outside the Tent of Meeting (vv. 8–9), eating of blood (vv. 10–12), hunting of animals (vv. 13–14), and purification (vv. 15–16). Much scholarship has focused on the diachronic relationship between Lev. 17 and Deut. 12.[20] From a participant-tracking point of view, another issue is likewise complicated. A simple participant-tracking algorithm may treat the references to אִישׁ as referring to the same participant. This procedure can indeed be followed in some instances. However, it is common in law texts to specify the referent if needed. In 17.3, 'anyone' is specified as someone belonging to the 'house of Israel', but in the remaining cases, additional phrases are employed to specify that 'anyone' is someone from 'the house of Israel or from the sojourners living

---

[20] Milgrom (2000, 1319–67), in particular, has argued for the priority of Lev. 17 over Deuteronomy (see also Kilchör 2015), while Otto (1999; 2008; 2015) has argued for the opposite view, namely, that the prohibition against profane animal slaughter in Lev. 17 is a revision of the Deuteronomic legislation. For a discussion of their views, see Meyer (2015a).

among them'. For this reason, participant tracking can be quite complicated, since it must take into account complex constructions, including restrictive relative clauses.

Lev. 25 provides a similar case that is even more difficult. The chapter contains nine attestations of אִישׁ 'a man/anyone'. The first two are found in v. 10, where the lexeme is used in two elliptic clauses and should probably be translated 'anyone': "And you shall return, anyone to his property; and anyone to his clan, you shall return." In neither of the cases is the reference further modified. The attestations in vv. 13, 14, and 17 are similar. In v. 26, a case law is introduced by the identical אִישׁ. In this case, however, the reference is followed by a description: 'Anyone without a kinsman redeemer' (lit. 'A man, when there is no kinsman redeemer for him'). To make things more complicated—at least for a computational algorithm—the description is not put in a typical relative clause but in a clause introduced by the conjunction כִּי 'that/when/for'. Thus, the participant is not directly specified, but only by means of a circumstantial or temporal clause. In the subsequent verse (v. 27), אִישׁ 'anyone' is now going to return the rest of his debt לָאִישׁ אֲשֶׁר מָכַר־לוֹ 'to the man to whom he sold [his property]'. The introduction of another אִישׁ is not arbitrary, because the reference comes with a restrictive relative clause specifying the other man as the buyer of the property. Nevertheless, as in Lev. 17, the algorithm needs to be able to include relative clauses in the computation to keep track of the various purviews of אִישׁ. Finally, in v. 29, another case law is introduced by אִישׁ 'anyone': "A man [anyone], when he sells a dwelling house of a walled city." Again, one wonders whether this 'anyone' is the same as the 'anyone' in v. 26. On the one hand, the references do not refer to 'real' participants, so the question remains hypothetical. On the other hand, a consistent participant analysis needs to ponder this question in order to disambiguate or collocate the references. In Talstra's dataset, the two references are indeed collocated, a reasonable choice given the lack of any restrictive relative clauses or complex phrases such as are found in the case laws of Lev. 17. The approach undertaken by the present analysis has been restricted to considering only complex phrases and relative clauses. Accordingly, אִישׁ refers to two different participants in Lev. 17 ('anyone of the house of Israel' and 'anyone of the house of Israel or of the sojourners') and to two different participants in Lev. 25 ('anyone' in vv. 10, 13, 14, 26, 29 and 'the man to whom he sold the property' in v. 27). For a more fine-grained analysis, other types of modifiers need to be brought into the computation, including temporal/circumstantial clauses, if possible.

## 3.5. References with Same Gender or Person

The rigidness, positively speaking, of the algorithm that produces the participant dataset of H prompts many interesting exegetical and linguistic questions. Because the program does not allow for ambiguity, every reference needs to refer explicitly to only one participant, even in cases where the text itself is ambiguous. Lev. 21.8 offers one such case in which the interpretation has rather significant implications. In this verse, a second-person reference suddenly appears in וְקִדַּשְׁתּוֹ D 'and you (Sg) shall consider him holy'. The addressees of the chapter are the priests, but they are for some reason addressed in the third person. The program, therefore, has linked the 2MSg reference to the most probable antecedent in this discourse, Moses. By contrast, most commentators interpret the reference as referring to the Israelites, even though they are not directly addressed in this particular speech (e.g., Milgrom 2000, 1808; Hartley 1992, 348).[21] To be sure, Moses is not an optimal antecedent, since 21.8 is part of Moses' speech to "the priests, the sons of Aaron" (21.1). On the other hand, since the addressees of Moses' speech are in the plural, Moses is the only referent so far having a 2MSg reference (21.1). The disagreement between the computer and human commentators should serve as a caution against far-reaching interpretations dependent upon this particular reference. It has been argued, for example, that the people is responsible for "transferring" holiness to the priests, thus diminishing the special status of the priests (Christian 2011, 368–69; see the discussion in chapter 2, §6.5). However, given the uniqueness of Lev 21.8 and the ambiguity of the text, one should be cautious about drawing historical and theological implications.

In some cases, a degree of ambiguity is apparently allowed for by the computer program in that a reference is not necessarily linked to a possible referent. The same verse (21.8) ends with a 2MPl suffix, which would logically refer to the priests as the addressees of the speech (see v. 1). However, for some reason, the dataset does not contain this connection, but simply labels the

---

[21] The Israelites, in the plural, are mentioned in 21.24 in a compliance report that seems to conclude chapters 17–21.

reference '2MPl', probably due to the fact that the priests have so far been referred to in the third person.

In sum, the rigidness of a computational procedure reveals complexities in the text which could easily be ignored by an ordinary reading of the text. In these cases, it may not be possible to decide on a referent with certainty. If more precise results cannot be achieved by further analysis, interpreters should at least treat these cases with caution.

## 3.6. Divine Communication Patterns

An important component of participant-tracking is the matching of participants across domains. By default, a quotation domain is introduced by a short narrative introduction specifying sender and addressee, for example, "YHWH spoke to Moses, saying" (Lev. 19.1). In the subsequent quotation, first-person references likely refer to the speaker (= sender) and second-person references to the audience (= addressee), for example, "Speak to all the congregation of the sons of Israel and say to them" (19.2ab), where the second-person imperative refers to Moses, the addressee of the narrative introduction.[22] In the next sentence, however, the pattern breaks down: "You shall be holy because I, YHWH your God, am holy" (19.2cd). According to the pattern, the first-person reference should refer to the speaker, Moses, as implied by

---

[22] There are exceptions to this pattern, e.g., the unexpected plural suffix in אֲבוֹתֵיכֶם 'your fathers' in Zech. 1.2, because the preceding speech introduction has the prophet Zechariah as the addressee. There is thus no antecedent to 'your' (Pl). For a discussion of this phenomenon, see Talstra (2018a) and Jensen (2016).

19.2ab, but that cannot be true. For some reason, Moses uses the first-person reference to refer to YHWH. While commentators have stressed the rhetorical and structural purposes of the *Selbstvorstellungsformeln* (Hartley 1992, 291–93; Milgrom 2000, 1517–18), the subtle breakdown of the normal communication pattern is not discussed in any commentary on Leviticus that I am aware of. But it is indeed curious that Moses frequently, though not exclusively, refers to YHWH in the first person. At times, YHWH is also referred to in the third person (19.5, 8, 21, 22, 24).[23] Thus, since there is no simple rule that YHWH only holds either first-person or third-person position, we need to study the phenomenon further.

The challenge for a participant-tracking analysis is that no rule seems to be able to account for this unusual communication pattern. As Talstra (2014, 551, 560) notes with respect to an identical phenomenon in Exod. 16, it is "a linguistically unmarked change of speaker" and a case "where linguistic analysis and literary interpretation meet." In fact, the only way to discern whether the first-person reference refers to Moses or YHWH is to look at the content of the utterances. Another surprising participant shift is found in 17.10, where a verb in the first person is employed to express that "I will set my face against that soul who

---

[23] As for the reference לַיהוה 'to YHWH' in 19.5, Milgrom (2000, 1619) notes that the referent has been explicitly specified because the Israelites were accustomed to sacrifice to goat-demons (see 17.7) and needed an explicit correction. However, a first-person suffix would be more suitable, since YHWH already holds the first-person position at this point in Lev. 19.

eats the blood, and I will remove it from the midst of its people." Does the 'I' refer to Moses, the direct speaker, or YHWH, the original speaker? Although all commentaries take it for granted that YHWH is the implied speaker, this interpretation is not the only option, since YHWH has frequently been referred to in the third person so far in the chapter (17.4 [×2], 5 [×2], 6 [×2], 9). With regard to the identical case in Exod. 16, Talstra (2014, 563) explains that the unmarked participant shifts between Moses and YHWH bear on a controversy as to who is responsible for the liberation from Egypt.[24]

Jacob Milgrom (2000, 1518, 1523) likens the *Selbstvorstellungsformel* 'I am YHWH' with the prophetic phrase נְאֻם־יהוה 'utterance of YHWH' and argues for a primarily structural function of the expression.[25] In fact, according to Milgrom, all but one of the *Selbstvorstellungsformeln* in Lev. 17–26 mark the end of a unit.[26] Some of these utterances, however, come in such close sequence that they are not likely to mark the end of a paragraph (e.g., 18.4, 5, 6). As for the possible prophetic parallel נְאֻם־יהוה 'utterance of YHWH', Glanz (2013) has analysed its distribution and function

---

[24] In several cases, Moses is actually blamed for the exodus (e.g., Exod. 14.11), even by God (Exod. 32.7; 33.1).

[25] De Regt (2019, 25–26) notes that the shift between third- and second-person references to YHWH in the Song of the Sea (Exod. 15) serves a structural purpose.

[26] The only exception is the one in 18.2b, where the phrase precedes a legal pericope (Milgrom 2000, 1518). Sailhamer (1992, 349) argues that Lev. 19 can be structured according to the *Selbstvorstellungsformeln*, which occur 14 times in the chapter.

in Jeremiah. He argues that the utterance is a "macro-syntactical marker" employed by the speaker to "remind the reader/listener in an objective way [...] that he is still speaking and demanding attention" (Glanz 2013, 264). In Jeremiah, the use of נְאֻם־יהוה often entails a participant shift from first person to third person. Glanz interprets the shift as a rhetorical means of "objectivization;" for example, when YHWH encourages the people to pray to him, it is never formulated with a first-person reference (e.g., 'pray to me'), but always in the third person, even in contexts where YHWH already holds the first-person reference (e.g., Jer. 29.7; Glanz 2013, 281). This particular participant shift is also used to mark discourse shifts, for example the shift from descriptive to explanatory discourse, with the latter argued to be more objective (Glanz 2013, 282).

Some of Glanz's observations resonate with the participant shifts in Lev. 17–26. For one thing, apart from the *Selbstvorstellungsformeln* and speech introductions, all proper-name references to YHWH concern cultic instructions, most frequently the numerous instructions regarding offering of sacrifices לַיהוה 'to YHWH'.[27] The third person is also used to mark YHWH as the beneficiary of sabbaths and feasts (23.3, 5, 6, 17, 34, 41; 25.2, 4) as well as of the rejoicing of the people (19.24; 23.40). The sacrifices are holy לַיהוה 'to YHWH' (23.20), and atonement is made לִפְנֵי יהוה 'before YHWH' (23.28). The kindling of the lampstand and the arranging of bread in the Sanctum are לִפְנֵי יהוה 'before YHWH (24.3, 4, 6, 8). Finally, the third person is used to denote

---

[27] 17.4, 5 (×2), 6, 9; 19.5, 21, 22; 22.3, 15, 18, 21, 22 (×2), 24, 27, 29; 23.8, 11, 12, 13, 16, 18 (×2), 20, 25, 27, 36 (×2), 37, 38; 24.7.

YHWH's ownership of the sanctuary (17.4), the altar (17.6), the sacrifices (19.8; 21.6, 21; 24.9), the holy feasts (23.2, 4, 37, 39, 44), and his name (24.16). This bias towards cultic contexts suggests that the distribution of the proper name YHWH is more than merely coincidental. In light of this pattern, only once is a first-person reference used where a third-person one would be expected:

(8) וַיְדַבֵּר יְהוָה אֶל־מֹשֶׁה לֵּאמֹר: דַּבֵּר אֶל־אַהֲרֹן וְאֶל־בָּנָיו וְיִנָּזְרוּ מִקָּדְשֵׁי בְנֵי־יִשְׂרָאֵל וְלֹא יְחַלְּלוּ אֶת־שֵׁם קָדְשִׁי אֲשֶׁר הֵם מַקְדִּשִׁים לִי אֲנִי יְהוָה:

'YHWH spoke to Moses, saying: Direct Aaron and his sons to deal respectfully with the sacred donations of the sons of Israel—so that they do not profane my holy name—which they dedicate to me. I am YHWH.' (Lev. 22.1–2)

In all other instances where YHWH is portrayed as the beneficiary of a sacrifice or as the 'owner' of his name, the proper name is used. The exception in 22.2, however, is due to the fact that the quotation is not one of direct speech but indirect speech.[28] In indirect speech, there are not normally participant-reference shifts, that is, the participants continue to hold the same grammatical person in the narrative introduction and the indirect speech event. Moses, the implicit speaker of the indirect speech, continues to hold the second-person role, while the addressees (Aaron and his sons) remain in the third person. It is thus logical that the direct speaker (YHWH) holds the first-person role in the indirect

---

[28] For the syntax of indirect speech in Biblical Hebrew, see Petersson (2017).

speech quotation.²⁹ The exception in 22.2 shows that reference to YHWH in the third person is the default, or neutral, option in direct speech. By implication, in cases where the third person would be expected (e.g., in Moses' direct speeches), first-person references to YHWH could most likely be rhetorical devices.

In general, first-person references to YHWH occur much more frequently in H than third-person references. Moreover, the first-person references occur in rather diverse semantic contexts compared to the third-person references, which occur exclusively in cultic contexts. Most first-person references to YHWH are found in chapter 26, the long exhortatory discourse where YHWH urges the Israelites to adhere to the law using promises and warnings. In the rest of H, all divine threats of punishment are formulated in the first person,³⁰ as well as all God's provisions, be it the atoning

---

²⁹ The only other example of an indirect speech in H is found in 24.2–4. This case illustrates that the implied speaker of the indirect speech, Moses, retains his second-person position. There is no first-person reference to the direct speaker (YHWH) within the indirect speech quotation. YHWH is referred to twice by a proper name (לִפְנֵי יהוה 'before YHWH'), which would seem to run counter to the argument made here. לִפְנֵי יהוה, however, is a frequent phrase in the priestly material (e.g., Lev. 1.3, 5, 11; 3.1, 7, 12; 4.4, 6, 7) and is generally thought of as indicating a place rather than referring to YHWH. As Milgrom (1991, 238) explains with reference to Lev. 4.7, "That 'before the Lord' can refer to the interior of the Tent is shown by Exod. 27.21; 28.35; 30.8; 34.34; 40.23, 25." J. W. Watts (2013, 188) does not want to distinguish between location and theology and treats the phrase as one of "ritual location," that is, when the worshipper stands before the Sanctum, he ritually stands before YHWH.

³⁰ 17.10 (×3); 18.25; 20.3 (×3), 5 (×3), 6 (×3); 22.3; 23.30.

blood (17.11), the land (20.24), the law (20.25), booths in the wilderness (23.43), or agricultural blessings (25.21). Whenever YHWH is presented as the saviour from Egyptian bondage, this is done in the first person (19.36; 25.38, 42, 55; 26.13, 45). Frequently, YHWH is portrayed as the 'owner' of the law,[31] as well as of the covenant (26.9, 15, 42 [×3], 44), the sabbath and holy feasts (19.3, 30; 23.2; 26.2), and the sanctuary (19.30; 21.23; 26.2, 11). The shifts to first-person references are strong rhetorical devices. Above all, they create the impression that YHWH speaks directly to his people, although the speeches are always mediated by Moses.[32] Through the use of first-person references, the addressees get the feeling of hearing YHWH himself. More specifically, the first-person references establish and strengthen the relationship between YHWH and the people, most explicitly stated in the *Selbstvorstellungsformel* 'I am YHWH your God'. This utterance is sometimes accompanied by reference to the exodus in order to further anchor the relationship in the shared history ("who brought you out of the land of Egypt;" e.g., 25.38). A few times, a first-person reference is used to redirect the speech, for example, "But I have said to you" (20.24; see also 17.12, 14), perhaps in order to enhance the contrast between the preceding verse and

---

[31] 18.4 (×2), 5 (×2), 26 (×2), 30; 19.19, 37 (×2); 20.8, 22; 22.9, 31; 25.18 (×2); 26.3, 15 (×2), 43 (×2).

[32] Even modern scholars can be persuaded by the reality-mimicking function of the first-person references, e.g., Christian (2011), who argues that the role of the priests is diminished because the Israelites have received direct revelation from YHWH, thereby overlooking the fact that Moses is in fact mediating the revelation (see chapter 2, §6.5 n. 67).

the following. The immanence of YHWH is likewise felt in the first-person warnings where YHWH personally promises to 'cut off' the culprits. The rhetorical force of the shift between third and first person is seen clearly in 23.28–30:

(9) וְכָל־מְלָאכָה לֹא תַעֲשׂוּ בְּעֶצֶם הַיּוֹם הַזֶּה כִּי יוֹם כִּפֻּרִים הוּא לְכַפֵּר עֲלֵיכֶם לִפְנֵי יְהוָה אֱלֹהֵיכֶם: כִּי כָל־הַנֶּפֶשׁ אֲשֶׁר לֹא־תְעֻנֶּה בְּעֶצֶם הַיּוֹם הַזֶּה וְנִכְרְתָה מֵעַמֶּיהָ: וְכָל־הַנֶּפֶשׁ אֲשֶׁר תַּעֲשֶׂה כָּל־מְלָאכָה בְּעֶצֶם הַיּוֹם הַזֶּה וְהַאֲבַדְתִּי אֶת־הַנֶּפֶשׁ הַהִוא מִקֶּרֶב עַמָּהּ:

'You shall not do any work during this whole day, because it is the day of atonement to atone for you before YHWH your God. For any soul, who does not humble himself during this whole day, he shall be cut off from his kinsmen. And any soul who does any work during this whole day, I will destroy that soul from the midst of his people.' (Lev. 23.28–30)

In 23.28–30, the reference 'YHWH' is neutral and to be expected from the fact that Moses is speaking. The shift to the first person adds a severe motivation for proper observance of the day of atonement, because YHWH personally confronts the listener with the warning of destruction.

In sum, the various instances of first-person references to YHWH within the speeches of Moses are pragmatic devices to create a strong impression of imminence. By making Moses refer to YHWH in the first person, YHWH comes closer to his audience and can thereby draw his audience into a personal dialogue.[33] By

---

[33] Similarly, "The אֲנִי יהוה-formula is at the core of this strategy since it makes the audience constantly aware that they are directly addressed

creating an impression of immanence, the frequent first-person references likely serve to strengthen the personal relationship between YHWH and the people and to enhance the motivations for strict adherence to the law. In this respect, the third-person references are the default references to YHWH in Moses' direct speeches and hardly carry any pragmatic significance. As argued, the first-person references to YHWH in the indirect speech of 22.2 support this idea. In conclusion, then, one can hardly expect a computer program to be able to attribute the first-person references in Moses' speeches to YHWH. On the other hand, a computational analysis can effectively identify occurrences of abnormal communication patterns that belong to the domain of rhetorical analysis.

## 3.7. The Audience

The Holiness Code contains interesting shifts between plural (2MPl) and singular (2MSg) references to the audience, בְּנֵי יִשְׂרָאֵל 'the sons of Israel'.[34] As explained in chapter 2, §6.1, the participant shifts have traditionally been interpreted as indicators of redactional activity, and more recently as intentionally-employed rhetorical devices. The participant shift is an obstacle for a participant-tracking algorithm, because the connection between the

---

by YHWH himself" (Müller 2015, 79). Müller (2015, 84) argues further that the full rhetorical effect of the אֲנִי יהוה-formula is only achieved by oral performance of the text.

[34] See chapter 2, §6.1, where the audience was defined as the sons of Israel, although Aaron and the sons of Aaron are at times also included in this group.

explicit addressee of the discourse (בְּנֵי יִשְׂרָאֵל) and the singular reference (2MSg) is vague. The references share gender (M), and the shift from third to second person can be accounted for by regular linking rules for linking narrative that introduces speech and direct speech (see step 4 in §2.1). The shift from plural to singular is unexpected and requires the semantic inference that the singular addressee is a member of the sons of Israel. For some reason, the linking procedure has had a successful outcome in some parts of Talstra's dataset. In Lev. 25, all second-person references are linked to the addressees of the text (בְּנֵי יִשְׂרָאֵל 'the sons of Israel') irrespective of grammatical number. In chapter 18, on the other hand, plural and singular addresses are distinguished, so that 2MPl references refer to the addressees (בְּנֵי יִשְׂרָאֵל 'the sons of Israel'), while 2MSg references refer to an unspecified singular addressee. It is not clear to me why the participant shifts are handled differently in different chapters, but it surely illustrates the complexity of the text.

As noted, it has become more common among scholars to emphasise the rhetorical function of this type of participant shift. In general, the second person address is considered a rhetorical device for persuading the hearers, since the "hearers and readers are likely to feel directly addressed and therefore obliged to respond" (Watts 1999, 64).[35] Norbert Lohfink (1963, 248) explained the participant shifts between plural and singular address

---

[35] In addition, Gane (2017) explains the participant-reference shifts with respect to the covenant: Y<small>HWH</small> has made a covenant with the people as a whole, but he has also made a covenant with each individual member of the people, and each of them is his covenant vassal. Accordingly, the

in Deut. 5–11 as markers of intensification. Thus, at critical places in the text, the singular address is employed to attract the attention of the hearer or reader. This interpretation was accepted by De Regt (1999b, 85–88), who also argued that the distribution of singular and plural addresses closely corresponds to the content matter of the book.[36] In his study of people and land in the Holiness Code, Jan Joosten (1996; see also 1997) likewise argued that the shifts between singular and plural addresses serve specific rhetorical and communicative purposes.[37] In particular, according to Joosten, the default address to the addressees is the plural reference, while the singular address is employed to address each member of the community personally. In one 'anomalous' case (25.7–9), the singular is apparently used to address the community (Joosten 1996, 48). Joosten admits that it is not possible to make a complete distinction, since Lev. 19 at least has a blend of plural and singular references, and he would not dare to postulate that "thou shalt rise up before the hoary head" (19.32) is more individualising than "ye shall not steal" (19.11). Nevertheless, Joosten shows that certain nouns such as שָׂדֶה 'field', כֶּרֶם 'vineyard', בְּהֵמָה 'cattle', עֶבֶד 'slave', רֵעַ 'neighbour', and family

---

"second-person address establishes a direct link between the speaker and the hearer/reader" (Gane 2017, 84).

[36] In particular, the plural addresses are applied in contexts of Israel's history, while singular references abound in passages dealing with cultic and ritual matters (De Regt 1999b, 86–87).

[37] See also Barbiero (1991, 206–8), who applies Lohfink's distinction in his analysis of rhetorical functions of the *Numeruswechsel* in Lev. 19.

members, occur with verbs and pronominal suffixes in the singular. By contrast, nouns such as מוֹשָׁבֹת 'dwelling places', דֹּרֹת 'generations', עָרִים 'cities', and מִקְדָּשִׁים 'sanctuaries' occur in contexts with plural verbs and pronominal suffixes (Joosten 1996, 49). According to Joosten, then, it means that the community is addressed as a group within the larger domains of the exodus, the cult, the festivals, the cities, and the land, while the members of the community are addressed individually within the domains of personal relations, property, and behaviour. Esias E. Meyer (2005), although not entirely convinced by Joosten's categorisation, likewise regarded the singular address as a rhetorical, individualising device.[38] Above all, Meyer (2005, 144) regards the number shifts as "power-conscious" devices, as the text "zooms in on those people who really have the power to make a difference."

In sum, even if a computer program can be developed to track the references to the addressees irrespective of number shifts, it is still useful to retain the distinction, insofar as the shifts are most likely intentional, rhetorical devices. If, in fact, Joosten

---

[38] Meyer (2005, 117) remarks with respect to Lev. 25 that "a word like אָח ['brother'] occurs with both the singular and the plural" and that "Even Joosten does not really know what to do with vv. 7–9, which according to his theory should be plural, but which are addressed to the singular." In his own attempt to solve the disturbing case of 25.7–9, Meyer (2005, 117–24) argues that the singular references are used both as a persuasive way of addressing the individual landowners and for the sake of making a smooth transition from the laws on the sabbatical year (addressed to the individual landowners) to the jubilee laws, which concern the community of landowners as a whole (plural references).

is right that the variation correlates with specific domains (communal vs personal), these participant shifts are within the interests of a social network analysis, which is concerned with the social domains of the participants. Thus, for the present analysis, the singular and plural references are kept distinct for further research (see chapter 7, §5.1.2).

## 3.8. Synonyms

Steps 7 and 8 of Talstra's participant-tracking procedure are concerned with semantic relationships beyond purely formal ones. More concretely, step 7 deals with different, yet synonymous, participant actors (PActs), while step 8 looks at participant actors with a certain amount of semantic overlap, essentially forming part-whole relationships. These two steps provide an obvious challenge for a computer program, since there are not necessarily linguistic cues (e.g., morphology or lexical identity) to suggest a semantic relationship. Nonetheless, since synonyms and part-whole relationships refer respectively to the same referent or membership of a referent, a profound participant analysis needs to take these phenomena into account. As a matter of fact, part-whole relationships have also been discussed with regard to SNA. In their SNA of *Alice in Wonderland*, Apoorv Agarwal et al. (2012) discuss whether a group of birds should be considered a group of which each bird is considered a member. And if so, if the group loses one member, should the remaining group of birds be marked as a new entity? These considerations are important for capturing the complexity and dynamics of a network of participants. The present study will therefore proceed a step further than Agarwal et al. by proposing a hierarchy of participants from which to extract participant information. The issue of part-whole relationships will be discussed in the next section (§3.9). The present section will consider synonyms.

To illustrate the issue of synonyms, I shall first discuss the cases found in Lev. 17. The most distinctive is the curious shift from אִישׁ 'anyone' to נֶפֶשׁ 'soul' in v. 10:

(10) וְאִישׁ אִישׁ מִבֵּית יִשְׂרָאֵל וּמִן־הַגֵּר הַגָּר בְּתוֹכָם אֲשֶׁר יֹאכַל כָּל־דָּם וְנָתַתִּי פָנַי בַּנֶּפֶשׁ הָאֹכֶלֶת אֶת־הַדָּם וְהִכְרַתִּי אֹתָהּ מִקֶּרֶב עַמָּהּ׃

'[If] anyone of the house of Israel or of the sojourners sojourning among them eats any blood, I will put my face against the soul who eats the blood, and I will remove it from the midst of its kinsmen.' (Lev. 17.10)

In (10), there is a subtle shift from 'anyone' to 'soul'.[39] The only explicit indication of co-reference is the participle הָאֹכֶלֶת 'eat', which relates 'soul' to the man of Israelite or foreign origin. While a reader will intuitively connect אִישׁ 'anyone' and נֶפֶשׁ 'soul', due to the fact that both participants are described as eating blood, the collocation is difficult to formalise. An algorithm would need to identify the clause בַּנֶּפֶשׁ הָאֹכֶלֶת אֶת־הַדָּם 'against the soul who eats the blood' with a complex clause 'anyone of the house of Israel or of the sojourners sojourning among them who eats any blood'. Although the two references clearly refer to the same person, one needs to consider the implications of collocation. As regards the shift from אִישׁ 'anyone' to נֶפֶשׁ 'soul', it may be that the

---

[39] I ignore for the moment the fact that the participant אִישׁ should rightly be labelled 'anyone of the house of Israel or of the sojourners' (see §3.4).

shift has a literary purpose. It has been suggested that נֶפֶשׁ 'soul' in conjunction with eating has to do with the root meaning of נֶפֶשׁ, which is 'throat/appetite' (Milgrom 2000, 1471), or that נֶפֶשׁ signals a deep connection between the blood, which is the נֶפֶשׁ 'life' of the animal (17.11), and the life of the human being punished by Y<small>HWH</small> as a revenge for eating blood/life (Wenham 1979, 244–45). In any case, these interpretations illustrate a consequence of participant tracking and, particularly, of participant clustering. Through the process of collocating semantically related participants, information is inevitably lost. On the other hand, by reducing the number of participants, other aspects of the text can be analysed. At this level of analysis, therefore, the granularity of the participant analysis must be defined by the aim of the researcher. The aim of the present study is not to explore the internal composition of the participants (i.e., word senses attached to individual participants) but rather to contrast distinct participants (e.g., the native Israelite and the sojourner). For this reason, אִישׁ 'anyone' and נֶפֶשׁ 'soul' are collocated, despite the possible theological significance attached to נֶפֶשׁ.

There is one important exception to this heuristic choice of granularity, because it is in fact relevant for investigating the internal composition of one participant, namely the addressees, the sons of Israel. Recall that the sons of Israel are sometimes addressed in the second person (singular and plural) and sometimes in the third person. The participant shifts may bear on certain rhetorical and theological concerns, as discussed above (§3.7). The second-person plural address likely refers to the Israelites as a group, while the second-person singular reference addresses each Israelite personally. In addition, the third-person reference is commonly used in case laws to exemplify a legal case. With respect to the addressees, therefore, a somewhat more fine-grained strategy is applied than for other participants in H. That is, the plural address to the Israelites (2MPl), the singular address (2MSg), and the singular, indirect address (3MSg) are handled separately. The benefit of this strategy is that it allows for analysis of the individual references independently within the network.

The participant tracking of Lev. 17 illustrates the trade-off between accuracy and simplicity well. Talstra's dataset of Lev. 17–26 contains 250 participant references for Lev. 17. Talstra's own analysis results in 34 participant actors (PActs). Still, some participants are semantically related and could reasonably be collocated, including, for example, אִישׁ 'anyone' and נֶפֶשׁ 'soul' (see above). Furthermore, if 'anyone' and 'soul' are collocated, the references to the kinsmen of 'anyone' (e.g., 17.4) and the kinsmen of 'soul' (e.g., 17.10) should likewise be collocated.

These considerations in mind, the list of participants in Lev. 17 can be reduced to 14 human/divine participants.[40] Figure 2 shows the resulting semantic hierarchy of the participants in Lev. 17. The semantic hierarchy captures both synonyms, marked by

---

[40] The 14 human/divine actors are אֶל־אַהֲרֹן וְאֶל־בָּנָיו וְאֶל כָּל־בְּנֵי יִשְׂרָאֵל 'to Aaron and to his sons and to all the sons of Israel', אַהֲרֹן 'Aaron', בְּנֵי יִשְׂרָאֵל 'the sons of Israel', אִישׁ מִבֵּית יִשְׂרָאֵל וּמִן־הַגֵּר 'anyone of the house of Israel or of the sojourners', בֵּית יִשְׂרָאֵל 'the house of Israel', הַגֵּר 'the sojourner', אִישׁ 'anyone', אִישׁ #2 'anyone', כָּל־נֶפֶשׁ 'any soul', מֵעַמָּיו 'from his [= 'anyone'] people', יהוה 'YHWH', מֹשֶׁה 'Moses', הַכֹּהֵן 'the priest', and שְׂעִירִם 'demon'. For the difference between אִישׁ and אִישׁ #2, see §3.9.

dashed boxes, and part-whole relationships, marked by lines. Part-whole relationships will be the topic of the next section.

Figure 2: Left-to-right hierarchy of human/divine participants in Lev 17. The lines represent part-whole relationships, and dashed boxes represent synonyms.

Another issue involving synonyms concerns the 'foreigners', which is a composite group in Leviticus. In the last part of Lev. 18, the audience is warned against pursuing a moral lifestyle similar to that of the people living in the land of Canaan before

## 3. Tracking the Participants

the conquest. These people are referred to as הַגּוֹיִם 'the nations' (18.24), יֹשְׁבֶיהָ 'its [= the land] inhabitants' (18.25), and אַנְשֵׁי־הָאָרֶץ 'the men of the land' (18.27). Previously, the audience had been warned against imitating the immoral deeds of the Egyptians (18.3). The Egyptians and the Canaanites are certainly two different ethnic groups and therefore not the same participant. However, in terms of ethics and their role in chapter 18, Egyptians and Canaanites are similar. That is, both groups represent a lifestyle not to be imitated by the Israelites, and they thus function as an ethical contrast to the sons of Israel. For this reason, it is sensible to collocate the references, even if some information is lost.

The final example is the well-known command to love one's fellow as oneself (Lev. 19.18). In the immediate context, a list of prohibitions concretises this rule. The list involves a range of participants, including אָחִיךָ 'your brother', עֲמִיתֶךָ 'your fellow countryman', בְּנֵי עַמֶּךָ 'sons of your people', and רֵעֲךָ 'your fellow'. It has been discussed whether these terms specify distinct persons to whom the individual addressee has distinct obligations (chapter 2, §6.3). Most commentators, however, hold that the references are 'near synonyms' (Milgrom 2000, 1655; see also Magonet 1983). The term 'near synonyms' illustrates well the point being made here. There are hardly any 'real' synonyms, because an author is likely to employ different words in order to accentuate a nuance in the portrayal of a participant. Therefore, the collocation of 'nearly synonymous' participants comes at the expense of accuracy. On the other hand, with these participants collocated, the text becomes readily accessible for analysis of the relationships among those participants that are relatively more distinct than near synonyms. Above all, the degree of granularity depends on the research question.

## 3.9. Part-Whole Relationships

The last step of Talstra's participant-tracking analysis concerns semantic relationships between participants that are not purely synonymous. In an example from Exod. 19, Talstra (2016b, 21) mentions הָהָר 'the mountain', הַר סִינַי 'mount Sinai', רֹאשׁ הָהָר 'top of the mountain', and תַּחְתִּית הָהָר 'bottom of the mountain', which form a cluster with 'the mountain' as the main actor and the remaining references as dependent actors. These relationships are still formal by nature in that they form *regens-rectum* constructions, and they can therefore probably be captured by a computer algorithm. Another kind of part-whole relationship is the member-group relationships which occur frequently in Lev. 17–26. The most apparent example is the complex addressee phrase in Lev. 17.2, as already discussed (see §3.1): 'to Aaron and to his sons and to all the sons of Israel'. In this example, three distinct members form a group of addressees. The members of this group can be tracked through the text by means of lexical or morphological marking. However, apart from semantic relationships like this one that are signalled by linguistic structure and grammatical marking, many part-whole relationships are almost entirely semantic. The recurrent reference אִישׁ 'a man/anyone' in Lev. 17 offers one such case. Lev. 17 consists of four major case laws, each unfolding an act undertaken by אִישׁ (17.3, 8, 10, 13). The issue of אִישׁ was already discussed in §3.4, where it was argued that, despite the identical lexemes, the reference does not always refer to exactly the same participant. While the first case law refers to a native Israelite alone, the remaining laws include the sojourner. This difference is difficult to capture by means of an algorithm, however, because the referential differentiation of אִישׁ is only signalled by complex constructions, including relative clauses.

Figure 3: Dependency tree of the native Israelite (אִישׁ 'anyone'), the sojourner (גֵּר), and the man being either native Israelite or sojourner (אִישׁ #2 'anyone'). Synonymous relationships are represented by dashed boxes.

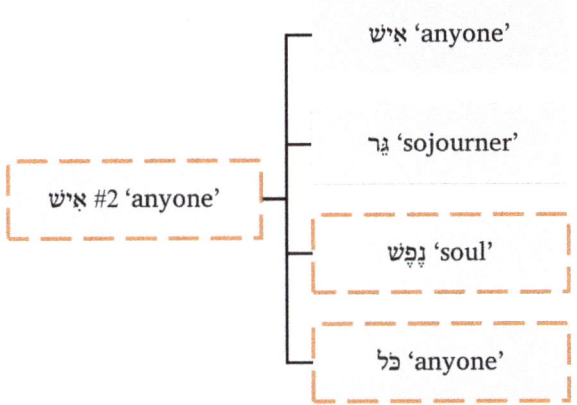

Nevertheless, even if an algorithm could successfully differentiate the two participants, some referential overlap must be retained, for the reason that the case laws which address both the sojourner and the native Israelite (17.8, 10, 13) pertain, by implication, also to the native Israelite alone, as mentioned in the first case law (17.3). Put differently, when reference is made to a group of participants, the reference pertains to each of the members. On the other hand, reference made to an individual does not necessarily pertain to the entire group. The relationship between the two participants אִישׁ (v. 3) and אִישׁ (vv. 8, 10, 13) is thus asymmetric. This asymmetric, partly overlapping relationship is illustrated in a dependency tree (Figure 3). The dependency tree illustrates both the symmetric and the asymmetric relationships pertaining to 'anyone, either native Israelite or sojourner' (אִישׁ #2 'anyone'). As for the symmetric relationships, it has already been explained that נֶפֶשׁ 'soul' is used synonymously with אִישׁ #2 (see §3.8). The same is true of כֹּל 'anyone'. By implication, the references tracked to נֶפֶשׁ and כֹּל can be mapped onto אִישׁ #2, and vice versa, as illustrated by the dashed boxes. Secondly, the references to אִישׁ #2 can be mapped onto each of its members, the native Israelite and the sojourner. More concretely, the laws concerning burnt offerings outside the sanctuary (v. 8), eating blood (v. 10), pouring blood on the earth (v. 13), and eating corpses (v. 15) apply to both the native Israelite and the sojourner.[41] Importantly, by implication of the asymmetric relationship, the first case law in v. 3 pertains only to the native Israelite (אִישׁ) and is not mapped onto the group אִישׁ #2, nor the other member of the group (גֵּר). In other words, the prohibition against profane sacrifices (v. 3) does not apply to the sojourner, nor to the 'group' consisting of the native Israelite and the sojourner, but exclusively to the native Israelite. This distinction is crucial when we want to map the participants with respect to the events

---

[41] The last case law (v. 15) uses the term כָּל־נֶפֶשׁ 'any soul' (כֹּל 'anyone' in the dependency tree), but, since this reference has been marked as synonymous to אִישׁ #2, the law already applies equally to the native Israelite and the sojourner.

in which they participate and the laws in which they are included.

Another example is found in Lev. 20. This chapter contains a long list of case laws establishing the punishment for engaging in incestual relationships, as well as adultery, homoerotic relationships, and bestiality. The case laws are characterised by a recurrent pattern where the perpetrator is introduced first (most frequently by the indefinite אִישׁ 'a man/anyone'), followed by another participant with whom the sexual act is committed. Finally, the two participants are subsumed in a plural reference, for example, מוֹת־יוּמְתוּ שְׁנֵיהֶם 'the two of them shall surely die' (20.11). A sophisticated algorithm might be able to track the participants because the two individual participants are now referred to in the plural. Even so, the participant tracking must account for the asymmetric relationships between the participants. Strictly speaking, while the death penalty applies to both individual participants, the sexual act does not apply equally to the two individuals, nor to the group reference. Rather, it is אִישׁ 'a man/anyone' who is described as the initiator of the sexual relationship and not the other participant. In other words, it is not 'the two of them' who instigate a sexual act but only 'a man/anyone'. This may seem to be an overcomplication, because both participants are apparently seen as equally guilty, given the death penalty stipulated for both. However, from the point of view of relational ethics, which is the topic of the social network analysis to be carried out (see chapter 7), it is important to distinguish between active instigators and passive undergoers as far as the text is concerned. In this light, asymmetric relationships between groups and members are immensely important for understanding the roles of the participants.

Another interesting case is found in Lev. 18. In v. 6, the Israelites are prohibited from coming near to כָּל־שְׁאֵר בְּשָׂרוֹ 'anyone of one's close relatives' to uncover their 'nakedness'.[42] The verse is often considered a general law heading the subsequent series of laws (Hartley 1992, 293; Milgrom 2000, 1532–33; Wenham 1979, 253; Levine 1989, 120). Logically, just as the general prohibition against sexual intercourse with a close relative subsumes the subsequent list of concrete laws, the participant reference in v. 6 subsumes the subsequent references to close relatives. Accordingly, the participant references referring to concrete family members can be mapped onto the general law in v. 6. This choice is obviously based on purely semantic and literary considerations, since there is no formal linking between the participant in v. 6 and those in the subsequent verses.[43]

In sum, the clustering of participants into hierarchical groups is a complicated, yet important task of participant tracking that aims to disambiguate the participants as much as possible without losing too much information. The classification of participants into asymmetric part-whole relationships allows for a controlled attribution of participant references to the members of a group.

---

[42] עֶרְוָה 'nakedness' is a euphemism for copulation (Milgrom 2000, 1534).

[43] Only family members are subsumed in the group of 'close relatives'; hence, only the participants in 18.7–15 are included.

## 3.10. The Human/Divine Participants of Lev. 17–26

The eight-step procedure for participant tracking documented above leads to a diminished list of participants. The overall objective of the present study is to investigate the roles and relations of the human and divine participants of the text. Hence, an additional step involves the exclusion of non-human and non-divine participants. In the end, a set of 74 unique human/divine participants can be identified in Lev. 17–26. These participants are listed in Table 2 below, along with their Biblical references.[44] The participants form the backbone of the social network analysis to be conducted in chapter 7, where the social relationships among the participants will be investigated on the basis of their interactions. It should be noted, however, that only 59 of the participants actually qualify for a SNA, since the participants need to occur in interaction with other human/divine participants.[45] Other restrictions apply as well, as explained in detail in chapter 7, §3.1.

A few participants in the resulting list have required additional disambiguation and/or collocation for the sake of the SNA. As an example, *mother* includes the mother of both *2MSg* (the individually addressed Israelite, e.g., Lev. 18.6) and the mother

---

[44] Only the first 10 references to each participant are listed for the sake of space. For all references, see https://github.com/ch-jensen/Roles-and-Relations/blob/main/Participants-and-references_Lev17-26.xlsx.

[45] The excluded participants are *son, father's_brother, Egyptians, blemished_man, resident_laborer, resident_with_priest, Shelomith, redeemer, Levite, sojourner's_descendants, ten_women, ancestors, Jacob, Isaac,* and *Abraham*.

of the third-person אִישׁ 'anyone' (e.g., 20.9). The same is true of the other relatives listed. As for the third-person אִישׁ itself, this participant is subsumed under *an_Israelite* along with its synonyms נֶפֶשׁ 'soul' and כֹּל 'anyone' (see the discussion in §3.8). Another case of collocation is the subsumption of all quasi-divine beings and idols under *idols*, including Moloch (18.21), goat-demons (17.7), and idols (19.4), as well as dead spirits and soothsayers (19.31). Thus, the list of human/divine participants could be much longer if the participants mentioned here were not collocated. However, for the sake of characterising the participants of Lev. 17–26 over against certain categories (e.g., family members or idols), these measures had to be taken.

Table 2: Human/divine participants in Lev. 17–26

| Participant | References (the first 10) | Participant | References (the first 10) |
|---|---|---|---|
| 2MPl | 21.8 | group_of_people | 20.5 (×3) |
| 2MSg | 18.7 (×3), 8 (×2), 9 (×2), 10 (×3)... | handmaid | 19.20 (×7); 25.6, 44 (×2)... |
| Aaron | 17.2 (×2); 21.10 (×7), 11... | human_being | 18.5 (×2); 22.5 (×2), 6; 24.17, 20, 21 |
| Aaron's_sons | 17.2 (×2), 5, 6 (×2); 19.22; 21.1 (×3), 2... | husband | 21.7 |
| Abraham | 26.42 | idols | 17.7 (×2); 18.21; 19.4, 31 (×3); 20.2, 3, 4... |
| Egyptians | 19.34, 36; 26.13 (×2), 45 | kinsmen | 17.4, 9, 10; 18.29; 19.8; 20.3, 5, 6, 18; 21.1... |
| Isaac | 26.42 | lay-person | 22.4, 10, 13, 14 (×4), 18, 21 (×2)... |
| Israelites | 17.2 (×2), 3, 5 (×4), 7 (×3)... | male | 18.22; 20.13 (×4) |
| Jacob | 26.42 | man | 19.20 |
| Levite | 25.32, 33 (×4), 34 (×2) | man/woman | 20.27 (×5) |
| Moses | 17.1, 2 (×2), 8; 18.1, 2 (×2); 19.1, 2 (×2)... | mother | 18.6, 7 (×3), 9, 13 (×2); 19.3; 20.9 (×2)... |
| Shelomith | 24.10, 11 (×2) | no-one | 26.17, 36, 37 |
| Yhwh | 17.1 (×2), 2 (×2), 4, 5 (×2), 6 (×2), 9... | offspring | 18.21; 20.2, 3, 4; 21.15; 22.13 |
| an_Israelite | 17.3 (×3), 4 (×5), 8 (×2)... | poor | 19.10, 15; 23.22 |
| ancestors | 26.39, 40 | purchaser | 25.27 (×2), 28 (×2), 30 (×2) |
| aunt | 18.6, 12 (×2), 13 (×2); 20.19 (×2) | redeemer | 25.25 (×3), 26 |
| aunt-in-law | 18.6, 14 (×3); 20.20 (×4) | relative | 21.2 (×2), 3 (×4) |

| | | | |
|---|---|---|---|
| blasphemer | 24.10 (×3), 11 (×4), 12, 14 (×2)... | remnants | 26.36 (×5), 37 (×2), 39 (×3)... |
| blemished_man | 21.18 (×2), 19 (×2), 20 | resident_laborer | 22.10 |
| blind | 19.14 | resident_with_priest | 22.11 (×2) |
| brother | 18.16 (×2); 19.11, 13, 15, 16 (×2), 17 (×3)... | rich | 19.15 |
| brother's_brother | 25.48, 49 | sister | 18.6, 9 (×2), 11 (×3); 20.17 (×4)... |
| brother's_uncle | 25.49 | sister_of_woman | 18.18 (×2) |
| children | 25.46 (×2); 26.29 (×2) | slave | 22.11 (×2) |
| clan | 25.10, 41 | sojourner | 17.8 (×3), 9 (×3), 10 (×4)... |
| corpse | 21.1, 11; 22.4; 26.30 | sojourner's descendants | 25.45 |
| daughter | 19.29 (×2); 21.9 (×5); 22.12 (×3)... | son | 18.10, 15 |
| daughter-in-law | 18.6, 15 (×3); 20.12 (×4) | son_of_brother | 25.41, 54 |
| deaf | 19.14 | sons_of_sojourners | 25.45 (×6), 46 (×2) |
| elderly | 19.32 (×2) | ten_women | 26.26 (×2) |
| father | 18.6, 7, 8 (×2), 9, 11, 12 (×2), 14; 19.3... | virgin | 21.13, 14 |
| father's_brother | 18.14 (×2) | widowed/expelled/ defiled_woman | 21.7 (×3), 14 (×2) |
| father's_wife | 18.6, 8 (×2), 11; 20.11 (×4) | witnesses | 24.11, 12 (×2), 14 |
| fellow's_wife | 18.6, 16 (×2), 20 (×2); 20.10 (×3), 21 (×2)... | woman | 18.17 (×4), 18 (×2), 19 (×2), 22, 23... |
| foreign_nations | 18.24, 25, 27 (×2), 28 (×2); 20.23 (×3), 24... | woman_and_her _daughter | 18.17 (×2) |
| granddaughter | 18.6, 10 | woman_and_her _mother | 20.14 (×2) |
| granddaughter _of_woman | 18.17 (×2) | woman_in _menstruation | 20.18 (×5) |

## 4.0. Conclusion

Although most participants in the Holiness Code can probably be correctly identified by everyday readers of the text, the contributions of the computational approach suggested in this chapter are significant. One of the main advantages of a formalised approach—apart from the resulting participant dataset itself—is the fact that an algorithm is not carried away by personal interests or scholarly consensus. The computer program will apply the same rules everywhere and is not sensitive to literary or theological considerations. That said, the computer is certainly not right everywhere. Participant tracking relies on semantics as well as syntax, and the former is difficult to formalise. However, discrepancies between the results of a computer and a human interpreter usually point to complexities in the text. Sometimes, these complexities can be resolved by improving the algorithm, but not always. If there are ambiguities in the text, they may signal literary conventions foreign to modern interpreters, or they may signal pragmatic issues, for example the deliberate conflation of YHWH and Moses in Moses' first-person references to YHWH.

Talstra's dataset does not reflect a complete tracking of participants. Neither does my own, despite the revisions documented in this chapter. Perhaps there is no such thing as a 'complete' or 'perfect' participant-tracking analysis. After all, participants of a text are not completely discrete entities, but often overlap to a certain extent. In H, this phenomenon is probably most evident in the claim that the Israelites are גֵּרִים וְתוֹשָׁבִים 'resident sojourners' in the land of YHWH (25.23). This reference is also used to describe the non-Israelite sojourners residing in the land and even as a description of how the poor Israelite fellow is to be treated: as a גֵּר וְתוֹשָׁב 'residing sojourner' (25.35). Thus, participant references are often conflated deliberately in order to convey a certain message, and the distinction between sojourners and Israelites is blurred. For this reason, participant tracking is not only about data production and clear-cut delineations of participants. Rather, participant tracking is an open-ended endeavour that continues to reveal complexities, literary conventions, curious abnormalities, and ideological concerns. In conclusion, then, I shall therefore echo a remark of Talstra's in one of his works on participant tracking: "It is clear that this research is very much in the experimental stage. That is, however, only a problem if one is just waiting for the final results to apply them. It is, in my experience, a much more fruitful attitude to accept that this ongoing research to enrich the Old Testament database is not just data production, but at the same time is also fundamental research in Hebrew language and in Old Testament texts" (Talstra 2016a, 242).

# 4. SEMANTIC ROLES AND DECOMPOSITION OF AGENCY

## 1.0. Introduction

A social network analysis of a law text like the one undertaken in the present work relies on the analysis of participants within their interactional contexts. Interactions, or transactions, are the means by which individuals attain specific roles, and a careful study of the interactions therefore holds the key to understanding the persons of the implied community of the Holiness Code and their respective roles (see chapter 2, §4.0). The challenge of doing so becomes readily apparent: there are 181 unique verbal predicates in the Holiness Code, corresponding to 181 different events, although some events may be semantically similar. With respect to social network analysis, the pertinent question is how these events can be quantified. For instance, how can a speech event be compared to a transaction event? How do these disparate events contribute to the construction of individual roles? The main argument of this chapter is that the concept of 'agency' is one possible measure, because all events naturally invoke some degree of agency. Agency relates to semantic parameters such as activity, volition, causation, and sentience, and each event can be quantified according to those parameters. Agency has received much attention in the linguistic literature, because the feature is quite intuitive but hard to decompose and measure. Scholars have generally been divided over whether verbal arguments and their roles are subcategorised for by the verb, that is, whether the verbal lexeme puts restrictions on the selection of arguments, or whether semantic roles are more loosely entailed by the verb on the basis of implicit notions of agency. This chapter will briefly discuss these approaches below, but will ultimately argue, with Role and Reference Grammar (RRG), that agency is neither subcategorised for by the verb nor a loose entailment. Rather, agency is compositional in nature and involves both lexical, morphological, syntactic, and pragmatic features. The implication of this is that agency is not subcategorised for by the verb, but that the lexical features of the verb nevertheless inform the agency of the event. As will be shown, the most important verbal features are dynamicity and causation, which will be analysed in turn in the two subsequent chapters.

Role and Reference Grammar is a linguistic theory which views syntax, semantics, and pragmatics as interactional components in language (Foley and Van Valin 1984; Van Valin and LaPolla 1997; Van Valin 2005).[1] While generative grammar views syntax as a self-contained object of study, RRG, like other functional theories, views language as "a system of communicative social action" which employs grammatical structures to express meaning (Van Valin 2005, 1). RRG, then, is a description of how syntax, semantics, and discourse-pragmatics interact, and it offers a 'linking algorithm' for representing the bidirectional links between syntax and semantics, including the role that discourse-pragmatic plays in the linking.

---

[1] A concise introduction to RRG is given in Van Valin (2015), while Pavey (2010) offers a beginner's introduction.

RRG grew out of an interest in how linguistic theory would look if it were based not merely on an analysis of English but on languages with diverse syntactic structures, such as Lakhota, Tagalog, and Dyirbal (Van Valin 2005, 1). For this reason, the theory is a good candidate for exploring the correspondence of syntax and semantics in an ancient language like Biblical Hebrew.[2] On the other hand, although RRG was developed for the purpose of describing languages with very diverse structures, for the most part, the languages under consideration were living languages, and the verbal analysis usually depended on the presence of native speakers. The main challenge for exploring the semantics of BH is the absence of native speakers, a challenge obviously shared by other methods used to investigate the semantics of BH. Consequently, the lexical decomposition carried out in the present study will diverge from traditional RRG approaches in the

---

[2] Some important work has already been done on describing a Role and Reference Grammar of Biblical Hebrew. The earliest work was Nicolai Winther-Nielsen's (1995) dissertation on interclausal connections in the Book of Joshua. Later works by the same author include studies on RRG decomposition of BH verbs (Winther-Nielsen 2016; 2017), information structure (Winther-Nielsen 2021), and the development of an RRG parser of the BH text (Winther-Nielsen 2008; 2009; 2012). At the time of writing, this work is carried on by Winther-Nielsen and the present author in cooperation with Laura Kallmeyer and her research team at the Heinrich Heine Universität in Düsseldorf on the TreeGraSP project, short for 'Tree rewriting grammars and the syntax-semantics interface: From grammar development to semantic parsing'. Finally, RRG was employed by the present author to explore the rhetorical structure of the book of Zechariah (Jensen 2017).

application of a quantitative corpus-linguistic basis for interpretation. In this chapter, the theoretical implications of applying RRG to the study of BH verbs will be discussed. Three related topics will be addressed in turn: 1) the correlation between lexical decomposition, semantic roles, and agency; 2) the methodological challenge of deriving the lexical aspect of verbs from an ancient corpus; and 3) the semantic representation of verbs in RRG logical structures.

## 2.0. Semantic Roles and Agency

The term 'agency' refers to the intuitive notion that some participants seem to be more controlling, instigating, volitional, and sentient than others. These participants are often labelled 'agents'. By contrast, non-controlling, non-instigating, and non-volitional participants are usually labelled 'patients'. A vast number of studies have scrutinised how agency relates to the semantic relationship between the predicate and its arguments, but with mixed results (e.g., Fillmore 1968; Delancey 1984; Talmy 1985; Van Valin and Wilkins 1996; Dowty 1991; Næss 2007; Rappaport Hovav 2008; Croft 2012). Indeed, as David R. Dowty (1991, 553) notes, the agent role "is one of the most frequently cited roles, and it is in some sense a very intuitive role, but it is one of the hardest to pin down." All agree that the agent role—and other semantic roles for that matter—expresses a semantic relationship between a participant and the predicate. But are semantic roles discrete entities or rather clusters of semantic properties? And moreover, is agency a specific property indexed by the predicate, or should agency rather be understood as a matter of degree entailed by the predicate?

Charles J. Fillmore (1968), in his classic *The Case for Case*, later published in a collection of his essays (2003), argued for the former position. Verbs, he argued, are related to specific deep cases (semantic roles) according to their inherent semantic properties. That is, verbs are selected according to the semantic environment of the sentence (called a 'case frame'), as expressed by the cases. A case frame with an agentive case, for instance, accepts only verbs that are subclassified for this feature, that is, the verb is required to accept an agentive case.[3] Thus, according to Fillmore's case system, each verb can be semantically classified according to the case frame(s) by which it is accepted. The strength and lasting influence of Fillmore's case system was its link between the semantic 'deep structure' and the syntactic 'surface structure' of a proposition. That is, the role of a participant is not determined by its surface case (be it the subject or object) but by its deep case. In many cases, the subject does indeed have the agent role, but not necessarily, as demonstrated by the following sentences (Fillmore 2003, 47):

(1) John opened the door.

(2) The door was opened by John.

It is evident from these examples that the subject need not be the agent. The passive construction in (2) expresses the agent with a prepositional phrase, while the subject is the semantic patient.

---

[3] The agentive case is "the case of the typically animate perceived instigator of the action identified by the verb" (Fillmore 2003, 46).

Thus, the sentences are deep-structurally identical, and the deep case structure determines the roles of the participants.

One of the major obstacles for Fillmore's thesis was the fact that a verb may be accepted by several case frames. For instance, the verb 'open' can, according to Fillmore (2003, 49), occur in at least four different case frames, including case frames with 1) an objective;[4] 2) an objective + an agent; 3) an objective + an instrument; and 4) an objective, agent, and instrument. To remedy this potential proliferation of case frames, Fillmore suggested that only the simplest frame should be considered obligatory (no. 1), while the remaining are optional extensions. Nevertheless, the approach lacks a controlled way of relating verbs and case frames. Moreover, there is no good reason why Fillmore's list of case roles should not be longer than the six suggested (agentive, instrumental, dative, factitive, locative, and objective), and he admits that additional cases are surely needed (Fillmore 2003, 46). But there does not seem to be an internal, methodological constraint upon the number and definitions of cases.

This lack of methodological control was brought to attention by Dowty (1991), who argued for completely abandoning the notion of discrete deep cases, or thematic roles, to use his

---

[4] In Fillmore's Case Grammar, the objective is the semantically most neutral deep case and is "the case of anything representable by a noun whose role in the action or state identified by the verb is identified by the semantic interpretation of the verb itself; conceivably the concept should be limited to things which are affected by the action or state identified by the verb" (Fillmore 2003, 46).

terminology.[5] In particular, Dowty (1991, 561) objected that existing theories of thematic role determination lacked a principled way to account for what kind of data motivates a thematic role type. For one thing, there was a tendency towards proliferation of lists of thematic roles. In addition, there was (and is) disagreement on the definitions of even the most familiar roles. According to Dowty, the lack of consensus as regards a shortlist of thematic roles seems to discount a view of thematic roles as argument-indexing.[6] Most important for Dowty's objections, however, are the theoretical and practical limitations of the case role system, because it requires each verb to clearly and definitely subcategorise for a particular thematic role. For the system to work, it cannot allow verbs to "hover over two roles, or to 'fall in the cracks' between roles" (Dowty 1991, 549). The solution to these problems, according to Dowty, is to view semantic roles not as discrete roles but as cluster concepts. That is, a verb does not determine a specific role, but rather imposes entailments on its arguments by virtue of the role the arguments play in the verbal event. Dowty proposed two proto-roles, the proto-agent and the

---

[5] Dowty considered Fillmore's case roles a theory among other argument-indexing views of thematic roles, that is, according to these theories, the predicate entails or indexes exactly one case/thematic role to each NP.

[6] The most common thematic roles are agent, patient, dative, instrument, benefactive, locative, associative, and manner (Givón 2001, I:107). However, in reality, the lists of thematic roles tend to grow wild, and one might want to add at least theme, goal, and source to Givón's list of semantic roles.

proto-patient, which correspond to two extremes of agency property entailment. For instance, the agent proto-role is characterised by volition, sentience, and causation, while the patient proto-role is characterised by undergoing change of state, stativity, and being causally affected. The verb may entail one or more of these properties to its arguments. Thus, in predicates with grammatical subject and object, the argument lexicalised as the subject is the argument for which the predicate entails the highest number of proto-agent features. The argument lexicalised as the object is the argument with the highest number of proto-patient features. As a result, in contrast to Fillmore's Case Grammar, Dowty's system does not depend on a specific list of semantic roles that can account for all kinds of verbal events, with the inherent risk of role proliferation. Rather, the semantic roles are determined on the basis of a more intuitive notion of agency.

One of the critiques raised against Dowty's proto-role theory is that there are no priorities among the entailments (Koenig and Davis 2001, 81–83). While Dowty (1991, 574) himself suggests that causation is the most important entailment for subject selection, in effect, according to his system, it is only the number of entailments that count. Since his lists of proto-role entailments are "preliminary" and not "necessarily exhaustive," the argument selection inevitably becomes a bit fuzzy (Dowty 1991, 572). In fact, Dowty (1991, 577) admits that his proto-roles are indeed "fuzzy" in that they are "higher-order generalization about lexical meanings." Nevertheless, Dowty is right to point out the compositional nature of agency, and in this respect, his work is also relevant for the present study.

More recently, Næss (2007) has offered another profound critique of traditional argument-indexing approaches. Her main objection is worth citing at length (Næss 2007, 107; italics original):

> The problem with thematic role theory is the absolute correlation it assumes between a verbal lexeme and the semantic properties of its arguments: a given verb must be taken to always subcategorise for the same set of thematic roles, and this leads to difficulties for verbs which seem to be compatible with several different role-types. A verb such as English *break*, for instance, may take a volitionally instigating subject argument, an agent: *John broke the window (on purpose)*. However, the property of volitionality is not actually required; *break* may equally well take a non-volitional subject argument (*John accidentally broke the window*), an inanimate force (*The bolt of lightning broke the window*) or even an instrument (*The hammer broke the window*). In the light of these data, which thematic role should one postulate for the subject argument of break?

Like Dowty, Næss abandons the concept of thematic roles. Rather, in a revision of Paul J. Hopper and Sandra A. Thompson's (1980) classic 'Transitivity Hypothesis',[7] she offers a 'Maximally

---

[7] According to Hopper and Thompson (1980), transitivity is best understood as an exchange or 'transfer' between two participants. The transfer may be more or less effective depending on the type of transfer (the lexical properties of the verb) and the participants involved. The effectiveness of the transfer correlates with an intuitive understanding of agency. A highly efficient exchange, e.g., 'John broke the window', requires a controlling and instigating agent and a totally affected patient. Less efficient exchanges, e.g., 'John sees Mary', imply a less instigating and volitional agent and a non-affected patient (see chapter 6, §4.0).

Distinguished Arguments Hypothesis' which she defines as follows (Næss 2007, 30):

> A prototypical transitive clause is one where the two participants are maximally semantically distinct in terms of their roles in the event described by the clause.

The two maximally distinct participants in transitive clauses are labelled 'agent' and 'patient'. That they are maximally distinct means that the properties of the agent are not shared by the patient, and vice versa. Importantly for the present discussion, Næss does not assume these semantic roles to be indexed or selected by the verb. According to Næss, verbs do not subcategorise for specific thematic roles (e.g., agent and patient), but rather for semantic properties (instigation, volition, and affectedness). Therefore, 'agent' and 'patient' are not thematic roles lexicalised by specific verbs, but clusters of properties exhibited by the arguments of the verb (Næss 2007, 37). To illustrate the implications of Næss' approach, compare the sentences with 'break' from the quotation above, repeated here:

(3)  John broke the window (on purpose).

(4)  John broke the window accidentally.

(5)  The hammer broke the window.

In terms of volition and affectedness, the three sentences differ. In the first sentence, John intentionally breaks the window and should be considered an agent. In the second, John is less agentive because he does not want to break the window. And, finally, in the third sentence, a physical object is used as an instrument to break the window. In sum, the subjects in the three sentences have different roles. Accordingly, Næss argues that 'break' does not subcategorise the subject for a certain semantic role, but rather a feature, the decisive feature being 'instigation', that is, the subject must be instigator of the event. Apart from verbal semantics, argument NP properties (including animacy, definiteness, and referentiality) and clause-level operators (most importantly negation and aspect) affect the degree of agency (Næss 2007, 111–19). In sum, within this framework, semantic roles are not seen as inherent properties subcategorised by the predicate, but as the relationship a participant has with the predicate.

In many respects a descendant of Fillmore's Case Grammar, Role and Reference Grammar offers a linking algorithm for deriving semantic roles from a logical decomposition of verbs.[8] In an early description of the theory, the agent role was considered a thematic relation on a par with relations such as instrument, experiencer, and patient (Foley and Van Valin 1984).[9] However,

---

[8] Fillmore's Case Grammar and RRG are similar in that they both have direct mapping between syntactic structure and semantic representation. Further, RRG inherited the original Case Grammar's view on grammatical relations like subject and object as non-universal features of natural language. One difference between Case Grammar and RRG is RRG's emphasis on the role of discourse pragmatics in the mapping between syntax and semantics (see Van Valin and Wilkins 1996, 305).

[9] In RRG, there is a significant distinction between 'thematic relations' and 'semantic macroroles'. 'Thematic relations' resemble Fillmore's case roles, but they differ in an important respect, because there is no listing of thematic relations in the lexical entry of a verb. By contrast, the thematic relationship between a verb and an argument is determined on the basis of the position of the argument in the logical structure representation. By implication, the RRG lexical representation of verbs is not

in an important discussion of agency and thematic relations, Robert D. Van Valin Jr. and David P. Wilkins (1996, 289) argued that the agent role is not a lexically determined role, but is compositional, and derived from the interaction of a number of "morphosyntactic, lexical, semantic, and pragmatic factors which coalesce at the level of the contextualized interpretation of the utterance." If agency were a lexical property, three different logical structures should be postulated for sentences (3) to (5) above, and that would indeed lead to a proliferation of logical structures, as critiqued by Dowty. Therefore, "while there are arguments which are 'pure' effectors, themes, and experiencers, there are no 'pure' agent arguments, because agents are always *composite*" (Van Valin and Wilkins 1996, 308; italics original). The RRG conceptualisation of agency was inherited from Dee A. Holisky (1987, 118–19), who argued that the meaning of the agent role is often not a property of the semantic structure of the predicate. Rather, the notion of the agent arises from the semantic intersection of predicate and actor NP. Moreover, she established an important pragmatic principle for interpreting the agent role (Holisky 1987, 119):

> Pragmatic principle: You may interpret effectors and effector-themes which are human as agents (in the absence of any information to the contrary).

---

dependent on a fixed list of thematic relations. For logical structures, see §4.0. There are two 'semantic macroroles', actor and undergoer, both of which subsume a number of thematic relations, and which can be considered generalisations of case roles. RRG offers a linking algorithm to derive the semantic macroroles (see Van Valin 2005, 53–67).

In RRG, the effector role is void of features like volition and control, and simply refers to the actor of an activity (represented as **do′**). Following Holisky, if the participant is human and the pragmatic context does not provide evidence to the contrary, the effector can be construed as the agent. Accordingly, sentences (3) to (5) all have an effector subject. Whether the effector is an agent depends on the pragmatic context. The first sentence does not provide evidence to the contrary, so John can be construed as an agent. In the second sentence, the adverb 'accidentally' cancels the pragmatic implicature of agency, while 'hammer' in the third sentence is not animate, so the agency inference is not applicable. Some verbs do in fact subcategorise for the agent role. In English, the verb 'murder' requires an agent actor, because the agency inference cannot be cancelled by an agency-cancelling adverb such as 'inadvertently' (e.g., '*Larry inadvertently murdered his neighbour'), unlike 'kill' (Van Valin and Wilkins 1996, 310). While English has a few verbs that subcategorise for the agent role, most verbs do not. Japanese, by contrast, seems to contain many more verbs that subcategorise for the agent role (Van Valin 2005, 56–57; see also Hasegawa 1996). Thus, despite objections to argument-indexing theories, thematic relations are retained in RRG. Importantly, however, the concept of thematic relations in RRG is not dependent upon a specific list or concrete definitions of relations. Rather, the meaning of the thematic relations is their logical positions within the semantic representation of the predicate, irrespective of any label one might postulate. RRG therefore offers a controlled framework for investigating the semantic relationship between predicates and arguments.

The overall purpose of this and the next two chapters is to establish a hierarchy of semantic roles on the basis of a structured verbal analysis. This objective transcends the logical analysis of verbs offered by RRG, because agency is compositional and arises from the intersection of predicate, arguments, and discourse pragmatics, as explained above. However, lexical decomposition of verbs is not irrelevant for an analysis of agency. On the contrary, the thematic relations derived from a semantic representation of the verb constrain the notion of agency, since only the effector role can possibly be an agent. Accordingly, this study will apply the RRG theory of lexical decomposition to derive logical structures and thematic relations from Biblical Hebrew verbs. On top of this framework, Næss' parameters of agency (instigation, volition, and affectedness) will be applied to determine the degree of agency exercised by each participant and to establish a hierarchy of semantic roles.

## 3.0. Decomposition of Verb Classes

Lexical decomposition is the task of decomposing lexemes into the most general categories possible in order to posit general criteria for how verbs function in the language. Ray Jackendoff (2002) likens lexical decomposition to physicists' quest to explain the composition of substances. A molecule is decomposed into atoms, and the atoms themselves can be decomposed into protons, neutrons, and electrons. Similarly, lexical decomposition is the task of decomposing lexemes into more generic sets of primitives. As with thematic roles, discussed above, there is in lexical decomposition an inherent risk of proliferation. Nevertheless, lexical decomposition is about positing the fewest and simplest primitives to account for the greatest lexical diversity.

With respect to verbs, Zeno Vendler (1957) famously proposed four verbal classes: states, activities, achievements, and accomplishments. Later, other classes were added, including the semelfactive, that is, a punctual event with no change of state implied (Smith 1991). In canonical RRG, six verbal classes have been proposed (including, apart from Vendler's classes, semelfactive and active accomplishment), each with a causative correspondent, because, as will be shown, causation interferes with the regular verbal classes. In RRG, the verbal classes are called *Aktionsart*, but other terms occur frequently in the literature: 'inherent aspect' (Comrie 1976), 'situation aspect' (Smith 1991), 'lexical aspect' (Olsen 1997), 'event ontology' (Parsons 1979), and 'internal structure of an event' (Goldfajn 1998). One of the main questions to address is where the aspectual meaning is 'located'. While Vendler admitted the possibility that other constituents in the sentence may affect the aspect of the verb, he did not explore this further. However, Henk J. Verkuyl (1972) was soon to argue that the aspect of the verb should in fact be assigned to the entire verb phrase, thus contending that aspect has a composite nature, including both the verb itself and other constituents in the phrase. Carlota S. Smith (1991) also argued for a compositional notion of aspect. For Smith, the verb is important, but it is not the only parameter. Nominals and prepositions also add to the resulting aspect of the sentence. Smith (1991, 54) argued for a set of "compositional rules" that might be used to calculate a "composite value" based on the composition of verb, arguments, and adverbials. In effect, Smith argued that the "intrinsic aspectual value" of the verb could be overwritten by other elements in the syntax. Accordingly, "Verbs have an intrinsic aspectual value, based on its [sic] aspectual contribution to a 'maximally simple sentence'" (Smith 1991, 54), that is, an intransitive sentence or a sentence with a direct object, and with quantised nominals; compare, e.g.:

(6)　Mary walked.

(7)　Mary walked to school.

Since the verb 'walk' appears meaningfully in the intransitive, atelic sentence (6), the verb is assigned the intrinsic aspectual value 'atelic'. The addition of the telic prepositional phrase 'to school' overwrites the atelic value and renders the sentence telic.

Until then, linguists had thought of aspect as a feature determined by equally valid oppositional components, e.g., the distinction between 'telic' and 'atelic', or 'durative' and 'punctual'. In other words, a verb was usually seen as either telic or atelic, dynamic or stative, and durative or punctual. Mari B. Olsen (1997, 19), however, argued that there is an intrinsic asymmetry between these components:

> [A] careful examination of the features on the basis of the semantic-pragmatic distinction reveals that the features have an asymmetry heretofore unnoticed in the literature: whereas positively marked lexical aspect features ([+telic], [+dynamic], [+durative]) are part of the semantics, interpretations generally attributed to negative features ([-telic], [-dynamic], [-durative]) arise as a result of conversational implicature.

For Olsen, a verb cannot be inherently atelic or inherently punctual, because these features are not lexical in nature, but pragmatic (or "conversational" in the quotation above). By implication, according to Olsen's theory, a verb need not be marked for telicity at all. In more general terms, Olsen views the semantic oppositions as 'privative', that is, the two opposed semantic features are not equally marked. In her semantic analysis, only positive features are marked, while negative features are optional. By contrast, the traditional view on semantic oppositions may be called 'equipollent', because the two opposed semantic features have equal weight or are equally marked.[10] The difference between the classical, 'equipollent' representation of aspect and Olsen's (1997, 21) 'privative' representation of aspect can be illustrated as follows:

(8) equipollent: run: [-telic, +durative, +dynamic]

(9) privative: run: [+durative, +dynamic]

In the traditional, equipollent analysis (8), the verb 'run' is marked atelic, while in the privative representation (9), the verb is simply unmarked for telicity. The equipollent analysis has a serious drawback, because it needs to posit an additional representation of the verb when it occurs with a telic complement, e.g., 'Mark ran a mile'. In the privative analysis, on the other hand, there is no need to propose a telic variant, since the telic interpretation does not arise from the verb but from the clausal context.

---

[10] For further explanation, see Olsen (1997, 17–22).

Olsen's 'privative oppositions' pose a fundamental challenge to the classical tests developed for diagnosing the *Aktionsart* of verbs. Dowty's (1979) test questions became a popular tool for decomposing verbs into aspectual classes, and they were later incorporated into RRG (Foley and Van Valin 1984; Van Valin and LaPolla 1997; Van Valin 2005). As an example, a test to distinguish states and activities is the progressive test, because only non-statives can normally occur in the progressive (Dowty 1979, 55):[11]

(10) *John is knowing the answer.

(11) John is running.

(12) John is building the house.

Similar tests include tests for agency, because states cannot have an agent. Therefore, states cannot occur with verbs such as 'force' and 'persuade', or as imperatives, according to this theory. Van Valin (2005, 36) adds to the pool of non-stative modifiers dynamic adverbs, including 'vigorously', 'gently', and 'powerfully'. If, however, Olsen is right in her claim that the dynamic feature is one of 'privative opposition', the validity of the tests is brought into question. The problem is that dynamicity and stativity are not symmetric. Stativity is a cancellable feature while dynamicity is not, and this asymmetry implies that states may have both stative and dynamic interpretations, in contrast to activities, which are always dynamic. By implication, stative verbs may respond positively to the tests given a pragmatic context that cancels out

---

[11] Some states can occur with the progressive aspect; see Van Valin 2005, 35 n. 3.

the stative interpretation, as in the following quotation from C. S. Lewis' *The Magician's Nephew*: "Digory was disliking his uncle more every minute" (see Olsen 1997, 37). In this example, the presence of the adverbials 'more' and 'every minute' cancels the stativity of the predicate, and the predicate expresses an incremental event. Olsen (1997, 37) adds the otherwise prototypically stative verbs 'know' and 'love' to the group of verbs that can occur in dynamic contexts. Because stativity is a cancellable feature, stative verbs may vary between a stative and a dynamic reading depending on the pragmatic context. A progressive test will therefore yield both states and activities. Obviously, the solution is not to propose opposite test questions, e.g., to test whether a verb can occur in a non-progressive form. Both stative and dynamic verbs can occur in the non-progressive, but the dynamic verb would still be interpreted as dynamic in contrast to the stative verb.

If it is inherently flawed to apply test questions for sorting states and activities in modern languages, it is even more so with respect to ancient languages, where there are no competent speakers to consult. One may be able to identify dynamic contexts, for example dynamic adverbs that suggest a dynamic interpretation of the sentence as whole. However, if Olsen is right, we should expect to find inherently dynamic as well as stative predicates in those contexts. Therefore, a verb is not necessarily inherently dynamic just because it happens to occur in a dynamic context. On the other hand, even if a verb never occurs in a dynamic context, it may still be dynamic, because we cannot assume of a limited corpus that it attests all possible types of construction. In this study, therefore, I shall explore a quantitative method for determining the *Aktionsart*, in particular as regards the dynamicity opposition (see chapter 5).

## 4.0. Logical Structures

In RRG, verb semantics is represented in so-called 'logical structures' according to *Aktionsart* (Van Valin 2005, 45). The purpose of the logical structures is to formally derive semantic roles depending on the *Aktionsart* of the verb. The semantic roles can then be mapped onto the syntax of the clause to determine the semantic roles of the arguments of the verb. There are six *Aktionsart* classes in RRG, each with a causative correspondent. As displayed in Table 3, the basic distinction is between states (represented as **predicate′** or simply **pred′**), and activities (**do′**). As Van Valin (2018, 77) explains, in RRG, "States and activities are taken as the primitive building blocks of the system; they are the only classes which take arguments." Moreover, unlike in the work of Dowty (1979), activities are not assumed to be derivable from states, but these are, rather, treated as two distinct primitives. The remaining classes are derived from this fundamental distinction. Accordingly, the ingressive aspect, the semelfactive aspect, and the resultative aspect are secondary operators modifying states or activities. The ingressive aspect (INGR) refers to instant change, the resultative aspect (BECOME) captures change over a span of time and a resulting state of affairs, while the semelfactive operator (SEML) denotes punctual iterations (Van Valin and LaPolla 1997, 104). Finally, CAUSE expresses the causal relationship between two individual logical structures.

Table 3: Logical structures for the *Aktionsart* classes (Van Valin 2005, 45). The variables x, y, and z represent the slots to be filled by lexical items from the syntax.

| *Aktionsart* class | Logical structure |
| --- | --- |
| State | **pred'** (x) or (x, y) |
| Activity | **do'** (x, [**pred'** (x) or (x, y)]) |
| Achievement | INGR **pred'** (x) or (x, y), |
| | or |
| | INGR **do'** (x, [**pred'** (x) or (x, y)]) |
| Semelfactive | SEML **pred'** (x) or (x, y), |
| | or |
| | SEML **do'** (x, [**pred'** (x) or (x, y)]) |
| Accomplishment | BECOME **pred'** (x) or (x, y), |
| | or |
| | BECOME **do'** (x, [**pred'** (x) or (x, y)]) |
| Active accomplishment | **do'** (x, [**pred$_1$'** (x, (y))]) & INGR **pred$_2$'** (z, x) or (y) |
| Causative | α CAUSE β, where α and β are logical structures of any type |

Later, Van Valin (2018) modified the representation of active accomplishments (most importantly, consumption and creation verbs). Whereas (active) accomplishments were traditionally conceptualised as BECOME **pred'** (x) or (x, y) or BECOME **do'** (x, [**pred'** (x) or (x, y)]) for states and activities respectively, the new representation adds additional nuances to the event structure. As a gradual process towards completion, an (active) accomplishment undergoes a process of change before reaching the point of completion. Accordingly, the BECOME operator has been split into a process (PROC) and a punctual endpoint (INGR), as exemplified below (Van Valin 2018, 85–86):

(13) Creation of a document: [**do'** (x, [**write'** (x,y)]) ^ PROC **create'** (y)] & INGR **exist'** (y)

(14) Motion to a goal: [**do'** (x, [**run'** (x)]) ^ PROC **cover.path.distance'** (x,(y))] & INGR **be-at'** (z, x)

In these examples the ^ means 'and simultaneously', and captures the meaning that when someone writes a letter, the letter is simultaneously undergoing a process of creation.

*Aktionsart* is often defined as the 'inherent temporal aspect' of a verb. For this reason, it may seem odd that the causative aspect is included in this model. After all, causation is a logical relation rather than a temporal one. However, according to Smith (1991, 21), *Aktionsart* (or, rather, 'situation type' in her terminology) is related to a super-ordinate 'causal chain':

Cause—Subject—Action—Instrument—Object—Result

As Smith (1991, 21) explains, stative situations typically cover only the Object–Result part of the chain, while activities usually cover the first part of the chain. A causative stative can therefore be expected to cover the Cause and the Object–Result parts of the chain. Moreover, causative verbs have an extra argument, namely the causer, and the extra argument has ramifications for the logical structure. When a causer is added, the logical structure must be expanded in order to include the causer, the causee, and the original non-causative object, if any. It is therefore reasonable to include causation in the study of *Aktionsart*.

The purpose of this study is to explore the correlation between Hebrew verbs (primarily those in Lev. 17–26) and agency. For this reason, not all aspects of the RRG logical structure theory are equally important. The two most important aspects are 1) the distinction between states and activities, because they subcategorise for different thematic relations; and 2) the distinction between causative and non-causative events, because causative events add an external causer and, by implication, a new set of thematic relations. The remaining operators add finer distinctions to the logical representation of the verb, but they do not influence the selection of thematic relations; hence, they do not affect the agency of the participants involved.

## 5.0. Annotation Procedure

Having discussed agency, lexical decomposition, and logical structures with respect to Biblical Hebrew, we are now in a position to sketch the analysis of verbal events to be carried out in the next two chapters. In general, given the obvious lack of native speakers of the language, the analysis will seek to employ quantitative methods as much as possible, without neglecting the importance of qualitative analysis. In chapter 5, dynamicity will be explored, and a quantitative method will be applied to distinguish states and activities. Despite promising results, many verbs are not captured by the quantitative model due to infrequency and low attestation of adverbials. These verbs will be manually annotated. In chapter 6, the Hebrew morphological and lexical causatives will be analysed in turn. A transitivity alternation model will be proposed to identify true morphological causatives

(§3.0). Next, lexical causatives will be analysed with respect to semantic transitivity (§§4.0–5.0). Finally, on the basis of verbal properties as well as argument and clausal features, the semantic roles and their corresponding agency scores will be computed (§6.0). The annotation procedure is sketched in Figure 4.

Figure 4: Annotation procedure

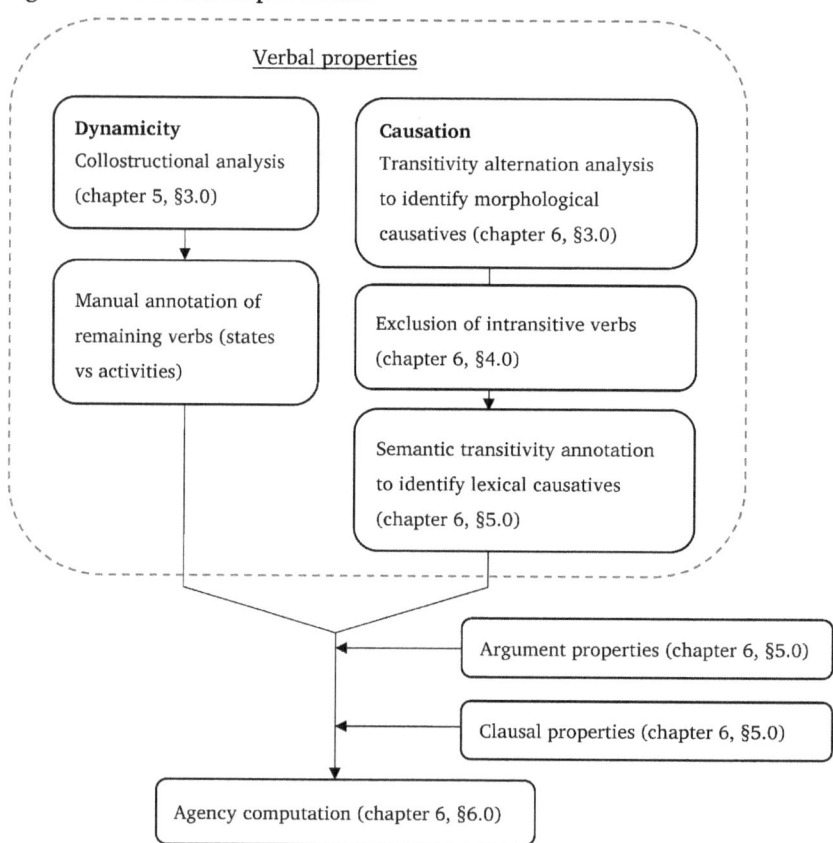

# 5. DYNAMICITY: A COLLOSTRUCTIONAL APPROACH

## 1.0. Introduction

Dynamicity refers to the universal opposition between situations of movement, activity, and change on the one hand, and situations of stativity and permanence on the other. Cognitive linguists generally consider the opposition between states and activities the most fundamental opposition with respect to verbal aspect (e.g., Dahl 1985, 28). Leonard Talmy (2000, 414), in his theory of force dynamics, treats the opposition between rest and motion as a language universal. In RRG, as explained in the preceding chapter, all *Aktionsart* classes are derived from the stative-dynamic opposition. For instance, a semelfactive verb is not simply a state or activity; rather, the semelfactive aspect is in fact projected as an operator modifying a state or activity, as exemplified in Van Valin (2005, 47):

(1)   Dana glimpsed the picture.

SEML **see′** (Dana, picture)

(2)   Mary coughed.

SEML **do′** (Mary, [**cough′** (Mary)])

Semitic languages, including Biblical Hebrew, support this notion of a fundamental opposition between states and activities. The verbal stem *qal* is attested in six vowel patterns, two of which are generally used for activities, another two for states, while the remaining two vowel patterns mix states and activities (Waltke and

O'Connor 1990, §22.3b). As discussed below, however, the correlation between morphology and *Aktionsart* is not so consistent as might be expected from the vowel patterns.

## 2.0. Previous Research on Dynamicity in Biblical Hebrew

As an ancient language, Biblical Hebrew is semantically much less accessible for contemporary research than modern languages. Stuart A. Creason (1995, 23–25) rightly notes the limitations for modern investigations of BH. Firstly, the corpus is limited, and since the corpus is ancient, the corpus cannot be expanded with additional evidence (unless archaeology uncovers related texts). Neither can one consult native speakers of BH. Secondly, due to the limited size of the corpus, many verbs are only attested a few times. And one may add that even relatively frequent verbs may not occur frequently with any particular adverbial modifier, so contextual evidence is sometimes scarce. Thirdly, the corpus contains a variety of literary genres (including prose, poetry, and prophetic literature) and is made up of texts from a range of historical periods.[1] Therefore, a verb may

---

[1] The question as to whether the Hebrew Bible contains evidence of well-defined stages of ancient Hebrew remains heavily debated. Recently, Hendel and Joosten (2018) have argued for three such stages of BH—namely, classic (CBH), transitional (TBH), and late Biblical Hebrew (LBH)—based on morphological and syntactic variations as well as synchronisations with extra-Biblical inscriptions. While CBH is most commonly associated with the Pentateuch and the Deuteronomic history (Joshua–Kings), other portions of the Bible are sometimes included: Isa. 1–39; Hosea; Amos; Obadiah; Micah; Nahum; Habakkuk;

be used differently in different parts of the HB.[2] Semantic decomposition of Biblical Hebrew verbs is thus a tricky endeavour, and

---

Zephaniah; and various Psalms (Hornkohl 2013). In this study, CBH is limited to Genesis–Kings. LBH includes Esther; Daniel; Ezra–Nehemiah; Chronicles; Ecclesiastes; the narrative framework of Job; and various Psalms. TBH is somewhat more debated, but it has been suggested that it contains the latter part of Kings; Jeremiah; Isa. 40–66; Ezekiel; Haggai; Zechariah; Malachi; and Lamentations (Hornkohl 2013). It has been objected that the syntactic variations between so-called CBH and LBH point rather to the coexistence of literary styles throughout the Biblical period (e.g., Young et al. 2008). For a recent overview of the *status quaestionis* and an extensive bibliography of the vast number of contributions published on this topic in recent years, see Rezetko and Young (2019).

[2] It has been common among Biblical scholars to posit a clear distinction between the usage of verbs in prose and poetry. In contrast to prose, poetic language was often considered "transcendent" and beyond "human understanding and analysis" (Van Peursen 2017, 378). According to Van Peursen, however, a number of recent studies on Biblical poetry in fact demonstrate the linguistic regularities of this genre, including Glanz's (2013) investigation of participant-reference shifts in Jeremiah (see chapter 3, §3.6), Oosting's (2013) analysis of the roles of 'Zion' and 'Jerusalem' in Isa. 40–55, Kalkman's (2015) study of verbal tenses in the Psalms, Bosman's (2019) dissertation on the relationship between syntactic and prosodic structure in BH poetry, and Erwich's (2020) analysis of participant-reference shifts in the Psalms (see chapter 3, §2.1). Moreover, it has been argued that the difference between these genres with respect to verbs is not one of grammar but "style" (Joosten 2012, 416) or "poetics" (Rogland 2003, 13 n. 70). One major difference between prose and poetry is the often "segmental nature" of the latter, which allows the author to shift perspective and theme (Siegismund 2018, 95). Furthermore, as Siegismund (2018, 94–97) explains, poetry

the following remark and question from Creason (1995, 22) capture the challenge—and sometimes frustration—that Hebraists face in their quest for meaning in Biblical Hebrew:

> The kinds of semantic distinctions which are discussed in this study are often subtle ones and this is especially true of the distinctions exhibited by verbs that are ambiguous in meaning. On what basis can one be at all certain that a particular verb does or does not exhibit the kind of semantic distinctions that are the focus of this study?

The traditional Dowtian approach is obviously difficult to apply to Biblical Hebrew. As noted in chapter 4, David R. Dowty's approach depends inherently on a principle of falsification by intuition, and we do not have such an intuition for Biblical Hebrew. There are no native language users to falsify our hypothetical juxtapositions of verbs and certain adverbials or our paraphrases of Hebrew sentences. One may wonder whether rare constructions are 'odd' (see Jero 2008, 56), but it is impossible to falsify this claim.

Previous research has (rightly) focused on how internal aspect relates to the morphology and syntax of Biblical Hebrew. If we are to decompose Biblical verbs in a consistent way, we need textual evidence—either the morphology of the verb, adverbial modifiers in the clause, or evidence from the discourse. In fact, for comprehensive analyses of the realisation of internal aspect, these parameters have often been combined. For the sake of

---

is more prone to textual corruption, due to the high degree of ambiguity often found in this genre, which also explains why it is often possible to posit alternative readings of the Hebrew verbs.

providing an overview of the research, however, I will focus on morphology and syntax separately.

## 2.1. Morphology

States and activities have traditionally been distinguished on the basis of vowel patterns (Waltke and O'Connor 1990, §22). Activities have an *a* theme vowel in the *qātal* and an *ō* theme vowel in the *yiqtōl*.[3] For stative verbs, the vowel pattern of the *qātal* is changed to *qātel* or, rarely, *qātōl*, whereas the vowel pattern of *yiqtōl* is changed to *yiqtal*. Although the morphological distinction seems to reveal a fundamental semantic distinction, the correlation between morphology and function is not straightforward. As John A. Cook (2002, 201) explains, the diagnostic theme vowel may be obscured by phonological factors, that is, the original theme vowel may be changed due to a pharyngeal or laryngeal in the second or third position in the verbal root. More importantly, the morphological 'stative' class does not always correlate with what we would assume to be semantically stative verbs. For example, the verbs ישב 'sit' and עמד 'stand' are morphologically dynamic but semantically stative (Jero 2008, 57–58). Therefore, while the morphological patterns certainly support the assumption that the distinction between stativity and activity is fundamental to Biblical Hebrew, the patterns themselves

---

[3] The 'theme vowel' is the vowel between the second and third consonant in the verbal root. The distinction between *qātal* and *yiqtōl* is most commonly associated with the opposition between perfect and imperfect/non-perfect aspect respectively (Van der Merwe et al. 2017, §19; Waltke and O'Connor 1990, §§30–31).

cannot be taken at face value. Cook (2002, 202–3), however, following G. R. Driver (1936), argues that some verbs must be classified as stative verbs despite their apparent dynamic use (e.g., קרב 'approach' and לבשׁ 'clothe'), because they reveal an original stative sense. Even if this reconstruction of a diachronic development in Hebrew verbs were true, one may argue that it is more fruitful to classify the verbs according to their present usage in the Hebrew Bible, rather than according to etymology. Etymology and cognate languages certainly provide useful background information, but verbs may take on new meanings and uses without necessarily changing theme vowels.

Within the last three decades, a number of scholars have sought to explore other morphological correspondences with internal aspect. Ronald Hendel (1996), in his analysis of the correspondence between verbal conjugations (in particular, *qātal* and *yiqtōl*) and internal aspect, argued that there is a complex relationship between *qātal* and *yiqtōl*, internal aspect, and relative tense. According to Hendel, stative verbs refer to relative non-future in *qātal* and to relative future in *yiqtōl*. By contrast, dynamic verbs refer to relative past in *qātal* and to relative non-past in *yiqtōl*. By implication, for example, in a simple present frame, a stative verb would normally be *qātal* and a dynamic verb *yiqtōl*. However, Hendel also acknowledged that *qātal* and *yiqtōl* correlate with both viewpoint aspect (perfect vs imperfect) and mood (indicative vs modal).[4] Thus, the Biblical Hebrew verbal system

---

[4] The correlation between relative tense and *qātal/yiqtōl* in BH has most recently been readdressed by Siegismund (2018), who argues that the *qātal* merely indicates that an event is anterior to a temporal reference

is multidimensional and cannot be reduced to a simple mapping of dynamicity and verbal conjugations.

One of the most promising studies on the relationship between the Hebrew stems, the so-called *binyanim*, and semantic features was carried out by A. J. C. Verheij (2000), who set out to explore the forms and functions of the *binyanim* on a quantitative basis.[5] It had long been postulated that certain stems are more telic than others, e.g., the *piʿel* is supposed to be telic while the *hifʿil* is progressive. To test this and other hypotheses, he analysed the dependence of the Hebrew stems on four semantic parameters: dynamicity, telicity, agency, and transitivity. He found that there is in fact a significant correspondence between agency and transitivity on the one hand and stem on the other hand. Dynamicity and telicity, by contrast, were far more dependent on the lexical root of the verb than its stem. The present study diverges from Verheij's in important aspects. Most importantly, whereas I will propose a quantitative model for distinguishing dynamic and stative verbs (§3.0), Verheij manually annotated his corpus with this feature. In other words, the features of dynamicity

---

point, in contrast to the *yiqtōl*, which is non-anterior. As for the frequent occurrence of present tense states in the *qātal*, Siegismund argues that the form is a relic from a pre-BH period where it expressed a simple predication of the subject. According to Siegismund (2018, 87), then, in BH, present tense states in the *qātal* were reanalysed within the new verbal system, e.g., 'I know' (יָדַעְתִּי) could be reinterpreted as 'I have come to know'. Apart from this particular verbal form, Siegismund does not incorporate inherent aspect into his grammar of the BH verbal system.

[5] For a concise introduction to the *binyanim*, see Dan (2013).

(as well as telicity, agency, and transitivity) are presupposed in his statistical analysis. At the basis of his work, therefore, lies a qualitative analysis of the verbs under consideration. My statistical model does not presuppose semantic features, but rather employs syntactic features to suggest semantic differentiation. Another important difference between Verheij's study and the present one is his concept of agency. It has already been explained that agency is a multifaceted concept and can hardly be thought of as a binary category (see chapter 4, §2.0). Verheij, however, treats all his semantic features as binary categories for the sake of his statistical model.[6] Moreover, each combination of root and stem is given only one set of features. This sort of annotation implies that all combinations of, e.g., הלך 'walk' and *qal* (1,412 attestations in Verheij's corpus) have exactly the same semantic properties (see Verheij 2000, 84). Thus, his annotations are contextually insensitive. However, as argued above, agency is a multifaceted parameter and rarely a lexical property. Therefore, the notion of agency depends on the linguistic context and not only on the verb. The sentences with 'break' (see chapter 4, §2.0) illustrate this well in that the notion of agency depends on the intentionality and animacy of the actor. Thus, considering agency

---

[6] Verheij (2000, 8) is well aware of the limitations of his model (and quantitative models in general). As he notes, "in-depth quantitative analysis [...] entails simplification. It cannot detail the semantic richness of individual words, the way philological scholarship can. In particular, it will reveal general trends and make claims against which counter-examples can be brought forward, as trends never account for all cases. The loss of nuance, however, is compensated by the gain in completeness and the generalizability of the results."

to be a binary, lexical property is a gross simplification of this semantic feature. In short, therefore, the present study diverges significantly from Verheij's in that Verheij presupposes semantic features for his study of *binyanim*, while my study aims to discern syntactic and morphological clues by which those semantic features might be identified. Nevertheless, Verheij was a pioneer of applying quantitative methods to the study of Biblical Hebrew, and his work has merit in that respect.

In a more recent study, Christopher Jero (2008) likewise explores the relationship between internal aspect and the morphology of Biblical Hebrew verbs. Although his study was limited to the lamentation psalms of the Psalter, the conclusions may be extended to the rest of the Hebrew Bible. Jero (2008, 87) observes that, for present temporal frames, "Activities and simple states appear as *yiqtol*. Resultative states, whether of resultative events or developmental verbs, appear as *qatal*." However, the proposed correlation between morphology and internal aspect does not include all verbs, and Jero (2008, 87–94) explicitly counts speech verbs, morphological states, verbs of location, and translocative verbs (motion verbs) among "exceptional" cases where the correlation is less than clear. The limits of the correlation are important, because, at least in CBH (Genesis–Kings), speech verbs, motion verbs, and locative verbs are abundant. At a more fundamental level, Jero's analysis relies on some of the same assumptions as did Hendel's earlier work. According to Jero (2008, 67), the largest correspondence between verb conjugation and internal aspect is observable in present temporal frames—but it is not clear how those present temporal frames are identified in the first place. Since Jero wants to compare the functions of present tense forms and modal forms (including various petitionary forms), he first needs to distinguish indicative and modal forms. He considers various textual evidence, including morphology (long and short forms of the *yiqtōl*) and word order. In the end, however, Jero (2008, 35) concludes that, although "deontic forms prefer first position" in the clause, he has "ultimately relied on [his] admittedly subjective interpretation of [...] each context." Jero's project demonstrates a general weakness in the study of the correspondence between morphosyntax and semantics. Our conclusions are only as strong as our data model, and if we cannot be sure that a particular use of the *qātal* or *yiqtōl* is present or past, indicative or modal, we can only guess as to its correspondence with the internal aspect of the verb.

In his grammar of the BH verbal system, Jan Joosten (2012) rejects a clear correspondence between verbal morphology and internal aspect. On the contrary, he proposes a number of syntactic constructions that correspond with internal aspect, at least to some extent. According to Joosten (2012, 90), the predicative participle (in the sequence Subj-PTC) "adds a nuance of ongoing action comparable to that of the English progressive tenses." One would expect this construction to be far more compatible with verbs of duration than verbs of punctuality. Joosten offers the difference between נבט H 'look' and ראה G 'see' as an example. The former never occurs as a predicative participle, while the latter does so frequently. A survey of the verbs in the Hebrew Bible for which the participle is attested at least 25 times sheds further light upon Joosten's thesis. The survey was carried out by exploring the syntactic role of participles based on the annotations of the ETCBC database. The ETCBC database distinguishes between part-of-speech and phrase-dependent part-of-speech. The former annotation is the result of a morphological analysis of the Hebrew text. The latter annotation is the result of a linguistic analysis of phrases in order to investigate whether a participle has a function above the phrase level (e.g., as a predicate), or whether it functions as a noun within a construct-chain of nouns. Put differently, the part-of-speech tagging comes from a distributional analysis, while the phrase-dependent part-of-speech annotation is the result of a functional analysis.[7] A participle may thus function as a predicate (3), adjective (4), or noun (5), as the following examples illustrate:

(3) וְדָוִד יֹשֵׁב בַּמִּדְבָּר

'But David was sitting in the desert' (1 Sam. 26.3)

(4) אִשָּׁה זֹנָה וַחֲלָלָה לֹא יִקָּחוּ

'They may not marry a prostituted or defiled woman' (Lev. 21.7)

(5) וַיֹּאמֶר מֶלֶךְ מִצְרַיִם לַמְיַלְּדֹת הָעִבְרִיֹּת

'And the king of Egypt said to the midwives of the Hebrews' (Exod. 1.15)

If the proportions of the part-of-speech functions are calculated for each verb, a graph can be plotted (Figure 5). As the graph shows, verbs such as אמר 'say', כתב 'write', and נגע 'touch' are only attested as predicates (= verb in the graph), and these verbs

---

[7] For a detailed account, see Talstra and Sikkel (2000).

are clearly associated with activity. At the other end of the graph, verbs like רצח 'kill' (in the sense of 'murderer'), חתן 'be father-in-law', בין 'understand', and איב 'be hostile' never, or rarely, occur as either predicate or adjective, but only as nouns, that is, as *nomen agentis* (see Waltke and O'Connor 1990, §37.2.a). Most interesting are participles occurring frequently as adjectives, such as רום 'be high', זוב 'flow', זנה 'fornicate', שמם 'be desolate'. These verbs support the hypothesis that verbs occurring as adjectival participles tend to be non-punctual.

Figure 5: Proportions of phrase-dependent part-of-speech for verbs in the *qal*

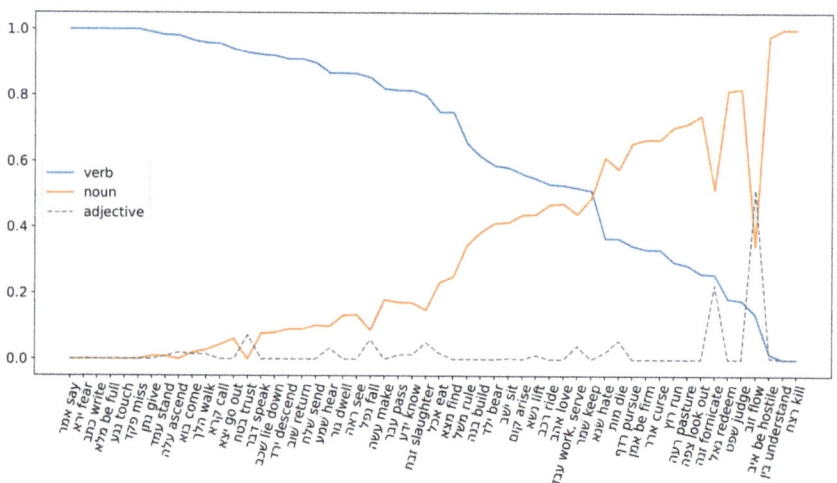

While the predicative participle may therefore serve as a clue to the internal aspect of the verb, an analysis along these lines is not uncontroversial, since the predicative participle may also be used with punctual verbs to denote duration or iteration of punctual events. The most striking case regards נפל 'fall', which is also found in the graph, despite its seemingly punctual nature. As Joosten (2012, 90) explains, נפל is typically used as a participle in order to express 'lying down' rather than 'falling'. Thus, even though participles, given their progressive and durative aspect, may be more frequently attested with non-punctual verbs, punctual verbs are not excluded *per se* from this construction. This observation compromises the use of participles as a diagnostic clue to the internal aspect of verbs.

## 2.2. Syntax

A number of Hebrew linguists have followed Henk J. Verkuyl (1972) in seeing *Aktionsart* as a compositional entity. In his treatment of *Aktionsart* in Biblical Hebrew, Creason (1995) explored how the respective properties of verb and arguments (called participants) contribute to the overall situation depicted in the sentence. He ends up with eight *Aktionsart* classes, including state, semelfactive, atelic achievement, telic achievement, unchanging activity, changing activity, accomplishment, and complex situation (Creason 1995, 72–73). In his study, Creason (1995, 5) sought to account for verbal ambiguity, that is, when there is a "potential for ambiguity which is inherent in the nature of a verb;" hence, said verb can refer to two or more different situations. Creason (1995, 73) explored stative verbs in detail because this verbal class offers a "primary example." According to Creason, stative verbs can refer to real states, but they can also refer to 'change of state' and to 'remain-in-state'. The first subclass, 'change of state', seems to cover the ingressive aspect, e.g., "The land became ritually unacceptable" (Lev. 18.25).[8] Importantly

---

[8] In RRG, the ingressive aspect is treated as an operator that can modify the *Aktionsart* of a given verb (see chapter 4, §4.0).

for the present discussion, Creason (1995, 75) offered two guidelines for distinguishing regular state and change of state, namely, a punctual adverbial in the clause, or a narrative context for the clause. It appears that the narrative context of Lev. 18.25 is the reason for Creason's interpretation of טמא 'unclean' ('ritually unacceptable' in Creason's translation) as a change of state. As for the subclass 'remain-in-state', it involves clauses where the state is entailed as having existed for some time, in contrast to regular states, where this particular aspect is not important. Creason offered Gen. 11.12 as an example: "When Arpachshad had been alive for/remained alive for/lived for 35 years, he begot Shelah." Creason (1995, 77) argued that the "example may be interpreted as referring to a state (be alive) or an event (remain alive/live)."

The so-called verbal ambiguity was later explained by F. W. Dobbs-Allsopp (2000) within the framework of 'privative oppositions' offered by Olsen (1997). Because stativity is a cancellable feature, states can be cancelled for stativity and thus become dynamic. The means of cancelling the stative aspect involve sentential complements and pragmatic contexts, such as a "narrative sequence" or a "punctiliar frame" (Dobbs-Allsopp 2000, 44–45). Above all, fundamental to this approach is the claim that the dynamic interpretation does not arise as a result of the verbal root itself or the conjugation of the verb, but is "implicated from the pragmatic context" (Dobbs-Allsopp 2000, 34).

Creason's and Dobbs-Allsopp's contributions explain well how the pragmatic context influences the situation expressed by the sentence at large. However, this particular approach also seems to presuppose a knowledge of which verbs are stative and which are dynamic. It is difficult to apply these criteria to identify states and activities respectively, because the same diagnostic clues can, according to the models of these two authors, yield both states and activities. A narrative sequence, for example, may cancel the stative aspect of a stative verb, but it may also simply be used with a dynamic verb. Consequently, given these theories, the *Aktionsart* of verbs can only be assumed, not falsified.

Relevant to this discussion are Janet W. Dyk's important studies of valence patterns in Biblical Hebrew. Together with her research team, she has published a series of articles discussing the meaning of verbs within the context of the clause (Dyk 2014; Dyk et al. 2014; Glanz et al. 2015; Oosting and Dyk 2017). Above all, their goal was to identify the syntactic circumstances under which a particular meaning of a verb is to be preferred (Dyk, Glanz, and Oosting 2014, 3). According to valence theory, verbs can be divided into groups of valency, that is, into groups characterised by a fixed number of arguments. For instance, the verb in 'he kicks the ball' has two arguments, a subject and an object, and is thus transitive (Dyk et al. 2014, 4). In order for a verb to be grammatically correct, it needs a certain number of arguments, depending on some lexical property of the verb. Thus, through analysis of valence patterns, a window is opened into the semantics of the verb. In natural language, however, verbs are normally attested in a variety of syntactic constellations of different transitivity. The verb 'eat', for example, may occur without an object, as in 'he eats', but it may also occur with an object, as in 'he eats an apple'. This phenomenon is called valence expansion or valence reduction, depending on which valence pattern is thought to be the inherent valence pattern of the verb. The project undertaken by Dyk and her team aimed to collect all valence patterns in the Hebrew Bible and thereby provide a quantitative basis for determining the inherent valence of any Hebrew verb (Dyk, Glanz, and Oosting 2014, 5). As a bottom-up approach, beginning with the syntactic constituents of the text and observing their distributional patterns, this valence approach is to be commended. At the end, however, we are confronted with a fundamental question: Is the most frequent valence pattern evidence of the core meaning of the verb, or should the core meaning of the verb rather be construed from its simplest construction? As an example, עשׂה 'make' occurs most frequently with a single object, but it is also attested without an object. The former view would construe the core meaning of עשׂה as 'do', 'make', 'perform', 'observe', while the latter view would interpret its core meaning according to its simplest pattern: 'act', 'take action' (Dyk, Glanz, and Oosting 2014, 18). Consequently, valence-pattern recognition provides a quantitative basis for identifying verbs of similar behaviour, but it does not by itself yield the core meaning of the verbs.

Recognising this fundamental problem, Nicolai Winther-Nielsen (2017) offered a different approach to verbal valence, exemplified in his account of נתן 'give' in Genesis.[9] In contrast to a bottom-up, distributional approach, Winther-Nielsen employed

---

[9] In a previous work, Winther-Nielsen (2016) classified the 100 most frequent verbs in the Hebrew Bible according to the RRG theory of *Aktionsart* and logical structures.

RRG as a framework for linking Hebrew syntax to universal semantic event structures. According to this framework, meaning cannot be captured simply by procedural rules or by semantic classification of the arguments. Rather, the meaning of a verb arises from mapping universal semantic roles onto language-specific structures. Essentially, and as explained earlier (chapter 4, §4.0), the semantic mapping is handled by lexical decomposition of the verb in order to retrieve its *Aktionsart* and logical structure. As an example, נתן 'give' retrieves from the lexicon its ditransitive logical structure, that is, a causative accomplishment of possession: [**do′** (x, Ø)] CAUSE [BECOME **have′** (z, y)]. Other senses of נתן are retrieved by modifying this basic logical structure into, e.g., causative accomplishment of location ('to place'): [**do′** (x, Ø)] CAUSE [BECOME **be-in′** (z, y)]. The strength of the RRG framework is its linking of syntax and semantics, and, consequently, its ability to account for a diversity of verbal senses while maintaining a core meaning of the verb. On the other hand, this approach seems to assume some existing knowledge of the lexicon, including the *Aktionsart* of the verb—knowledge that we cannot always take for granted.

## 3.0. A Collostructional Analysis of Verbs and Spatial Modifiers

As discussed above, qualitative approaches to lexical decomposition have serious drawbacks for a language like Biblical Hebrew. Therefore, the purpose of what follows is to propose and demonstrate a quantitative analysis of Biblical Hebrew verbal predicates. A quantitative approach takes seriously the frequency of a constellation, based on the assumption that frequency more or less reflects "degrees of conventionalization" of linguistic units or structures (Schmid 2010, 117; see also 2000). This assumption may not always hold, of course, but the assumption seems important for a language like Biblical Hebrew where we do not have access to the lexicon apart from the extant text. Roughly speaking, if a verb occurs more frequently with a directional adverbial than with a locational adverbial, the verb would be assumed to be dynamic rather than stative. In fact, as will be unfolded below, the statistical computation is more sophisticated than merely counting frequencies. Nonetheless, frequency matters, and it is the most controlled way of analysing verbal aspect.[10] In some respects, the proposed method aligns with Dyk's valence approach in that it looks for patterns and emphasises the role of frequency (see §2.2). On the other hand, I shall not argue that a Biblical Hebrew lexicon can be created on the basis of strict, generative rules. Rather, it is my contention that a quantitative analysis of verbs and their modifiers can serve as a falsifiable basis for understanding the most primitive notions of internal aspect, in particular the dynamicity opposition. In this respect, a quantitative

---

[10] It is a common misunderstanding, however, that quantitative, corpus-linguistic methods are not subjective. On the contrary, they are indeed subjective, because the annotation of the corpus, the choice of which features to explore, the size of the corpus, and the statistical algorithms employed are all subjective choices. Nevertheless, as Glynn (2010, 242) argues, "It is not objectivity that quantitative analysis offers us, but a better and more varied way of verifying the results. Seen from this perspective, quantitative methods are all the more important for subjective semantic analysis."

analysis is only the first step towards creating a Biblical Hebrew lexicon. Understood this way, the primitive semantic notions derived from a quantitative analysis can inform the RRG logical structures and thereby justify a full-fledged verbal analysis within the framework of RRG.

The analysis proposed is a so-called collostructional analysis of predicates and their spatial modifiers. The collostructional analysis was developed by Anatol Stefanowitsch and Stefan Th. Gries (Stefanowitsch and Gries 2003; see also Gries and Stefanowitsch 2004; Stefanowitsch and Gries 2005) within the framework of Construction Grammar.[11] The constructions to be considered in this study are verbal predicates in the *qal* and complements headed by one of five different prepositions (אֶל 'to', לְ 'to', בְּ 'in', מִן 'from', and עַל 'upon'), as well as complements containing the so-called directional ־ָה. Three examples of these constructions are:

(6) וַיֹּאמֶר אֶל־הָאִשָּׁה

'And he said to the woman' (Gen. 3.1)

(7) בְּתִרְצָה מָלַךְ שֵׁשׁ־שָׁנִים׃

'He reigned in Tirzah for six years.' (1 Kgs 16.23)

(8) וַיֵּרֶד אַבְרָם מִצְרַיְמָה

'And Abram went down to Egypt' (Gen. 12.10)

---

[11] Construction Grammar is characterised by the assumption that all levels of grammatical description—not only the lexicon, as traditionally stated—are symbolic units of form and meaning. For a recent introduction to Construction Grammar, see Hoffmann and Trousdale (2013; see also Goldberg 1995; Fillmore 1988).

In what follows, the method, corpus, and results will be discussed in turn.

## 3.1. Method

A collostructional analysis is similar to traditional collocational analyses to the extent that it measures the strength of association of the word under investigation with another word in the constructional context. However, traditional methods do not take the syntactic structure into account, but simply measure the strength of association between two items within a certain distributional distance. A collostructional approach, on the other hand, takes syntax into account and looks specifically at the relationship between the target word and another word in a particular syntactic position (Stefanowitsch and Gries 2005, 5). Thus, a collostructional method enhances the likelihood of capturing significant relationships within a well-defined construction. Importantly, the analysis is not based on the raw frequencies of collexemes. On the contrary, the analysis applies distributional statistics in order to compare the frequency of a target word in a particular construction to the frequency of the word in other constructions and the frequency of the construction with other words. In practice, the researcher creates matrices containing the cross-tabulations of the two variables under consideration. Table 4 below shows the contingency table (Stefanowitsch and Gries 2005, 6–7):

## 5. Dynamicity

Table 4: Contingency table of collostructions

|  | Construction X | ¬X (all other constructions) |
|---|---|---|
| Word L | 1. freq. (L + X) All attestations of the word in the given construction | 3. freq. (L + ¬X) All attestations of the word outside the given construction |
| ¬L (all other words) | 2. freq. (¬L + X) All other words in the given construction | 4. freq. (¬L + ¬X) All other words and all other constructions in the corpus |

As an example, the predicate אמר 'say' and the prepositional complement phrase headed by אֶל 'to' are considered (see example 6 above). The frequencies are extracted from the corpus (Genesis–Kings; see below). As can be seen in Table 5, there are 928 constructions in the corpus where someone talks to someone. Although אֶל is a frequent preposition, there remain only 829 attestations of it with other verbs. In addition, it is calculated how many times the verb occurs with other complement phrases (385), and finally, the frequency of all other complements and all other verbs (38,440).

Table 5: Contingency table of אמר 'say' and אֶל 'to'

|  | אֶל 'to' | ¬ אֶל 'to' (all other complement phrases) | Row totals |
|---|---|---|---|
| אמר 'say' | 928 | 385 | 1,313 |
| ¬ אמר 'say' (all other verbs) | 829 | 38,440 | 39,269 |
| **Column totals** | 1,757 | 38,825 | 40,582 |

On the basis of contingency tables like this one, two important statistical measures can be computed: Attraction and Reliance. The former reflects the degree to which the construction attracts the target word; the latter reflects the degree to which the lexeme depends, or relies, on the construction (Schmid 2000, 54–57). In this concrete example, we would expect a high attraction score as well as a high reliance, because the construction occurs most frequently with this particular predicate, and because the predicate occurs most frequently in this particular construction. It is common, however, to use the Fisher-Yates Exact test, which provides a uniform measure of association strength, that is, the lower the value, the stronger the association (Stefanowitsch and Gries 2003, 218). Another measure is ΔP (Ellis 2006; Ellis and Ferreira-Junior 2009), which is preferred here because it maintains the bidirectional association strength and includes the corpus size (in contrast to Attraction and Reliance).[12] However, as has been demonstrated, each measure has its own advantages and drawbacks, so the use of multiple scores enhances the robustness of the analysis (Schmid and Küchenhoff 2013).

---

[12] ΔP 'delta P' is a bidirectional, statistical measure of the probability that a given construction attracts a lexeme (ΔP Attraction) and that a given lexeme relies on a construction (ΔP Reliance). Thus, in contrast to Fisher-Yates Exact, which gives one measure of association, ΔP provides two measures, seen respectively from the construction and from the lexeme. Both measures are important, because they are not necessarily reciprocal, that is, a lexeme may rely heavily on a construction, but the association may not be mutual, since the construction may attract other lexemes more heavily. For a technical description, see Ellis (2006, 11). For an evaluation of statistical measures commonly applied in collostruction analysis, see Schmid and Küchenhoff (2013).

## 3.2. Corpus

The corpus selected for the analysis is the Classic Biblical Hebrew (CBH) corpus, i.e., the books of Genesis–Kings.[13] The corpus consists of 40,582 clauses, 6,403 of which have a predicate, a single complement phrase and no object. The great majority of the complement phrases are prepositional phrases (5,882).[14] The five most frequent prepositions (אֶל 'to', לְ 'to', בְּ 'in', מִן 'from', and עַל 'upon') have primarily spatial senses. Each of them, however, can be used in a diversity of ways. בְּ 'in', for instance, is deployed in the very first sentence of the Hebrew Bible as a temporal modifier (Gen. 1.1). The five prepositions each form one distinct construction type in this analysis. Another, less frequent, type is the complement with a directional ה-. The directional ה- is an adverbial suffix with a distinct directional meaning, roughly equivalent to the English *-ward* (e.g., 'upward'; Waltke and O'Connor 1990, §10.5). This directional ה- is the sixth complement type for this collostructional analysis. An overview of the constructions, including their frequencies in the corpus, syntax, and primary functions, is given in Table 6. As for the predicates, only predicates

---

[13] Although it is common to distinguish CBH and LBH (see n. 1), "the Hebrew Bible exhibits a remarkable degree of linguistic uniformity" (Hornkohl 2013). Nevertheless, the two corpora exhibit morphological, syntactical, and lexical deviations (see examples and discussion in Hornkohl 2013). For this reason, it is appropriate to limit the research to CBH, in which Leviticus is contained.

[14] The remaining complement phrases are adverbial phrases (269), nominal phrases (126), proper noun phrases (119), and interrogative phrases (7). Due to low frequency, these phrases are not included.

attested at least 10 times with these constructions were included.[15] Accordingly, 62 verbs were included, with a total of 4,933 attestations.

Table 6: Overview of constructions considered for the collostructional analysis of verbs in CBH

| Preposition | Frequency | Syntax | Primary function(s) |
|---|---|---|---|
| אֶל 'to' | 1,717 | - | directional, addressee |
| לְ 'to' | 1,124 | verb + complement phrase headed by preposition | recipient, beneficiary, directional |
| בְּ 'in' | 907 | - | place, instrumental, temporal |
| מִן 'from' | 594 | - | source, comparative |
| עַל 'upon' | 367 | - | place, adversary |
| directional ה- | 224 | verb + complement phrase including a word with directional ה- | directional |

One might raise an objection to this research design to the effect that the constructions under consideration need not be directional or locational; hence, how can we be sure that the outcome

---

[15] A minimal frequency of 10 attestations has been chosen in order to avoid the statistical inaccuracies demonstrated for collocations of low-frequency words (Evert 2004, esp. chapter 4). According to Evert (2008, 1242), "Theoretical considerations suggest a minimal threshold of f[requency] ≥ 3 or f[requency] ≥ 5, but higher thresholds often lead to even better results in practice."

of the analysis corresponds to an opposition of activities and states? As a matter of fact, the prepositions considered are used in a multiplicity of ways in the Hebrew Bible, including in instrumental, temporal, adversative, and benefactive senses, among others. Even if the spatial sense is the primary sense in terms of cognition and frequency, the analysis most likely plots other senses as well. It might be tempting to manually annotate the constructions beforehand to sort spatial from non-spatial senses. However, this procedure would be hazardous for at least two reasons. Firstly, semantic annotations are commonly acknowledged as the most difficult type of annotation because they involve a great deal of subjective interpretation.[16] Secondly, and importantly in the context of this study, predicates and complements are not independent. Consequently, the complement cannot be ascribed a semantic role (goal, beneficiary, location, source, etc.) independently from investigating the meaning of the predicate. In other words, since semantic roles reflect the interpretation of the predicate, complement annotations would compromise a quantitative analysis, because the verbs would (unconsciously) have been interpreted prior to the analysis itself. The method proposed here is therefore simply a pattern recognition analysis and does not directly address the dynamicity opposition. However, because we investigate several constructions, we can

---

[16] For VerbNet, for instance, it was found that expert annotators agreed on the sense of verbs less than 80% of the time (Rayson and Stevensen 2008, 565; see also Fellbaum, Grabowski, and Landes 1998). If this is true for modern languages, it is even more so for ancient languages where we cannot rely on native speakers.

observe patterns of predicates that behave similarly with respect to this particular aspect.

## 3.3. Results

Extracts of the results of the collostructional analysis are given in the tables below. A variety of statistical measures are provided, most importantly ΔP Attraction and ΔP Reliance, which are the preferred measures here.[17] The tables also provide the raw frequencies of the words in the constructional patterns with respect to their frequencies in the corpus.

Table 7: Top 10 verbs relying on the אֶל 'to' construction (ranked according to ΔP Reliance)

|  | freq. in pattern | Fisher-Yates Exact | ΔP Attraction | ΔP Reliance | Odds Ratio |
|---|---|---|---|---|---|
| צעק 'cry' | 17/17 | 6.126e-24 | 0.0097 | 0.9571 | inf |
| זעק 'cry' | 11/12 | 1.121e-14 | 0.0062 | 0.8736 | 244.60 |
| נגש 'approach' | 18/20 | 4.595e-23 | 0.0102 | 0.8571 | 200.92 |
| שלח 'send' | 36/45 | 3.503e-41 | 0.0203 | 0.7575 | 90.22 |
| פנה 'turn' | 17/22 | 1.312e-19 | 0.0095 | 0.7298 | 75.86 |
| קרב 'approach' | 24/32 | 1.217e-26 | 0.0135 | 0.7073 | 67.20 |
| אמר 'say' | 928/1313 | 0.000e+00 | 0.5183 | 0.6857 | 111.77 |
| בוא 'come' | 269/476 | 8.091e-240 | 0.1478 | 0.5280 | 33.73 |
| שוב 'return' | 62/140 | 1.442e-46 | 0.0333 | 0.4009 | 18.17 |
| שמע 'hear' | 56/142 | 7.820e-39 | 0.0297 | 0.3523 | 14.83 |

Table 7 shows the top 10 verbs relying on the אֶל 'to' construction according to the ΔP Reliance score. The list is dominated by motion verbs, but three speech verbs appear as well (צעק 'cry', זעק 'cry', and אמר 'say'). These speech verbs often attract אֶל 'to' in order to express the addressee of the speech. The verb שמע

---

[17] For explanation and evaluation of the other statistical measures, Fisher-Yates Exact and Odds Ratio, see Schmid and Küchenhoff (2013).

'hear' also appears in this table, probably because the verb does not always simply refer to simple perception, but also attentive listening, signalled by אֶל.

The picture is different for the בְּ 'in' construction (Table 8). Some quite different verbs rely on this construction, including seemingly dynamic verbs, such as תקע 'blow', רחץ 'wash', פשׂה 'spread' (?), דבק 'cling/cleave to', פגע 'meet', and נגע 'touch'. Two stative verbs, רעע 'be evil' and ישׁב 'sit', also rely significantly on this preposition. Unlike with the אֶל construction, which was relied on predominantly by dynamic verbs, one cannot easily find a pattern of verbs relying on the בְּ construction.

Table 8: Top 10 verbs relying on the בְּ 'in' construction (ranked according to ΔP Reliance)

|  | freq. in pattern | Fisher-Yates Exact | ΔP Attraction | ΔP Reliance | Odds Ratio |
|---|---|---|---|---|---|
| תקע 'blow' | 27/27 | 7.335e-43 | 0.0239 | 0.9728 | inf |
| רחץ 'wash' | 16/16 | 1.161e-25 | 0.0142 | 0.9726 | inf |
| פשׂה 'spread' | 12/12 | 2.030e-19 | 0.0106 | 0.9725 | inf |
| חפץ 'desire' | 10/10 | 2.671e-16 | 0.0089 | 0.9724 | inf |
| דבק 'cling/ cleave to' | 17/18 | 5.583e-26 | 0.0150 | 0.9170 | 603.13 |
| פגע 'meet' | 24/26 | 1.121e-35 | 0.0212 | 0.8958 | 428.43 |
| משׁל 'rule' | 12/13 | 2.572e-18 | 0.0106 | 0.8955 | 423.84 |
| נגע 'touch' | 32/35 | 6.509e-47 | 0.0283 | 0.8872 | 383.59 |
| רעע 'be evil' | 15/17 | 5.456e-22 | 0.0132 | 0.8549 | 265.60 |
| ישׁב 'sit' | 129/172 | 3.123e-164 | 0.1132 | 0.7253 | 118.23 |

In Table 9, the picture is consistent. All of the top 10 verbs relying on the directional ה- construction are motion verbs, a result consistent with the common understanding of the sense of this morpheme.

Table 9: Top 10 verbs relying on the directional ה- construction (ranked according to ΔP Reliance)

|  | freq. in pattern | Fisher-Yates Exact | ΔP Attraction | ΔP Reliance | Odds Ratio |
|---|---|---|---|---|---|
| נוס 'flee' | 18/49 | 1.829e-28 | 0.0775 | 0.3621 | 110.43 |
| ירד 'descend' | 17/84 | 6.437e-22 | 0.0723 | 0.1971 | 47.99 |
| שכב 'lie down' | 3/18 | 1.377e-04 | 0.0127 | 0.1611 | 35.54 |
| נפל 'fall' | 12/75 | 1.569e-14 | 0.0506 | 0.1546 | 35.20 |
| בוא 'come' | 70/476 | 1.006e-78 | 0.2943 | 0.1431 | 43.05 |
| עבר 'pass' | 12/82 | 4.807e-14 | 0.0504 | 0.1410 | 31.68 |
| הלך 'walk' | 31/242 | 1.301e-32 | 0.1296 | 0.1232 | 29.64 |
| עלה 'ascend' | 17/142 | 7.599e-18 | 0.0708 | 0.1145 | 25.68 |
| שוב 'return' | 14/140 | 8.206e-14 | 0.0577 | 0.0947 | 20.69 |
| פנה 'turn' | 2/22 | 6.856e-03 | 0.0082 | 0.0853 | 17.69 |

On their own, the six constructions reveal the attraction and reliance of verbs and constructions. If, however, the six reliance scores for each verb are seen as six variables, statistical methods can be applied to measure the correspondences of these variables and plot the constructions and verbs according to similarity. Principal component analysis (PCA) is one such method.[18] PCA was developed as a method for exploring multiple independent quantitative variables and reducing the variation, or spread, of these variables to the smallest possible number of dimensions, called 'principal components'. In short, the purpose of the method is to trade a little accuracy for simplicity. The method has been widely used for a diversity of data types, including linguistic data. In this case, the 62 verbs and the six constructions form a dataset of 62 rows and six columns. Using PCA, a two-

---

[18] For introductions to PCA, see Levshina (2015, 351–66) and Jolliffe (2002).

dimensional map captures 64.05% of the variation in this dataset.[19] The first component accounts for the largest possible variation, and the second for the second-largest variation. The resulting two-dimensional map projects the data according to their contributions to the component, as seen from the perspective of the centre of the plot. Accordingly, the data points near the extremes of the map are those that contribute the most to the component. The first two components are plotted in Figure 6 below. The first component accounts for 38.5% of the variation and captures the variation caused by the constructions בְּ 'in' on the right side, and אֶל 'to' and מִן 'from' on the left side. Significantly, all prepositions associated with direction, source, or goal are projected on the left side, while the preposition associated more with stative location is projected on the right side. The projection of individual verbs supports the notion of this opposition. Except perhaps for קצף 'be angry', חזק 'be strong', ירא 'fear', and צרר 'wrap/be narrow', all verbs on the left side of the plot are seemingly dynamic verbs. The lower left side of the plot is dominated by motion verbs. The constructions of directional ־ה and עַל 'upon' are situated close to the centre of the map, which is to be expected, since the frequencies, and, accordingly, the contributions of these variables are smaller than those of the other constructions.

As for the right side of the map, the picture is mixed. As would be expected, given the frequent locative use of בְּ 'in', prototypical stative verbs are found in this side of the plot, including

---

[19] A three-dimensional map captures 85.15% of the variation.

ישב 'sit', שכן 'dwell', חנה 'encamp', שכב 'lie down', רעע 'be evil', יטב 'be good', and ראה 'see'. Curiously, a number of verbs do not easily fit into this pattern of stative verbs; in fact, most of the verbs clustering near בְּ in the plot do not. First, פשׂה 'spread' is, among the constructions under consideration, only attested with בְּ 'in'. It occurs only in Lev. 13 and 14, and the complement headed by בְּ signals the location of where a (skin) disease spreads.[20] Thus, the verb can easily be construed as an activity, and the preposition merely designates the location of that activity. The same is true of רחץ 'wash', where the preposition בְּ marks the location of bathing. That רחץ should be construed as an activity is supported by the frequentative temporal phrase 'seven times' in 2 Kgs 5.10.[21] Another predicate, דבק 'cling/cleave to' occurs frequently with בְּ to mark the object or place to which someone or something clings.[22] Similarly, בְּ is employed with נגע 'touch' to mark the object or place to be touched.[23] Finally, to conclude these examples, תקע 'blow' usually denotes blowing a

---

[20] See Lev. 13.5, 6, 7, 8, 34, 35, 36, 51, 53; 14.39, 44, 48.

[21] "Go, and bathe (רחץ 'wash') seven times in the Jordan" (2 Kgs 5.10). רחץ occurs frequently with בְּ, always referring to the location of bathing; see Lev. 14.8; 15.5, 6, 7, 8, 10, 11, 18, 21, 22, 27; 17.15; Num. 19.19; Deut. 23.12; 2 Kgs 5.12.

[22] See Gen. 2.24; 34.3; Num. 36.7, 9; Deut. 10.20; 11.22; 13.5, 18; 28.60; 30.20; Josh. 22.5; 23.8, 12; 2 Sam. 20.2; 1 Kgs 11.2; 2 Kgs 5.27; 18.6.

[23] See Gen. 3.3; 32.26, 33; Exod. 19.12, 13; Lev. 5.2, 3; 6.11, 20; 7.19, 21; 11.8; 12.4; 15.5, 11, 12; 22.5, 6; Num. 16.26; 19.16, 22; Deut. 14.8; Josh. 9.19; Judg. 6.21; 1 Sam. 6.9; 10.26; 2 Sam. 5.8 (?).

trumpet or horn, and בְּ marks the object to be blown.[24] In sum, these predicates employ the preposition בְּ 'in' for quite different reasons, and the preposition does not by itself indicate a stative interpretation of the verb.

Figure 6: PCA two-dimensional map of verbs and constructions according to ΔP Reliance scores

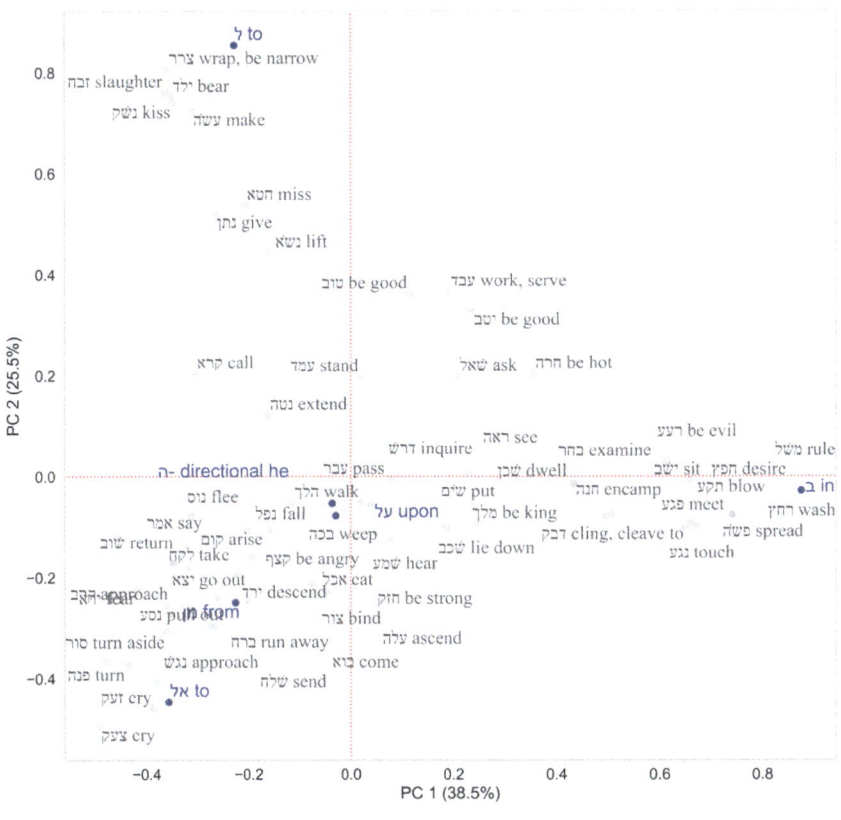

[24] See Num. 10.3, 4, 8, 10; Josh. 6.4, 8, 9, 13 (×2), 16, 20; Judg. 3.27; 6.34; 7.18 (×2), 19, 20; 16.14; 1 Sam. 13.3; 2 Sam. 2.28; 18.16; 20.1, 22; 1 Kgs 1.34, 39; 2 Kgs 9.13. There is only one exception, namely Gen. 31.25, where the verb should be translated 'pitch' (a tent), because the object is inferred from the context.

Thus, the first component exhibits an asymmetry, in that presumably dynamic verbs occur across the range of the component, while stative verbs are almost entirely restricted to the right side of the plot. These observations demonstrate the usefulness of a quantitative approach. While it may still hold true that stative verbs can become dynamic given the right pragmatic context, the observations so far demonstrate that dynamic verbs are more likely to occur with certain prepositions.

As for the second component, there is an interesting contrast between the constructions אֶל 'to' and לְ 'to'. Apparently, the opposition between those two constructions is not one of activity but between directionality on the one hand and benefaction/malefaction on the other hand. A closer inspection of the verbs clustering around לְ 'to' supports this interpretation, as illustrated by the representative examples (9) to (13) below. Other examples that illustrate this interpretation are given in footnotes:

(9) וַתֵּ֤צֶר לְדָוִד֙ מְאֹ֔ד

'It was a great danger for David' (1 Sam. 30.6)[25]

(10) וְנִזְבְּחָ֖ה לַיהוָ֥ה אֱלֹהֵֽינוּ:

'Let us sacrifice to YHWH, our God.' (Exod. 3.18)[26]

---

[25] See also Gen. 32.8; Judg. 2.15; 10.9; 11.7; 1 Sam. 13.6; 28.15; 2 Sam. 1.26; 13.2; 24.14.

[26] See also Exod. 5.3, 8, 17; 8.4, 21, 22, 23, 24, 25; 32.8; 34.15; Deut. 16.2; 32.17; Judg. 2.5; 1 Sam. 1.3; 15.15, 21; 16.2, 5; 1 Kgs 8.63; 2 Kgs 17.35, 36.

(11) וְשָׂרַי֙ אֵ֣שֶׁת אַבְרָ֔ם לֹ֥א יָלְדָ֖ה לֽוֹ

'Sarai, Abram's wife, did not bear [any children] for him' (Gen. 16.1)[27]

(12) וַיִּשַּׁ֥ק הַמֶּ֖לֶךְ לְאַבְשָׁלֽוֹם׃

'The king kissed Absalom.' (2 Sam. 14.33)[28]

(13) וַיֵּ֕דַע אֵ֛ת אֲשֶׁר־עָ֥שָׂה־ל֖וֹ בְּנ֥וֹ הַקָּטָֽן׃

'and he knew what his youngest son had done against him.' (Gen. 9.24)[29]

The verb צרר consistently means 'be in trouble/danger' in this pattern (see example 9). The sentence is difficult to translate literally into English, but the person in trouble or danger is always marked by the preposition לְ, which suggests a malefactive interpretation. The constructions exemplified in (10) and (11) are always benefactive, that is, the participant marked by לְ benefits from the event (unless, of course, the sentence is negated, as in 11). נשק 'kiss' seems to be an exception to the pattern established so far. One may construe the object marked by the preposition לְ as a beneficiary, but perhaps more precisely as an experiencer. Finally, עשה 'make' almost always uses לְ to mark the beneficiary

---

[27] See also Gen. 6.4; 17.21; 21.3, 9; 24.24, 47; 25.12; 30.1; 34.1; 41.50; 46.15, 20; 2 Sam. 12.15; 21.8 (×2).

[28] See also Gen. 27.26, 27; 29.11; 48.10; 50.1; Exod. 4.27; 18.7; 2 Sam. 15.5; 19.40; 20.9; 1 Kgs 19.18, 20.

[29] There are 166 attestations of this collostruction; see, e.g., Gen. 16.6; 19.8; 21.1; 27.45; 30.30; 39.19; 42.25; 50.12; Exod. 5.15.

or maleficiary of the event, as in (13).[30] In sum, apart from perhaps נשק 'kiss', the five verbs forming a cluster around ל mark their beneficiary/maleficiary with this preposition.

Figure 7: Second and third component of the PCA

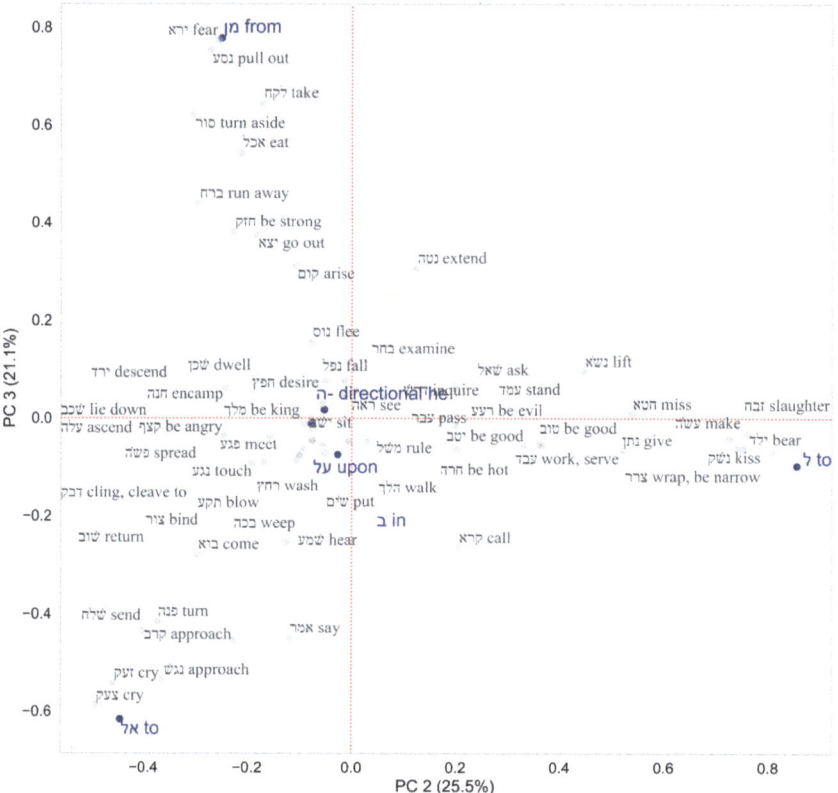

The third dimension accounts for 21.1% of the variation, and contrasts source (מִן 'from') and goal (אֶל 'to'), as visualised in Figure 7. Verbs easily associated with a point of departure are

---

[30] This observation corresponds with one made by Dyk et al. (2014, 13–14), where ל is said to mark either location or the argument affected by the event. Their observations, however, were made for עשה 'make' in ditransitive frames (with two objects).

found in the top left corner of the map, including נסע 'pull out', סור 'turn aside' (or rather, 'depart'), ברח 'run away', יצא 'go out', נוס 'flee', נפל 'fall', and ירד 'descend'. The verb לקח 'take' marks the source from where something is taken with מִן (14), while ירא 'fear' is exceptional in this context, because the object to be feared is marked by this preposition (15).

(14) וְלָקַחְתָּ֞ מִן־הַדָּ֗ם אֲשֶׁ֣ר עַל־הַמִּזְבֵּ֒חַ֒

'And you shall take of the blood that is on the altar' (Exod. 29.21)[31]

(15) וְיָרֵ֖אתָ מֵּאֱלֹהֶ֑יךָ

'And you shall fear your God' (Lev. 19.14)[32]

In sum, the three most important components explored here correspond largely to lexical senses, although there is not an unambiguous distinction between states and activities. Importantly, however, the first component shows a distinction between directional/goal senses on the one hand and non-directional/non-goal senses on the other hand. The second component distinguishes direction and benefaction/malefaction, while the third component differentiates source and direction. Given the choice of adverbials to consider, it is not surprising that the directional sense dominates the picture, but it is instructive to observe how this sense is distinguished from other lexical senses.

---

[31] There are 50 attestations of this collostruction; see, e.g., Gen. 2.22; 3.6; 8.20; 14.23; 23.13; 28.11; 43.11; 48.22.

[32] See also Exod. 9.30; Lev. 19.32; 25.17, 36, 43; Deut. 1.29; 2.4; 5.5; 7.18; 20.1; 28.10; Josh. 10.8; 11.6; 1 Sam. 7.7; 18.12, 29; 21.13; 28.20; 1 Kgs 1.50; 3.28; 2 Kgs 1.15; 19.6; 25.24, 26.

With respect to Lev. 17–26, 31 verbs from the collostructional analysis are attested in this text. Not surprisingly, a number of these are motion verbs: עלה 'ascend', בוא 'come', שוב 'return', יצא 'go out', קרב 'approach', נגש 'approach', נוס 'flee', קום 'arise'. These verbs all rely on directional adverbials and are therefore found in the directional half of the PCA model (the left half in Figure 6). Other presumably dynamic verbs are likewise found in this area of the graph (עשה 'make', אכל 'eat', אמר 'say', נשא 'lift', קרא 'call'). A handful of presumably stative verbs are found in the right side of the plot as expected (עמד 'stand', שכב 'lie down', שמע 'hear', ישב 'sit', ראה 'see'). A number of verbs diverge from the pattern. Most surprisingly, הלך 'walk' and עבר 'pass' are situated on the right side of the plot, albeit near the centre. As a motion verb, הלך would be expected to be associated more strongly with directional adverbials. On the other hand, the preposition בְּ is commonly used to denote the location of the event, sometimes figuratively as in (16).

(16) וּבְחֻקֹּתֵיהֶם לֹא תֵלֵכוּ׃

'And you must not walk in their instructions' (Lev. 18.3)

Another verb is שׂים 'put', a transfer verb often denoting the translocation of an entity. Although expressing an activity, the verb is situated on the right side of the plot among presumably stative verbs. The reason is that the preposition בְּ designates the location where the entity is put or, as an adversative, the entity against which something is put, as in (17).

(17) וְשַׂמְתִּי אֲנִי אֶת־פָּנַי בָּאִישׁ הַהוּא וּבְמִשְׁפַּחְתּוֹ

'I will put my face against that man and against his clan' (Lev. 20.5).

The case of שׂים illustrates a more general complication for the methodology applied here. As a transfer verb, שׂים involves a dynamic event and a static endpoint, and cannot therefore be considered *either* an activity *or* a state. Thus, the methodology applied here works best with simple verbs that express either a dynamic event or a static situation. For complex events, including transfer verbs, a distributional analysis must at least be accompanied by a more logical interpretation of the verb, so as to conceptualise the internal composition of the semantics of the verb.[33]

## 4.0. Conclusion

The collostructional analysis of Hebrew verbs proposed in this chapter was an attempt to take a step backwards and consider how broad semantic notions can be gleaned from the Hebrew Bible on a more objective basis than has usually been achieved. The collostructional analysis was carried out on 62 verbs and six constructions with assumed spatial notions (directional or locational). A principal component analysis of the collostructions yielded significant distinctions between directionality and non-directionality (first component), directionality and benefaction/ malefaction (second component), and goal and source (third component).

---

[33] Other surprising verbs have already been discussed, including ירא 'fear', נגע 'touch', and רחץ 'wash', also attested in Lev. 17–26.

The analysis provided modest results with respect to Lev. 17–26. Most verbs of the text were not captured by the collostructional analysis because of the obvious bent of the model towards directionality. More generally, the challenge remains that many Hebrew verbs occur infrequently, and are rarely found with adverbial modifiers. Thus, like other approaches, this methodology applies most effectively to frequently attested verbs. On the other hand, most verbs in H targeted by the analysis conformed to the distinction between directionality and non-directionality. To yield more semantic distinctions, more collostructions could—and should—certainly be considered. Temporal adverbials, for instance, could contribute important temporal distinctions that might help to support or falsify the observations made in this analysis.

# 6. CAUSATION: INSTIGATION, VOLITION, AFFECTEDNESS, AND A HIERARCHY OF AGENCY

## 1.0. Introduction

As explained in chapter 4, dynamicity and causation are the two most important verbal features with respect to agency. The former was explored in the preceding chapter, and the latter will be the topic of the present one. In essence, causation concerns the interference of two entities, one entity *causing* another entity towards rest or activity (Talmy 2000). Traditionally, 'cause' was seen as an irreducible, atomic primitive, as illustrated in James D. McCawley's (1968) now classic decomposition of 'kill' into [CAUSE [BECOME [NOT [ALIVE]]]]. A similar understanding of cause is found in RRG, where the following explanation of causative verbs is found (Van Valin 2005, 42):

> Causative verbs have a complex structure consisting of a predicate indicating the causing action or event, usually an activity predicate, linked to a predicate indicating the resulting state of affairs by an operator-connective CAUSE, e.g. [**do'** ...] CAUSE [BECOME **pred'** ...].

However, Van Valin (2005, 42 n. 5) also admitted that this notion of causation was "a gross oversimplification," because causation involves such various connections as "direct coercive" (e.g., 'Pam made Sally go'), "indirect non-coercive" (e.g., 'Pam had Sally go'), and "permissive" (e.g., 'Pam let Sally go'). Consequently, in later works, linguists working within the framework of RRG have reconceptualised causation and added important nuances to this complex matter (in particular Nolan et al. 2015). These nuances are especially important when analysing the role and agency of linguistic participants. The classical, atomic notion of causation would imply treating all types of causatives as simply involving an effector (Van Valin 2005, 58), even though the degree of this participant's agency can be perceived as being quite different depending on whether the participant is forcing another entity towards a particular state of affairs, or whether the participant is simply permitting the other entity without being further involved. In short, a fine-grained analysis of participant roles requires fine distinctions in causative types.

There are three formal types of causal realisations within the sentence. These are lexical, morphological, and syntactic causatives (Kulikov 2001, 886–87).[1] Lexical causatives are causatives which cannot be derived morphologically from non-causative counterparts. One example is the pair 'kill'–'die', expressing causation and non-causation, respectively, but without any morphological connection. Biblical Hebrew also contains lexical causatives, such as הרג G 'kill'. A morphological causative

---

[1] The syntactic causative is sometimes called the 'periphrastic causative' (e.g., Castaldi 2013), or 'analytic causative'. Kulikov (2001, 887) adds 'labile verbs' to lexical causatives as a subcategory. Labile verbs are causatives that are indistinguishable from their non-causative counterparts, such as 'open' and 'move'.

is formally derivable from its non-causative counterpart. The BH prototypical morphological causative is the *hifʿil* stem formation, which is frequently used to denote the causing of an undergoer to perform an event. Less prototypically, the *piʿel* stem often expresses a factitive event, that is, an external causer causes an entity to enter a new state (see further discussion below). Finally, the syntactic causative is defined as a causative construction formed by two verbs, hence the frequent label 'periphrastic causative'. Here, the causative morpheme is a free form, in English 'cause', 'make', 'let', in German *lassen*, or in French *faire*. This causative type is absent from Biblical Hebrew.

The aim of this chapter is to explore the Biblical Hebrew causatives in light of recent, general treatments of causation, in particular Talmy's (2000) concept of 'force dynamics', Van Valin's (2005) Role and Reference Grammar (see also Van Valin and LaPolla 1997), and Næss' (2007) theory of 'prototypical transitivity', the three of which offer means by which causatives can be further distinguished. More concretely, the chapter will include 1) a general introduction to causation; 2) classification and comparison of the BH verbal stems *hifʿil* and *piʿel* in terms of causation; and 3) a discussion of the lexical causatives appearing in Lev. 17–26. Finally, a hierarchy of agency will be proposed on the basis of the analysis of dynamicity and causation in this and the preceding chapter.

## 2.0. Causation and Force Dynamics

Causation has been researched and debated intensively, and it is not the aim of this chapter to summarise this long history of research.[2] As Suzanne Kemmer and Arie Verhagen (1994, 116) note, linguists have apparently come to see causation not only as an interesting, complex issue on its own, but as "fundamental to an understanding of clause structure as a whole." The phenomenon of causation appears at almost all levels of grammar, from grammatical affixes, to lexemes, syntax, and discourse. Not only is causation related to many grammatical levels; causation is often only implied. A causative reading may be suggested by the mere juxtaposition of two sentences. As Vera I. Podlesskaya (1993, 166) summarises, a "causal relation between clauses can be encoded: (a) by the mere juxtaposition of clauses; (b) by non-specialized, or contextual, converbs, [...] i.e. with medial verbal forms that are semantically unspecific; and, (c) by non-specialized conjunctions." Often, a great deal of cultural knowledge is required to decode a causal relationship.[3] It

---

[2] For overview and discussion, see Kulikov (2001). Important works on syntactic and semantic parameters of causation include Shibatani (1976a), Aissen (1979), Comrie and Polinsky (1993), Song (1996), Talmy (2000), Escamilla (2012), Copley and Martin (2014), and Nolan et al. (2015).

[3] For interclausal relationships including causal relations, see Renkema (2009).

is therefore not surprising that it has been difficult to form a unitary, monistic theory of causation.[4]

In essence, a causal relation refers to a certain type of relationship between two events, a causing event and a caused event (Shibatani 1976b, 1). Not all linguists accept this definition (e.g., Dixon 2000, 30), and it is not without problems. Even the word 'causing' should be qualified, because it can refer to many specific kinds of relationships. For this reason, causation is better viewed within the framework of 'force dynamics', a theory proposed by Talmy in several publications (1976; 1988; 2000) and further developed by Phillip Wolff and others (Wolff and Song 2003; Wolff 2007; Wolff et al. 2010). Force dynamics is about how entities interact with one another in terms of force: coercion, resistance, assistance, and permission. Talmy (2000, 409) explains the relationship between causation and force dynamics as follows:

> [Force dynamics] is, first of all, a generalization over the traditional linguistic notion of 'causative': it analyzes 'causing' into finer primitives and sets it naturally within a framework that also includes 'letting', 'hindering', 'helping', and still further notions not normally considered in the same context.

Accordingly, force dynamics, or 'force theory' in Wolff's terms, goes beyond traditional notions of causation, even to the extent

---

[4] Some linguists have proposed what is often referred to as 'causal pluralism', in acknowledgement that there are many sorts of causation (see Wolff 2014, 101).

of including modal verbs, such as 'may' and 'can', within the framework.

Essential to the concept of 'force dynamics' is the assumption of an entity upon which another entity exerts force. The first entity, the element of primary attention, has an intrinsic tendency towards either rest or motion, or, in other words, towards either stativity or activity. The other entity, the so-called antagonist, exerts an opposing force to overcome the intrinsic tendency of the former entity, the agonist. If the antagonist is stronger than the agonist, the agonist will succumb to the impingement of the antagonist. But the opposite scenario is also possible. The agonist may be stronger than the antagonist and therefore remain in its initial state *despite* the antagonist's impact. The latter example explains why concepts that are somewhat unrelated to traditional accounts of causation, such as 'hindering, 'letting', 'trying', and 'preventing', among others, can be regarded as equally important for a force dynamics framework (Talmy 2000, 430).

Force dynamics offers a framework or a certain perspective on discourse. While other frameworks account for participant viewpoints or temporal and spatial parameters, force dynamics concerns "the forces that the elements of the structural framework exert on each other" (Talmy 2000, 467). As molecules exert forces on one another when they collide, linguistic discourse entities (participants) affect each other, either directly and physically, or indirectly and psychologically.[5] Stronger participants will overcome the intrinsic resistance of weaker participants, and will themselves resist the forces of weaker participants. Taken this way, force dynamics provides a framework for analysing the interactions between participants and, by implication, the relative strength (agency) of each participant in an interaction. The term 'relative strength' indicates that the framework does not offer an account of the independent or absolute strength of a participant, because strength is only visible in interaction. The comparison with colliding molecules implies a scale of force. The force of molecules is dependent on their mass and speed, but how can the force of linguistic entities be measured, other than by recording the (binary) outcome of each linguistic 'collision'?

To answer this question, linguists have proposed a variety of criteria in order to quantify causative events and divide them into more accurate subtypes. For example, based on one of Talmy's (1976) early accounts of force dynamics, Verhagen and Kemmer (1997, 71) argued for two significant dimensions in categorising causative events. The first dimension is the distinction between the 'initiator' and the 'endpoint' of the causal event. This distinction relates to a distinction between intransitive causatives (e.g., 'He made the baby cry') and transitive causatives (e.g., 'She had him bake a cake'). In the former case, the state of the causee is the 'endpoint' of the event, while in

---

[5] Croft (2012, 203) has argued that empirical data on language use suggest that there is a continuum between physical and psychological (volitional) causation.

the latter case, the causee is an intermediary affecting the so-called 'affectee' (i.e., 'a cake'). The second dimension is the distinction between animate and inanimate participants. Verhagen and Kemmer (1997, 71) noted that there is a "very marked asymmetry" between animate and inanimate participants in that animate participants can only interact with each other "via the intervening physical world," usually by verbal communication. In other words, as a psychological being, an animate participant "cannot reach into another person's mind and *directly* cause him or her to do, feel, or think something," but relies on communication to indirectly cause him or her to do, feel, or think something (Verhagen and Kemmer 1997, 17; italics original). By contrast, physical entities interfere directly with one another (e.g., a rock causing the window to break). Verhagen and Kemmer's account raises an important question as to how direct, physical causation and indirect, psychological causation could be related in terms of agency. Volition (a feature only applicable to human beings) has often been seen as the most significant parameter in terms of agency. If a participant is volitional, the participant can be seen as more involved and hence more agentive. On the other hand, as Verhagen and Kemmer highlight, mental participants can only affect one another indirectly, in contrast to non-volitional, physical entities, which impact directly on one another.[6]

---

[6] In fact, Diedrichsen (2015), in a recent application of Verhagen and Kemmer's parameters, suggested two scales of causation: one for animate participants and one involving inanimate participants.

Another influential typology was offered by Robert M. W. Dixon (2000), who proposed nine semantic parameters related to all three parts of the causative construction, i.e., the verb, the causee, and the causer (Dixon 2000, 62):

Verb
    1. State/activity
    2. Transitivity

Causee
    3. Control
    4. Volition
    5. Affectedness

Causer
    6. Directness
    7. Intention
    8. Naturalness
    9. Involvement

While the parameters for the causer and the causee are labelled differently in Dixon's typology, they are oriented towards some overlapping core notions, including the mental attitude (volition and intention), the degree of physical involvement (control and directness), and the affectedness (affectedness and involvement) of each of the participants. Dixon's parameters have become highly influential in recent scholarship, although some of the parameters have turned out to be less significant in terms of grammaticalisation.⁷ Dixon (2000, 63) also illustrated in his work that languages may have two or more causative 'mechanisms'; for example, in Bahasa Indonesian and Malay, the causative suffix *-kan* applies to stative and process verbs only, while causative constructions are always periphrastic with activities (see Tampubolon 1983, 45). Dixon's framework applies well to Biblical Hebrew, which also has two different morphological causatives, *hifʿil* and *piʿel*. In light of Dixon's typology, we should expect the *hifʿil* and *piʿel* to express different kinds of causation, or to be associated with different types of verbs (e.g., state vs activity) or participants (e.g., animate vs inanimate). It will be the aim of what follows to investigate how morphological causatives can be identified in the first place, and how the two stems, *hifʿil* and *piʿel*, can be semantically distinguished.

In sum, then, Talmy's framework of force dynamics has led to a multifaceted conception of causation. Causation can be further subdivided into particular types and degrees of causation, e.g., force, permission, assistance, and non-intervention. Force dynamics has important implications for the analysis of agency, since the agency invested by a participant depends not only on whether the participant instigates a causative event, but rather on what type of causative event is instigated. Dixon's typology offers concrete means by which to differentiate causative events and helps to explain why languages often have more than one causative type, as is the case in Biblical Hebrew. A

---

⁷ For example, in a large study of 114 constructions in 50 different languages, the parameter of the causee's affectedness was not found to be crucially encoded; see Escamilla (2012).

simplified model of Dixon's typology will be presented in the discussion of lexical causatives and related to force dynamics (§§4.0–5.0). For the time being, I shall investigate the BH morphological causatives attested in Lev. 17–26 with respect to whether they express different kinds or degrees of causation.

## 3.0. Morphological Causatives in Biblical Hebrew

Biblical Hebrew has two inflectional stems associated with causation and morphologically derived from the 'default' stem, the *qal*. The two stems are the *hifʿil* and the *piʿel*, and both stems have passive counterparts, namely, the *hofʿal* and *puʿal* respectively. The *hifʿil* is the prototypical morphological causative, since it causes an event (example 2). By contrast, the *piʿel* most frequently functions as a factitive in that it causes a state (example 4).[8] Here, both stems are termed morphological causatives, although the term 'causative' has typically been reserved for the *hifʿil* in studies of Biblical Hebrew. It is generally acknowledged, however, that the *piʿel* is associated with causation (Waltke and O'Connor 1990, §24.1i), and both stems are characterised by the addition of an external causer *vis-à-vis* the *qal*. This morphological process may imply the addition of a prefix (*hifʿil*), the doubling of a consonant (*piʿel*), and vowel change (*hifʿil* and *piʿel*).[9] In this respect, both stems can be considered morphological causatives. The internal *quality* of a mor-

---

[8] These definitions of 'causative' and 'factitive' follow those of Waltke and O'Connor (1990, 691).

[9] For a general overview of morphological processes for marking causatives, see Dixon (2000, 33–34).

phological causative, however, may vary, in that it may denote either a factitive or a 'real' causative. Note the variation between *qal* and *hifʿil* (causative) in examples (1) and (2), and the variation between *qal* and *piʿel* (factitive) in examples (3) and (4).

(1) וַיֵּצְאוּ אֶל־מִדְבַּר־שׁוּר

'and they went out to the desert of Shur' (Exod. 15.22)

(2) וְכִי אוֹצִיא אֶת־בְּנֵי יִשְׂרָאֵל מִמִּצְרָיִם:

'so that I should bring the sons of Israel out of Egypt?' (Exod. 3.11)

(3) כָּל־הַנֹּגֵעַ בַּמִּזְבֵּחַ יִקְדָּשׁ:

'anyone touching the altar becomes holy.' (Exod. 29.37)

(4) וַיִּמְשַׁח אֹתוֹ לְקַדְּשׁוֹ:

'and he anointed him to sanctify him.' (Lev. 8.12)

Not all verbs occurring in the *hifʿil* or *piʿel*, however, can be classified as morphological causatives. In a number of cases, the relationship between the verbal root in the *qal* and *hifʿil/piʿel* cannot be explained in terms of causation or factivity. In particular, the meaning of the *piʿel* has been heavily disputed, and various functions have been ascribed to it, including resultative/telic, intensifier, and factitive. Therefore, in what follows, the *hifʿil* and *piʿel* verbs of Lev. 17–26 will be investigated with an eye to two factors: Do the verbs in fact form morphological causatives (in the sense that they add an external causer)? And, if so, can the causative dynamics be analysed into narrower primitives (e.g., causative and factitive) that would account for the existence of the two stems?

## 3.1. *Hifʿil*

To form the perfect of the *hifʿil*-stem, a prefix (ה) is added to the verb and the second vowel is changed to *ī*. In the imperfect, the vowel of the prefix is typically changed to *a* and the second vowel to *ī* (Van der Merwe et al. 2017, §16.7). Examples of the *hifʿil* being used as a causative are abundant and include הוֹצִיא 'bring out' from יָצָא 'go out', הֵקִים 'erect' from קָם 'rise', and many others.[10]

Not all uses of the *hifʿil* are causative, however. A word like אזן H 'listen' is certainly not causative. It is sometimes used in parallel with שמע G 'hear', e.g., "Hear, O heavens, listen to me, O earth" (Isa. 1.2). To be sure, אזן does not qualify as a morphological causative, despite the *hifʿil* stem formation, because it has no correspondent in the *qal*, at least not in the Hebrew Bible, our main source for ancient Hebrew. To qualify as a morphological causative, therefore, the verb has to appear in both the *hifʿil* and the *qal*. Lev. 17–26 contains 47 different *hifʿil* verbs. Some of these also appear in the *qal* in those chapters, but this small corpus is obviously limited. To test whether these verbs may indeed qualify as morphological causatives, their attestations in the remaining CBH corpus are included. More specifically, a verb is considered a potential morphological causative if it occurs at least five times in the *qal* and at least five

---

[10] For more examples, see Joüon and Muraoka (1993, 162).

times in the *hifʿil* in the CBH corpus.¹¹ Consequently, as far as concerns Lev. 17–26, of the 47 *hifʿil* verbs in those chapters, 21 potentially form morphological causatives.

In order for a verb to be classified as a morphological causative, in addition to being attested in the *qal* and *hifʿil* forms, it should also add an external causer in the *hifʿil* that would distinguish the *hifʿil* sense from its non-causative *qal* equivalent. In other words, we may expect an increase in transitivity for morphological causatives, while the remaining *hifʿil* verbs that do not form morphological causatives should not exhibit such an increase. Accordingly, the 21 potential morphological causatives in Lev. 17–26 were tested for transitivity alternation between *qal* and *hifʿil*. All instances of the verbs in the CBH corpus were collected, along with the syntactic frames (intransitive, transitive, or ditransitive) in which they occur. Intransitive, transitive, and ditransitive verbs are defined as follows:¹²

---

[11] Only verbs in simple predicate phrases (excluding participles) and verbs with object/subject suffixes are included in the dataset.

[12] Some caution is in order at this point. Firstly, in BH, objects need not be explicit, but can be inferred from the context. However, to decide whether an object should be inferred from the discourse context, or whether the predicate expresses a distinct lexical sense by means of valence decrease, is not always easy to decide (see Winther-Nielsen 2017, 379). For the present analysis, only phrases marked as direct objects (lexical or suffix) are included. Secondly, the ETCBC database does not always distinguish between direct objects and predicative complements, both of which are accusative, but only the former of which contributes to transitivity. A predicate complement denotes a

**Intransitive**: A verb with one argument, the subject only. Since the subject is not obligatory in BH, intransitive frames include here both clauses with explicit subject and clauses without explicit subject, e.g.:

(5) מַדּוּעַ לֹא־יִבְעַר הַסְּנֶה

'Why does the bush not burn?' (Exod. 3.3)

**Transitive**: A verb with two arguments: the subject and an object (lexical or suffix), e.g.:

(6) וַיְקַדֵּשׁ אֶת־הָעָם

'and he sanctified the people' (Exod. 19.14)

**Ditransitive**: A verb with three arguments: the subject and two objects (one suffix + one lexical, or two lexical objects), e.g.:

(7) וְלַמְּדָהּ אֶת־בְּנֵי־יִשְׂרָאֵל

'Teach the Israelites it' (Deut. 31.19)

---

property of a participant, e.g., 'He seemed a nice guy / nice' where 'a nice guy' does not refer to a participant but expresses a property of the subject (Huddleston and Pullum 2002, 253). For the present analysis, this distinction influences the analysis of מלא 'be full' and will be explained more thoroughly there (§3.2.2). Thirdly, complement phrases sometimes mark indirect objects, e.g., וַיְדַבֵּר יְהוָה אֶל־מֹשֶׁה 'and YHWH spoke to Moses' (Lev. 17.1) and sometimes non-arguments, e.g., לָכֵן כֹּה־אָמַר יְהוָה עַל־אַנְשֵׁי עֲנָתוֹת 'therefore, thus says YHWH concerning the men of Anathoth' (Jer. 11.21). Since the ETCBC database simply marks both phrases as complements without further distinction, in the present analysis, oblique objects are missed. In short, the results of the quantitative model cannot stand alone, but must be followed by a more thorough analysis, as below.

Any verb may occur in any of these frames and in both of the stems. Thus, a verb may appear in six different syntactic constellations (e.g., intransitive *qal*, etc.), although, in reality, this is rarely the case. On the basis of these syntactic constellations, a simple alternation ratio can be computed. If the ratio of any constellation is given as the sum of all attestations of a verb in a particular stem and frame proportional to the sum of all constellations of that verb and stem, the alternation ratio (R) would be computed by multiplying the ratio of a *qal* constellation with the ratio of a *hif'il* constellation:

$$\frac{\sum verb(Qal, frame)}{\sum verb(Qal)} \times \frac{\sum verb(Hiphil, frame)}{\sum verb(Hiphil)} = R$$

If, for instance, a verb is always intransitive in *qal* and always transitive in *hif'il*, the alternation ratio between these two would be 100%. This makes sense, because there would be a 100% chance (on the basis of the corpus, of course) that the particular lexeme would always be *qal* intransitive and *hif'il* transitive. In most cases, however, the picture is less clear. A verb may occur in different frames in the same stem. For instance, it may be 30% intransitive and 70% transitive in the *qal* and 50% intransitive, 40% transitive, and 10% ditransitive in the *hif'il*. So, in order to compute the overall alternation ratio between the *qal* constellations and the *hif'il* constellations, we need to compute the alternation ratios of any constellation in the *qal* and any constellation in the *hif'il* and compare these. In particular, we want to calculate whether the verb generally alternates to lower or higher transitivity when it alternates from *qal* to *hif'il*. An alternation from an intransitive frame to a transitive frame is an alternation towards higher transitivity. In fact, there are three alternations possible for alternating towards higher transitivity: intransitive → transitive, intransitive → ditransitive, and transitive → ditransitive. The opposite alternations would be alternations towards lower transitivity. As noted, a verb may occur in all six constellations (three in the *qal* and three in the *hif'il*), which means that there are nine possible alternations from *qal* to *hif'il*. The overall alternation ratio is computed by subtracting the sum of all negative alternation ratios (towards lower transitivity) from the sum of all positive alternation ratios (towards higher transitivity). This computation is exemplified in Table 10 below. The scale goes from -100% (an argument is always dropped in the *hif'il*) to 100% (an argument is always added in the *hif'il*). If the result is 0%, the transitivity neither increases nor decreases when the verb alternates from *qal* to *hif'il*. As shown in Table 10, הלך 'walk' (99%) has a much higher transitivity alternation ratio than ילד 'bear' (25.6%). In other words, הלך 'walk' has a higher tendency towards adding an extra argument in the *hif'il* than does ילד 'bear'. We may therefore hypothesise that the *hif'il* of הלך 'walk' is more likely to form a morphological causative than that of ילד 'bear'. In fact, since ילד only adds an extra argument in 25.6% of its alternations from *qal* to *hif'il*, in the majority of cases, it does not add an extra argument, and it probably does not, therefore, form a morphological causative in the *hif'il* according to this hypothesis.

Table 10: Calculation of the overall transitivity alternation ratio for two concrete verbs[13]

|   |   | הלך 'walk' (%) | ילד 'bear' (%) |
|---|---|---|---|
| 1 | Intransitive *qal* → Transitive *hif'il* | 99.3 | 29.7 |
| 2 | Intransitive *qal* → Ditransitive *hif'il* | 0.0 | 0.0 |
| 3 | Transitive *qal* → Ditransitive *hif'il* | 0.0 | 0.0 |
| 4 | Ditransitive *qal* → Transitive *hif'il* | 0.2 | 0.0 |
| 5 | Ditransitive *qal* → Intransitive *hif'il* | 0.0 | 0.0 |
| 6 | Transitive *qal* → Intransitive *hif'il* | 0.0 | 4.1 |
|   | Transitivity increase (row 1 + 2 + 3) | 99.3 | 29.7 |
|   | Transitivity decrease (row 4 + 5 + 6) | 0.2 | 4.1 |
|   | Total (increase-decrease) | 99.0% | 25.6% |

Along with the remaining verbs in H attested in both *qal* and *hif'il*, הלך 'walk' and ילד 'bear' are plotted in Figure 8. The majority of the verbs show a tendency towards higher transitivity. Two verbs show only a minor tendency towards higher transitivity, that is, less than 50%, which means that the majority of their alternations neither increase nor decrease in transitivity. Three verbs even have an overall tendency towards transitivity decrease when alternating from *qal* to *hif'il*.

---

[13] The computation is done by calculating all individual alternations from one combination of stem + frame to another. The table shows that הלך 'walk' occurs predominantly in the intransitive *qal* and transitive *hif'il* combinations, resulting in an alternation ratio of 99.3% between these two constellations. The overall alternation ratio is computed by adding the scores of rows 1–3 and subtracting the scores of rows 4–6. It should be noted that alternations between two similar frames (e.g., Intransitive *qal* → Intransitive *hif'il*) are not included in

In total, 22 different verbs that qualify as potential morphological causatives in the *hifʿil* are attested in Lev. 17–26. All attestations of these verbs in the *qal* and in the *hifʿil* have been collected from the entire CBH corpus, resulting in a dataset comprising 2,657 clauses corresponding to 17.94% of all relevant cases.[14] The verbs display a combined tendency towards increased transitivity of 70.97%. This tendency supports the common understanding of the *hifʿil* as a morphological causative. To evaluate the hypothesis of a correlation between causation and transitivity increase, all verbs have been inspected manually. In what follows, the verbs will be investigated in order to discern whether the transitivity hypothesis adequately accounts for morphological causatives. Moreover, the finer semantic properties of the events will be conceptualised using RRG logical structures.

---

the computation. It becomes evident that ילד 'bear' has a lower alternation ratio towards higher transitivity than הלך 'walk' because most of its alternations are between similar frames.

[14] The relevant cases are constituted by all verbs in the CBH corpus attested at least five times in both the *qal* and the *hifʿil*: 14,808 cases. Only verbs in predicate phrases, possibly with object/subject suffixes, are included (excluding participles). The verbs must also occur in one of the three transitivity frames described above.

Figure 8: Transitivity alternation ratios for verbs in the *qal* and in the *hifʿil*. Red bars signal that the transitivity alternation ratio is below 50%; hence, the verbs in question are hypothesised not to form morphological causatives in the *hifʿil*.

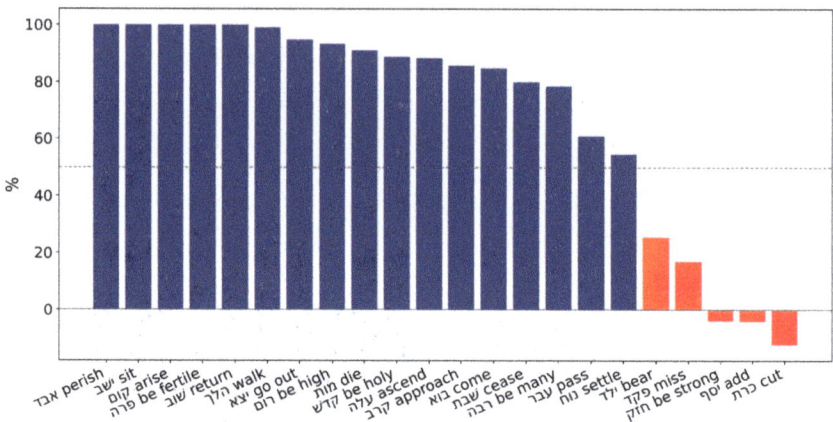

### 3.1.1. *Hifʿil* Verbs in Lev. 17–26

אבד 'perish'

אבד 'perish' is one of a few verbs with an overall alternation ratio of 100%, which means that it always occurs in higher transitive frames in the *hifʿil*. The verb clearly forms a morphological causative in the *hifʿil*, since the state of non-existence denoted by the *qal* (8) can be turned into a causative event using the *hifʿil* (9). Curiously, the verbal root also occurs frequently in the *piʿel* (10), and, at first glance, this form appears to carry the same meaning as the *hifʿil*.

(8) וַאֲבַדְתֶּם בַּגּוֹיִם

 'and you shall perish among the nations' (Lev. 26.38)

(9) וְהַאֲבַדְתִּי אֶת־הַנֶּפֶשׁ הַהִוא

'and I will destroy that soul [from the midst of his people].' (Lev. 23.30)

(10) וְאִבַּדְתֶּם אֵת כָּל־מַשְׂכִּיתָם

'you shall destroy all their figured stones' (Num. 33.52).

Ernst Jenni (1967), in an important study of the difference between the *hifʿil* and the *piʿel*, dedicated his discussion to the meaning of אבד. Since the verb has practically the same meaning in both stems, it provides an important case for considering the respective meanings of the stems. Rejecting the classical understanding of the *piʿel* as an intensifier, because both the *hifʿil* and the *piʿel* equally denote destruction and extinction, Jenni noted important differences between the uses of the two stems. Most importantly, Jenni argued that the *hifʿil* is a real causative, because the causee is caused to undergo a process towards destruction. By contrast, the *piʿel* denotes a much simpler event in that the undergoer is simply put into a state-of-being, and there is thus an exclusive focus on the resulting state. According to this interpretation, the *hifʿil* is a real causative, while the *piʿel* is factitive. Jenni supports this interpretation by noting that the *hifʿil* is only used with human undergoers, in contrast to the *piʿel*, which also accepts inanimate undergoers.[15] That the *hifʿil* only accepts human undergoers is reason-

---

[15] Although in agreement with Jenni, Waltke and O'Connor (1990, §27.2) caution that the association of human undergoers with the *hifʿil* and inanimate undergoers with the *piʿel* should not be exaggerated. Jenni (1967, 153) argues further that the *hifʿil* is only used in so-called

able if the undergoer is also the undersubject, that is, the undergoer is not simply put into a state but is the subject of the caused event. The distinction between factitive and causative implies that the relationship between the causer and the resulting event is less immediate in the *hifʿil*, where the undersubject performs the process of destruction. This difference is captured in RRG logical structures by differentiating these caused events into one of incremental process with a termination (*hifʿil*) [**do′** (x, Ø)] CAUSE [PROC **degenerate′** (y) & INGR NOT **exist′** (y)] and one of simple accomplishment (*piʿel*) [**do′** (x, Ø)] CAUSE [INGR NOT **exist′** (y)].

ישׁב 'sit'

This verb belongs to a class of stage-level predicates which is characterised by sometimes referring to temporary events

---

occasional contexts, i.e., case laws and concrete narrative situations. By contrast, the *piʿel* is also used in habitual contexts, such as apodictic laws. Finally, the relationship between the event and the undergoer in the *hifʿil* is 'substantial', which means that the undergoer undergoes the event by logical necessity. The *piʿel*, on the other hand, assumes an 'accidental' relationship between event and undergoer, because the destruction or extinction happens as an accidental consequence of previous events. This difference is illustrated by comparing Deut. 12.3 and 7.24. In the former case, אבד D serves to sharpen the rhetoric, i.e., "blot out the names of the idols" is a consequence—but not a necessary consequence—of breaking down the altars and burning the sacred poles, hence accidental. In the latter case, אבד H in "blot out the names of the kings" is a critical part of the destruction. For this and other examples, see Jenni (1967, 154–55).

(Winther-Nielsen 2016, 81).[16] The situation described in sentence (11) is temporary and lasts for only seven days. In (12), ישב H denotes a causative event where the undersubject is caused or allowed to live in booths in the wilderness. With these stage-level predicates, the *hifʿil* is not used to express the bringing about of a state (factitive) but the causing of an event (causative). The contrast is readily seen with another stage-level predicate, שכן 'dwell', which occurs in both *piʿel* and *hifʿil* and offers an opportunity for comparison. When the *piʿel* is used, the focus is on the state of dwelling and not on the fact that the undergoer performs an act of settling down (e.g., Deut. 16.6).

(11) בַּסֻּכֹּת תֵּשְׁבוּ שִׁבְעַת יָמִים

'You shall live in booths for seven days' (Lev. 23.42)

(12) כִּי בַסֻּכּוֹת הוֹשַׁבְתִּי אֶת־בְּנֵי יִשְׂרָאֵל

'that I made the sons of Israel live in booths' (Lev. 23.43)

קום 'arise'

Many motion verbs have high transitivity alternation scores, including the verb קום 'arise' (100%). In the *qal*, the verb is used

---

[16] Stage-level predicates are predicates depicting stative situations that are not necessarily permanent. While some situations are necessarily permanent, such as 'The city lies at the base of the mountains', other situations are temporary, e.g., 'The book is lying on the table'. In English, the progressive *-ing* does not normally occur with stative verbs, but it can occur with stage-level predicates, e.g., 'The book is lying on the table'. Besides ישב 'sit', other frequent BH stage-level predicates are עמד 'stand', שכב 'lie', שכן 'dwell', גור 'dwell', and לין 'spend the night' (Winther-Nielsen 2016, 81).

of the activity of rising up or taking a stand (13). The *hifʿil* derives a causative event from the *qal* and is frequently translated 'erect', as in (14). Motion verbs like קום tend to be causative in the *hifʿil*, and these verbs generally score highly with respect to transivitity alternation. The motion verbs found in Lev. 17–26 are שוב 'return' (100%), הלך 'walk' (99%), יצא 'go out' (95%), עלה 'ascend' (89%),[17] קרב 'approach' (86%), בוא 'come' (85%), and עבר 'pass' (61%).

(13)  וַיָּקָם לִקְרָאתָם

'and he rose to meet them' (Gen. 19.1)

(14)  וּמַצֵּבָה לֹא־תָקִימוּ לָכֶם

'and you may not erect standing stones for yourselves' (Lev. 26.1)

מות 'die'

מות 'die' forms a morphological causative in the *hifʿil* because the original subject in the *qal* (15) becomes the undersubject in the *hifʿil* (16). Traditionally, this verb is interpreted as a process

---

[17] Although עלה most frequently means 'ascend' and denotes physical activity, the verb also appears frequently in cultic contexts. For instance, sacrificing an offering is commonly expressed by עלה H (e.g., Gen. 8.20; 22.2, 13; Exod. 24.5; 30.9; 40.29; Lev. 14.20; 17.8). Although one might be tempted to see the cultic use as a metaphorical extension of the causative of 'ascend', that is, to cause the sacrifice to ascend to YHWH, it should be noted that the same verb is also used to express the kindling of a lamp (e.g., Exod. 25.37; 27.20; 40.25; Lev. 24.2). Therefore, the verb is best translated 'burn' or 'kindle' in the contexts of sacrifice and lamp kindling; see Milgrom (1991, 172–74).

leading towards an instant change of state in the *qal*, that is, an accomplishment, BECOME **dead'** (x) (see Winther-Nielsen 2016, 88), although in some cases it might indicate a pure state-of-being (Winther-Nielsen 2008, 471). The meaning of (15) does not so much refer to the state of death than to the childless process towards that state. In the *hif'il*, the verb refers to the act of killing, a causative accomplishment [**do'** (they, Ø)] CAUSE [BECOME **dead'** (him)], yet less brutally than הרג 'kill', which would be translated 'murder'.[18]

(15) עֲרִירִים יָמֻתוּ׃

'They will die childless.' (Lev. 20.20)

(16) לְבִלְתִּי הָמִית אֹתוֹ׃

'and do not put him to death.' (Lev. 20.4)

שבת 'cease'

For other verbs, it is less clear whether, or to what extent, the *hif'il* is derivable from the *qal*. One such case is שבת 'cease', which occurs six times in Lev. 17–26. In the *qal*, the root typically means 'rest' or 'cease' from activity (17). However, when the verb appears in conjuction with the noun שבת 'sabbath', the idea of observing the sabbath is expressed (Lev. 23.32; 25.2; 26.35). In the *hif'il*, a similar idea of 'cease' exists, but it is not

---

[18] The decomposition of killing verbs is discussed in Winther-Nielsen (2008, 469–71). It has also been noted (Gerleman 1984) that when מות H forms parallel expressions with נכה H 'strike', the verb does not refer to death so much as to the act leading to death (see Josh. 10.26; 11.17; 2 Sam. 4.7; 18.15; 21.17; 1 Kgs 16.10; 2 Kgs 15.10, 30).

immediately derivable from the *qal*. In (18), the idea is that YHWH hinders wild animals from being in the land, or, put differently, YHWH causes the animals to *cease* from being in the land. In general, שבת H appears to denote causation of absence, either by removal or hindrance of access. Obviously, by implication, removal or hindrance of access means ceased activity.[19]

(17) אָ֥ז תִּשְׁבַּ֖ת הָאָֽרֶץ

'Then the earth shall rest.' (Lev. 26.34)

**rest'** (earth)

(18) וְהִשְׁבַּתִּ֞י חַיָּ֤ה רָעָה֙ מִן־הָאָ֔רֶץ

'I will keep the wild animals from the land.' (Lev. 26.6)

[**do'** (I, Ø)] CAUSE [NOT **be-LOC'** (land, wild animals)]

## 3.1.2. *Hifʿil* Verbs with <50% Transitivity Alternation Scores

The verbs investigated so far scored higher than 50% in transitivity alternation and were hypothesised to form morphological causatives in the *hifʿil*. A minority of verbs scored less than 50% and are thus less likely to form morphological causatives in the *hifʿil*, because they are less likely to add an external causer. These verbs will be discussed in what follows.

ילד 'bear'

This verb occurs in Lev. 17–26 once in the *hifʿil* and never in the *qal*. It occurs frequently in both stems elsewhere, however, par-

---

[19] See Exod. 5.5; 12.15; Lev. 2.13; Deut. 32.26; 2 Kgs 23.5, 11.

ticularly in genealogies (e.g., Gen. 5 and 11). It is common to differentiate between *qal* 'bear a child' and *hifʿil* 'cause to bring forth' or 'beget' (Köhler et al. 1994, ילד; Kühlewein 1984), thereby underscoring the role of the *hifʿil* as adding an external causer to the event. One would expect the *qal* to have female subjects and the *hifʿil* male subjects, but this is not always the case. Even though female subjects tend to be used with the *qal* and male subjects with the *hifʿil*, male subjects can occur with both stems, e.g., (19).

(19) וְעִירָד יָלַד אֶת־מְחוּיָאֵל

'and Irad bore Mehujael' (Gen. 4.18)

(20) וַיּוֹלֶד מִן־חֹדֶשׁ אִשְׁתּוֹ אֶת־יוֹבָב

'By Hodesh, his wife, he begot Jobab' (1 Chr. 8.9)

If the *hifʿil* is indeed the causative equivalent of *qal*, the full causal chain is rarely fully syntactically expressed, e.g., 'a man causing a woman to bear a child'. The absense of a full syntactic causal chain is illustrated well by the low transitivity alternation ratio (26%), because a full causal chain in the *hifʿil* would increase the transitivity alternation ratio. The example in (20) provides an exception to the common simplified syntax (although outside the actual corpus of the present analysis). If this interpretation is true, the *qal* event is best understood as a causative accomplishment of existence (see Winther-Nielsen 2016, 88), while an extra causer is added in the *hifʿil*: [**do'** (x, Ø)] CAUSE [[**do'** (y, Ø)] CAUSE [BECOME **exist'** (z)]].

### פקד 'miss'

פקד 'miss' has a small tendency towards higher transitivity in the *hif'il* (17%). The most common meanings of the verb in the *qal* are 'visit', 'summon' (an army), and 'avenge' sin. In the *hif'il*, the verb can similarly mean 'summon' (e.g., 'summon terror against you' in Lev. 26.16), or 'install' in an official position. Winther-Nielsen (2016, 85) contrues the verb as expressing a simple, non-causative event, that is, **do'** (x, [**visit'** (x, y)]) or **do'** (x, [**summon'** (x, y)]), depending on the actual use. In any case, the difference between the *qal* and the *hif'il* cannot be explained in terms of causation.

### חזק 'be strong'

חזק 'be strong' has a negative tendency towards higher transitivity in the *hif'il* (-4%). The fact that the *hif'il* cannot always be seen simply as a causative equivalent of the *qal* is also demonstrated by examples from the corpus:

(21) וַיְהִי כִּי חָזְקוּ בְּנֵי יִשְׂרָאֵל

'When the sons of Israel became strong' (Josh. 17.13)

(22) וְהֶחֱזַקְתָּ בּוֹ

'you shall seize it [= the hand]' (Lev. 25.35)

(23) הַחֲזֵק מִלְחַמְתְּךָ אֶל־הָעִיר

'Intensify your war against the city!' (2 Sam. 11.25)

In the *qal*, the verb regularly expresses a situation of being strong (21). The *hif'il* can be used to express the causative counterpart of 'be strong', namely, 'strengthen' or 'intensify', as in

(23). However, the *hifʿil* also frequently occurs with 'hand' or another object to be seized (22). Jenni (1968, 46) argues that חזק + oblique object is best paraphrased "(die Hand) an etwas fest sein lassen," that is, letting the hand be firm on something, or simply, grasping or seizing. This construal comes close to a regular causative. Jenni does not, however, provide examples, and I have only been able to identify one example where a direct object seizes an oblique object: "Let your hand be firm on/seize him [= the boy], because I will make him a great nation" (Gen. 21.18).[20]

יסף 'add'

יסף 'add' also has a tendency towards lesser transitivity when alternating from *qal* to *hifʿil* (-4%). It occurs four times in Lev. 17–26, three times in the *qal* and once in the *hifʿil*. The few examples in Lev. 17–26 yield a variety of meanings. The verb is used in the *qal* in the sense of 'add' (24), but also in the sense of 'continue' (25). In the *hifʿil*, the verb is used to mean 'increase' (26), which seems similar to 'add'. In any case, the relationship between the *qal* and the *hifʿil* is not one of causation.

(24) וְיָסַף חֲמִשִׁיתוֹ עָלָיו

'and he shall add its fifth to it' (Lev. 22.14; cf. 26.21)

(25) וְיָסַפְתִּי לְיַסְּרָה אֶתְכֶם שֶׁבַע

'and I will continue to discipline you sevenfold' (Lev. 26.18)

---

[20] A slightly different example is found in Judg. 7.20: "And they seized the torches with their left hands," where 'with their left hands' is a PP.

(26) לְהוֹסִיף לָכֶם תְּבוּאָתוֹ

'in order to increase its produce for you' (Lev. 19.25)

כרת 'cut'

כרת 'cut' has the lowest transitivity alternation score among the verbs considered here (-15%), and a closer inspection of the verb supports the hypothesis that the verb does not form a morphological causative in the *hifʿil*. כרת is frequently deployed in the *qal* to denote 'cutting down', e.g., of trees (Judg. 9.48). It is also used to express the initiation of a covenant or treaty. In the *hifʿil*, it expresses destruction or removal (e.g., extermination of a person, see Lev. 17.10), a meaning somewhat similar to the *qal* meaning of 'cutting down'. Interpreted this way, the event is a causative accomplishment of non-existence.

### 3.1.3. Summary

To conclude, then, of the 17 verbs hypothesised to form morphological causatives in the *hifʿil*, two were marked ambiguous (שבת 'cease', עלה 'ascend'). For the remaining verbs, the relationship between the *qal* and the *hifʿil* could reasonably be explained in terms of causation. The five remaining verbs in this corpus were hypothesised not to form morphological causatives in the *hifʿil* due to their low transitivity alternation ratios. On the basis of closer analysis, this hypothesis held true in most cases, since the variation between the stems could not easily be accounted for by causation. ילד 'bear' provided an exception in that the *hifʿil* stem formation could in fact be construed as adding an extra causer to an existing causative event of giving birth. Moreover, חזק H 'be strong' could be construed as a morphological causative in a number of cases, perhaps even the use of חזק H as 'seize/grasp', if an object (most likely 'hand') with which to seize something is inferred.

### 3.2. *Pi'el*

While the *hif'il* is the prototypical morphological causative in BH, another stem, the *pi'el*, also seems to carry a causative sense insofar as alternation between *qal* and *pi'el* often involves the addition of an external causer. Morphologically, the *pi'el* is typically formed by doubling of the second stem consonant and by vocalisation changes. In the perfect, the stem vowel is *i*. In the imperfect, the prefix vowel is reduced, and the stem vowel is *a* (Van der Merwe et al. 2017, §16.4).

The great diversity of meanings associated with the *pi'el* often perplexes linguists. Traditionally, the *pi'el* was primarily seen as an intensifier, although other functions were acknowledged as well. Inspired by Albrecht Goetze's (1942) study of the Akkadian D-stem, Jenni (1968) embarked on a close analysis of all 415 BH verbs attested in the *pi'el*, the Hebrew D-stem. He came to the conclusion that with verbs that are intransitive in the *qal*, the *pi'el* is factitive, while with transitive verbs, the *pi'el* is resultative. Waltke and O'Connor further developed Jenni's classification. They divided the factitive into a 'real' factitive and a 'psychological/linguistic' factitive. The 'real' factitive refers to an objective event which can be seen apart from the participants involved (Waltke and O'Connor 1990, §24.2.e). The 'psychological/linguistic' factitive refers to a subjective event where the resultant state of affairs cannot be seen (Waltke and O'Connor 1990, §24.2.f). To the latter category belong 'declarative' and 'estimation', which do not bring about an objective state but *declare* or *esteem* an undergoer to be in a certain state.

Most recently, John C. Beckman (2015) has challenged the explanation of the *pi'el* given by Waltke and O'Connor and revived the classical interpretation of the *pi'el* as an intensifier. In particular, Beckman argues that a close inspection of the *pi'el* verbs does not support the claim that the *pi'el* is primarily used with a factitive/resultative meaning. On the contrary, the *pi'el* is far more often used to describe processes, a grammatical aspect otherwise attributed to the *qal* by Waltke and O'Connor (Beckman 2015, 247). Moreover, the problem for both Jenni and Waltke and O'Connor is that they cannot account for syntactically intransitive verbs in the *pi'el* (Beckman 2015, 21). These verbs include דבר 'speak' and צוה 'command', which are the two most frequent lexemes found in the *pi'el* and which are certainly not factitive.

Beckman relies on N. J. C. Kouwenberg's (1997; 2010) diachronic work on the Akkadian D-stem. Kouwenberg had argued that the D-stem was originally formed by geminate adjectives and was marked for intensity in contrast to the regular G-stem (which was only formed by simple adjectives).[21] According to Beckman, this Proto-Semitic development explains the association between the *pi'el* and intensification. Later, the D-stem category was broadened to include other expressions of verbal

---

[21] For a summary of Kouwenberg's thesis, see Beckman (2015, 12–13).

plurality. Kouwenberg considers 'verbal plurality' a broad category including not only plural subjects and objects but also intensive action, iteration, and continuation. Moreover, since the D-stem was marked for intensity, it evolved into being marked for high semantic transitivity.[22] In other words, because intensity is associated with high affectedness of the participants involved, the D-stem became marked for high semantic transitivity with highly affected participants. In effect, "because a factitive meaning has a higher semantic transitivity than a stative meaning, the D stem became preferred for a factitive meaning, and the G stem lost its factitive meaning" (Beckman 2015, 13).

Diachronic considerations aside, although some verbs in the *piʿel* stem formation are indeed factitive in contrast to their non-factitive *qal* correspondents, the *piʿel* should not, according to Beckman, be considered a factitive stem. Rather, the *piʿel* is more fundamentally associated with verbal plurality and high semantic transitivity. In this respect, the intensification often associated with the *piʿel* can be explained as an implication of verbal plurality (Beckman 2015, 248). The fact that the *piʿel* more often has a factitive meaning than the *qal* is not because the *piʿel* is a factitive stem. Rather, according to Beckman

---

[22] Semantic transitivity contrasts with syntactic transitivity (see Hopper and Thompson 1980; Givón 2001, I:109–10). Whereas syntactic transitivity relates to the number of syntactic arguments, "Semantic transitivity is a multivalued property of a clause; the more the agent of the clause affects the patient, the higher the semantic transitivity of the clause" (Beckman 2015, 13 n. 9). Further explanation is given below (§5.0).

(2015, 244), the reason for the *pi'el* more often being factitive lies in the fact that the *pi'el* prefers high-semantic-transitivity contexts while the *qal* prefers low-semantic-transitivity contexts. This argument is underscored by the observation that verbs with the same meaning in the *qal* and the *pi'el* prefer the *qal* in low-semantic-transitivity contexts and the *pi'el* in high-semantic-transitivity contexts. Beckman's thesis explains a number of *qal-pi'el* alternations, e.g., זבח 'slaughter', which can occur in both the *qal* and the *pi'el* with a plural subject but never in the *pi'el* with a singular subject (Beckman 2015, 222). In fact, of the 138 verbs with similar meaning in the *qal* and the *pi'el*, 49 are marked for verbal plurality in the *pi'el* but not in the *qal* (Beckman 2015, 220). These verbs thus support Beckman's intensification/plurality thesis. If the criteria are tightened to include only those verbs that occur at least five times in each stem, 27% of the verbal roots show "some level of evidence" of being marked for plurality in the *pi'el* and not in the *qal*, while 15% show "strong, unambiguous evidence" of being so marked (Beckman 2015, 222). While Beckman should certainly be commended for his empirical approach, most verbal roots are not well accounted for by his thesis of verbal plurality. Beckman (2015, 224) provides evidence of a tendency towards higher semantic transitivity in the *pi'el* than in the *qal*, but it should be noted that the most frequent verbs have been sampled, which means that infrequent verbs are given more statistical weight. The verb דבר 'speak', for instance, occurs 1,085 times in the *pi'el*, always in low-transitivity contexts, but only 90 of these instances are included. Due to the sampling, Beckman can demonstrate a stronger tendency towards higher semantic transitivity in the *piʿel* than if he had included all instances.

The general challenge of investigating the function(s) of the *piʿel* is the vast number of infrequent verbs. In the Hebrew Bible, only 77 roots occur more than five times in both the *qal* and the *piʿel* out of 302 roots occurring in both of these stems. Consequently, for most verbs, we cannot know whether we are observing a language pattern in our corpus, or whether the relative frequencies are merely accidental. Moreover, while both of the two interpretations of the *piʿel*, the factitive/resultative interpretation and the intensifier interpretation, succeed in accounting for a good portion of the verbal roots, neither of them accounts well for all of the roots. The purpose of this study is not to provide a resolution to this deadlock, as this task would require a study of its own. Rather, the purpose of the following survey is two-fold. Firstly, the verbs of Lev. 17–26 that potentially form morphological causatives in the *piʿel* will be identified on the basis of transitivity alternation between *qal* and *piʿel*. In this respect, the procedure is similar to that carried out for the *hifʿil* (see §3.1). Secondly, the *piʿel* verbs of Lev. 17–26 will be conceptualised in RRG logical structures in order to discern finer causative distinctions and derive semantic roles.

### 3.2.1. *Piʿel* Verbs in Lev. 17–26

Morphological causatives are constructions marked by a morphological process applied to the verb by which an external causer is added to the clause. Accordingly, to discern whether a verb in the *piʿel* forms a morphological causative, we can test for transitivity increase between its *qal* stem formation and its *piʿel* stem formation. On this basis, we can examine whether a verbal root occurring in both *qal* and *piʿel* forms a morphological causative in the *piʿel*, or whether the relationship between the *qal* and the *piʿel* should be construed differently.

Accordingly, the *piʿel* verbs in H were analysed for transitivity alternation, similarly to the *hifʿil* verbs documented above. In total, nine different verbs occur in the *piʿel* in these chapters, and all attestations of these verbs in the *qal* and the *piʿel* across the entire CBH corpus have been collected, resulting in a dataset comprising 590 clauses, that is, 39.81% of all relevant cases.[23] Since the number of roots under consideration is small, the remaining verbs from the larger corpus have been included in the graph for comparison (Figure 9). The syntactic frames for each clause have been recorded (intransitive, transitive, ditransitive), and the alternation ratios between *qal* frames and *piʿel* frames were computed for each verb. The verbs displayed in the graph exhibit a combined alternation ratio towards higher transitivity of 63.4%; that is, slightly lower than that of the *hifʿil* (70.97%). As shown in Figure 9, the verbs קדש 'be holy' and טמא 'be unclean' offer the most convincing examples, with alternation ratios at, or close to, 100%. In terms of

---

[23] The relevant cases are constituted by all verbs in the CBH corpus attested at least five times in both the *qal* and the *piʿel*: 1,482 cases. Only verbs in simple predicate phrases and predicates with object/ subject suffixes are included. Hence, participles are not included, and some *piʿel* cases will inevitably be missing for this reason.

alternation ratio, these verbs are similar to verbs such as טהר 'be clean', כבד 'be heavy', חזק 'be strong', למד 'learn', and חטא 'miss'. In what follows, each case from Lev. 17–26 will be explored in detail in order to investigate 1) whether the transitivity hypothesis holds; and 2) how the verbs can be conceptualised with RRG logical structures.

Figure 9: Transitivity alternation ratios for verbs in the *qal* and *piʿel*. Verbs not occurring in Lev 17–26 are less opaque.

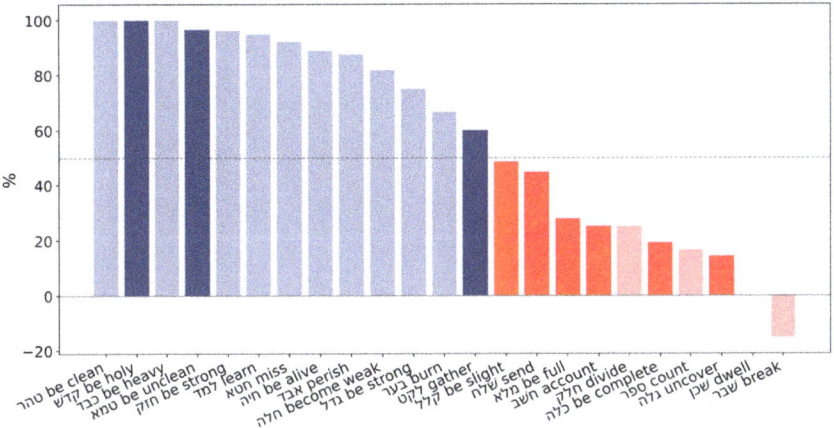

## קדשׁ 'be holy'

קדשׁ G 'be holy' most frequently denotes a change of state from profane to holy. In fact, this change may often be punctual, as illustrated in (27). The lexical root also occurs in the *piʿel* and *hifʿil* with different meanings. In the *piʿel*, there are two dominant uses. Firstly, the *piʿel* is used in a factitive sense, that is, an external causer causes the undergoer to enter a state of holiness (28). This event is hardly punctual, but requires a strict ritual procedure within an incremental process of sanctification. A fitting logical structure for this type of event is the causative accomplishment. Secondly, the *pi'el* is often used in an estimative sense, that is, an actor does not cause a process of sanctification but merely acknowledges that the undergoer is already holy. The estimative is a subset of the declarative and may also be labelled a 'psychological/linguistic' factitive (see Waltke and O'Connor 1990, §24.2f). In RRG, the declarative may be called a 'propositional attitude', which is a two-argument stative with a judger and a judgment (29). The factitive and the declarative are thus given quite different logical structures, and the arguments are ascribed different semantic roles. Only the factitive involves an external causer. Finally, the root also appears in the *hif'il* (30). Like the factitive *pi'el*, the *hif'il* adds an external causer. However, there appears to be an important difference between those two senses. The *hif'il* sense does not so much indicate a ritual *procedure* as rather a ritual *transfer* of an entity from the profane to the holy sphere (see Jenni 1968, 61). This interpretation is underscored by the frequent appearance of the complement לַיהוה 'to YHWH' (or לִי 'to me') by which the recipient of the ritual transfer is marked (Müller 1984, 592).[24] Moreover, in Lev. 27.9, the *hif'il* is used interchangeably with נתן 'give'.[25] If this interpretation is correct, the *pi'el* and *hif'il* stems of קדש 'be holy' both involve a causer, but in two different

---

[24] The *pi'el* is also used once with this meaning (Exod. 13.2).

[25] "Anything which one may give (נתן G) to YHWH shall be holy" (Lev. 27.9). Similar expressions are produced with קדש H 'holy' in Lev. 27, e.g., "a man, if he consecrates (קדש H) his house to YHWH" (27.14; cf. vv. 16, 22). Both terms depict the transfer of an entity to YHWH, and they can therefore be used interchangeably in this respect.

ways. In the former stem, the undergoer of the causation is a patient undergoing a process of becoming holy. With *hifʿil*, the undersubject is not simply a patient, coming into a state-of-being, but a recipient who comes into possession of the entity ritually transferred.[26] This difference is important, because it suggests that *piʿel* and *hifʿil* subcategorise for different semantic roles.

(27) כָּל־הַנֹּגֵעַ בַּמִּזְבֵּחַ יִקְדָּשׁ׃

'everyone who touches the altar becomes holy.' (Exod. 29.37)

INGR **holy'** (everyone touching the altar)

(28) כִּי אֲנִי יְהוָה מְקַדְּשׁוֹ׃

'because I am YHWH who sanctifies him.' (Lev. 21.15)

[**do'** (I, ∅)] CAUSE [PROC **holy'** (him) & INGR **holy'** (him)]

(29) וְקִדַּשְׁתּוֹ

'And you shall consider him holy' (Lev. 21.8)

**consider'** (you, **holy'** (him))

(30) אֲשֶׁר יַקְדִּישׁוּ בְנֵי־יִשְׂרָאֵל לַיהוָה

'[the holy donations] which the sons of Israel sanctify to YHWH' (Lev. 22.3)

[**do'** (Israelites, ∅)] CAUSE [BECOME **have'** (YHWH, holy donations)]

---

[26] For the semantic difference between 'patient' and 'recipient', see §6.0.

## טמא 'be unclean'

טמא G 'be unclean' refers to a state of ritual impurity (31). In the *pi'el*, the verb is factitive in that an external causer causes an undergoer to become ritually impure (32). In contrast to the ritual process of sanctification, as expressed by קדש D 'be holy', there is no evidence that the causation of becoming unclean is incremental in nature. A person or object cannot be more or less impure. Rather, even the slightest exposure to impurity requires a full cleansing ritual; hence, the causation of impurity should probably be understood as a punctual event. If this interpretation is accepted, the logical structure would be a causative achievement [**do'** (x, Ø)] CAUSE [INGR **unclean'** (y)]. Finally, this verbal root in the *pi'el* is also frequently used in a declarative sense, that is, the unclean state of an entity is acknowledged and declared by the actor (e.g., Lev. 13.3).

(31)  וְטָמֵא עַד־הָעָרֶב

'and he is unclean until evening' (Lev. 17.15)

(32)  וְלֹא יְטַמְּאוּ אֶת־מַחֲנֵיהֶם

'and they may not defile their camp' (Num. 5.3)

## לקט 'gather'

לקט 'gather' has a small tendency towards higher transitivity in the *pi'el* (60%). However, the meaning of the verb is the same in both stems, namely 'to gather'. Beckman (2015, 198) notes that this verb belongs to a group of verbs for which there is a tendency towards a plural object (grammatically and semantically) in the *pi'el*, in contrast to the *qal*, which prefers singular objects.

According to Beckman, then, this tendency, albeit modest, supports a semantic transitivity hypothesis of the *piʿel*, rather than the classical factitive interpretation. One wonders, however, why the writer of Gen. 31.46 chose the *qal* form when the object is clearly plural (33). Jenni (1968, 188–89) explains the difference between the *qal* and the *piʿel* by pointing to the definiteness of the object. In the *qal*, the object is less definite, e.g., 'stones' in (33), while the object in the *piʿel* is usually well defined, e.g., 'the leftovers' in (34)—cf. Lev. 23.2—or 'the grapes of your vineyard' (Lev. 19.10). Thus, the *piʿel* appears to be more resultative. To be sure, resultatives are also associated with high semantic transitivity. A logical structure may capture the resultative sense by adding the complete removal of the object gathered to the causative accomplishment: [**do′** (x, ∅)] CAUSE [BECOME **have′** (x, y) & INGR NOT **be-at′** (z, y)].

(33) וַיֹּאמֶר יַעֲקֹב לְאֶחָיו לִקְטוּ אֲבָנִים

'and Jacob told his fellows to gather stones' (Gen. 31.46)

(34) וְלֶקֶט קְצִירְךָ לֹא תְלַקֵּט:

'and you may not gather the leftovers of your harvest.' (Lev. 19.9)

### 3.2.2. *Piʿel* Verbs with <50% Transitivity Alternation Scores

For the remaining *piʿel* verbs with *qal* equivalents, the transitivity alternation ratios are below 50%, which means that the verbs are not likely to form morphological causatives in the *piʿel*.

קלל 'be slight'

קלל 'be slight' has an alternation ratio slightly below the 50% threshold (49%). The root is used in the *qal* to denote a stative situation, 'be small' or 'be insignificant', e.g., 'be insignificant in her eyes' (Gen. 16.5). In the *pi'el*, the verb is used exclusively as a declarative, that is, to declare someone small, or to curse someone (Gen. 19.14; Köhler et al. 1994, קלל; Jenni 1968, 41). Beckman (2015, 100), however, argues that eight instances of קלל in the *pi'el* require a process interpretation rather than a factitive/declarative interpretation. Two of these cases are found in Leviticus (24.14, 23).[27] In both cases, the verb is a nominal participle referring to the 'one cursing' (35). Beckman argues that these examples focus on the action and not the affected undergoer, as would be expected for a factitive interpretation. In other words, according to Beckman, a factitive reading of קלל D requires at least an affected undergoer, because the undergoer is the 'one deemed insignificant'. It should be noted, however, that of the nine attestations of the קלל D participle in the HB, six take a direct object (e.g., 36).[28] In these cases, we should certainly understand the *pi'el* as a nominal declarative. In the two cases of Lev. 24, the object is probably implied, because the undergoer of the curse, YHWH, is present in the context (24.11, 15).

---

[27] The remaining cases are: Exod. 21.17; 1 Sam. 3.13; 2 Sam. 16.5, 7; Ps. 62.5; Eccl. 7.21.

[28] See also Gen. 12.3; 2 Sam. 16.7; Jer. 15.10; Prov. 20.20; Eccl. 7.21.

(35) הוֹצֵא אֶת־הַמְקַלֵּל אֶל־מִחוּץ לַמַּחֲנֶה

'Bring the curser out of the camp' (Lev. 24.14)

(36) וּמְקַלֵּל אָבִיו וְאִמּוֹ מוֹת יוּמָת׃

'And the one cursing his father or his mother shall surely be put to death.' (Exod. 21.17)

שלח 'send'

שלח 'send' has almost the same meaning in both *qal* and *pi'el*. Jenni (1968, 193–96), however, has suggested a distinction along the lines of process and result. While the *qal* is frequently employed to express 'stretching' (37), the *pi'el* is used in contexts where an undergoer is sent away (38). Thus, the *pi'el* is distinguished by separation as the result of the event. An RRG logical structure captures this distinction by adding a punctual endpoint to the representation of the *pi'el* sense.

(37) וַיִּשְׁלַח אַבְרָהָם אֶת־יָדוֹ וַיִּקַּח אֶת־הַמַּאֲכֶלֶת לִשְׁחֹט אֶת־בְּנוֹ׃

'And Abraham stretched out his hand and took the knife to slaughter his son.' (Gen. 22.10)

[**do'** (x, ∅)] CAUSE [**do'** (y, [**move.away.from.ref.point'** (y)])]

(38) וַיְשַׁלַּח אֶת־הַיּוֹנָה

'and he sent out the dove' (Gen. 8.12)

[**do'** (x, ∅)] CAUSE [**do'** (y, [**move.away.from.ref.point'** (y)]) & INGR NOT **be-at'** (z, y)]

מלא 'be full'

Despite its low alternation score (28%), מלא 'be full' should be considered a factitive. The model used for calculating the alternation scores does not always distinguish between nominal phrases that function as direct objects and NPs with other functions. מלא 'be full' is one of several verbs where some property of a participant may be expressed by an NP.[29] Unlike direct objects, predicative NPs do not realise participants but express properties, like adjectives (Huddleston and Pullum 2002).[30] In (39), then, the NP זִמָּה 'loose conduct' is not a direct object, but rather a predicative complement that denotes the state-of-being of the land. The sentence is therefore intransitive. While Hebrew expresses the property with an NP, English uses a preposition 'with' or 'of'.[31] The *pi'el* realises an external causer with a direct object (40). Therefore, the *pi'el* is rightly considered a factitive in contrast to the stative 'be full of...' in the *qal*.

---

[29] Other such verbs include קרא (e.g., וַיִּקְרָא אֶת־שְׁמוֹ גֵּרְשֹׁם 'and he called his name Gershom', where 'Gershom' is a predicative NP denoting a property of 'his name'), and לבש (e.g., וַיַּלְבֵּשׁ שָׁאוּל אֶת־דָּוִד מַדָּיו 'and Saul clothed David with his armour', where מַדָּיו is a predicative NP). Other verbs of wearing/undressing and abundance/scarcity apply as well: פשט 'strip' (e.g., Gen. 37.23; Lev. 16.24; 21.10), שבע 'be sated' (Exod. 16.12; Isa. 1.11), חסר 'lack' (e.g., Deut. 2.7; Isa. 32.6), שכל 'be derived' (e.g., Gen. 27.45; Mal. 3.11).

[30] Predicative NPs may express depictive properties, e.g., 'the land is full of loose conduct', or resultative properties, e.g., 'he makes the land full of loose conduct'.

[31] In LXX, the property is often in the genitive, e.g., Λάβετέ μοι τέσσαρας ὑδρίας ὕδατος 'Take me four jars of water' (1 Kgs 18.34).

(39) וּמָלְאָה הָאָרֶץ זִמָּה׃

'and the land becomes full of loose conduct.' (Lev. 19.29)

(40) מִלְאוּ אַרְבָּעָה כַדִּים מַיִם

'Fill four jars with water' (1 Kgs 18.34)

## חשב 'account'

חשב 'account' has a transitivity alternation score of 25% and occurs three times in Lev. 17–26 (exclusively in the *pi'el*); see (41). While the *pi'el* is employed to express the mental activity of calculating, the *qal* has a less technical meaning, e.g., 'intend/count' (42). חשב D forms neither a morphological factitive nor a resultative. Given the fact that חשב D exclusively denotes calculation, we might consider this construction lexicalised for this particular meaning.

(41) וְחִשַּׁב אֶת־שְׁנֵי מִמְכָּרוֹ

'And he shall count the years since his sale' [lit. 'years of his sale'] (Lev. 25.27; cf. 25.50, 52)

**do'** (x, [**count'** (x, y)])

(42) וַיַּחְשְׁבֶהָ לּוֹ צְדָקָה׃

'and he counted it to him as righteousness.' (Gen. 15.6)

**consider'** (x, y)

## כלה 'be complete'

This verb occurs four times in Lev. 17–26 (exclusively in the *pi'el*) and carries the meaning of 'completing' an undergoer, that is, completely destroying an undergoer (43) or completely harvesting a field (Lev. 19.9). In the *qal*, the verb can be used to denote a water-skin that has been 'finished' or emptied (Gen. 21.15). It also refers to the accomplishment of a task (44). Both the *piʿel* and the *qal* focus on the result of an event, either termination (43) or completion (44), rather than the process. The *piʿel* frequently involves an external causer that brings about the termination or completion of an entity. Therefore, in one of its uses, at least, כלה D may be regarded as a factitive correspondent to the *qal*.

(43) וְלֹא־גְעַלְתִּים לְכַלֹּתָם

'and I will not abhor them to terminate them' (Lev. 26.44)

(44) וּבַשָּׁנָה הָאַחַת עֶשְׂרֵה בְּיֶרַח בּוּל הוּא הַחֹדֶשׁ הַשְּׁמִינִי כָּלָה הַבַּיִת
לְכָל־דְּבָרָיו וּלְכָל־מִשְׁפָּטוֹ

'And in the eleventh year, in the month of Bul, which is the eighth month, he completed the house according to all his words and all his judgments' (1 Kgs 6.38)

## גלה 'uncover'

Finally, with a transitivity alternation score of 14%, גלה 'uncover' generally has two meanings in the *qal*. Firstly, the verb frequently denotes exile (e.g., 2 Kgs 25.21), an activity. Secondly, the verb often denotes revelation, literally 'open [the ears]', as in (45). These two meanings cannot easily be reconciled, so we should accept two different meanings in the *qal*. In the *piʿel*, the verb is almost exclusively used in the anti-incestual laws of Lev. 18 and 20 as a prohibition against uncovering, or exposing, the 'nakedness' of close relatives (46).³² In one case, the verb in the *pi'el* denotes revelation (47).

(45) וַיהוָ֗ה גָּלָ֥ה אֶת־אֹ֖זֶן שְׁמוּאֵ֑ל

'And YHWH opened Samuel's ear' (1 Sam. 9.15)

(46) לֹ֥א תְגַלֵּ֖ה עֶרְוָתָֽהּ׃

'You may not expose her nakedness.' (Lev. 18.7)

(47) וַיְגַ֣ל יְהוָה֮ אֶת־עֵינֵ֣י בִלְעָם֒

'And YHWH opened Balaam's eyes' (Num. 22.31)

As illustrated by the examples, גלה 'uncover' can have a factitive meaning in both the *qal* and the *pi'el*, that is, to cause something to become open, or to expose/uncover something. Although Jenni (1968, 202) argues for a resultative meaning in the *pi'el* versus a process meaning in the *qal*, the examples in (45) and (47) do not support such a strict distinction. In both cases, the event is a causative accomplishment. In sum, גלה D 'uncover' should not be considered a morphological causative.

### 3.2.3. Summary

In conclusion, three verbs were hypothesised to form morphological causatives in the *pi'el*, due to their alternation ratios of more than 50%. Among these verbs, there was one false positive (לקט 'gather'), because the verb was found to be causative in both the *qal* and the *pi'el*. Nevertheless, all three verbs could be explained along the lines of factivity, that is, a state-of-being

---

[32] עֶרְוָה 'nakedness' is a euphemism for copulation (Milgrom 2000, 1534).

caused by an external causer. The remaining verbs under consideration were hypothesised not to form morphological causatives in the *pi'el*, because their alternation ratios were lower than 50%. Of the six verbs considered, two were concluded to be false negatives: כלה D 'complete' and מלא D 'fill' were both found to form morphological causatives. The remaining verbs supported the hypothesis that verbs with a low, or negative, transitivity alternation ratio (below 50%) are not likely to form morphological causatives in the *pi'el*.

In sum, there seems to be a correlation between syntactic transitivity alternation and the function of the *pi'el* as a causative morphological derivation of its non-causative *qal* equivalent. Nevertheless, the statistical basis is not strong, so this conclusion would have to be validated on a larger scale.

## 4.0. Lexical Causatives in Biblical Hebrew

Lexical causatives are inherently causative verbs not morphologically derivable from a non-causative equivalent. For this reason, lexical causatives are also more complicated to identify than morphological causatives, which, as we have seen above, can be predicted to some extent by their transitivity alternation ratio. In RRG, a paraphrasing test is often employed to identify lexical causatives (adapted from Van Valin and LaPolla 1997, 97):

(48) The dog frightens the boy. → The dog causes the boy to be afraid.

Since 'The dog causes the boy to be afraid' is an appropriate paraphrase of 'The dog frightens the boy,' the verb in question can reasonably be considered a lexical causative. The test is constrained by the requirement that the paraphrase is only allowed to contain as many NPs as the original sentence, in order to rule out false paraphrases, e.g., '*Mary caused herself to run' as a paraphrase of 'Mary ran'. Importantly, what follows from this test is that intransitive verbs are ruled out by default, because causatives require at least two participants. As for the concrete case of Lev. 17–26, of the 181 different verbs, 161 verbs are potentially causative (27 of which form morphological causatives).[33] We can thus exclude 20 verbs.[34] The transitivity constraint is obviously only a partial solution, but it is a valid starting point because it filters out intransitive and, hence, non-causative verbs.

---

[33] The transitivity constraint is found by extracting all verbs from the CBH corpus and analysing the syntactic frames in which they occur. If a verb only occurs in intransitive frames (with an explicit or implicit subject), it is considered intransitive. If the verb also occurs in transitive or ditransitive frames, it is considered (di)transitive. Obviously, an otherwise intransitive verb could potentially be transitive if the rest of the Hebrew Bible were included in the analysis. In any case, the transitivity analysis is only hypothetical insofar as we cannot expect all possible verbal patterns to be attested in the corpus. An inherently transitive verb may only occur in intransitive frames in the selected corpus and thereby falsely be considered intransitive.

[34] The excluded intransitive verbs are היה 'be', גור 'dwell', כחש 'grow lean', שקר 'do falsely', לין 'spend the night', חרף 'spend autumn', חפש 'be free', סלח 'forgive', נחש 'divine', קוץ 'loath', רמש 'creep', צרע 'have skin-disease', נצה 'fight', פרש 'explain', מוך 'grow poor', מוט 'totter', חוה 'bow down', אבה 'want', כשל 'stumble', and מקק 'putrefy'.

While the transitivity constraint limits the number of possible lexical causatives, the paraphrasing test is difficult to apply more concretely to the Biblical Hebrew cases. The corpus does not contain syntactic causatives equivalent to lexical causatives, as could be found in an English corpus, e.g., 'cause to be afraid' equivalent to 'frighten'; see (48). Moreover, it is methodologically flawed to hypothesise paraphrases of Biblical verbs, because the paraphrase would most likely merely reflect verb patterns in the target language (e.g., English) rather than in the source language. The issue is the same as with all other tests for verbal *Aktionsart* (see chapter 4, §3.0). If a given form does not exist in the corpus, how can it be analysed?

The most valid approach is to analyse the parameters actually attested in the corpus. The most important parameters in terms of transitive clauses are the parameters of the participants involved, that is, the actor and the undergoer. In what follows, I shall argue that semantic analysis of the transitive frames provides valid criteria for distinguishing lexical causatives.

## 5.0. Causation and Semantic Transitivity

A transitive construction is a construction with a verb and two arguments. Semantically speaking, the transitive construction expresses an exchange, or transfer, from an agent to a patient (Hopper and Thompson 1980, 251). The nature of the exchange may be communication ('John spoke to Mary'), translocation ('John moved the wheelbarrow'), or creation ('John wrote a song'), among others. The exchange is not always equally efficient, as may be intuitively sensed from the examples below:

(49) 'I am YHWH who brought you out of Egypt' (Lev. 19.36)

(50) 'You shall love your neighbour as yourself' (Lev. 19.18)

The exchange in (50) is much less concrete than that in (49), where the semantic undergoer is moved from one location to another. In (50) the undergoer is not moved and hardly knows of the 'exchange'. Based on this intuitive notion of varying transitive 'effectiveness', Hopper and Thompson (1980) presented 10 components that constitute what they call the Transitivity Hypothesis. Each of the components involves different degrees of intensity or effectiveness, as shown in Table 11. The parameters concern both the verb (kinesis, aspect, punctuality, mode) and the participants involved (volitionality, agency, affectedness, individuation), as well as the sentence as a whole (participants, affirmation). A highly transitive sentence has many components of high intensity, while a less transitive sentence has more components of low intensity. Importantly for the present argument, the transitivity hypothesis also relates to causation. As Hopper and Thompson (1980, 264) explain, "causatives are highly Transitive constructions: they must involve at least two participants, one of which is an initiator, and the other of which is totally affected and highly individuated." Curiously, Hopper and Thompson do not list 'initiator' as one of the components of transitivity, but 'agency' is probably intended to capture the initiator role: The causer must be high in agency in order to be able to cause the event. The undergoer, on the other hand, is defined as a participant totally affected and highly individuated.[35]

Table 11: The Hopper-Thompson model of semantic transitivity (adapted from Hopper and Thompson 1980, 252)

|  | High intensity/ effectiveness | Low intensity/ effectiveness |
|---|---|---|
| A. Participants | two/more participants | one participant |
| B. Kinesis | action | non-action |
| C. Aspect | telic | atelic |
| D. Punctuality | punctual | non-punctual |
| E. Volitionality | volitional | non-volitional |
| F. Affirmation | affirmative | negative |
| G. Mode | realis | irrealis |
| H. Agency | agent high in potency | agent low in potency |
| I. Affectedness of object | totally affected | not affected |
| J. Individuation of object | highly individuated | non-individuated |

Recently, Næss (2007) has readdressed the transitivity hypothesis in her *Prototypical Transitivity*, the result of which is a somewhat simpler model that aims to explain the most fundamental criteria for distinguishing agent and patient. Recall her definition, "A prototypical transitive clause is one where the two participants are maximally semantically distinct in terms of their roles in the event described by the clause" (Næss 2007, 30; see also chapter 4, §2.0). The two maximally distinct participants are the prototypical agent and the prototypical patient, and the distinction can be explained in terms of instigation, volition, and affectedness:

---

[35] Although Hopper and Thompson (1980, 253) distinguish between affectedness and individuation, in reality the features overlap. According to them, an entity is more completely affected if it is definite, that is, more individuated.

Table 12: The Næss model of semantic transitivity (Næss 2007, 44)

|  | Agent | Patient |
|---|---|---|
| **Instigation** | + | – |
| **Volition** | + | – |
| **Affectedness** | – | + |

In short, a prototypical transitive sentence is a sentence with an agent who instigates and intends the event without being affected by the event, and a patient which is totally affected by the event. For the sake of simplicity, the parameters are binary (+/–), although Næss (2007, 44) readily admits that the parameters are actually continuous. Positive values therefore refer to high values and negative values to low values. While the majority of Hopper and Thompson's 10 components are left out, some of them are at least implicated by Næss' model. For example, while Næss does not include the kinetic component, her instigation parameter only applies to activities, and kinesis is thus implied. Moreover, when analysing concrete sentences, Næss applies the affirmation criterion, because negation cancels instigation and affectedness, that is, a negated event does not happen, so the actor does not instigate it (despite his/her intention), and the undergoer is not affected. The simplicity of Næss' model, its explanatory power, and the fact that both participants are evaluated according to the same criteria have made it popular. In the study of Biblical Hebrew, the model has been applied by Beckman (2015) in his analysis of the *piʿel* stem (see §3.2).

It is also my contention that semantic transitivity is a valuable framework for scrutinising Biblical Hebrew causatives. Granted, the model does not capture all fine-grained aspects of causative events. It does, however, serve as a useful starting point for distinguishing causatives and non-causatives, which is the primary aim of this study. In light of Hopper and Thompson's earlier definition of causation, Næss' prototypical transitive construction may correspond well with causation: if one participant instigates the event, and the other participant is totally affected, then the construction may be regarded as a causative construction. This hypothesis will be tested on the H data.

It should be noted, however, that simplicity often comes at the cost of accuracy. This is also the case with Næss' model. For example, although volition is presented as a category relating to both participants, in reality, to evaluate whether a participant is volitional, different aspects of volition (intentionality and benefaction) must be considered. Moreover, the binary values in the model come at the cost of evaluating different degrees of each of the three parameters. In particular, the affectedness parameter is more fine-grained than it appears to be in the model. In what follows, therefore, each parameter will be introduced and evaluated on the basis of the Hebrew data.

## 5.1. Instigation

The first parameter is 'instigation', which fundamentally concerns the bringing about of an event. In Næss' (2007, 42) terms,

> the property of instigating or causing an event is central to our whole understanding of what an agent is; a simplistic description of a transitive event might refer to it as an act where one participant 'does something to' another.

Instigation implies Hopper and Thompson's (1980, 252) 'kinesis', which is concerned with the distinction between states and activities. If a situation is stative, there is no exchange between the two participants and, by implication, no instigating actor. The correlation with kinesis is important because it reveals how instigation relates to the semantics of the verb: activities have an instigating actor, while states do not.[36] Instigation is not restricted to animate or human agents. Physical forces also instigate events (Næss 2007, 93). Even physical objects may instigate events if they can be reasonably interpreted as instruments. As an instrument, the physical object plays a dual role in that it causes an event to happen, but only by being manipulated itself by an independent agent. Thus, an instrument is both an instigator and affected by an independent agent.[37] Næss (2007, 97) describes the instrument as having a 'mediating role' in the event, which explains why the instrument can be realised as both actor and undergoer.

In RRG, instigation is captured by **do'**, which distinguishes activities from states. In other words, activities, in contrast to states, have instigating actors. Inherently stative verbs, however, may have their stativity cancelled due to pragmatic implicature (see chapter 4, §3.0). There are 24 such cases in Lev. 17–26, including the famous command in (51), where the stativity of the verb is cancelled due to its occurrence in a prescriptive sentence.

---

[36] See also Creason (1995, 134), who seems to capture the parameter of instigation with his notion of volition and claims that "stativity and volitionality are incompatible."

[37] For affectedness, see §5.3.

(51) וְאָהַבְתָּ לְרֵעֲךָ כָּמוֹךָ

'but you shall love your fellow as yourself' (Lev. 19.18; cf. 19.34)

(52) וְאִם־בְּאֵלֶּה לֹא תִוָּסְרוּ לִי

'And if by these things you will not let yourselves be admonished by me' (Lev. 26.23)

Verbs in the Hebrew passive stems, *nifʿal* and *puʿal*, may sometimes be used as reflexives or reciprocals. Seven such cases were identified, including the one in (52).[38] This particular case is curious, because the agent of admonishment is clearly the oblique object ('me', i.e., Yhwh). The addressees are urged to let themselves be admonished, although the exhortation is only indirect insofar as it is not phrased as a command but as a warning. Thus, in this particular case, there seems to be a shared responsibility for the admonishment: Yhwh is the one who chastises the people, but the people themselves are given the blame for not allowing the admonishment.

Like simple activities, causative events are usually represented with **doʹ** (x, ∅) in RRG, with reference to an unspecified action causing another event. However, causation may also involve non-instigating actors. In these cases, the event happens because the actor allows it without further participation in the event, or even by accident. As Elke Diedrichsen (2015, 55) explains, non-intervention "may be something that happens by

---

[38] The remaining reflexive/reciprocal verbs are שבע N 'swear' (19.12), ענה Dp 'be lowly' (23.29), נצה N 'fight' (24.10), גאל N 'redeem' (25.49), חוה Hst 'bow down' (26.1), and אסף N 'gather' (26.25).

not paying enough attention. It may also happen on purpose, in which case there is a component of 'allowing' in the statement, if the causee argument is animate." עזב G 'leave' may be one Hebrew example of purposeful non-intervention:[39]

(53) לֶעָנִי וְלַגֵּר תַּעֲזֹב אֹתָם

'you shall leave them to the poor and the sojourner.' (Lev. 19.10; 23.22)

[do' (x, Ø)] LET [BECOME have' (poor and the sojourner, them)]

In (53), the addressees are ordered to leave the harvest for the poor and the sojourner; hence, the leftovers of the harvest are left in the fields on purpose. Diedrichsen (2015, 91), in her treatment of the German causative *lassen*, offers an analysis of the sentence 'Hans ließ mir den Mantel hängen', which is similar to the Hebrew sentence under consideration in that it also includes a benefactor.[40] In her analysis, she marks the agent for control and authority, because the agent has control over the situation and performs it for the benefit of another (Diedrichsen 2015, 93). Therefore, although the presence of an instigating agent is required for 'real' causative events, more subtle causative events are not captured by the ± instigation feature. A

---

[39] פרע G 'let loose' (21.10) is another example. The priests are commanded not to let their hair hang loose.

[40] The two sentences differ in that the Hebrew example is phrased as a command. It may therefore be construed as an event of enablement rather than simply non-intervention; hence, there is a higher degree of instigation involved.

more fine-grained concept of the involvement of the causer is needed, including features such as control, authority, and order/permission/direct causation, as proposed by Diedrichsen. Talmy's (2000) concept of 'impingement' is also helpful for distinguishing real causative events with direct, physical impingement from indirect causative events with no impingement.

## 5.2. Volition

Unlike instigation, which is the primary parameter for distinguishing actor and undergoer, volition is applicable to both participants. Volition normally pertains only to human (and divine) beings, because they are the only ones that have the cognitive capacity to will an event to occur. Because Næss uses one label, one might be tempted to treat volition as a uniform parameter. Dixon (2000, 62), however, distinguishes between volition exercised by the actor and volition pertaining to the undergoer. While the latter is called 'volition', the former is called 'intention', emphasising that only actors can intend an activity. Volition is thus multifaceted, and I will therefore discuss it with respect to both actor and undergoer.

An actor is the instigator of an event. If the actor is human or divine, it is capable of volitionality. Physical forces, on the other hand, do not have the capacity to will an event to occur and are not marked for volition. With respect to Talmy's differentiation of causative events, in most cases, a causing actor (human/divine) would also be volitional. Sometimes, however, an actor may accidently instigate the event, perhaps due to clumsiness or neglect; or perhaps the event may happen as an unexpected side-effect of a previous event. The latter option may capture the meaning of Lev. 18.30:

(54) וְלֹא תִטַּמְּאוּ בָּהֶם

> '[And you shall keep my obligations so that you never do any of those abominable customs that were practised before you], so that you do not make yourselves unclean by them.' (Lev. 18.30)

In (54), causing oneself to be unclean (a reflexive factitive) seems to be an unintentional side-effect of practising those abominable customs enumerated in the chapter. By practising these customs, the actor thus instigates an event of becoming unclean, but probably unintentionally. Thus, while most causative events involve an intentional causer, some do not (see also Diedrichsen 2015, 93).

As for the undergoer, volition concerns involvement. While an undergoer cannot intend an event, it can nevertheless be volitionally involved in the event in various ways. Due to their mental and sensory capacities, human/divine participants are involved in experiencer events (Næss 2007, 41). Thus, a participant may be volitionally involved in an experiencer event, e.g., 'I heard a sound', even though the participant does not intend the event. This distinction is captured in RRG by two different logical structures. The **do'** in (56) marks the event as one of directed, intentional perception, in contrast to the undirected, unintentional event of perception in (55):

(55) **hear'** (x, y)

(56) **do'** (x, [**hear'** (x, (y))])

Undergoers can also be involved in events by filling other semantic roles. Apart from experiencer roles, participants in recipient and beneficiary roles are also involved, hence volitional (Næss 2007, 90–91). Firstly, only participants with a capacity of volition can reasonably be said to possess something, and, by implication, to be recipients. Secondly, beneficiaries are participants who benefit from an event. By implication, only human/divine beings can normally be beneficiaries, because they possess the cognitive capacity to deem an event good or bad. Although an undergoer might have the capacity for volitionality, this capacity is not realised in all cases, as demonstrated in (57).

(57) כִּי־אִישׁ אִישׁ אֲשֶׁר יְקַלֵּל אֶת־אָבִיו וְאֶת־אִמּוֹ מוֹת יוּמָת

'Any man who curses his father or mother, he shall surely die' (Lev. 20.9)

(58) אֲנִי יְהוָה אֱלֹהֵיכֶם אֲשֶׁר־הוֹצֵאתִי אֶתְכֶם מֵאֶרֶץ מִצְרָיִם:

'I am YHWH your God who brought you out of the land of Egypt.' (Lev. 19.36)

In (57), a human being is sentenced to death. As Næss (2007, 40) explains, as a human being, the undergoer of the death penalty is capable of being volitional, but during the event, he does not "exercise this volitionality." Moreover, his role within this event is not dependent on him being volitional. Roughly speaking, the participant would die whether he wills it or not. By contrast, in (58), the undergoer benefits from the event. The given translation, which is preferred by most Bible translations (e.g., New Revised Standard Version, New American Standard Bible, and King James Version), suggests that the undergoers (the Israelites) are simply carried away from Egypt, whether they like it or not.[41] However, the Israelites have a personal interest in the event and benefit from it. Therefore, since the event has a positive outcome for the Israelites, we can consider them volitional.

In sum, volition is a multifaceted property and involves intention, sentience, recipience, and benefaction. In particular, intention and benefaction involve subjective interpretation of how the event was conceptualised by the author. Moreover, the given examples show that the kind of volition in question is not an inherent property of which human/divine participants are capable, but rather a relational property (see Næss 2007, 40). Accordingly, for each potentially volitional participant, it must be determined manually whether the participant intends the event or benefits from the event.

## 5.3. Affectedness

Affected participants are participants "that undergo a change in posture, place, shape, state, or existential status" (Frajzyngier and Shay 2016, 144). In Næss' (2007, 42) terms, "a patient is generally defined as the participant which in some way undergoes a change of state as a result of the event." In practice, however, it has proved difficult to differentiate affectedness. John Beavers (2011, 2) makes the criticism that high and low

---

[41] The verbal event (יצא 'go out') in the *hifʿil* could also be translated 'made/let you go out' to emphasise the role played in the event by the undergoers. The *hifʿil* stem does not by itself entail a specific type of causation.

affectedness, as defined by Hopper and Thompson, "are hard to define precisely, and are usually left to intuition." He offers the following examples to demonstrate the subtle distinctions in affectedness:

(59) John ate the apple up. → Apple is completely gone.

(60) John cut the apple. → Apple cut, not necessarily to a particular degree.

(61) John kicked the apple. → Apple impinged, not necessarily affected.

(62) John touched the apple. → Apple manipulated, not necessarily impinged.

For evaluation of the Hebrew data, four sub-parameters proved to be instructive: 1) material vs immaterial; 2) definite vs indefinite; 3) direction of event; and 4) affected vs effected. These sub-parameters have implications for determining the affectedness of the participants in the sentences below:

(63) וְאֶת־מִצְוֺתַי תִּשְׁמְרוּ

'and [if] you keep my commandments' (Lev. 26.3)

**do'** (you, [**observe'** (you, commandments)])

(64) וְאִישׁ אִישׁ מִבֵּית יִשְׂרָאֵל וּמִן־הַגֵּר הַגָּר בְּתוֹכָם אֲשֶׁר יֹאכַל כָּל־דָּם

'And any man from the house of Israel or from the sojourner who sojourns among you who eats any blood' (Lev. 17.10)

[**do'** (man, [**eat'** (man, blood)]) ∧ PROC **consumed'** (blood)]

(65) וְאָכַל֙ אֶת־כָּל־הָעֵ֣ץ הַצֹּמֵ֥חַ לָכֶ֖ם מִן־הַשָּׂדֶֽה׃

'and they [lit. 'it'] shall devour all the trees which sprout for you out of the field.' (Exod. 10.5)

[**do'** (they, [**eat'** (they, trees)]) ∧ PROC **consumed'** (trees)] & INGR **consumed'** (trees)

(66) וְאָפ֨וּ עֶ֤שֶׂר נָשִׁים֙ לַחְמְכֶם֙ בְּתַנּ֣וּר אֶחָ֔ד

'and ten women shall bake your bread in one stove' (Lev. 26.26)

[**do'** (ten women, [**bake'** (ten women, bread)]) ∧ PROC **create'** (bread)] & INGR **exist'** (bread)

In (63), the undergoer ('commandments') is an immaterial, abstract entity and cannot be affected by being observed by a human being. It is therefore appropriate to construe the event as a single activity of performance. In (64), by contrast, the undergoer ('any blood') is a physical entity which can be affected. In this case, however, 'any blood' is indefinite and non-referential, which means that it is not totally affected (see Pavey 2010, 124–25).[42] The contrast is readily seen in (65), where the un-

---

[42] For the function of כָּל 'all/every/any', see Doron (2020); Naudé (2011). Prototypically, כָּל denotes the entirety of a group, e.g., "all the words of God" (1 Sam. 8.10), which refers to the sum of words revealed to Samuel in vv. 7–9 of that chapter. "All the trees that sprout for you out of the field" (65) is less specific as to the number of trees in question. Nevertheless, the definite article and the object marker make clear that the entirety of the trees is in view. In (64), כָּל does not mean 'all' as in 'all blood' but 'any blood'. כָּל receives here a free choice reading because it is satisfied by any member of the group, or

dergoer ('all the trees') is completely consumed. In RRG logical structures, the difference is captured by adding a punctual endpoint to express the accomplishment of the event. If we consider the actors in (64) and (65), they would perhaps intuitively be viewed as prototypical actors that perform an event without being affected themselves. However, while eating, an actor becomes affected insofar as he/she becomes full. Put differently, it is not so much the undergoer that determines the scope of the event, but the actor, who performs the event until he/she is full (see Næss 2007, 56). This interpretation is supported by the observation that the phenomenon in question is grammaticalised in a number of languages. In a cross-linguistic study on passive participles, Martin Haspelmath (1994) showed that both agents and patients of consumption verbs, experience verbs, and verbs of wearing may be grammatically encoded as affected.[43] Evi-

---

rather, any drop of blood (Doron 2020; see also Menéndez-Benito 2010).

[43] Haspelmath's study concerns passive participles across languages. According to him, it is widely attested that participles "can be directed toward the patient of transitive verbs or the subject of unaccusative intransitive verbs" (Haspelmath 1994, 157). The semantic constraint for forming a passive participle is whether the participant described by the participle can be characterised by a resultant state of the event. Therefore, the participant in question must necessarily be affected, and this is the reason that only patients are normally described by passive participles. However, a number of languages do have transitive active resultative participles, i.e., participles of active verbs describing the resulting state of the agent presumably affected by the event. These verbs include the Latin *cenatus* 'having eaten' and *potus* 'having drunk' but also the Hindi-Urdu *dekh-naa* 'see', *siikh-naa* 'learn',

dence is also found in Biblical Hebrew, where participles are divided into active and passive participles. The passive participle can be used as either an attributive or an adjective and generally refers to the coming of an entity into a state (Waltke and O'Connor 1990, §37.4). Interestingly, לבשׁ 'wear/clothe' occurs a few times as a passive participle (לָבוּשׁ G or מְלֻבָּשִׁים Dp), always referring to the actors who wear the garments (1 Sam. 17.5; 1 Kgs 22.10; Ezra 3.10; 2 Chr. 5.12; 18.9).[44] Thus, Biblical Hebrew adds support to the notion that people wearing clothes are affected participants. (66) provides an example of a creation verb. Although one might think that the undergoer ('bread') is affected because it comes into existence, Næss (2007, 103–4) argues that, strictly speaking, the undergoer does not undergo a change of status but rather acquires a status. Put differently, there was no bread to be affected prior to the event.[45] Thus, it is important to distinguish between *affected* and *effected* undergoers.

The sentences examined above illustrate the nuances of affectedness. We will now turn to sentences in which the un-

---

and *pahan-naa* 'wear'. These grammaticalisations suggest that verbs of consumption, wearing, and experiencing involve affected agents (Haspelmath 1994, 157–61).

[44] See also the discussion in Van Peursen (2004, 208 n. 41).

[45] Levinson (2006, 491) argues that an effected object is a "prototypical patient," in contrast to affected objects, which are much less affected. However, as argued by Hopper (1986, 69), objects resulting from an event "cannot be said to 'undergo' the action of the verb, and therefore cannot be described as Patients." See also Fillmore (2003, 24–25).

dergoer is completely affected, in order to discuss the correlation of affectedness with causation. The sentence in (67) depicts a transfer of land. The actor transfers the land to the undergoer, who comes into possession of that land. The land is itself an undergoer of the event and is completely affected by being transferred from one participant to another. The event is causative because the undergoer ('you') is caused to come into possession of the land. Or, put differently, an external causer is the reason, or cause, for the event to take place. Other BH transfer verbs include שׂים G 'put', ערך G 'arrange', לקח G 'take', מכר G 'sell', קנה G 'buy', and probably נחל HtD 'take possession'.[46] The various verbs of harvest or gathering in Lev. 17–26 could also be construed as transfer verbs, that is, causing oneself to come into possession of the produce. These verbs are בצר G 'gather grapes', עלל D 'deal with'—or rather, 'pick bare'; see Milgrom (2000, 1627)—קצר G 'harvest', and אסף G 'gather'.

---

[46] נחל HtD 'take possession' occurs once in H (Lev. 25.46). Milgrom (2000, 2230) quotes Rashi in support of paraphrasing the verse 'Take (them) for yourselves (for the benefit of your children)'. Rashi denies a causative interpretation, because the *hitpaʿel* form is reflexive; hence the sentence could be translated 'You should keep them as an inheritance'. However, it is in fact entirely possible to have a reflexive causative, e.g., קדשׁ HtD 'sanctify yourselves' (Lev. 20.7). Moreover, the words 'take' and 'keep' suggest a causative reading, because the undergoer is either taken from one place to another or prevented from leaving, respectively.

(67) כִּי תָבֹאוּ אֶל־הָאָרֶץ אֲשֶׁר אֲנִי נֹתֵן לָכֶם

'When you come into the land which I am giving you' (Lev. 25.2)

[**do'** (I, Ø)] CAUSE [BECOME **have'** (you, land)]

(68) עַם הָאָרֶץ יִרְגְּמֻהוּ בָאָבֶן׃

'The people of the land shall stone him with stones.' (Lev. 20.2)

[**do'** (people, Ø)] CAUSE [[**do'** (stones, Ø)] CAUSE [BECOME **dead'** (him)]]

(69) וְאִישׁ כִּי יַכֶּה כָּל־נֶפֶשׁ אָדָם מוֹת יוּמָת׃

'Any man, when he strikes any human being, he shall surely die.' (Lev. 24.17)

[**do'** (he, Ø)] CAUSE [BECOME **dead'** (any human being)]

(70) וְרָדְפוּ מִכֶּם חֲמִשָּׁה מֵאָה

'And five of you shall pursue a hundred' (Lev. 26.8)

[**do'** (five of you, Ø)] CAUSE [**do'** (hundred, [**flee'** (hundred)])]

Sentence (68) describes a capital penalty by stoning. In abstract terms, the undergoer ('him') is caused to enter the state of death. The stones function as the instrument of the execution and are represented as "manipulated inanimate effector[s]" in the RRG logical structure (Van Valin 2005, 59). Put differently, the instrument is caused to cause an event. Needless to say, the undergoer is completely affected by the event. A number of other verbs similarly denote an event of annihilation, including הרג G 'kill' (specifically, intentional killing or murder), שחט G 'slaughter', זבח G 'slaughter', and שרף G 'burn'. Another verb, נכה H 'strike', often expresses a fatal blow, as in the *lex talionis* of Lev. 24.15–22 (69). Sometimes, however, the verb seems to express a hit which does not affect the undergoer permanently. In Lev. 26.24, for example, Y<small>HWH</small> threatens to strike the Israelites seven times. In this case, the outcome is not death but repeated or increased punishment. The event in (70) is a persecution, which amounts to causation of running away. The undergoer is affected because it is forced to flee.

In other cases, it is not so easy to determine whether the event is causative or not. Consider the following examples:

(71) וּפְאַת זְקָנָם לֹא יְגַלֵּחוּ

'neither shall they shave off the edge of their beard' (Lev. 21.5)

**do'** (they, [**shave off'** (they, edge of beard)])

(72) בְּצֶדֶק תִּשְׁפֹּט עֲמִיתֶךָ׃

'With justice you shall judge your fellow.' (Lev. 19.15)

**do'** (you, [**judge'** (you, your fellow)])

(73) צַו אֶת־בְּנֵי יִשְׂרָאֵל וְיִקְחוּ אֵלֶיךָ שֶׁמֶן זַיִת זָךְ כָּתִית לַמָּאוֹר

'Command the sons of Israel to take to you pure, beaten olives for the lamp' (Lev. 24.2)

[**do'** (you, [**express.**(you).**to.**(sons of Israel)])] CAUSE [[**do'** (sons of Israel, ∅)] CAUSE [BECOME **have'** (you, oil)]]

There is a group of verbs that look similar to regular extinction verbs. One of these is גלח 'shave'; see (71).[47] The verb denotes an act of shaving, and one wonders whether the act should be conceptualised as an act of removal or 'extinction' of the beard. In that case, the verb would be inherently causative. However, while the object of shaving here is 'the edges of the beard', on other occasions the direct object is simply ראש 'head' (e.g., Lev. 14.9; Num. 6.9, 18; Deut. 21.12; 2 Sam. 14.26). Therefore, we should not understand the undergoer of the verb as an object to be removed, but simply as the theme of an activity. Accordingly, the RRG representation would be a two-argument performance structure.

Sentence (72) depicts a public, juridical exchange between two participants, rather than a personal estimation or judgement. For that reason, the undergoer must at least be affected due to his experience of the encounter. However, whether the undergoer is affected on a more fundamental level (i.e., whether his social status is permanently changed) is less clear. שפט G 'judge' occurs frequently in the HB and is used to denote concrete lawsuits between two parties, as well as referring to the just rule of kings and judges (Liedke 1984). In the particular case of Lev. 19.15, the meaning is a lawsuit. Given the lack of contextual evidence, it is hard to determine whether the undergoer is permanently affected. In cases like this, it is best to con-

---

[47] Other such verbs include נקף H 'go around' (or 'trim'; see Lev. 19.27), and שחת H 'destroy' (Lev. 19.27). Similar considerations pertain to זמר G 'prune', which is used in the context of pruning a vineyard, that is, trimming the branches (Lev. 25.3, 4).

strue the event in simplest terms possible. Therefore, it is represented as a two-argument activity.

Finally, speech verbs are not normally causative. Van Valin and La Polla (1997, 118) describe 'tell' as a causative of becoming aware. צוה D 'command' is probably also causative, as illustrated in (73). Firstly, the addressees of the command are not marked as an oblique object, as for regular speech verbs, but with an object marker. Secondly, the speech event forces or persuades the Israelites to bring olive oil.[48] Therefore, the entire event is given as a double causative structure: a command causing the Israelites to cause Moses to come into possession of olive oil.[49]

## 5.4. Summary and Discussion

The annotation of participants with Næss' three semantic parameters—instigation, volition, and affectedness—has led to a discussion of the compositionality of each parameter. A summary of the discussion and its implications for annotation and conceptualisation of causation is given in Table 13 below. In theory, Næss' concept of semantic transitivity is compelling, because it treats actors and undergoers of transitive events according to the same criteria. In practice, however, neither volition nor affectedness is self-evident. In particular, volition refers to

---

[48] Petersson (2017) argues that the speech event in Lev. 24.2 is an indirect command that involves an element of causation, because the agent is seeking to manipulate an addressee to perform an event.

[49] Another example with a causative צוה D 'command' is found in Lev. 25.21: "and I will command my blessings to you in the sixth year."

rather different notions with respect to actor and undergoer. The decisive criteria of volition are intention with regard to the actor and involvedness with regard to the undergoer. Moreover, affectedness is a complex feature involving the definiteness and inherent properties of the undergoer (material vs immaterial), in addition to considerations pertaining to whether the undergoer is indeed *affected* or merely *effected*, and whether the actor is also affected (direction).

With regard to *Aktionsart* and semantic roles, instigation applies only to the actor role. Affectedness prototypically applies to the undergoer of events, but also relates to specific situations where the actor is affected by the event, e.g., events of eating, drinking, and wearing. Finally, volition, due to its compositionality, pertains to both actor and undergoer insofar as the respective participant is human/divine.

Table 13: Summary table of Næss' (2007) semantic parameters of transitivity, including their alleged components and their correlations with semantic roles and causation

|  | Components | Correlations with semantic roles | Correlations with causation |
| --- | --- | --- | --- |
| **Instigation** | ± impingement<br>± authority | actor | real causation [+ impingement, ± authority]<br>indirect causation [± control, ± authority] |
| **Volition** | ± intention<br>± involvedness | actor, undergoer | intended causation [+ intention, ± involvedness]<br>permission [+ intention, + involvedness]<br>neglection [− intention, ± involvedness] |
| **Affectedness** | ± material<br>± definite<br>± effected<br>direction | undergoer, actor | real causation [+ material, ± definite, − effected, directed] |

With regard to the correlation of causation with semantic transitivity, Hopper and Thompson's (1980, 264) simple definition must be reconsidered. For convenience, their definition is repeated here:

> [C]ausatives are highly Transitive constructions: they must involve at least two participants, one of which is an initiator, and the other of which is totally affected and highly individuated.

To begin with, the discussion so far has revealed that the definition accounts well for 'real', or physical, causatives, that is, direct causation of a concrete, material undergoer by an impinging causer. In this case, the undergoer can rightly be considered completely affected, and the causer initiates the event (regardless of intentionality). However, as Talmy (2000) has demonstrated, causation is a much broader concept and involves persuasion, coercion, permission, neglect, and hindrance, besides direct causation. These derived causative events are not captured simply by considering the semantic transitivity parameters offered by Næss or Hopper and Thompson. Rather, the defining criterion of a causative event must be whether the event can logically be thought of as two individual events connected by a causative operator (see Shibatani 1976b, 1). The logical decomposition of verbal aspect offered by RRG is therefore a fruitful framework for analysing Biblical Hebrew verbs. We may not be able to avoid the RRG paraphrasing test for causation completely, since causation is a logical relation and, in the case of lexical causatives, is not realised morphologically or syntactically. Nevertheless, by annotating the semantic parameters of the participants using Næss' parameters (with modifications), we have independent criteria for investigating the roles of the participants in any given event. As shown, by combining RRG logical structures with semantic parameters, the decomposition of BH verbs can be carried out on a more informed basis.

## 6.0. Agency and a Hierarchy of Semantic Roles

We are now in a position to return to the overall purpose of decomposing Hebrew verbs, namely, to be able to compute a measure of agency for the sake of a social network analysis of the Holiness Code. It was argued in chapter 4 that dynamicity and causation were the two features contributing most significantly to agency, and the long detour around dynamicity (chapter 5) and causation was crucial in order to detect morphological and syntactic parameters correlating with agency. Given that agency is a multifaceted feature, a verbal complement can exhibit it to a lesser or greater degree. This is especially apparent for causation in light of Næss' three parameters (instigation, volition, and affectedness) because, for example, a participant may be instigating an event volitionally or involuntarily, the latter event naturally being less agentive. In other words, participants can be differentiated semantically by discerning the level of agency invested in an event. This will prove particularly important in chapter 7, where agency will be considered one of several parameters on the basis of which the social roles of the participants in Lev. 17–26 may be differentiated. In order to differentiate the participants according to agency, we first need to establish a hierarchy of semantic roles with corresponding agency scores. Accordingly, the insights gained in chapters 4–6, in particular Næss' (2007) semantic features, will be combined in order to establish a hierarchy of semantic roles according to the degree of agency associated with each role.

In the history of linguistic research, a variety of hierarchies of semantic roles have been proposed. Traditionally, the hierarchies were created for the sake of argument selection. That is, the critical question was how the semantic roles relate to grammatical relations. Charles J. Fillmore (1968; 2003), with his concept of deep cases, explained how the deep semantic structure of propositions is decisive for selecting the surface structure cases of NPs. In fact, he offered a simple hierarchy of semantic roles to explain the selection of subject in unmarked sentences (Fillmore 2003, 55):

> If there is an A[gentive], it becomes the subject; otherwise, if there is an I[nstrumental], it becomes the subject; otherwise, the subject is the O[bjective].

In other words, the case roles Agentive, Instrumental, and Objective form a hierarchy by which case roles can be linked with grammatical relations. Later, Ray Jackendoff (1990) offered a more elaborate hierarchy of semantic roles: Actor > Patient /Beneficiary > Theme > Location/Source/Goal. Dowty (1991) proposed yet another hierarchy based on his proto-role distinction: Agent > Instrument, Experiencer > Patient > Source, Goal (usually). In fact, one of the criticisms levelled against thematic-role approaches to argument selection concerns the differing hierarchies (see Croft 2012, 181). RRG also offers a hierarchy of thematic relations based on their positions in the logical structure representations of the verbs (see chapter 4,

§4.0). The hierarchy is used to determine the macroroles of a proposition, actor, and undergoer. The RRG hierarchy of thematic relations, however, is not relevant for this study, because I am not only interested in thematic relations but also in semantic roles beyond the thematic relations. The hierarchy I shall propose shortly depends on both thematic relations and the semantic parameters of the arguments (see Næss 2007). Accordingly, in the context of the present study, a hierarchy of semantic roles serves two purposes. Firstly, as in traditional approaches, the hierarchy is the basis for determining the actor and undergoer of a proposition. Secondly, since the hierarchy correlates with a measure of agency associated with each semantic role, it allows for the quantification of events involving two interacting participants, by means of the positions of the participants in the hierarchy.

Adopting the semantic features proposed by Næss (2007), I suggest a hierarchy of semantic roles based on instigation, volition, and affectedness. Within Næss' framework, Agent and Patient are the two most distinguished participants. Consequently, they represent the two extremes of a scale of agency. The defining features of an Agent are instigation and volition, while the Patient is prototypically characterised by affectedness. Thus, if the eight semantic roles proposed by Næss are sorted according to these parameters, a hierarchy is established (Table 14).

Table 14: A hierarchy of semantic roles and their corresponding agency scores

| Role | Parameters | Score | Examples |
| --- | --- | --- | --- |
| Agent | +VOL<br>+INST<br>–AFF | 5 | I am Y<small>HWH</small> your God who brought you out of the land of Egypt (Lev. 19.36) |
| Force | –VOL<br>+INST<br>–AFF | 4 | The land vomited out its inhabitants (Lev. 18.25) |
| Affected Agent | +VOL<br>+INST<br>+AFF | 3 | Anyone of the house of Israel or of the sojourners sojourning among them who eats any blood (Lev. 17.12)<br>You shall love your neighbour as yourself (Lev. 19.18) |
| Instrument | –VOL<br>+INST<br>+AFF | 2 | I will bring terror upon you, disease and fever, which destroy the eyes… (Lev. 26.16) |
| Frustrative | +VOL<br>–INST<br>–AFF | 1 | You may not let some of it remain until morning (Lev. 22.30) |
| Neutral | –VOL<br>–INST<br>–AFF | 0 | You shall love your neighbour as yourself (Lev. 19.18) |
| Volitional Undergoer | +VOL<br>–INST<br>+AFF | -1 | I am Y<small>HWH</small> your God who brought you out of the land of Egypt (Lev. 19.36)<br>A man who takes his sister as wife and sees her nakedness… (Lev. 20.17) |
| Patient | –VOL<br>–INST<br>+AFF | -2 | The people of the land shall stone him with stones (Lev. 20.2) |

At the top of the scale is the prototypical agent role, followed by non-volitional Force. Force represents natural, physical forces such as lightning. Curiously, in H, אֶרֶץ 'land' is sometimes presented as a force that can vomit out its inhabitants (e.g., Lev. 18.25).[50]

---

[50] The role of the land can also be interpreted differently. It can be construed as a personified participant having its own will (Agent) or

Further, an Affected Agent is a volitional agent that is affected by the event (e.g., consumption events). Since an Affected Agent is volitional, it is ranked higher than an Instrument, which is also affected but not volitional.

The last four roles are non-instigating. These include the Frustrative, which expresses the denial or hindrance of an event willed by a participant.[51] This role applies well to the many prohibitions given in the law texts of Leviticus. The Neutral exhibits none of the agency parameters and includes the traditional semantic roles: source, goal, location, and manner. Since this role is neutral, it is given the agency score 0, from which the agency scores of the other roles are derived.

The Volitional Undergoer is a sentient and/or beneficiary participant, and the role thus subsumes the experiencer, recipient, and beneficiary roles. The example of 'seeing' from Lev. 20.17 (see Table 14) illustrates an interesting implication of the hierarchy. A man who sees his sister's 'nakedness' (euphemism for copulation) is a Volitional Undergoer insofar as he perceives his sister's nakedness. There is no hint in the text that he intentionally observes her but, rather, that the uncovering and perception of her nakedness is the effect of marrying her. The 'nakedness', on the other hand, is the object perceived and is therefore semantically neutral. It is neither instigating nor volitional

---

as an instrument executing the will of YHWH (Instrument). Since these two interpretations are not supported directly by the text, the Force role appears to be the most convincing.

[51] The Frustrative is typically derived from other roles by the presence of a negative clause operator (see Næss 2007, 116–17).

and presumably remains unaffected during the event. This interpretation has important ramifications for the attribution of actor and undergoer in the sentence. As explained, the hierarchy of semantic roles allows for deciding which participant is the actor and which is the undergoer. The most agentive participant is the actor, while the least agentive is the undergoer. In the present case, 'nakedness' is rated higher than 'man' because Neutral arguments rank higher than Volitional Undergoers; hence, 'nakedness' is the actor of the event, while 'man' is the undergoer. This might seem odd, since one would expect a human being who sees an object to be more agentive than the object seen. Strictly speaking, however, the event does not originate from the experiencer but from the object that stimulates the observation. Understood this way, the object perceived is construed as the actor and the Volitional Undergoer as the undergoer of the event.

Finally, the prototypical Patient concludes the list of roles. This role is the least agentive of all roles and refers to participants who are totally and non-volitionally affected by the event.

The agency hierarchy allows us to explore the distribution of semantic roles, agency, and participants in Lev. 17–26. As an example, all human/divine participants that occur at least 20 times in Lev. 17–26 have been cross-tabulated with their roles (Table 15). Given the agency scores, the mean agency for each participant can be calculated. Interestingly, the two main speakers of the speeches comprising the text, Moses and YHWH, are the two participants with the highest mean agency scores. By contrast, Aaron, the sons of Aaron, and the brother have much smaller agency means, a fact indicating that these participants obtain less agentive roles in the events in which they partake. Finally, the Israelites and the 2MSg ('you'), which refer respectively to the entire community of the Israelites and to its individual members, are frequently attested in the Frustrative role. This is to be expected, since the frequent prohibitions in the text are primarily directed to the Israelites, either as a group or as individuals.

Although the distribution of semantic roles is suggestive of a *social* hierarchy, the semantic roles do not by themselves establish this hierarchy. Even if YHWH is agent-like, the frequencies of semantic roles do not inform us about the situations in which he is agentive and with respect to whom. To explore how the participants relate to one another, we need to analyse the semantic roles within a framework of actual social exchange among concrete participants. This framework is called social network analysis and will be the topic of the next chapter. In that chapter, the hierarchy of semantic roles and the corresponding agency scores will serve as the means by which the interactions among the participants of the social network are quantified.

Table 15: Semantic roles and mean agency scores obtained by the most common participants in Lev. 17–26

| | Agent | Force | Affected Agent | Frustrative | Neutral | Volitional Undergoer | Patient | Mean Agency |
|---|---|---|---|---|---|---|---|---|
| Moses | 36 | 0 | 1 | 0 | 1 | 19 | 0 | 2.877 |
| YHWH | 118 | 0 | 1 | 8 | 29 | 30 | 17 | 2.645 |
| an Israelite | 60 | 0 | 22 | 7 | 4 | 6 | 38 | 2.182 |
| 2MSg ('you') | 21 | 0 | 10 | 57 | 8 | 8 | 2 | 1.698 |
| Israelites | 99 | 0 | 44 | 72 | 28 | 83 | 31 | 1.569 |
| sojourner | 45 | 0 | 16 | 5 | 13 | 9 | 38 | 1.532 |
| Aaron's sons | 16 | 0 | 6 | 22 | 5 | 17 | 5 | 1.310 |
| Aaron | 16 | 0 | 11 | 31 | 1 | 19 | 10 | 1.193 |
| brother | 11 | 0 | 3 | 1 | 16 | 10 | 13 | 0.611 |
| remnants | 3 | 2 | 4 | 0 | 2 | 5 | 13 | 0.138 |
| foreign nations | 3 | 0 | 1 | 0 | 5 | 3 | 10 | -0.227 |

# 7. PARTICIPANTS IN SOCIAL NETWORKS

## 1.0. Introduction

The preceding chapters laid the groundwork for exploring participants in social networks. Chapter 3 discussed the complex task of participant tracking, with the aim of establishing a comprehensive dataset of all participant references. Chapter 4 introduced a theoretical framework for capturing the agency of participants according to their semantic roles, and chapters 5–6 applied the theory based on the two most significant contributors to agency: dynamicity and causation. All these data come together in the social network analysis of the Holiness Code to be carried out in this chapter. At this point, we are not only interested in the semantic roles of the participants, as in the preceding chapters, but rather in what could be called 'network roles'. While semantic roles pertain specifically to the role of a participant in a particular event, network roles generalise beyond semantic roles and consider the roles of participants in a network of events. The framework of this undertaking is the relational sociology introduced in chapter 2, §4.0. With 59 human/divine participants, Lev. 17–26 poses a real challenge for understanding the social relationships among these participants. Who are the most important participants? Who are the most peripheral? Do some participants play the role of an intermediary between different social groups? And further, how do the specific roles of the participants correlate with the ethical obligations formulated by the Holiness Code? Are the laws simply arbitrary, or does the content of the laws hinge on the nature of the participants and the social roles constrained by the network? These are the questions to be addressed in this chapter.

## 2.0. Social Network Analysis

### 2.1. Brief History

Social network analysis is an umbrella term for theories and tools that aim to describe social networks and the roles of the participants within the network. The most important research questions investigated with SNA relate to the ties between participants. What kinds of ties are they? Friendship ties, ties of trust, or of economical transaction? Furthermore, how strong are they? The importance of investigating these questions lies in the fact that the performance of a team with the same members differs depending on the relationships between the members of the team (Borgatti et al. 2009).

The history of SNA is long and complex, and its roots can be traced back to the *Gestalt* tradition of psychology in the 1920s and 1930s.[1] By the 1970s, 16 centres of research into social networks had emerged, but none of these succeeded in providing a generally accepted paradigm for the study of social networks (Freeman 2014). Finally, with the rise of the seventeenth centre led by Harrison C. White at Harvard University, SNA became a more standardised paradigm and began to have immense impact

---

[1] For more comprehensive accounts of the history of SNA, see in particular Freeman (2004; 2014) and Scott (2017, 11–39).

on the social sciences. However, SNA did not only attract attention from sociologists, psychologists, and anthropologists. In the 1970s, mathematicians and computer scientists became interested in subjects related to SNA, such as network groups and communities, in particular with respect to their special interests, namely graphs and graph partitioning. Later, in the 1990s, physicists entered the scene (e.g., Watts and Strogatz 1998; Barabási and Albert 1999) and "revolutionized" the area of research, as Linton C. Freeman (2014) puts it. At that time, physicists and biologists were facing huge amounts of structured data to be analysed, and they started applying (and sometimes reinventing) the statistical methods developed in SNA. The 'revolution', however, was not applauded by all members of the SNA community. As Ann Mische (2014) explains, the cultural theorists in the field felt that the physics bent reduced the social and cultural richness of network analysis to a matter of 1s and 0s. In short, SNA was always a very diverse field of research, despite numerous attempts to bring the methodologies and terminologies into line. Even today, social network analysts disagree as to the nature of SNA. Is SNA basically "a collection of theoretically informed methods" (Scott 2017, 8), or is it a theory in its own right (Borgatti et al. 2009)?[2]

Today, SNA has become a huge field of research. Its evolution is partly owed to the development of Web 2.0 and the still recent, but enormously influential, phenomenon of social media, including Facebook, X, and Instagram, to name but a few. Each

---

[2] See also Mische (2014) for a discussion of whether SNA is a theory.

Facebook user participates in a huge social network, and the inbuilt application of friend suggestions on Facebook uses SNA-based algorithms for predicting new relationships on the basis of existing ones. Similar algorithms are known from Amazon and other web-shops, where products are recommended based on previous purchases and, importantly, on purchases of users with a similar profile. These advanced websites thus apply SNA methods in order to create social network profiles of their users, for the purpose of predicting behaviour and targeting products and advertisements.

With its emphasis on networks, clustering, prediction of behaviour, and role profiling, SNA is related to a broad range of network approaches in various research areas. These include physics and computer science (e.g., Watts and Strogatz 1998; Barabási and Albert 1999; Newman 2010), psychology (e.g., Westaby et al. 2014), biology (e.g., Luczkovich et al. 2003), and economics (e.g., Jackson 2011). Importantly, SNA has also found its way to the study of literature, where it provides a methodological framework for revealing subtle connections among participants and patterns of interaction (see §2.3).

## 2.2. Main Concepts

A great number of introductions to SNA have been published, both theoretical and practical ones (Borgatti et al. 2018; Scott 2017; Newman 2010), as well as highly technical (Brandes and Erlebach 2005). Moreover, several practical introductions to analysing social networks with Python have been published in recent years (Al-Taie and Kadry 2017; Raj P. M. et al. 2018). In what follows, I will introduce the main concepts of SNA relevant for the present research. The interested reader is referred to more general introductions.

**Nodes**: The constituents or participants of a social network are called nodes.[3] The nodes can denote many different entities: typically individuals, but also companies, organisations, terror cells, teams, etc. Within the broader applications of network analysis, a node may be a computer, a blood cell, or a neuron, depending on the network under scrutiny. In this study, the participants of Lev. 17–26 form the nodes of the network; hence 'participants' and 'nodes' will be used interchangeably.

**Edges**: The nodes in a network are connected by edges, often also called ties. An edge denotes the type of relationship between two nodes, e.g., friendship, kinship, enmity, trust, wedding, economical transaction, etc. The values of the edges may be binary (e.g., wedding ties) or continuous (e.g., degree of trust or amount of money transferred). The edges can be undirected (e.g., wedding ties) or directed, e.g., one person may regard another as a friend, but the friendship or trust may not be mutual. The same nodes may even be connected by multiple, different edges.

**Degree**: The degree is the number of edges tied to a node, e.g., a node with three edges has a degree of three. For directed

---

[3] In computer science and graph theory, the nodes are also called vertices.

edges, incoming ties produce the indegree, while outgoing ties produce the outdegree.

**Graph**: The nodes and edges form a graph. Depending on the type of edges (undirected vs directed) and number of overlapping edges (singular vs multiple), the graph may be either a simple graph (singular, undirected graph), a directed graph, or a multiple directed graph. Graphs efficiently visualise network structures and can be modified with colour-coding of both nodes and edges, as well as scaling of nodes and edges according to their respective values. However, although graphs give a visual impression of the network, they can be difficult to interpret, especially for large networks with multiple directed ties. Therefore, it is common to transform the graph into adjacency matrices or vectors that allow for statistical computations of the structural properties of the graph. Moreover, recent approaches to studying network properties apply neural deep learning (Zhang et al. 2019; Wu et al. 2020) and so-called random walks (see §4.2).

**Walk**: The network graph can be traversed by following the edges between the nodes. Such traversing is called a walk and is essentially a sequence of edges connecting two nodes. The walk must respect the directions of the edges (if directed). The concept of the walk provides information about the connectivity of the network and the environment of individual nodes. If a node can be reached by a number of different walks from another node, the two nodes are well connected. Other nodes may only be linked by a single sequence of edges and are therefore only loosely connected.

**Ego**: One can view a network from the viewpoint of the network at large or from the viewpoint of a single node, called ego. When exploring real-world data, one may not have access to the complete network because of lack of data. Instead, one can learn general network features by focusing on the individual nodes, the egos of the network. From the viewpoint of the ego, a node with a tie to the ego is called an alter.

**Ego-network**: An ego-network consists of an ego and its alters. The ego-network is, thus, a subset of the entire social network.

**Neighbourhood**: A neighbourhood consists of all adjacent nodes with immediate ties to the ego. This neighbourhood is called a first-order neighbourhood. By contrast, a second-order neighbourhood includes nodes within a distance of two edges from the ego.

## 2.3. Related Research

A number of social network analyses have been dedicated to historical social networks, the best-known example probably being the Medici-family network in Renaissance Florence (Padgett and Ansell 1993). Another important study is Charles Tilly's (1997) analysis of the parliamentarisation of Great Britain in 1758–1834. By systematically cataloguing numerous newspaper articles into categories of event, people, and action, among others, Tilly created a large dataset that could be explored to investigate changing relations among people groups. The procedure was tedious, because each event had to be transcribed into an actor, the activity itself, and the undergoer of the activity, if any.[4] At the same time, Roberto Franzosi (1997) categorised 15,146 newspaper articles from the 'Red Years' (1919–20) that preceded the Fascists' rise to power in Italy. Relying on the works of William Labov and Joshua Waletsky (1967) and M. A. K. Halliday (1970), among others, the articles were classified according to actors and events. More pieces of information, such as time, space, number of actors in a particular group, and instrument, were also added to the dataset. For both Tilly and Franzosi, the ultimate goal was to create a searchable database of the texts in order to query actors and events. In other words, the building blocks were semantic triplets of participants (actor and undergoer) and event. Today, computational methods enable automatic or semi-automatic classification of all sorts of text, but Tilly's and Franzosi's works demonstrate the basic requirements in preparing natural text for SNA.

Somewhat related to the present study is Steven E. Massey's (2016) network analysis of Moses and his relations with other Biblical characters in the Pentateuch. The underlying structural patterns revealed by his network analysis show that Moses and YHWH are unusually highly connected, that is, given that the degree of participants tends to correspond to the number of participants, Moses and YHWH have surprisingly many connections.

---

[4] See also Tilly's (2008) later work in which he unfolds his approach in detail.

Massey suggests that this fact may be due to authorial emphasis on these two participants.

Other social network analyses have focused on novels and mythological texts (e.g., Beveridge and Shan 2016; Waumans et al. 2015; Carron and Kenna 2012). M. E. J. Newman and Michelle Girvan (2004) explored algorithms for detecting communities in social networks, including in Victor Hugo's famous *Les Misérables*. SNA has also been applied to the study of the literary characters in the Greek tragedies collected and digitised by the Perseus Digital Library (Rydberg-Cox 2011). Finally, Agawar et al. (2012) carried out a study of *Alice in Wonderland* in which they explored the narrative roles of the participants in terms of authority, degree centrality, and structural hubs. Moreover, although a text is static (in terms of network structure), by modelling each chapter as a separate network, they demonstrated how the network evolves over the course of the novel.

SNA has also been applied to the study of ancient corpora. In particular, Assyriologists have employed SNA for the research of Neo- and Late Babylonian archives (Waerzeggers 2014b; Wagner et al. 2013; Still 2019). The Babylonian archives contain thousands of tablets which record the activity of thousands of people, including economical transactions and marriages. By itself, a tablet gives a glimpse of a social world, but may not provide an extensive impression of the social roles of the participants recorded on the tablet. However, some participants occur in several tablets and possibly in different roles, e.g., witnesses or traders. Therefore, through the mapping of tablets and persons, a social network emerges, allowing for the exploration of social connectivity in Babylonian society, flows of communication, and even "potential for mobilizing rebellions" (Waerzeggers 2014b, 209). In fact, the construction of a two-mode social network (i.e., a network with two types of nodes: tablets and persons) can even be used for the dating of tablets (Allon Wagner et al. 2013). In his dissertation, Bastian Still (2019) analysed 3,500 cuneiform tablets in order to map the social world of Babylonian priests and investigate how the Babylonian priesthood interacted with other social groups. To complete this short survey of SNA studies of cuneiform tablets, it is worth noting that Judean-Babylonian connections during the Judean exile in Babylon have also been mapped and explored (Alstola 2017; Waerzeggers 2014a).

All the social network studies of cuneiform tablets mentioned here essentially employ two-mode networks, that is, they involve two sets of nodes (tablets and persons) to be mapped. In this respect, they can reveal connections between persons across different tablets. By contrast, the present study is a one-mode network, because there is only one text, the Holiness Code. Therefore, the present analysis diverges from the archive approach in several respects. Most importantly, the participants in H are not assumed to be connected simply because they appear in the same text, but only if interactions are explicitly recorded.

Much more relevant for the present study is Chebineh Che's (2017) text-syntactic and literary analysis of Gen. 27–28, in which he applied SNA to a short, self-contained text, not unlike the present study of H. In his dissertation, the social network was modelled on the basis of the speeches recorded in order to quantify the relationships and roles of the participants in dialogue.

The methodology was adopted from Franco Moretti (2011; 2014), who argued that narrative plots can be quantified according to SNA centrality measures. In particular, like Jan A. Fuhse (2009; see also chapter 2, §4.0), Moretti pointed to the significance of the network edges, because it is not enough to simply record who is speaking to whom. Rather, according to Moretti (2011), speeches need to be quantified according to the space occupied by them, that is, the extent of communication. In this respect, participants with multiple or long dialogues will carry more weight than participants with just a single utterance. In his application of Moretti's methodology, then, Che demonstrated how SNA centrality measures can be used to identify different participant roles in a narrative.

## 3.0. The Social Network of the Holiness Code

Unlike the related research described above, the purpose of the present study is to examine a social network implied by a single, legal text. To my knowledge, it is the first attempt to model a law code as a social network. A number of issues arising from this endeavour have already been addressed (chapter 2, §5.0). Most importantly, despite Lev. 17–26 being a law text, the chapters constitute an apt candidate for SNA, because the legal basis is one of common law. Therefore, we can expect the laws to be dialogical and interactional in nature, as a reflection of their social context and as concretisations of the expectations and values of the author.

Another difference to the related research referenced above is the conceptualisation of the ties among the participants. It is common to count co-appearance as a tie—for instance, if two participants are present in the same text or in the same chapter—or to quantify the interaction as the length of speech between two conversing participants. To my knowledge, no social network analysis has so far quantified the interaction between two participants by means of agency, as is done in the present study. The notion of agency allows for the inclusion of a vast range of interactions apart from merely dialogue or specific types of transactions. The procedure for capturing agency will be unfolded below.

Finally, the present SNA is the first attempt at taking the discourse structure of the text into account. The ETCBC database contains annotations of the syntactic hierarchy of the BH text, which allow the discourse structure to be considered another dimension of the network. When applied to texts, SNA is regularly employed to model the text as a two-dimensional network. Thus, the complexity of the text is often reduced to whether two participants appear in the same text or section of the text, or whether two participants are interacting. Texts, however, are not two-dimensional. They have an inherent 'depth' in that interactions are embedded in a discourse structure. Accordingly, the interaction of two participants may be conditioned by the interaction of another set of participants. Understood this way, the 'world' of the text is a three-dimensional space, and in order to capture the meaning of the network, the internal relationships of the participants are best understood within this space. This feature will be the topic of §3.5 and will be demonstrated concretely in the discussion of the role of *Moses* (§5.2.1).[5]

---

[5] Italics are used to mark participants, e.g., *Moses*, as network participants. Thus, the role of *Moses* is not (necessarily) the role of the 'real'

## 3.1. Data Modelling

The data used for deriving the social network of Lev. 17–26 are participant references and verbs. Together, these two types of data form semantic triplets of actor, undergoer, and event. Both sets of data have been documented in the preceding chapters and form the backbone of the present investigation. However, not all data produced in the participant tracking and semantic role analyses are included. A more precise definition of the data types is therefore in place:

**Nodes**: The nodes of the network are human/divine participants. In addition, body parts and expressions referring to a human/divine being, e.g., soul, are also included. The choice of including body parts is reasonable, given that they are frequently employed as references to persons, e.g., 'his hand' in "a man, if he has no redeemer, but his hand prospers..." (Lev. 25.26).[6] All non-human and non-divine participants have been excluded.

**Edges**: The edges of the network are the interactions taking place among the participants (i.e., the nodes). These interactions include speech, trade, marriage, execution, and fighting. The interactions also include cultic transactions, such as defilement and sanctification, as well as affective

---

Moses outside the text or outside the bounds of Lev. 17–26, but the role of the participant within the social network derived from H.

[6] Consequently, in the New Revised Standard Version, 'hand' is simply omitted, and the verb refers to the man: "If the person has no one to redeem it, but then prospers..."

relations, such as love and hate, and perceptual relations, such as hearing. Not all of these relations are actually transactions, but they capture different sorts of relationships (Borgatti et al. 2018, 5). In SNA, it is common to restrict the edges to representing only one type of interaction or connection, e.g., trade connections or marriage ties, in order to simplify the analysis. To justify the present approach, however, the events are also quantified in terms of agency. As explained in chapter 6, each participant is given an agency score according to its semantic role in a particular interaction, and this procedure effectively distinguishes highly agentive participants, such as traders or speakers, from less agentive participants, such as recipients or benefactors. The agency scores are computed on the basis of the semantic role hierarchy in chapter 6, §6.0 (see examples in Table 16 below). Since each interaction involves two participants, there are also two agency scores. The squared difference between these two scores produces a combined agency score for each interaction. In other words, the network edges are conceptualised as the agency difference between two interacting participants (see example in Figure 10).[7]

---

[7] While most interactions involve two participants, some actually involve three. More precisely, the three-argument sentence in Figure 10 involves three participants ('I', 'that soul', and 'his people') that are connected by edges; hence, there are three edges to represent the event going on between the three participants: Yhwh → an Israelite, Yhwh →

Figure 10: A schematic representation of the derivation of a semantic triplet from a clause in Lev 23.30. Agency scores are computed on the basis of the respective agency scores of the participants (YHWH = 5, an Israelite = -2). The difference is seven, and the squared difference is 49.

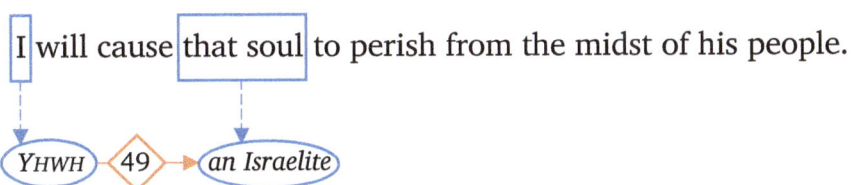

The constraint on participants (i.e., only human and divine participants) resulted in a reduced list of potential edges. Moreover, since only semantic triplets are of interest here, many sentences were dropped because they involved only one participant. The semantic triplets were automatically extracted from the database according to the presence of human/divine participants. A few interactions were not captured by this approach, including, e.g., Lev. 25.14, where the addressees are prohibited from oppressing their fellows, literally 'You (Pl) may not oppress, a man his brother'. Since this event is formed by two clauses ('You may not oppress' and 'a man his brother'), it was not captured as a semantic triplet by the present approach. For the sake of consistency, only one-clause semantic triplets were included.

In sum, 479 semantic triplets were extracted from the text, which consists of 1,176 clauses. To be sure, some clauses generated multiple triplets, because a participant reference may refer

---

his people; his people → an Israelite. The agency scores of the participants decide the direction of interaction.

to multiple participants, e.g., 'mother and father' in "any man (of you) shall fear his mother and his father" (Lev. 19.3). A sample of the resulting data is given in Table 16, and the resulting network is illustrated in Figure 11.

Table 16: A sample of the semantic triplets extracted from Lev. 17–26

| Event ID (clause) | Actor | Undergoer | Event | Agency |
|---|---|---|---|---|
| 439721 | YHWH (Agent) | Moses (Volitional Undergoer) | speak (דבר D) | 36[8] |
| 440521 | 2MSg (Affected Agent) | YHWH (Neutral) | fear (ירא G) | 9 |
| 439855 | 2MSg (Agent) | YHWH (Patient) | defile (חלל D) | 49 |
| 439740 | sojourner (Frustrative) | mother (Neutral) | approach (קרב G) | 1[9] |
| 440045 | foreign nations (Neutral) | YHWH (Volitional Undergoer) | loath (קץ G) | 1 |

The network has 59 nodes, corresponding to the number of participants, and 479 edges. The edges refer to concrete verbs as well as to agency scores derived from the respective agency degrees of the participants in an interaction. Moreover, the edges are directional (from actor to undergoer) and multiple according to the number of interactions between the participants. The purpose of what follows is to explore the network by means of standard statistical measures. These measures include 1) network cohesion;

---

[8] The agency score is calculated as the squared difference between the actor score (5 for Agent) and the undergoer score (-1 for Volitional Undergoer). The difference is six, and the squared difference is 36.

[9] The clause would normally involve an agentive actor. In this particular case, however, the event is prohibited, i.e., negated. Strictly speaking, therefore, the event does not take place, and the actor is left frustrative (agency = 1) and the undergoer untouched (= 0).

2) reciprocity; and 3) centrality. Finally, the discourse structure of the text will be related to the social network. The visualisations and calculations were carried out with the Python package NetworkX.[10]

Figure 11: The social network of Lev 17–26

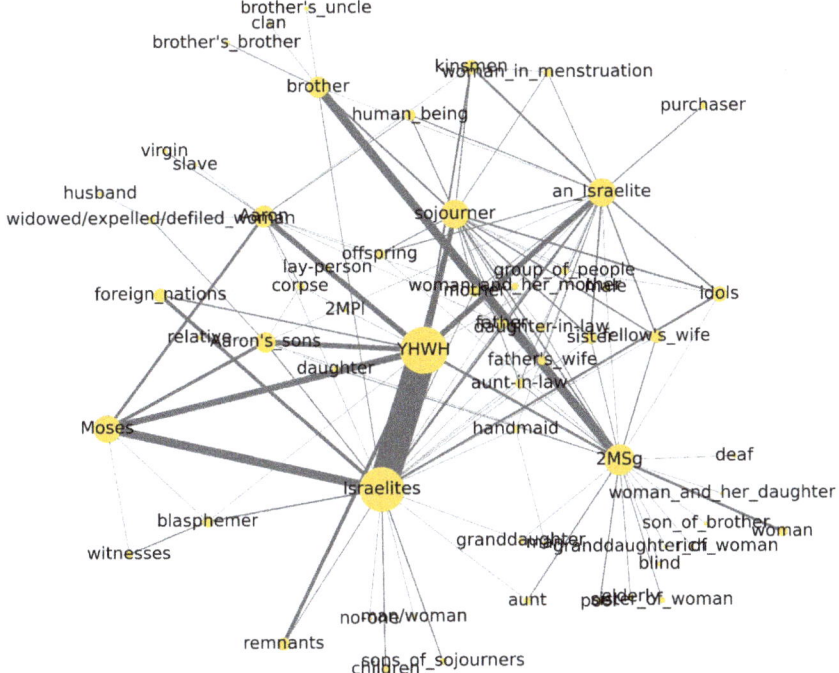

## 3.2. Cohesion

Cohesion is a measure of the 'knittedness' of a network, that is, how well connected it is (Borgatti et al. 2018, 174–79). A network with many interconnected nodes has a high degree of cohesion,

---

[10] For a practical guide to analysing social networks with Python and NetworkX, see Al-Taie and Kadry (2017). For a summary introduction to SNA and computational methods, see Tang (2017).

while networks with long paths between the nodes, as well as isolates (unconnected nodes), are less cohesive. In this respect, cohesion does not concern the nature of connections, whether the connections or relations are positive or negative (e.g., friendship or hate). A network may be structurally cohesive but sociologically fragmented if the connections are relations of enmity.

One of the simplest measures of cohesion is average degree.[11] The average degree is the average ingoing and outgoing ties of each node in the network. In the H network, the average degree is 16.23 if all connections are included (including multiple edges). The edges are far from evenly distributed in the network. As Figure 12 below illustrates, a large number of nodes (32) do not have outgoing ties, that is, more than half of the participants do not function as actors in the network but only as undergoers. By contrast, only eight nodes have no ingoing edges. The graph illustrates a common phenomenon for social networks in that the vast majority of the participants have few ties to other participants (Massey 2016).[12] A few participants are very well connected in the network. YHWH, for instance, has 115 outgoing ties and 76 ingoing ties and has the highest overall degree within the network (191). This is not surprising, since he is recorded as the divine speaker and frequently appears within the speeches

---

[11] Another measure is density, which is the number of edges in the network proportional to the number possible (Borgatti et al. 2018, 174). The Leviticus network has 59 nodes and 128 edges (undirected and unweighted), corresponding to a density of 0.075.

[12] 52.54% of the nodes have three or fewer ingoing ties (77.97% for outgoing ties).

themselves as recipient of sacrifices or as one under threat of ritual pollution (see §5.1.1). Other frequent participants include the collective group of *Israelites* (degree = 165), the singular 'you' labelled *2MSg* (78), the *sojourner* (66), the singular *an Israelite* (65), and *Moses* (61). These participants account for 65.34% of the interactions. Thus, the Holiness Code network is hierarchical, with a small set of very connected participants in crucial positions and a large number of peripheral participants dependent upon intermediating participants for their embeddedness in the network.

Figure 12: Degree distribution (multiple, directed graph). Dashed lines are cumulated degree.

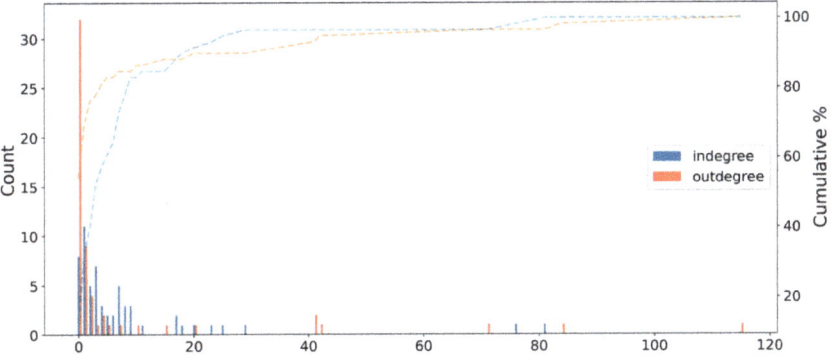

## 3.3. Reciprocity

The edges of the H network are directional, and some of them are reciprocal. Strictly speaking, reciprocity need not imply that one action is a response to another action. Reciprocal actions may not be directly related, since interactions can be captured from anywhere in the corpus. Reciprocity, however, gives an indication of whether the relationships of the network are mutual or one-sided. For a law text like the Holiness Code, the degree of reciprocity shows whether the obligations prescribed by the law are mutual or whether one party benefits more than the other. In the H network, only 24.66% of the relationships are mutual,[13] while the remaining ones are only one-way interactions (see Figure 13).[14] Participants in reciprocal interactions include the most recurrent participants but also infrequent ones, e.g., *foreign nations* and *fellow's wife*. At this point, it can only be concluded that the benefits provided by the law are not equally distributed among the members of the network. To investigate whether this apparent inequality is arbitrary or meaningful, we need to dive into the smaller networks of concrete participants and their interactions (see §5.0).

Figure 13: Reciprocity (singular, directed graph)

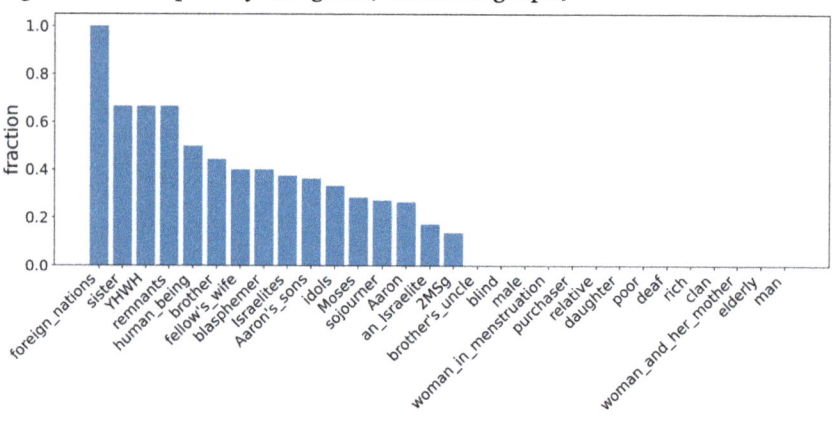

---

[13] This measure excludes multiple ties. If multiple ties are included, 32.57% of the interactions are reciprocal.

[14] A participant with no reciprocal relations may be transmitter in one relation and receiver in another relation.

## 3.4. Centrality

In real-world social networks, people tend to cluster in smaller, cohesive groups within the larger network. The reason for this phenomenon usually relates to different sociological factors, such as homophily,[15] geographical concentration, and a tendency to connect with the relations of one's relations (Borgatti et al. 2018, 180). The indegree and outdegree scores recorded above already indicated a small core of highly connected participants and a majority of less connected participants forming a periphery of the network. A range of statistical measures have been developed to calculate the centrality of individual participants in the network. Four of these measures have been computed for the H network, and the top-ten scores for each measure are displayed in Figure 14.

The first two measures are indegree and outdegree, already introduced above. Here, the degrees are calculated as degree centralities.[16] There is a marked difference between the outdegree and indegree scores. First of all, while the indegree ratios appear more evenly distributed across the participants, a few participants have strikingly high outdegree scores. The singular 'you' (*2MSg*), and the *Israelites* both have very high outdegree ratios and are thus very active in the network. They are the actors of many events and therefore occupy central positions in the network. *An Israelite* (Sg), the *sojourner*, Y*HWH*, and the priests (*Aaron*

---

[15] Homophily is the tendency of participants to bond with similar participants, e.g., same gender or same age.

[16] Degree centrality is computed as the sum of ties normalised by the maximum number of ties possible. In simple graphs, the score is between 0 and 1.

and *Aaron's sons*) also have high outdegree ratios. As noted, the indegree ratios are less varied. YHWH has the highest indegree ratio, probably because he is the benefactor/recipient of offerings as well as the undergoer of reverence. While some of the outdegree top scorers also have relatively high indegree ratios (e.g., the *Israelites*, the *sojourner*, *an Israelite*, *Aaron's sons*), some participants score high in indegree but not in outdegree. These are the *brother*, the *mother*, the *father*, the *idols*, and the *daughter-in-law*. Except for the *idols*, these participants are all defined from the point of view of the Israelites (most frequently the singular Israelites). They occur relatively frequently in the network and thus have relatively high indegree ratios, but they occur predominantly as undergoers. These participants thus fall somewhere between infrequent, peripheral participants and frequent, active participants.

Figure 14: Top-ten distributions of centrality measures

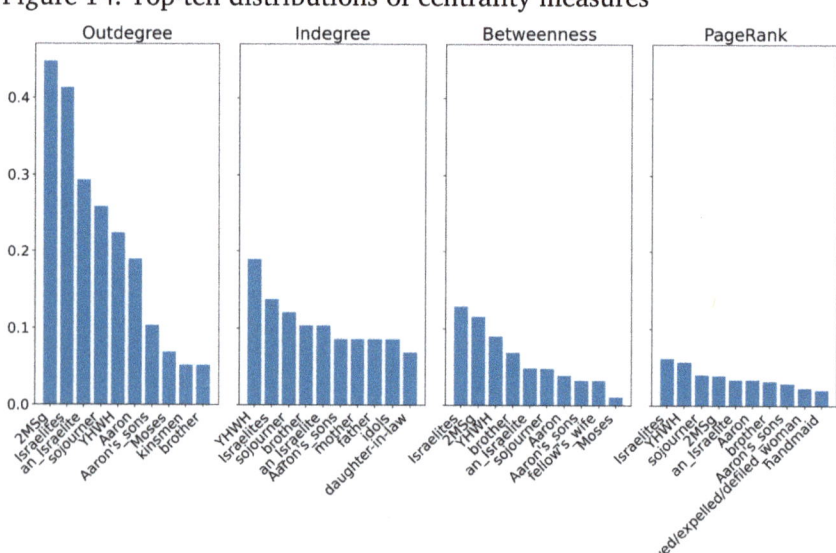

The third measure is betweenness (Freeman 1978), where centrality is understood as how often a node is positioned along the shortest path between two nodes. Betweenness centrality is typically interpreted as an index of control, because nodes with high betweenness ratios occur at critical junctures of the network and function as 'gatekeepers' (Brass 1984). If these nodes fall out of the network, the network becomes fragmented, because a number of nodes will no longer have any connections with the network. In general, the H network does not exhibit high betweenness scores. This fact indicates that the network is generally well connected. The *Israelites*, *2MSg*, and Yhwh have the highest betweenness scores in the network. In particular, *2MSg* and the *Israelites* are both connected to unique sets of participants and they therefore have an intermediary role in the network. Yhwh also has a high betweenness ratio, because he is involved in interactions with many different parts of the network, which would otherwise be less cohesive.

The fourth measure is the PageRank centrality, which was developed by Lawrence Page et al. (1998) and became one of the main ingredients of Google's search engine at that time (Koschützki et al. 2005, 53). The algorithm rates a node according to the number of ties from other nodes and, importantly, the centrality of those nodes. In other words, a node (e.g., a website) is considered central if it is linked to by other central nodes. As for the H network, one recognises several top scorers from the other centrality measures. The *Israelites* have the highest PageRank ratio, followed by Yhwh, the *sojourner*, *2MSg*, an *Israelite*, and *Aaron*. The *Israelites* are the direct addressees of Yhwh's speech to *Moses,* and they are therefore directly connected to other important participants, unlike *2MSg,* which is only indirectly connected by being referred to within the speeches. As recipients of divine revelation, the *Israelites* would be assumed to be a central figure within the law text.

In sum, the first explorations into the Holiness Code network have shown a highly hierarchical network with a small set of very connected participants in crucial positions and a large number of peripheral participants dependent upon intermediating participants for their embeddedness in the network. The addressees of the law code, namely the *Israelites* and *2MSg* (and less frequently, *Aaron* and *Aaron's sons*), occupy central positions in the network. They are very active (high outdegree), and they have direct ties with other important participants, including *YHWH*. *Moses* does not score high in centrality, despite his role as the intermediary of *YHWH's* speeches. This observation is curious and needs further investigation below.

## 3.5. Discourse Structure

As explained above, the purpose of SNA is to reduce the complexity of a social setting into a two-dimensional map consisting of nodes and edges. The same approach applies to SNA of texts, which have traditionally been analysed with SNA by modelling the participants and their internal connections on the basis of some criteria. Edges may be conceptualised as the cooccurrence of participants in the same chapter, newspaper article, or tablet, but also as concrete dialogue between participants (e.g., Che

2017). These traditional approaches tend to run counter to a fundamental feature of texts, namely the internal syntactic structure of texts. Texts are not one-dimensional, but are structured according to the discourse of the text, so that each sentence is structurally related to other sentences in one way or another. The dialogical structure of Lev. 17–26 illustrates this phenomenon well, e.g., "And YHWH spoke to Moses, saying: Speak to the sons of Israel and say to them: I am YHWH your God" (18.1–2). These two verses contain several layers. The first layer is a narrative introduction by the author of the text (18.1). Embedded in the narrative context, YHWH's speech is a command to Moses to speak to the people of Israel (18.2ab). Finally, Moses' speech begins in 18.2c with a quotation of YHWH. Thus, the first two verses of Lev. 18 contain three levels of discourse: narrative introduction (level 1) > YHWH's command to Moses (2) > Moses' speech to the Israelites (3). Most interactions occur at the third discourse level (Figure 15). This level usually contains the content of Moses' speeches and comprises the body of the legislation. Moses himself is by far most active at the second level, that is, the level where YHWH typically commands Moses to speak. Consequently, the interactions contained in the laws of Lev. 17–26 are *conditioned* by the speeches of Moses; they are the content of what he says. Ultimately, the legal interactions and Moses' speeches are the content of YHWH's speeches to Moses and, of course, the content of the author's narrative. In a word, then, interactions on one domain are *controlled* or *conditioned* by the higher-level domains. Obviously, this phenomenon has implications for how we understand the importance and roles of participants, because higher-level participants are in control of lower-level interactions.

Figure 15: Frequency of participants (actors) as a function of textual domain in Lev. 17–26

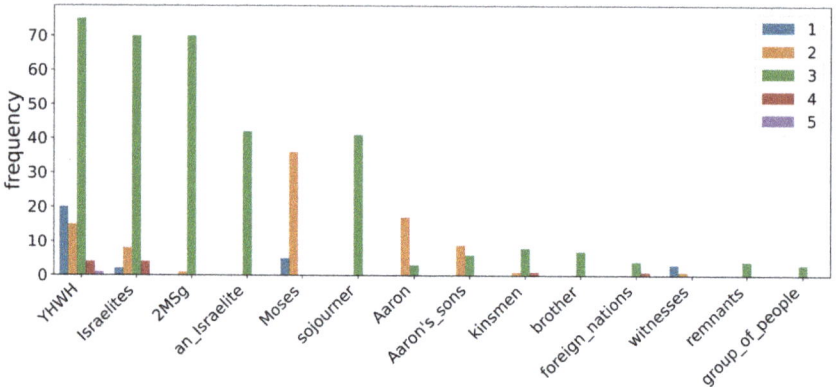

As shown in Figure 15, there are five discourse levels in Lev. 17–26.[17] On a more fundamental level, however, the structural hierarchy of a text is not limited to the embedding of speeches but

---

[17] The five discourse levels are as follows.

Level 1: 17.1; 18.1; 19.1; 20.1; 21.1a, 16, 24; 22.1, 17, 26; 23.1, 9, 23, 26, 33, 44; 24.1, 10–13, 23; 25.1; 26.46.

Level 2: 17.2ab, 8a, 12a; 18.2ab; 19.2ab; 20.2a; 21.1b–15c, 17ab; 22.2a–3a, 4a–16d, 18ab, 27a–33c; 23.2ab, 10ab, 24ab, 27a–32c, 34ab; 24.2a–9d, 14a–15b, 22; 25.2ab.

Level 3: 17.2cde, 8b–11f, 12b–14d; 18.2c–24c, 26a–27b, 28a–30e; 19.2c–37c; 20.2b–23c, 24e–26b, 27; 21.17c–23f; 22.3b–h, 18c–25d; 23.2c–8c, 10c–22f, 24c–25b, 34c–43d; 24.15c–21d; 25.2c–20a, 21–55; 26.1a–13c, 14–45.

Level 4: 17.3–7, 14e–16c; 18.25, 27c; 20.23d–24a, 26cd; 25.20bcd; 26.13de.

Level 5: 20.24bcd.

applies to all sorts of interaction. Indeed, one sentence in a text is structurally conditioned by another sentence. In a narrative, for instance, one event is conditioned by the preceding event, and the narrative is thus formed by a series of successive and conditional events. In the case laws of Lev. 17–26, the apodosis is conditioned by the protasis, for instance, the sentence "If the people of the land should hide their eyes from this man" conditions "I will put my face upon that man and his clan" (Lev. 20.4–5).[18] This information is stored as the 'mother' feature in the ETCBC database of the Hebrew Bible. If this feature is retrieved and mapped onto the SNA-model of the text, 39 levels appear. If one event conditions another one, it is reasonable to consider the *actor* of the former event to condition the latter event, including the participants participating in the latter event. We can represent this conditional relationship as a directional edge going from the actor of the former event to the participants involved in the conditioned event. For example, insofar as *YHWH's* speech in 18.2ab conditions *Moses'* speech in 18.2c, an edge can be drawn from *YHWH* to *Moses* to represent the conditional relationship between the two participants. Put differently, *Moses* is embedded in *YHWH's* domain, and *YHWH's* 'domain ownership' can be represented as a directional edge from *YHWH* to *Moses*. If such edges are drawn from all controlling actors in the network to all their respective conditioned participants, another type of network emerges, representing the syntactic structure as a network. In this

---

[18] To be sure, a clause need not be conditioned by the immediately preceding clause, because two clauses may both depend on the same higher-level clause.

network, the nodes are still participants, but the edges are not interactions but direction of embeddedness. The syntactic hierarchy thus establishes a third dimension to the network of Lev. 17–26 and can be represented as a network on its own (Figure 16).

Figure 16: A multiple, directed network of domain ownership/control. Node size corresponds to outdegree.

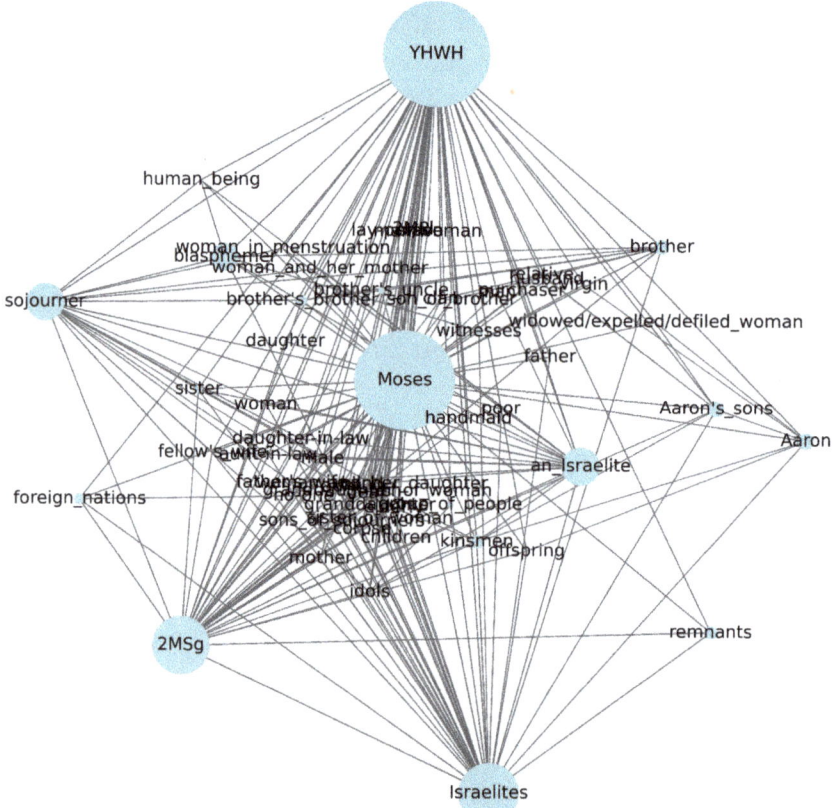

Compared to the regular social network of Leviticus (Figure 11), the main participants still dominate the network. The centrality of *Moses*, however, is significantly increased, as illustrated by the size of his node. He has the second highest outdegree (826) in the entire 'control network', that is, he conditions or controls the interactions of 826 participants.[19] The high outdegree values are also reflected in the centrality measures displayed in Figure 17. Put differently, *Moses* and YHWH dominate the network because they control most of the interactions. This observation will be considered along with the general discussion of *Moses'* role in the network (§5.2.1). Other main participants follow, e.g., the *Israelites*, *2MSg*, *an Israelite*, and the *sojourner*. Interestingly, the *blasphemer* appears among the top scorers, despite his less than central role in the regular network (see §5.2.3). YHWH also dominates the indegree scores, presumably because he not only instigates the speeches but also has *Moses* referring to him within the speeches. In other words, YHWH is embedded in his own speeches, a phenomenon already discussed in chapter 3, §3.6.

Figure 17: Centrality measures of the control network

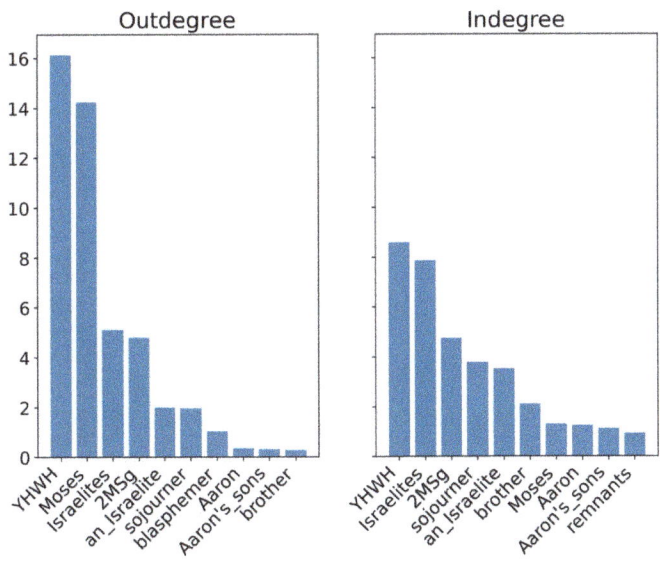

---

[19] The number does not correspond to 826 unique participants, but to 826 participant references in the interactions controlled by *Moses*.

## 4.0. Role Assignment

Complex networks are hard to pin down, because the edges of the network may be directed and weighted. In the Holiness Code network, the edges represent various different types of interaction, which further complicates the analysis. This complication, however, is partly mitigated by conceptualising the edges as degrees of agency rather than diverse events. A crucial objective of network analysis is to reduce the complexity of the network in order to capture and visualise the most important features. An abundance of methods for network reduction have been proposed and need not be summarised here (Borgatti et al. 2018; Brandes and Erlebach 2005). The goal of network analysis is the classification of nodes according to their structural position in the network (Lerner 2005). Some nodes are peripheral, others central, and yet others may be 'bridges' and connect otherwise unconnected communities of nodes. Node classification first arose in sociology, where the structural roles of nodes were used to explain their social functions. More recently, the emergence of big data and graph theory has led to new explorations into node classification and role discovery, and network analysis has become subject to highly advanced mathematical scrutiny (see Rossi and Ahmed 2015).

An abundance of methods has been developed to detect the network roles of nodes. The wealth of methods also reflects the increasing interdisciplinary interest in graphs and networks, which means that traditional, small-scale sociological models now exist alongside highly advanced computational algorithms for role detection in huge networks. Nevertheless, the methods can be divided into roughly three groups (Rossi and Ahmed 2015): 1) graph-based; 2) feature-based; and 3) hybrid approaches. Firstly, graph-based role detection has been the most common approach among sociologists and aims to detect roles directly from the representation of the graph. Secondly, feature-based approaches have become increasingly popular with the rise of computational methods. These methods basically involve two steps: 1) transformation of the graph into vectors, each node being described as a vector; and 2) statistical analysis of the vectors for role detection. Thus, in contrast to graph-based methods, feature-based methods only compute roles indirectly from the graph. Thirdly, hybrid approaches combine graph-based and feature-based approaches. In what follows, I shall try out two role detection methods on the H network. The first of these is a graph-based method called structural equivalence. The second method is a feature-based algorithm called node2vec.

The purpose of this section is not to introduce the applied methods in detail, as this has been done elsewhere. The selected methods will only be introduced in general terms, and the main focus of this section will be on their implications for understanding the participants of H.

## 4.1. Graph-Based Role Discovery

A social network essentially consists of a group of participants connected by various ties. Intuitively, some of the participants appear more similar than others because they have similar roles in the network. In networks of families, for instance, some of the participants are parents while others are children. In order to identify participants with similar roles, social network analysts have developed a range of statistical tools. One of these tools is derived from what is called structural equivalence (Lorrain and White 1971).[20] In simple terms, two participants can be said to be structurally equivalent if they have exactly the same ties with exactly the same third-parties. The two participants need not be connected themselves. Sociologists have noted that structurally equivalent participants tend to show a certain amount of homogeneity. As Stephen P. Borgatti, Martin G. Everett, and Jeffrey C. Johnson (2018, 240) explain, "one mechanism underlying the relationship between structural equivalence and homogeneity is the idea that persons adapt to their social environments, and therefore actors with similar social environments will tend to have certain similarities." Now, structural equivalence is a mathematical ideal, clearly defined in theory but a rare phenomenon in real data. In the real world, people rarely have exactly the same relationships, even if they have the same formal roles, e.g., teacher or father. In practice, then, if one wants to examine the social networks of teachers, for example, it is more useful to look for structural *similarities* rather than complete equivalence. The concept of structural equivalence has therefore been relaxed in order to cope with real data. Nevertheless, in order to identify similar participants, structural equivalence provides a strong theoretical framework. Essentially, all participants are compared on the basis of their ties to one another. Two structurally equivalent participants would be two participants that have the same ties to

---

[20] For a recent explanation of structural equivalence and applied methods, see Borgatti et al. (2018, 240–53).

the same third parties. Two structurally *similar* participants, on the other hand, would be two participants with a low degree of internal variation. Thus, statistical methods can be applied to cluster participants on the basis of similarity. This type of analysis is frequently conducted with hierarchical clustering, such as the dendrogram in Figure 18.[21] Accordingly, all participants in the H network are grouped into a hierarchy of clusters.

Figure 18: A dendrogram of the participants in Lev 17–26. The clustering is computed with the Ward algorithm.

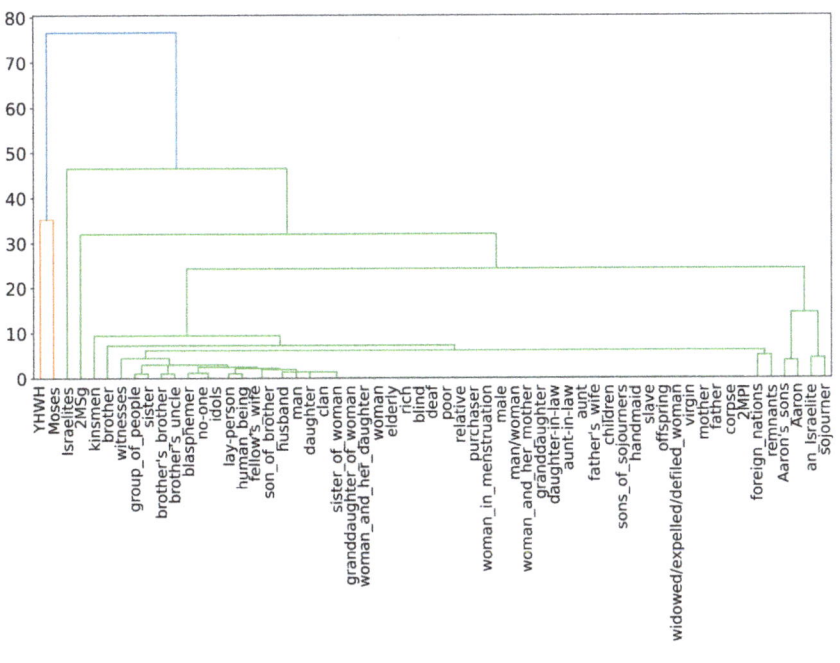

[21] In this analysis, the H network is considered a network with multiple, directed ties, i.e., the ties between the participants are weighted on the basis of frequency. The values of the ties (e.g., event type or degree of agency), however, are not taken into account. The clustering itself is computed with the 'Ward' algorithm.

Two major clusters appear: one consisting of YHWH and *Moses*, the other consisting of all remaining participants. The YHWH-*Moses* cluster is not strongly cohesive, as it exhibits large internal variation. However, they are still more similar to each other than to the rest of the participants. The largest cluster is dominated by a great number of infrequent participants, e.g., the *poor*, the *blind*, the *deaf*, etc. Many of these participants occur only once, so they are statistically insignificant. Some of these may be structurally equivalent because they have one third party that happens to be the same. The right side of the dendrogram is more interesting. Firstly, *Aaron* forms a cluster with *Aaron's sons*. This observation is interesting because both participants are priests; hence, there appears to be an integrated group of priests with similar roles. Secondly, *an Israelite* and the *sojourner* form another cluster. This observation is curious, because we might expect the two parties to be in opposition. However, this clustering procedure does not take into account the nature of the ties, only the fact that they are tied to the same third parties. Thirdly, a similar relationship is found between the *foreign nations* and the *remnants*, both of which appear in the same context in Lev. 26. Due to the complex relationships among the participants (i.e., multiple, directed, and valued ties), it is highly complicated to compare all relationships at once. In the dendrogram above, then, the cluster analysis was carried out on a network of multiple, directed ties, ignoring the values (i.e., the agency scores) of the ties. It is also possible to explore structural similarity with respect to the mean agency score of each relationship in the social network (see the semantic hierarchy of semantic roles and corresponding agency scores in chapter 6, §6.0).²² In this way, the semantic roles derived in chapter 6 now represent the interactions among the participants; hence, the semantic roles—along with the structural properties of the graph—now serve to yield the network roles of the graph. The resulting structural similarity is plotted in Figure 19 using multidimensional scaling (MDS), a dimension reduction method for high-dimensional data.

Figure 19: MDS of the H-network (edges conceptualised as agency scores)

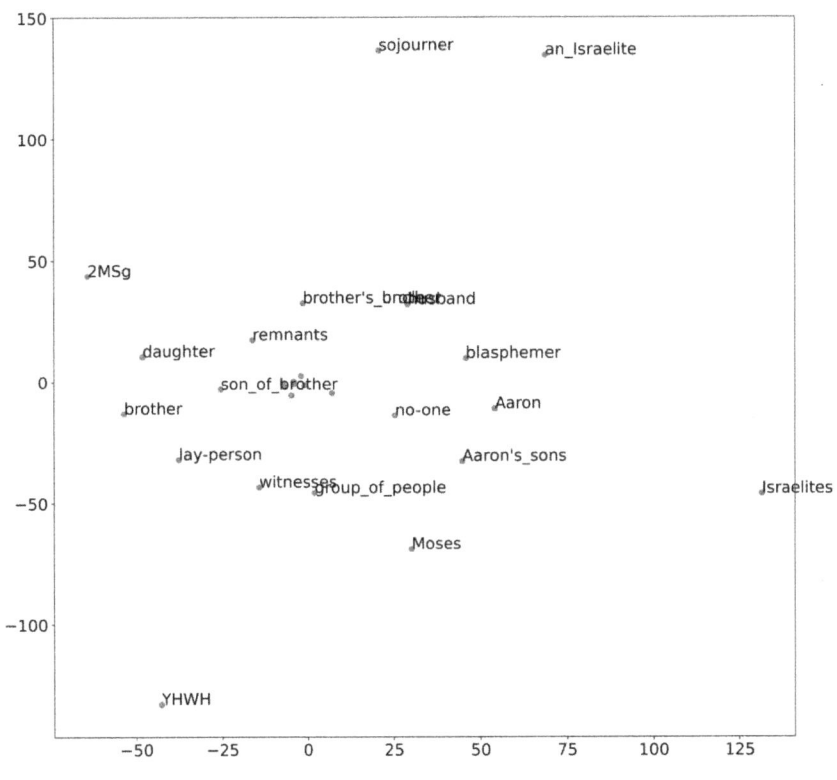

²² Unlike in chapter 6, §6.0, where the mean agency referred to the mean of all interactions pertaining to a particular participant, the mean

The graph shows the two dimensions accounting for the most variation in the data. In the graph, accordingly, participants situated close together are structurally similar, in contrast to participants that are situated far away from one another. In the centre of the plot is a large group of infrequent participants. Their labels have been removed for convenience. Participants exhibiting more variation are situated further from the centre of the plot. At the extremes of the plot, therefore, are those participants who are highly distinctive in the network. As we dive into the details of the plot, interesting features become apparent. To begin with, most of the major participants of the network are isolated, in particular the *Israelites* and *YHWH*, who lie towards the extremes of the plot. However, as with the dendrogram above, *an Israelite* and the *sojourner* occur more closely together. They are thus structurally similar as regards the frequency of ties to the same third parties, as well as the agency scores invested in those shared ties. In this plot, *Aaron* and *Aaron's sons* are also situated relatively close to each other. Thus, apart from their sharing many third parties, the agency invested in these interactions is similar. Finally, the *brother's brother* and the *brother's uncle* have a complete overlap. This observation is not unexpected, since these participants occur in the same context and involve the same third party, the *brother*.

As can be inferred from the dendrogram and the MDS two-dimensional plot, participants that are structurally similar are not

---

agency score refers here to the mean of the concrete interactions between pairs of participants with respect to the social network (see the computation of combined agency scores in §3.1).

only similar but also proximate (see Borgatti and Everett 1992). That is, in order to be structurally similar, the participants need to be proximate in the network, because they need to tie in with the same third parties. In some social networks, proximity is indeed an important factor. For instance, in a contagion network, proximate persons are more prone to the same infections, because they are exposed to the same persons. However, in other networks, proximity is irrelevant. A teacher has the role of a teacher irrespective of whether he/she is related to the same students as other teachers. In other words, two participants have the same role (e.g., teacher, mother, etc.) because they have a *similar* relationship with participants with *similar* roles (e.g., pupil, child, etc.). This notion of similarity implies an abstraction from structural equivalence, because the specific position in the network is no longer important. Two participants may be similar, even if they are not neighbours or second-degree neighbours in the network. There have been several strategies for abstracting from structural equivalence, e.g., regular equivalence, where two nodes are considered structurally equivalent if they are connected to the same class of nodes (Borgatti and Everett 1993; see also White and Reitz 1983; Audenaert et al. 2018). Recently, the methods for abstract role partitioning have exploded, largely thanks to the rise of computer technology and the overwhelming interest in graphs and networks in a variety of research areas, including computer science. Thus, rather than detecting the roles of nodes directly from the graph (i.e., graph-based methods), it has become much more common to transform the graph into vectors by means of which the structural features of the graph can be coupled with a large variety of other features (i.e., feature-based methods). One of the recent algorithms for transforming graphs into vectors is called node2vec and will be the focus of the next section.

## 4.2. Feature-Based Role Discovery

With the rise of computational methods, new approaches are constantly being developed for classifying node roles and reducing the complexity of graphs. Many of these new approaches fall under the category of feature-based role discovery.[23] Unlike graph-based role equivalence, which is based on the derivation of node properties directly from the graph, feature-based role discovery involves the transformation of the graph into a feature representation to be analysed. More specifically, each node in the graph is transformed into a vector, and nodes with similar vectors are ascribed the same role. In general terms, the approach has two steps: 1) computation of feature vectors on the basis of user-defined criteria; and 2) assignment of roles according to the computed features. The advantage of transforming a graph into a set of vectors is that any node, irrespective of how well it is embedded in the network, is represented in the same shape, and vectors are therefore a well-suited input for machine-learning algorithms. A feature-based approach allows for the consideration of a diversity of data, as the input data are not restricted to the structural properties of the graph, but may also include node val-

---

[23] For an overview of feature-based approaches, see Rossi and Ahmed (2015).

ues (e.g., attributes of neighbour nodes), edge features (e.g., attributes of the walk from the target node to the neighbour nodes), and non-relational features (attributes not dependent on the relations of the target node; Rossi and Ahmed 2015).[24] One of the most recent tools for capturing graph features is node2vec, developed by Aditya Grover and Jure Leskovec (2016). In technical terms, it is "a semi-supervised algorithm for scalable feature learning in networks" (Grover and Leskovec 2016, 856). In less technical terms, the method aims to balance two different concepts of role similarity. The first concept concerns homophily, that is, two nodes are considered similar if they belong to the same community within the larger network. As for the second concept, two nodes are considered similar if they have the same structural role, irrespective of their community. Thus, people from different communities can have the same role within their respective structural neighbourhoods (e.g., different teachers largely have the same role, although they have different pupils). This notion of structural role similarity resembles that of regular equivalence mentioned above. Since real-world networks commonly exhibit both types of equivalence, a realistic representation of node equivalence should take both perspectives into account (Grover and Leskovec 2016). As the name suggests,

---

[24] Here, 'neighbour' is not restricted to the immediate neighbours of the target node. The neighbours may be nodes within a certain distance from the target node. One could even rank the neighbours, so that the features of more adjacent neighbours are given greater weight than those of more distant neighbours.

node2vec is an algorithm designed to transform a graph into numerical vectors, each vector representing the features of a node.[25] The features of the H network relevant for the algorithm include the direction of ties, the number of ties, and the agency values. Having been transformed into vectors, the nodes can now be compared by means of traditional statistical methods, including hierarchical clustering, k-means clustering, and MDS. A two-dimensional projection was computed with MDS, as shown in Figure 20.

---

[25] What sets node2vec apart from most other node-to-vector transformation algorithms is its search strategy. Node2vec is a further development of DeepWalk, which was developed to learn the features of a network by performing a series of short random walks through the graph (Perozzi et al. 2014). A random walk is a walk from one node to another following a random path of edges (Brandes and Erlebach 2005, 14–15). Node2vec is a further development produced by applying two additional parameters to be adjusted by the user. The two parameters ($p$ and $q$) control how fast the random walk explores and leaves the neighbourhood of the target node, hence a semi-supervised algorithm. The two parameters seek to balance two different notions of equivalence (homophily vs connectivity-independent structural roles), e.g., if $q > 1$, the random walk is biased towards exploring the immediate neighbourhood of the target node and thus towards similarity in terms of homophily. In short, the different notions of equivalence can be prioritised by adjusting the parameters. For the present purposes, the connection-independent structural roles have been prioritised. The random-walk algorithm was set to walk length $= 4$, $p = 1$, $q = 1$, and dimensions $= 16$. 150 walks were conducted. The parameters have been set according to the comprehensive analysis of the algorithm by Hermansen et al. (2017).

7. *Participants in Social Networks* 313

Figure 20: Structural role similarity based on feature vectors learned by node2vec

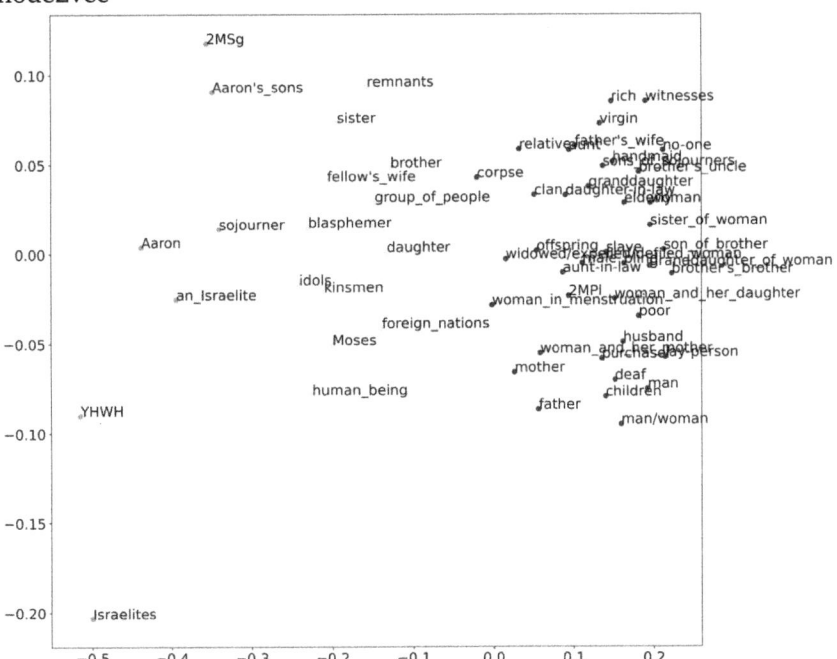

Three groups of structurally similar nodes appear, here coloured according to a k-means clustering of the vectors. One cluster includes peripheral participants (purple), the members of which are most often participants that are undergoers of events. That the participants are peripheral does not necessarily mean that they are socially marginalised, since the *rich* is included in this group. However, most participants may be considered vulnerable, e.g., a woman during her menstruation. Another cluster is formed by the most recurrent participants, namely *YHWH*, *2MSg*, the *Israelites*, *an Israelite*, the *sojourner*, *Aaron*, and *Aaron's sons* (green). As shown in the figure, these participants are more dispersed than the participants in the purple group, testifying to greater diversity among these participants. Nevertheless, the members of this group are characterised by having a core role in the network, that is, they are highly connected with one another as well as with less connected nodes. The last group (yellow) is less easy to characterise. The members of this group include *Moses*, the *blasphemer*, the *daughter*, the *brother*, and the *fellow's wife*, among others. They are less frequent than the core participants, but generally more frequent than the peripheral participants. What characterises this group is the participants' relatively frequent interactions with core participants. They are both recipients and transmitters of events and are therefore more embedded in the network than are the peripheral members. Some of these participants function as bridges between core participants and peripheral participants, e.g., the *brother*, who interacts with several core participants, including the *Israelites*, *2MSg*, *an Israelite*, and the *sojourner*, as well as peripheral participants, such as the *brother's uncle*, *brother's brother*, and *clan* (see Figure 21).

Figure 21: Ego-network of the *brother*

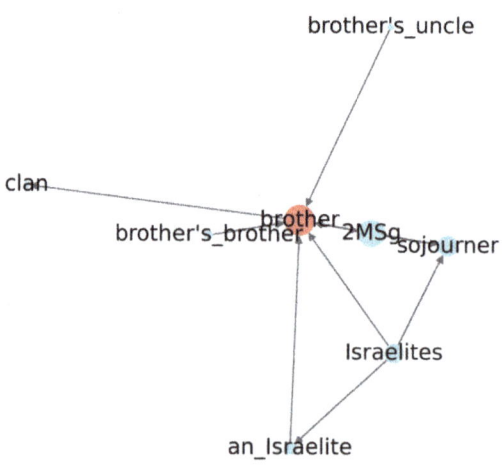

## 5.0. Law-Text Roles

Identification of clusters of participants helps to delineate the complex social network of the Holiness Code. But a structural analysis does not explain *why* the participants occur in these specific positions and *how* these structural positions relate—if they do—to the ethical values and expectations underlying these ancient prescriptions of right behaviour. These questions will need to be addressed by scrutinising individual participants according to their structural positions in the network, their concrete interactions, and the degree of agency invested in the events. Not all 59 participants of the Holiness Code-network will be explored. Instead, informed by the cluster analyses conducted above, important representatives from each group will be investigated.

## 5.1. Core Participants

There are seven core participants in the network. They are the main literary characters and the most frequently attested participants of Lev. 17–26. The group includes Y*HWH*, the *Israelites*, *2MSg, an Israelite*, the *sojourner*, *Aaron*, and *Aaron's sons*. The distinction between the *Israelites* (2nd Pl), *2MSg* (2nd Sg), and *an Israelite* (3rd Sg) is somewhat arbitrary, since there is a considerable semantic overlap between those participants. However, although they all refer to the people of Israel or members of the Israelite community, each of them may reflect a certain perspective on how the laws relate to different segments of the group. In fact, if Joosten (1996; 1997) is right, the distinction between 'you' in the plural (= the *Israelites*) and 'you' in the singular (= *2MSg*) bears on a crucial rhetorical thrust. This hypothesis will be tested by projecting each of the participants as individual nodes in the network.

In what follows, all core participants will be discussed with respect to their roles in the network and how their roles relate to the intention ('expectations', see §2.4) of the law and the ethical obligations associated with the participants.

### 5.1.1. Yhwh

The most important participant in the Leviticus network is Yhwh. This claim can be demonstrated by a so-called 'elimination test' (see Che 2017). An elimination test measures the density of a network that results when one of the participants is removed. Density is a measure of the cohesion of the network (see §3.2). Therefore, if the network becomes less dense as a result of removing a certain participant, this participant is important for the cohesion of the network. If that participant were missing, the network might become fragmented. On the other hand, if the resulting network becomes denser, the participant under consideration is peripheral and not structurally important. Here, elimination tests are applied to the entire network or a subset of the network (i.e., the ego-networks of particular participants), and the density of the network is computed while excluding one participant at a time. In the end, the participants can be compared with respect to who causes the highest loss or gain of density. The result of the elimination test carried out on the entire H network is shown in Figure 22, where the participants are ordered according to their effect on the network density.

Figure 22: Elimination test of the H network. Only the 15 most important participants with respect to density are shown. The dashed line represents the original density of the network.

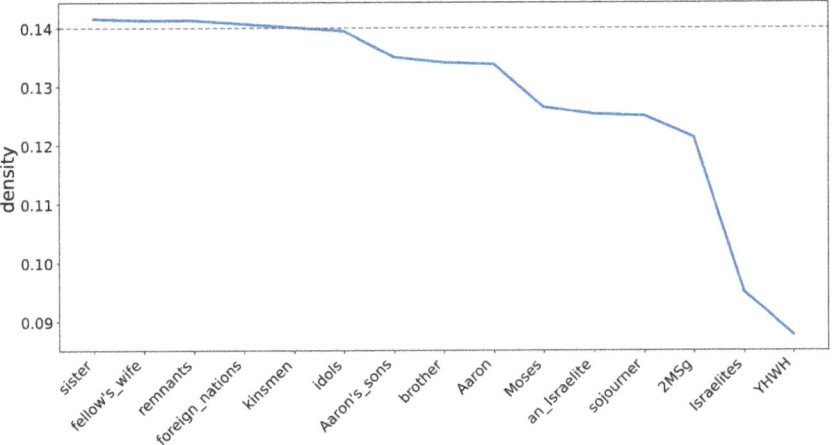

As shown in the elimination test, YHWH is the most important participant. If he were removed from the network, the resulting density would be smaller than it would be if any one of the other participants were removed. YHWH is also the participant involved in most interactions (degree = 191), although he is not related to the most participants. While YHWH is connected to 15 participants, the sojourner and the three different configurations of the Israelites (i.e., the *Israelites*, *2MSg*, and *an Israelite*) are all connected to more participants.[26] Thus, the network is hierarchical insofar as the most important participant, YHWH, is only the fifth-most connected participant. By implication, most participants of the network only have an indirect connection to YHWH. A closer look at the participants interacting with YHWH reveals that he

---

[26] *2MSg* has 27 different connections, while the *Israelites* have 26, *an Israelite* 21, and the *sojourner* 19.

interacts with all other core participants, six intermediate participants (*Moses, kinsmen, foreign nations, remnants, blasphemer, group of people*) and three peripheral participants (*corpse, 2MPl, and lay person*). By contrast, *2MSg* is only connected to three other core participants, five intermediate participants, and 19 peripheral participants. In fact, YHWH is the only participant who is connected to all other core participants. For this reason, it is safe to conclude that the divine speaker is in fact the most important figure in terms of network cohesion. At another level, moreover, YHWH is even more significant. If the syntactic structure of the text is taken into account, YHWH is by far the most important participant, because almost all recorded interactions in Lev. 17–26 are the products of the divine speeches. This dimension will be unfolded below (§5.2.1).

Figure 23: Mean agency invested by YHWH in all his interactions. The black bars show the confidence intervals (95%).

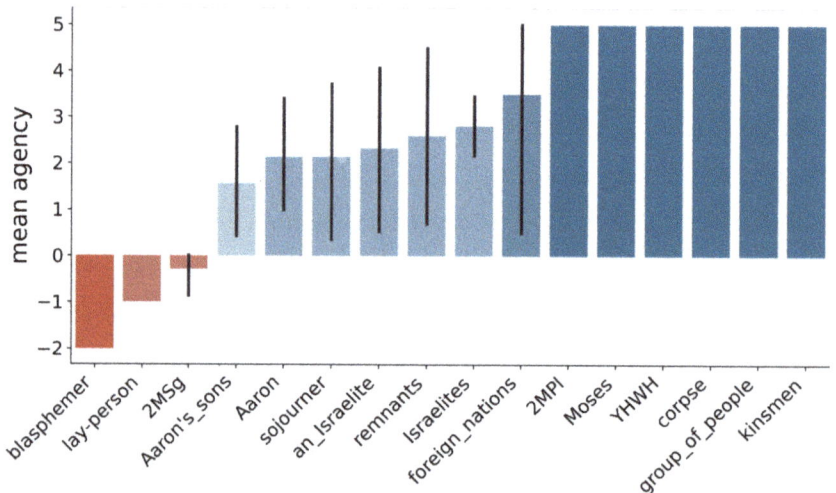

YHWH fulfils a variety of roles in his interactions. Figure 23 shows the mean agency scores invested by YHWH in all his relationships.

To begin with, YHWH is a Patient or a Volitional Undergoer in his interactions with the *blasphemer*, the *lay person*, and *2MSg*. The *blasphemer* curses YHWH (24.11), which makes YHWH the Patient of the interaction (-2 in agency), and this interaction is never directly returned. The *blasphemer* is punished but not directly so by YHWH. Other participants are directly punished by YHWH, resulting in high agency scores for YHWH. These participants include a *group of people* (20.5), the *sojourner* (17.10; 20.3, 5, 6), and *an Israelite* (17.10; 20.3, 5, 6; 23.30). YHWH's one interaction with the *lay person* results in a negative agency score, because YHWH is portrayed as the recipient of a sacrifice (22.21). By contrast, the interactions with *2MSg* are more diverse, since YHWH is sometimes depicted as a participant under threat of defilement (18.21; 19.12) and sometimes as someone to be feared (19.14, 32; 25.17, 36, 43). Interestingly, no interaction between YHWH and *2MSg* is recorded where YHWH is the actor. By contrast, the relationship between YHWH and the *Israelites* (the collective reference to the people) is more varied. In most cases, YHWH is the recipient or beneficiary of an event, mostly sacrifices.[27] However, YHWH is also someone to be listened to (26.14, 18, 21, 27) and to be considered holy in the midst of the *Israelites* (22.32). Therefore, the *Israelites* are not to "walk in opposition" (i.e., be resistant or stubborn) to YHWH (26.21, 23, 27), nor to defile his name (22.32), e.g., by abusing his name in a false oath (19.12). Rather, they have to let themselves be admonished by YHWH (26.23), so that

---

[27] 17.5; 19.5; 22.2, 3, 15, 22 (×2), 24, 29; 23.8, 16, 25, 27, 36 (×2), 37, 38, 40.

he will not abhor them (26.11, 30). Y*HWH* is also frequently recorded as the actor in his interactions with the *Israelites*. On the positive side, he is portrayed as the God who made the *Israelites* go out of Egypt (19.36; 22.33; 23.43; 25.38, 42, 55; 26.13) and made them live in booths in the wilderness (23.43). He also removed the previous inhabitants of the promised land (18.24; 20.23) to let the *Israelites* inhabit the land (18.3; 20.22, 24; 23.10; 25.2, 38). He will bless the people (25.21), e.g., by making them fertile (26.9), and he will establish a covenant with them (26.9), place his sanctuary in their midst (26.11) and walk among them (26.12). The latter expression is likely an allusion to God's presence with Adam and Eve in the garden of Eden (Harper 2018, 194–95). He sanctifies the *Israelites* (20.8; 22.32) and provides blood for atonement (17.11). Just as he separated the people from the surrounding foreign nations (20.24, 26), he has separated clean animals from unclean for the benefit of the people (20.25). A few times Y*HWH* is also recorded as speaking directly to the *Israelites* (17.12, 14; 20.24). On the negative side, Y*HWH* responds to the unfaithfulness of the people by punishing them (26.16, 21, 24), in particular by sending wild animals (26.22), famine (26.26), sword (26.25, 33), and plague (26.25). He admonishes the *Israelites* (26.18, 28) and walks in opposition to them (26.24, 28) as they do to him. Finally, he even threatens to scatter the people among those nations from which they were separated (26.33). The conflict between the *Israelites* and Y*HWH* is carried on by the *remnants* of the people who eventually confess their sins and humble their hearts (26.40–41).

The connection between YHWH and Moses is simple, because the only type of interaction recorded is the recurrent speech by YHWH to Moses. As will be demonstrated below, this type of interaction leaves Moses in a quite distinct intermediary role (see §5.2.1). The relationship between YHWH and the *sojourner* will also be discussed later. The priests, *Aaron* and *Aaron's sons*, are connected to YHWH primarily by means of the sacrifices of which YHWH is the recipient (22.22 [×2], 24, 29; 23.11, 20).[28] Moreover, the priests are prohibited from defiling the name of YHWH (21.6; 22.2, 32). YHWH, on the other hand, is portrayed as sanctifying the priests (21.15, 23; 22.9, 16, 32), but he also threatens the offspring of the priests with being 'cut off' (נִכְרְתָה N) if they mistreat the sacrifices of the people (22.3). Finally, the priests are included in the large group of people brought out of Egypt by YHWH (22.33).

In sum, YHWH is the central-most participant insofar as he is the participant involved in most interactions and the only participant connected to all other core participants. He is not the participant connected with most participants, but he performs a large variety of roles in those interactions in which he is involved. He is frequently depicted as a recipient of sacrifices but also once as a Patient of cursing. He is a speaker and a direct causer of extinction. The relationship with the *Israelites* is probably the most complex relationship in the whole network, because of the dynamics of blessings and curses unfolded in Lev. 26 in particular. This perspective will be explored further below.

---

[28] Other related cultic activities are the kindling of the golden lampstand and the arranging of the 12 breads (24.3, 8).

### 5.1.2. The People

H refers to the people of Israel in many ways. Apart from a few outsiders, including the *sojourner*, the *handmaid*, and the *foreign nations*, all participants are presumably part of the people. More specifically, the people is addressed in either the plural or the singular. It has been argued that the participant shifts between the plural and the singular are a rhetorical device (see chapter 3, §3.7). Although the participant shifts do not implicate a semantic difference, the different rhetorical aspects pertaining to each of the participant references are worth exploring in depth. Thus, the distinction is retained in the H network, where the two types of references are conceptualised as individual participants. It is the objective of the network analysis to explore whether the distinction bears on subtle differences in the characterisation and the roles of the participants. In particular, two aspects will be discussed. Firstly, is there any difference in terms of content and agency with respect to those relationships that are shared by the two participants? Secondly, what do the non-shared relationships imply for the characterisation of the two participants?

The *Israelites* and *2MSg* share 14 relationships, several of which are the result of a single verse (Lev. 18:6): "You (Pl) may not approach anyone near of kin." This expression functions as a summary statement of the following incestual laws in Lev. 18, and, as a result of the semantic hierarchy of the participants, all family members in this list of laws are subsumed under 'anyone near of kin' (see §3.9).²⁹ Consequently, the interactions and the agency invested are the same with respect to this group of shared relationships, except for *father, mother,* and *brother*. The remaining shared participants are YHWH, the *idols*, *Aaron's sons*, the *sojourner*, and the *fellow's wife*. The *Israelites* and *2MSg* relate quite differently to YHWH, as described above, since the *Israelites* have a much more substantial and dynamic relationship with YHWH than does *2MSg*. This difference may explain the difference between the ways in which the two participants interact with the *idols*, a category that includes Moloch (18.21), goat-demons (17.7), and idols (19.4), as well as dead spirits and soothsayers (19.31). While *2MSg* is only prohibited from giving his son to Moloch (18.21), the *Israelites* are warned against sacrificing to the goat-demons, attending dead spirits and soothsayers, and casting idols. The latter practice, in particular, stands in a marked contrast to the right worship of YHWH (19.2–3). Therefore, because the relationship between the *Israelites* and YHWH is more substantial, the relationship with the idols is also more explicated in order to contrast true and false worship. The same context in Lev. 19 also includes the command to fear one's *father* and *mother* (Lev. 19.3). In this case, the law is directed to the *Israelites* as a group, the reason for which may be the context of right worship of YHWH. As for the interactions with *Aaron's sons*, the priests, the two participants differ slightly. While the *Israelites* are recorded as bringing sacrifices to the priests (Lev. 17.5; 23.10), *2MSg* is

---

²⁹ The shared family members include *mother, father, sister, brother, father's wife, daughter-in-law, aunt, aunt-in-law,* and *granddaughter*.

commanded to consider the priests holy (21.8), depending on how the reference is interpreted (see chapter 3, §3.5).

Figure 24: Mean agency invested by the *Israelites*

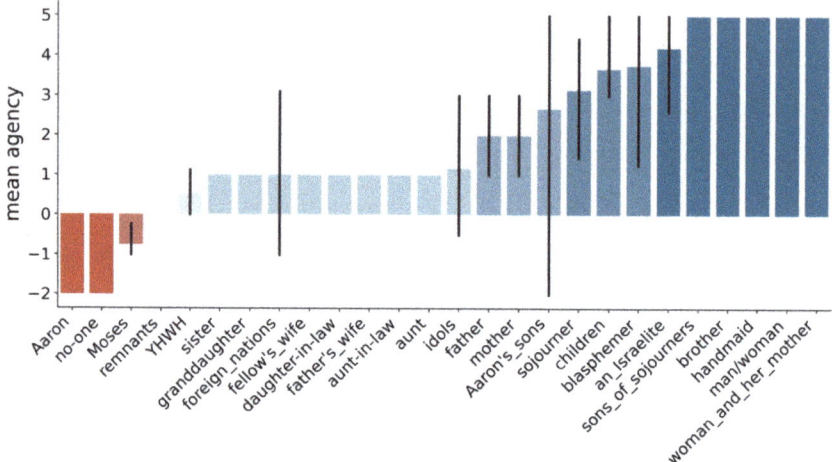

Figure 25: Mean agency invested by *2MSg*

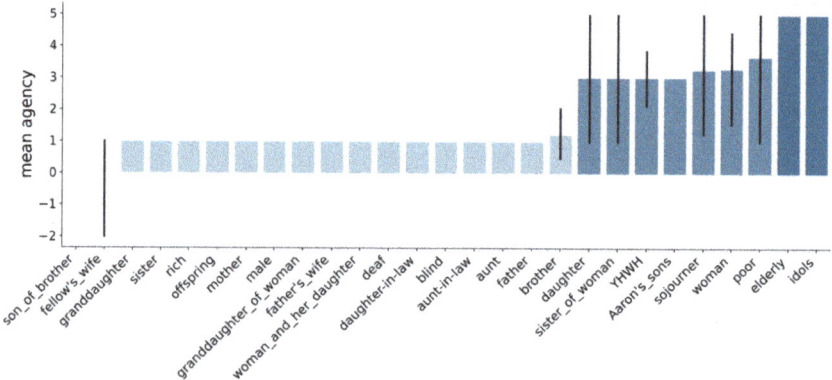

The mean agencies of the *Israelites* and *2MSg* in their interactions with the *sojourner* are similar, although both scores show internal variation, indicating diverse interactions. Interestingly, *2MSg* is consistently commanded to show love and compassion towards the *sojourner* (19.10, 34; 23.22), whereas the actions of the *Israelites* are more varied. While they may not oppress the *sojourner*

(19.33), they are nevertheless commanded to execute the death penalty for idolatry and blasphemy (20.2, 14; 24.16). Again, the difference can be explained in light of the relationship with YHWH. As a group, the *Israelites* have to take responsibility for the right worship of YHWH.

The *Israelites* and *2MSg* are related quite differently to the *brother*. While the *Israelites* have no interactions with the *brother* apart from a general description of a transaction between the two parties (25.14),[30] *2MSg* is repeatedly commanded to love and care for his *brother*, or fellow, and treat him with justice.[31] This difference supports Joosten's claim that exhortations to the individual concern individual relationships.

The *Israelites* and *2MSg* each have a number of unique relationships. There is a striking contrast between these relationships, since all of *2MSg*'s 13 unique relationships regard individual, unnamed members of the society, including family members.[32] The *Israelites* have 12 unique relationships, two of which resemble the individual, unnamed members of the society related to *2MSg*.[33] The *Israelites* are also related to concrete individuals,

---

[30] This single case of interaction between the *Israelites* and the *brother* may be due to the parallel structure of the verse, where two plural references envelop two singular suffixes (Jensen 2019).

[31] 19.13, 15, 16, 17 (×3), 18 (×2); 25.15, 35 (×2), 36 (×2), 37, 39, 43, 46.

[32] These relationships include the *deaf, blind, poor, rich, daughter, elderly, woman, son of brother, granddaughter of woman, sister of woman, woman and her daughter, offspring,* and *male*.

[33] The *woman and her mother* and *man/woman*.

namely, *Moses, Aaron,* and the *blasphemer,* whose mother is named (24.11). The only interaction with *Aaron* recorded, however, is in a context where *Aaron* and his offspring are warned not to eat the sacrifices of the *Israelites*, which would cause the *Israelites* to incur guilt (22.16). The relationship with *Moses* will be discussed below (§5.2.1). The connection with the *blasphemer* follows the pattern observed above, where the *Israelites* as a community are commanded to execute the death penalty for blasphemy.[34] The same kind of interaction pertains to the relationship with *an Israelite,* who must be executed as punishment for child sacrifice (20.2, 4, 14) or blasphemy (24.16).[35] Three of the *Israelites'* unique relationships regard relationships with outsiders, including the *foreign nations* (that is, foreigners from surrounding countries, as well as enemies), the *sons of sojourners,* and the *handmaid* of foreign descent. The relationship with foreign peoples is dynamic. On the one hand, the *Israelites* can buy *handmaids* from the *foreign nations* (25.44), as well as chattel slaves, labelled *sons of sojourners* (25.45, 46). Moreover, as part of the covenantal blessings given in Lev. 26, the *Israelites* are promised that they will be able to pursue and fight down their enemies from the surrounding nations (26.7, 8). On the other hand, if the *Israelites* fail to obey YHWH, the *foreign nations* will now pursue and fight down the *Israelites* (26.17, 25, 38). These interactions support the idea that the people are addressed as a

---

[34] The interactions are recorded in 24.14, 23 ($\times 2$).

[35] The punishment applies to *an Israelite* as well as the *sojourner* (see §§5.1.2–5.1.3).

group in cases of foreign affairs. Moreover, the dynamic relationship with the foreigners is placed in a context of curses and blessings as implications of the relationship between YHWH and the people.[36]

In sum, the network analysis largely supports and qualifies Joosten's thesis of a pragmatic distinction between community and individual in H. For one thing, the unique relationships of the *Israelites* are qualitatively different from those of *2MSg* in that they include relationships with concrete, named participants and non-domestic participants. On the other hand, both the *Israelites* and *2MSg* have relationships with the *father* and the *mother*, as well as other domestic participants. The most important difference is that the recorded interactions between the *Israelites* and YHWH are much more substantial than those between *2MSg* and YHWH. The individual Israelite (the *2MSg*) is to fear YHWH and be cautious not to defile his name, but the responsibility of right worship lies with the people as a whole. Thus, the individual ethical obligations are embedded in a collective identity, most importantly the collective covenantal relationship with YHWH. This

---

[36] The remaining unique relationships of the *Israelites* include the *children* (25.46; 26.29), the *remnants* of the *Israelites* (26.36, 39), and *no-one* (26.17). While the latter is hardly a participant at all, the *children* are the *Israelites*' *children* whom the *Israelites* are threatened with being forced to eat due to hunger because of their rebellion against YHWH. The relationship with the *remnants* is not interesting in terms of interaction, because the 'interaction' is only one of qualification.

identity has ramifications for the communal responsibility for adherence to the law and punishment of perpetrators, as well as for foreign affairs.

### 5.1.3. The *Sojourner*

Probably one of the most curious participants of the H network is the *sojourner*. Despite generally being considered a person on the margins of society, the sojourner appears prominently in the core of the network. Many laws apply equally to the *sojourner* as to the native *Israelite* (see 18.26; 24.22). However, the *sojourner* is never directly addressed, so it is not accurate to handle the *sojourner* and the *Israelites* alike. The *sojourner* is clearly not thought of as belonging to the plural 'you' (the collective *Israelites*), because the *sojourner* is described as residing 'in your midst' (Lev. 18.26).

The structural importance of the *sojourner* can be computed by conducting an elimination test of the *sojourner* and his ego-network. The result of the test is illustrated in Figure 26 below. It should be noted that the *Israelites* represent a merger of *Israelites, 2MSg,* and *an Israelite* in this part of the analysis, because it is less important to distinguish different notions of the native Israelites (e.g., plural and singular) than to distinguish the native Israelites and the *sojourner*. In the elimination test, therefore, the *sojourner* is found to be only the third most important participant within his ego-network. The *Israelites* and Y*HWH* are far more important, and the density of the network would drop drastically if they fell out. On the other hand, the *sojourner* is more important than the *brother*, among many other participants.

Figure 26: Elimination test of the *sojourner*'s ego-network

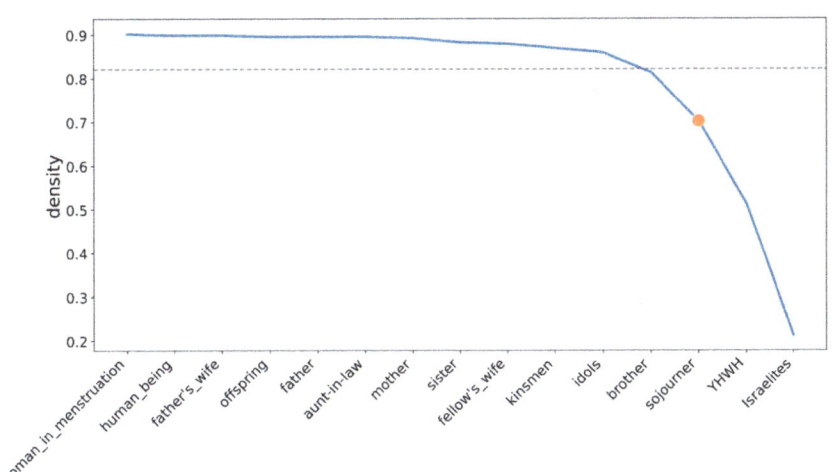

The *sojourner* and the *Israelites* are related to many of the same participants. In fact, all the *sojourner*'s connections are shared by the *Israelites*, and this fact explains why the density of the network only decreases slightly if the *sojourner* falls out. By contrast, the *Israelites* have ties that are not shared by the *sojourner*. Moreover, the internal relationship between the *sojourner* and the *Israelites* is markedly asymmetric. The *sojourner* is never the instigating participant in interactions with the *Israelites*. By contrast, the *Israelites* have many outgoing ties to the *sojourner*.[37] The ties are of very different kinds and include the command to leave remains from the harvest to the *sojourner* (Lev. 19.10; 23.22) and the prohibition against oppressing *sojourners* living among the *Israelites* (19.33). As a more general command, the *Israelites* are commanded to love the *sojourner* (19.34). However, if the *so-*

---

[37] 19.10, 33, 34; 20.2, 4 (×2), 14; 23.22; 24.16.

*journer* partakes in child sacrifices to Moloch (Lev. 20.2, 4), blasphemy (24.16), or incest (20.14), the *Israelites* are commanded to execute him.[38] The *sojourner* is not granted this legal right or duty, so we see here a marked difference between the legal rights of the *sojourner* and those of the *Israelites*. The asymmetry is supported by the mean agency scores illustrated in Figure 27. In his interactions with the *Israelites*, the *sojourner* is generally the undergoer.

Figure 27: Mean agency invested by the *sojourner*. The *women* comprise all female participants in the network.

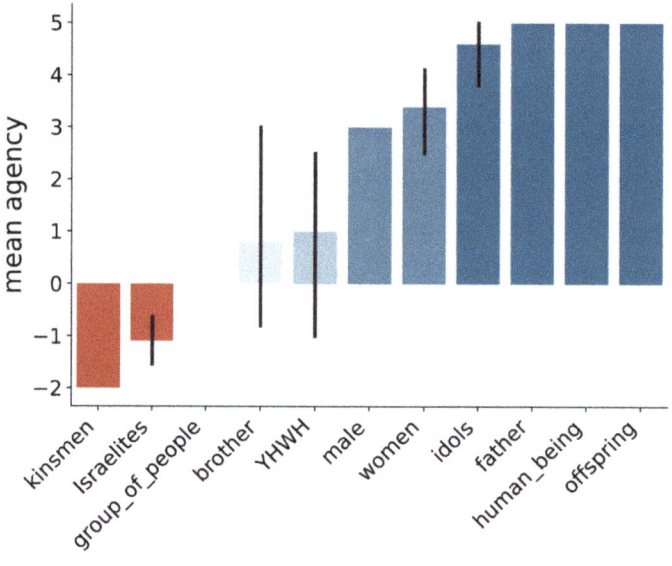

---

[38] Strictly speaking, it is not the plural addressees who must execute capital punishment (20.2, 4), but the עַם הָאָרֶץ 'the people of the land'. The term 'the people of the land' has attracted attention, because it functions elsewhere as a technical term referring to an active political group in the history of the Judaic monarchy (Joosten 1996, 42). Within the context of Leviticus, it has been argued that the term refers to "the male populace at large" (Milgrom 2000, 1730) or ordinary citizens in

An SNA should not focus exclusively on the ego and its alters. Equally important—and often more informative—are the ties among the alters. For instance, if two alters were to become enemies, the enmity would affect the relationships between the ego and each of the two alters, because the ego would likely need to pick a side.

The two most important participants in the ego-network of the *sojourner* are the *Israelites* and Y*HWH*. A closer look at the ties between these two participants and the *sojourner* reveals that the *Israelites* have many more and more important ties with Y*HWH* than does the *sojourner*. The *sojourner* is portrayed similarly to the *Israelites* to the extent that he can offer sacrifices to Y*HWH* and that he can potentially defile or blaspheme the name of Y*HWH*.[39] However, the references to the *Israelites* offering sacrifices are much more numerous, partly because the *sojourner* is not mentioned in the speeches concerning the holy convocations (Lev. 23).[40] Therefore, although the *sojourner* can partake in the cult,

---

contrast to elders and judges; see Lev. 4.27 (Wenham 1979, 278; Hartley 1992, 333). The parallel between עַם הָאָרֶץ 'the people of the land' and הָעֵדָה 'the congregation' has been noted (Joosten 1996, 44). Thus, it is generally accepted that 'the people of land' is used non-technically in Leviticus as a way of referring to native Israelites as opposed to non-Israelite sojourners.

[39] 17.9; 20.3; 22.18; 24.15, 16. The *Israelites* have many more outgoing ties to Y*HWH*: 17.5, 9; 18.21; 19.5, 12 (×2), 14, 32; 20.3; 22.2, 3, 15, 18, 22 (×2), 24, 29, 32 (×2); 23.8, 16, 25, 27, 36 (×2), 37, 38, 40; 24.15, 16; 25.17, 36, 43; 26.11, 14, 18, 21 (×2), 23 (×2), 27 (×2), 30.

[40] In fact, it is explicitly stated that the אֶזְרָח 'native' is supposed to celebrate the Feast of Booths by living in booths for seven days (Lev.

his participation is presumably limited to common sacrifices. Moreover, only the *Israelites* are portrayed as being expected to listen to YHWH (26.14, 18, 21, 27) and to be admonished by him (26.23). The actions of YHWH towards the *Israelites*[41] are also more numerous than and qualitatively different from the actions of YHWH towards the *sojourner*. As for the relationship between YHWH and the *sojourner*, all actions instigated by YHWH concern punishment.[42] To be sure, YHWH does also threaten the *Israelites* with severe punishments for violating the divine laws.[43] But the overall image of the relationship between YHWH and the *Israelites* is one of greater complexity. On the one hand, YHWH intends to bless the *Israelites* for their faithfulness by commanding his agricultural blessings upon them (25.21) and by making them fruitful (26.9) and numerous (26.9). On the other hand, YHWH also threatens the *Israelites* with chastisement (26.18, 28) and curses, such as plague (26.25), wild animals (26.22), and exile (26.33), if they do not obey him. Thus, YHWH's punishments, despite their harshness, are more nuanced than mere annihilation. The *Israelites* are pictured as children who need to be disciplined. When

---

23.42). By implication, the sojourner is not supposed to participate in this feast.

[41] 17.10, 11, 12, 14; 18.3, 24; 19.36; 20.3, 5, 6, 8, 22, 23, 24 (×3), 25, 26; 22.32, 33; 23.10, 30, 43 (×2); 25.2, 21, 38 (×2), 42, 55; 26.9 (×3), 11, 12, 13 (×2), 16 (×2), 17, 18, 21, 22, 24 (×2), 25 (×2), 26, 28 (×2), 33 (×2), 46.

[42] 17.10; 20.3, 5, 6.

[43] 17.10; 20.3, 5, 6; 23.30; 26.16 (×2), 17, 18, 21, 22, 24 (×2), 25 (×2), 26, 28 (×2), 33 (×2).

comparing the *sojourner* and the *Israelites*, we should keep in mind that the sojourner is portrayed as an individual, while the *Israelites* sometimes refer to an individual (who can certainly be annihilated; see 17.10; 20.3, 5, 6) and sometimes to the people at large. It is the people at large which is said to be disciplined and not the individual Israelite. The composite picture of the relationship between YHWH and the *Israelites* is based on the covenant between these two parties. The *sojourner* is never said to have been freed from slavery in Egypt. By contrast, the *Israelites* are repeatedly reminded of their status as liberated slaves.[44] As liberated slaves, the *Israelites* are separated from the nations as a unique community (20.24, 26), and YHWH sanctifies the people and considers them his own (20.8; 22.32).

To sum up, then, the overall picture of the *sojourner* is somewhat complex. On the one hand, he is certainly more agentive than peripheral participants, such as the *women* (§5.3.1) of the text, and than the *brother* (§5.2.2). The *sojourner* has ethical obligations, can partake in certain ritual activities, and is threatened by divine punishment for violating the law. Given his interactions with both YHWH and the *Israelites*, the *sojourner* is situated safely in the core of the network. The role of the *sojourner* is most clearly seen in contrast with the relationship between YHWH and the *Israelites*, which is stronger and more complex. The *Israelites* have a deeper and more intimate relationship with YHWH, because it is rooted in a covenant. In this light, the *sojourner* serves to mark the boundary of the covenantal community.

---

[44] 19.36; 22.33; 23.43; 25.38, 42, 55; 26.13.

### 5.1.4. The Priests

The priestly class is formed by the high priest *Aaron* and his sons, labelled *Aaron's sons*. Although one might expect a book like Leviticus to emphasise the role of the priests (which is indeed the case in the first half of the book), in this part of the book, the priests play a less central role. Elimination tests show that both *Aaron* and *Aaron's sons* are only the fourth most important participants in their respective networks. With YHWH, the *Israelites*, or *Moses* removed, the networks become less cohesive than they do when any of the priestly participants is removed. In fact, the removal of *Aaron's sons* results in a *more* cohesive ego-network, a fact that demonstrates the less important structural role of this participant. If the two participants are combined in a node called *priests*, the structural importance of the priestly participants increases, as shown Figure 28.

Figure 28: Elimination test of the *priests* (comprising *Aaron* and *Aaron's sons*)

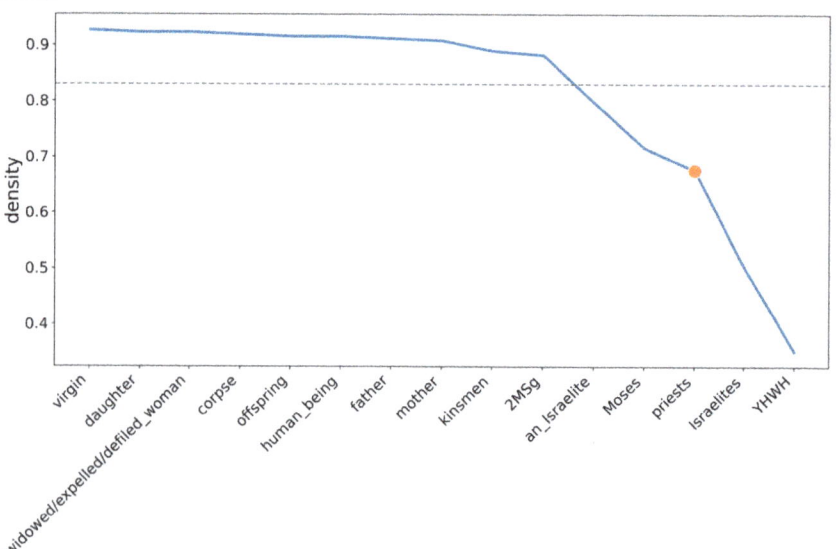

The *priests* interact with a range of participants, most frequently their relatives (*daughter, father, mother, offspring,* and *relative,* the latter of which is the virgin sister of a priest), and (non)potential wives (*widowed/expelled/defiled woman* and *virgin*). These and the remaining participants interacting with the *priests* are displayed in Figure 29, along with the mean agency invested by the *priests* in the interactions.

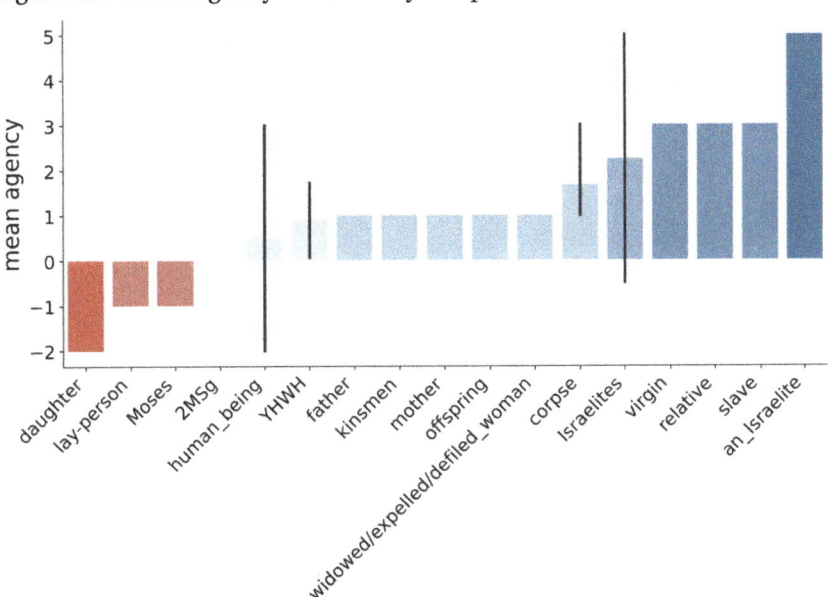

Figure 29: Mean agency invested by the *priests*

With regard to the *priests,* the major concern of the text is the threat of defilement. All interactions with family members and potential wives are fraught with the risk of defilement.[45] In this respect, the *priests* are set aside as a distinct group within the community, because they are not allowed to be as involved in

---

[45] The same concern regards the interactions with *corpses* and the *human being* (i.e., an unclean person; see 22.5).

daily-life activities as regular people. Moreover, there are serious constraints as to whom they can marry. The only kind of interaction recorded between *Moses* and the *priests* is the communication of divine revelation from *Moses* to the *priests*.[46] Interestingly, while the cult is therefore maintained by the *priests*, divine revelation is not mediated by the *priests* but by *Moses*.

The most substantial relationship between the *priests* and another participant is their relationship with YHWH. On the one hand, their interactions with YHWH demonstrate their unique privileges. They are sanctified by YHWH and are thereby set aside as a distinct group (21.15, 23; 22.9, 16, 32). The most prominent privileges include their role in the offering of sacrifices to YHWH (22.29; 23.11, 20),[47] as they are the recipients of the sacrifices offered by the *Israelites* (17.5; 23.10) and the *lay person* (22.14). In fact, they can cause the *Israelites* to incur guilt by mistreating the sacrifices (22.16). Moreover, they are in the crucial position of mediating atonement to *an Israelite* (19.22). However, in terms of frequency, other types of interactions are more significant. While the *priests* certainly have the role of handling sacrifices and providing atonement, most interactions recorded emphasise what is required of the *priests*. They are to be cautious not to defile the name of YHWH, e.g., by becoming impure through contact with a dead person, by shaving their beards, or by marrying a prostitute or a divorced woman (21.1–7). Moreover, by mistreating the sacrifices, they also defile YHWH's name (22.2, 32). The

---

[46] 17.2 (×2); 21.1 (×2), 17, 24; 22.2, 3, 18 (×2).

[47] In addition, *Aaron* is to arrange the golden lampstand and the 12 breads (24.3, 8).

punishment for defiling the name of YHWH is to be 'cut off' from the presence of YHWH (22.3).

In sum, the *priests* form a distinct class in the community. They are set aside by YHWH for cultic service and are responsible only to YHWH. Nevertheless, within this particular text, there is a marked limit to the domain of the *priests*, since YHWH never speaks directly to the *priests*, but only to *Moses*, who is outside the priestly class. It is therefore fair to conclude that the *priests* have a 'facilitator' role in that they facilitate the relationship between YHWH and the Israelite community, although that relationship does not originate with the *priests* but with YHWH himself in his exodus-intervention. This conclusion has implications for the ongoing debate on the authorship of Leviticus. Watts (2013, 98) has argued that Aaronide priests produced the book in order to legitimise their cultic monopoly. However, while the priests do facilitate the sacrifices of the Israelites and thereby have an important role, the main focus of the text (or Lev. 17–26 at least) is not on the prerogatives of the priests but on their responsibilities. It is not likely that a priestly class authored this legislation which lends so much significance to direct interaction between YHWH and the *Israelites* outside the cultic activities of the *priests*, and which attributes divine revelation solely to a person outside the priestly class, namely *Moses*.[48]

---

[48] This conclusion aligns with Gane's (2015, 219) argument that "the priestly role is part of a tightly controlled ritual system that makes it possible for holy YHWH to reside among and be accessible to his faulty and often impure people for their benefit without harming them." Thus, according to Gane (2015, 220–21), "There is no question that Leviticus

## 5.2. Intermediate Participants

12 participants belong to the cluster called 'intermediate participants'. These participants are not as embedded in the network as the core participants. Nevertheless, they do interact with both core participants and peripheral participants, so they obtain a kind of middle position in the network. The 12 participants are *Moses, kinsmen, blasphemer, foreign nations, remnants, group of people, human being, brother, idols, sister, fellow's wife,* and *daughter.* Some of the participants have rather simple roles, such as the *kinsmen*, which almost always represent the extended family from which a member is removed because of capital punishment.[49] Several participants may be 'cut off' from their *kinsmen*, which makes *kinsmen* a somewhat structurally connected entity. This explains why the *kinsmen* belong to the 'intermediate participants', although they are entirely inactive. Other participants have been discussed with regard to core participants, e.g., *foreign nations* and *remnants* (§§5.1.1–5.1.2). The three women of this

---

can be regarded as 'priestly' in the sense that much of its teaching concerns matters that involve priests. However, it is less certain that the author(s) belonged to the priestly profession, or at least primarily wrote in a priestly capacity. It is true that in Leviticus the priests are responsible for teaching laws to the other Israelites, but the priests receive these laws from Moses, whose reception of them from YHWH is what makes them authoritative (e.g., 10.11)."

[49] 17.4, 9, 10; 18.29; 19.8; 20.3, 5, 6, 18; 23.29, 30. The only exception is 21.15, where the *kinsmen* are the group of people to which the offspring of the high priest belongs and who are all defiled as a result of the high priest marrying a woman outside his own kin (see Milgrom 2000, 1820).

group will be discussed along with the peripheral women in the network (§5.3.1). Three participants will be discussed here, namely, *Moses*, the *brother*, and the *blasphemer*.

### 5.2.1. *Moses*

It may come as a surprise that *Moses* is not listed among the core participants of the network. After all, he is the mediator between YHWH and the *Israelites*, and he controls the divine revelation. Within the larger narrative of the Pentateuch, Moses is explicitly described as the covenantal 'broker' between YHWH and the people, e.g., in Exod. 20.19, where the people want Moses to mediate the covenant, so that they themselves can escape YHWH's direct speech (cf. Exod. 24.2; Deut. 5.25–27). In H, except for YHWH's command that *Moses* is to bring the *blasphemer* out of the camp for execution (Lev. 24.14), all *Moses*' actions are speeches. *Moses* speaks to the *Israelites*,[50] *Aaron*,[51] and *Aaron's sons*.[52] *Moses* is primarily the undergoer of YHWH's speeches.[53] However, he is also the central participant when the *witnesses* bring the *blasphemer* to him (24.11), and when the *Israelites* are to bring pure olive oil to him (24.2). To sum up, *Moses* has a central role in terms of

---

[50] 17.2 (×2), 8; 18.2 (×2); 19.2 (×2); 20.2; 21.24; 22.18 (×2); 23.2 (×2), 10 (×2), 24, 34, 44; 24.2, 15, 23; 25.2 (×2).

[51] 17.2 (×2); 21.17, 24; 22.2, 3, 18 (×2).

[52] 17.2 (×2); 21.1 (×2), 24; 22.2, 3, 18 (×2).

[53] 17.1; 18.1; 19.1; 20.1; 21.1, 16; 22.1, 17, 26; 23.1, 9, 23, 26, 33; 24.1, 13, 23; 25.1.

revelation, special legal cases, and in some cultic activities.⁵⁴ Important as these activities are, they are not enough to cast *Moses* as a main participant of the text with respect to a regular social network analysis. An elimination test of *Moses'* ego-network shows that *Moses* is only the third most important participant next to YHWH and the *Israelites* (Figure 30). Without *Moses*, the density would only be slightly smaller than in the original network.⁵⁵

Figure 30: Elimination test of *Moses'* ego-network

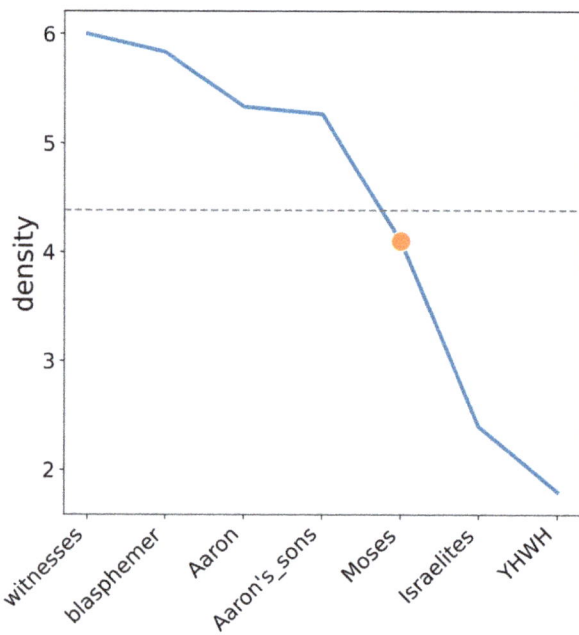

---

⁵⁴ Moses is also commanded to bake 12 loaves and put them on the table in the Sanctum. However, Aaron is to regularly arrange the table every sabbath, and the people is to deliver the bread, so Moses is apparently only involved at the time of the inauguration of the cult (see Milgrom 2001, 2095).

⁵⁵ The original density of *Moses'* ego-network is 4.38, whereas the removal of *Moses* results in a density of 4.10.

*Moses* has a slightly more important role than *Aaron* and *Aaron's sons* in this subset of the network, because *Moses* has more interactions with the *Israelites* and the *sojourner*, the latter not interacting with the priests at all. However, the *Israelites* and YHWH are much more important for the cohesion of the network than is *Moses*. For one thing, the *Israelites* and YHWH interact with many of the same participants as *Moses*, including the *blasphemer*, *Aaron*, and *Aaron's sons*. Secondly, while *Moses* is clearly a broker for revelation, the *Israelites* and YHWH interact in multiple other ways. Their relationship, being covenantal in nature, is multifaceted and involves both negative and positive interactions. On the positive side, the *Israelites* can offer sacrifices to YHWH without the mediation of *Moses*. Strictly speaking, the sacrifices are brought to the priests, who are the sacrificial mediators.[56] However, in many cases, YHWH is explicitly mentioned as the beneficiary or recipient of those sacrifices, so even delivering sacrifices to the cult may be viewed by the author as a direct interaction between the offeror and YHWH. While the facilitating role of the priests is implied and often fleshed out, in many cases the priests are simply omitted, e.g., "and you shall bring fire offerings to YHWH" (23.25).[57] The number of such cases suggests that the immediacy of the covenantal relationship between YHWH and the

---

[56] The priestly 'brokerage' role is emphasised in Lev. 22, where the priests are commanded to treat the sacrificial gifts of the Israelites properly.

[57] See also 19.5; 22.2, 3, 15, 22 (×2), 24, 29; 23.8, 16, 27, 36 (×2), 37, 38.

*Israelites* should not be overlooked. The intimate relationship between Y*HWH* and the *Israelites* is also underscored by Y*HWH's* unmediated response to the *Israelites'* conduct, already elaborated upon in §5.1.1.

Perhaps the most important expression of the immediate relationship between Y*HWH* and the *Israelites* is the recurrent reference to Y*HWH's* deliverance of the people from Egypt[58] and his granting a land to them.[59] In neither of these cases is *Moses* mentioned as the mediator, despite his obvious role, according to Exodus, in confronting the Egyptian Pharaoh and delivering the people from bondage.

Nevertheless, in order to present a balanced picture of the role of *Moses*, we must consider his role in the control network (see §3.5). While *Moses* is only an intermediate participant with a limited brokerage role in the regular network, he is the second-most important participant in the control network, because he controls most of the interactions recorded. The elimination plot of the control network illustrates this (Figure 31). While *Moses* is only the sixth-most important participant with respect to the cohesion of the regular network (see Figure 22 above), he is the second-most important participant in the control network. Thus, to explain the role of participants in a text more accurately, their role in the social network must be balanced by their role in the discourse structure.

---

[58] 19.36; 22.33; 23.43; 25.38, 42, 55; 26.13.
[59] 18.3; 20.22, 24; 23.10; 25.2, 38.

Figure 31: Elimination plot of the entire 'control network', displaying the 15 most important participants for the cohesion of the network

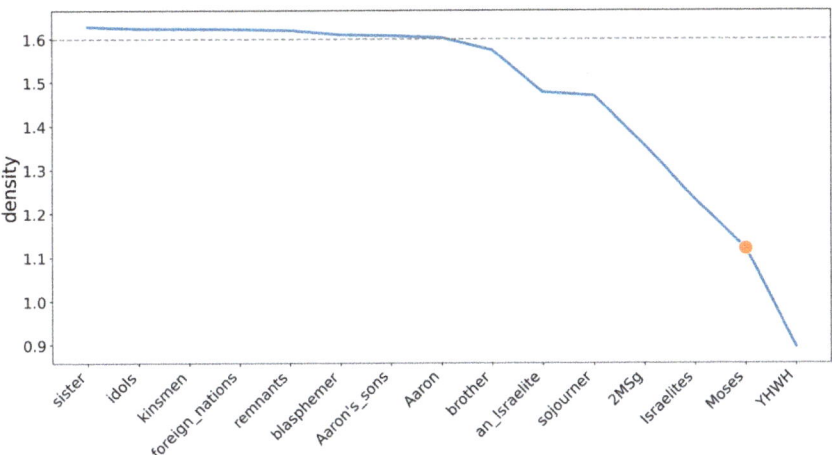

To summarise, in spite of *Moses'* obvious role as a mediator or 'broker' of the revelation of YHWH, he is not particularly important in the regular social network. Even in his own ego-network, the *Israelites* and YHWH are far more important. If *Moses* were removed from the network, the network would remain relatively stable, and the *Israelites* and YHWH would remain closely connected. This view is balanced by *Moses'* role in the control network, where he is the second-most important participant. We are thus left with a tension between an ordinary SNA of *Moses'* role and a discourse-structural analysis. To be sure, much interaction takes place between YHWH and the *Israelites*, but these interactions are nevertheless the content of *Moses'* speeches. In that sense, he is the 'broker' of divine blessings and curses, and he is more important than the *priests* with respect to authority. We are thus justified in claiming *Moses* to be a mediator.

## 5.2.2. The *Brother/Fellow*

The *brother* receives much attention in H. In the network analysis, the references to אָחִיךָ 'your brother' are collocated with references to nearly synonymous participants, namely, רֵעֶךָ 'your fellow', עֲמִיתֶךָ 'your fellow countryman', and בְּנֵי עַמֶּךָ 'sons of your people', all of which occur in parallel in 19.17–18 (see chapter 3, §3.8). Understood this way, the *brother* is not merely a close family member, but represents any person belonging to the *Israelites*, literally, 'the sons of Israel'. Indeed, the sons of Israel are portrayed as an extended family comprising the entire people. The *brother* is related to three groups of participants, including his close relatives (*brother's brother*, *brother's uncle*, and *clan*), members of Israelite society (*Israelites*, *2MSg*, and *an Israelite*), and the *sojourner* (see Figure 32). As such, the *brother* is constructed as a figure in the social sphere between family, society, and foreigners.

Figure 32: Mean agency invested by the *brother*

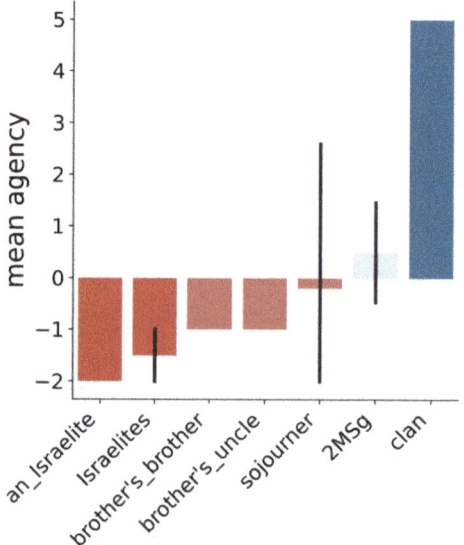

The mean agency invested by the *brother* is generally relatively low (see Figure 32). His only highly agentive interaction is with his *clan*, to which he returns after his release from debt slavery (25.41). Understood this way, the jubilee redemption is an act of empowering the *brother*, and his regained status as a free agent is expressed directly in his autonomous return to the *clan*. Most of the interactions of the *brother* are interactions with *2MSg*, one of the addressees of the text. First of all, *2MSg* is prohibited from oppressing, slandering, and hating the *brother* (19.16, 17). On the contrary, he must treat him with justice and honestly reprove him if he finds anything wrong with him (19.15, 17). In short, *2MSg* is to love his *brother* as he loves himself (19.18). These commands show that the *brother* is to be seen as an equal with equal legal rights. This concern is concretised in the jubilee discourse (Lev. 25). Here, the *Israelites* are commanded not to oppress one another (lit. 'one's brother') when they sell or buy property from one another in case of debt (25.14). In this chapter, the *brother* is portrayed as a fellow Israelite who has fallen into poverty and reaches out for help from *2MSg* (25.35). When the *brother* reaches out, *2MSg* is to seize him (25.35) and help him. He can buy his property but not in perpetuity (25.23). Moreover, if the situation of the *brother* is worsened and he needs to borrow money, *2MSg* may lend him money but not take interest (25.36–37). Finally, if the financial situation of the *brother* is so grave that he needs to sell himself to *2MSg* as a debt slave, *2MSg* must treat him not as a slave but as a hired worker (25.39), and he may not treat the *brother* with violence (25.43). Under these circumstances, the *brother's brother* (25.48) and the *brother's uncle* (25.49) must be allowed to redeem the *brother* from his debt slavery. In this chapter, the *brother* also has interactions with the *sojourner*. The *sojourner* is depicted as a rich man to whom the *brother* may reach out for help. The *sojourner* can buy him as a debt slave, but he is not allowed to treat him with violence (25.53). Indeed, the command is not directed to the *sojourner*, but to *2MSg*, who is commanded not to allow the *sojourner* to treat the *brother* with violence. Thus, while the author does not assume that *2MSg* has authority over the rich *sojourner*, he demands that *2MSg* take responsibility for the *brother*, even when he is in the hands of the *sojourner*.

In sum, the *brother* represents a member of Israelite society. He is not actively involved in many interactions and does not pose a threat to the society. Rather, the aim of the text is to protect the legal rights of the *brother*, as well as to constrain the power of *2MSg* who is thereby constructed as a person in a powerful position with the ability to take advantage of marginalised and impoverished fellows. In the jubilee discourse, in particular, the *brother* is portrayed as a lonely figure on the margins of family and society. He can hope that his family will relieve him, but he has no guarantee. The *brother* may even drift away from the community and reach out to the *sojourner* in desperation. Indeed, we may construe the *brother* as a 'transitional' figure with an innate tendency towards drifting away from the community. The lawgiver wants to retain the order of society by regulating the behaviour of the *Israelites* towards their needy fellows. The interactions between *2MSg* and the *brother* thus reflect the author's expectations of equality between the members of the covenantal community, explicitly argued for in the frequent references to the common history of the *Israelites*, the exodus (19.36; 22.33; 23.43; 25.38, 42, 55; 26.13). The *Israelites* are not to jeopardise the covenantal community by oppressing fellow members or closing their eyes to injustice.

### 5.2.3. The *Blasphemer*

The *blasphemer* is an intriguing figure in the Holiness Code. Curiously, he is never named, but is consistently designated הַמְקַלֵּל 'the curser' (24.14, 23). By contrast, his mother is known as 'Shelomith, daughter of Dibri, of the tribe of Dan' (24.11). The *blasphemer* has been considered a paradigmatic outsider, based on the gendered language applied in the portrayal of this figure (Rooke 2015; see also chapter 2, §6.6). Within the network structure, however, the *blasphemer* occurs among the intermediate participants. After all, he is actively involved in an event, and he has interactions with YHWH, Moses, and the *Israelites* (see Figure 33). The structural roles in the network analysis do not take into account the content of the interactions, only the agency invested. It is crucial, of course, whether the ties are positive or negative.

The ties of the *blasphemer* are entirely negative. His only act, apart from 'going out in the midst of the Israelites', is the cursing of YHWH (24.11). YHWH never responds directly to the blasphemy, but *witnesses* to the event bring the *blasphemer* to Moses and into custody (24.11–12). YHWH's response is given to Moses, who is ordered to bring the *blasphemer* outside the camp to stone him (24.14). The execution is carried out by the entire community (labelled *Israelites* in the network), who bring out the *blasphemer* and stone him to death, after the *witnesses* have laid their hands on his head (24.14, 23).

Figure 33: Ego-network (left) and mean agency invested by the *blasphemer* (right)

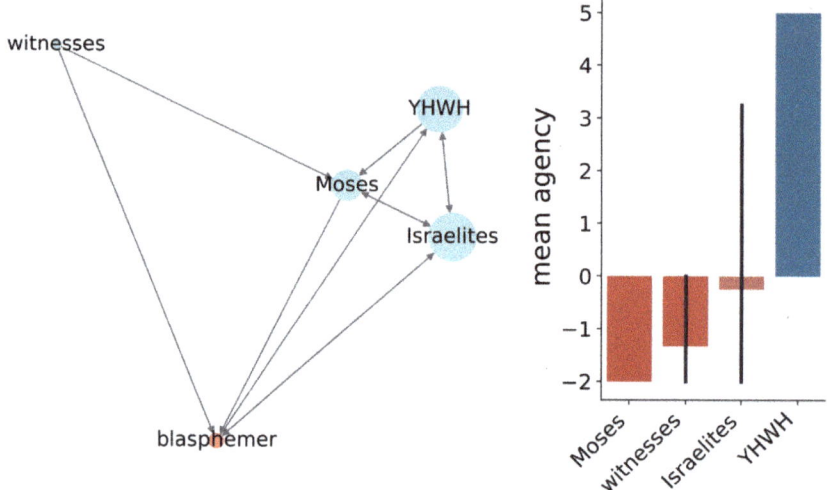

In short, the entire story of the *blasphemer* is fraught with enmity. It is not accurate, however, to describe the *blasphemer* as a paradigmatic outsider in the sense of being a "victim of impossible demands" (so Holguín 2015, 99). The relatively high agency invested by the *blasphemer* in his interactions sets him apart from other so-called marginalised participants (e.g., the *women*). Rather, the *blasphemer* is cast as a rebel who poses a threat to the community, not because of his ethnic origins, but because of his blasphemy against YHWH.[60] In other words, the pericope describes

---

[60] As explained in chapter 2, §6.6, the confusion pertaining to the case of the blasphemer relates to whether half-Israelites are subject to Israelite law. Since the blasphemer is only half Israelite, he could have been

a rebellion gone wrong. The first event recorded is when the *blasphemer* 'goes out' (וַיֵּצֵא G) in the midst of the Israelite camp. At the end, he is himself brought outside the camp (וַיּוֹצִיאוּ H) by the *Israelites*. That the *blasphemer* should not be understood simply as a paradigmatic outsider is underscored by his structural role in the discourse. In fact, in the so-called 'control network', the *blasphemer* plays a rather important role, which is indicated by his relatively high outdegree score (see Figure 17 in §3.5). By initiating the narrative of 24.10–23, the *blasphemer* 'controls' (or, at least, is responsible for) the narrative, in a total of 21 interactions.

In short, the *blasphemer* is not the paradigmatic outsider, but the paradigmatic rebel, and the function of the *blasphemer* within the Holiness Code is to illustrate what the community needs to do when the borders of the covenantal community are transgressed. Since the *lex talionis* applies equally to native *Israelites* and non-Israelite *sojourners*, it also applies to the half-Israelite *blasphemer*. Indeed, it is emphasised that the law applies to anyone within the domain of the covenantal community, regardless of ethnic descent.

---

exempt from punishment. The divine speech prompted by the blasphemy, however, states that both Israelites and non-Israelite sojourners are within the scope of the law (24.16, 22). By implication, therefore, the half-Israelite blasphemer must be punished insofar as the blasphemy was pronounced in the midst of the camp (24.10).

## 5.3. Peripheral Participants

Most of the participants are situated in the periphery of the network. They are generally characterised by having minimal ties to other participants, and most of them only occur once or twice in the text. Of the 40 participants, 17 are women.[61] Another three women are in the group of intermediate participants (*sister, fellow's wife*, and *daughter*), but all women will be treated as one group below. Most other participants have already been mentioned in relation to core or intermediate participants, including the *witnesses* in relation to the *blasphemer* (§5.2.3), the *lay person* in relation to the *priests* (§5.1.4), and the *brother's brother, brother's uncle*, and *clan* in relation to the *brother* (§5.2.2). Therefore, apart from the *women*, only the *father* and a small group of vulnerable members of the society (the *poor*, the *blind*, the *deaf*, and the *elderly*) will be considered.

### 5.3.1. The *Women*

There are 20 women in the H-network, about one third of the human/divine participants. The vast majority of these are relatives of the core participants of the text, in particular *2MSg*, the

---

[61] These include the *mother, virgin, widowed/expelled/defiled woman, handmaid, father's wife, aunt, aunt-in-law, daughter-in-law, granddaughter, woman and her mother, man/woman, woman in menstruation, relative, woman, woman and her daughter, granddaughter of woman*, and *sister of woman*. The remaining peripheral participants are the *corpse, 2MPl, lay person, witnesses, father, offspring, slave, sons of sojourners, children, no-one, male, purchaser, deaf, blind, poor, rich, elderly, son of brother, brother's brother, clan, brother's uncle, man*, and *husband*.

*Israelites, an Israelite,* the *sojourner, Aaron,* and *Aaron's sons.* Indeed, all core participants but YHWH interact with at least some of the women in the network. Although it might not be entirely correct to treat the women as a group, given that some of the women are related to the priests and others to regular Israelites, it is nevertheless the case that, by considering the women as a group, we can investigate whether a pattern of interaction and social status emerges. In general, the *women* have low mean agency scores in the network, indicating that they are typically portrayed as semantic undergoers rather than instigating actors. Curiously, the participants with whom the *women* are most agentive—although still low agency—are all core members of the network (see Figure 34).

Figure 34: Mean agency invested by the *women*

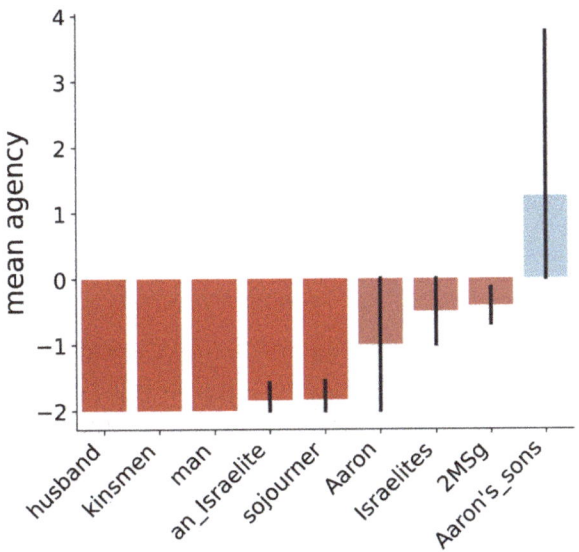

The three participants with whom the *women* have the lowest mean agency (-2) are the *husband*, the *kinsmen*, and the *man*.

These are all peripheral participants, so the interactions to report are scarce. The interactions include expulsion by the *husband* (21.7), removal from their *kinsmen* by means of capital punishment (20.18), and engagement to a *man* (19.20). The remaining participants are all core participants, and the *women* have a little higher mean agency with this group. The most common interaction is sexual intercourse, expressed with the verbs קרב G 'approach', גלה D 'uncover' [nakedness], ראה G 'see' [nakedness], נתן G 'give' [copulation], and שכב G 'lie with'. Related interactions are לקח G 'take' (here, 'marry') and נאף G 'commit adultery'. An *Israelite* and the *sojourner* are both prohibited from having sexual intercourse with close relatives, as well as the wife of another man (i.e., the *fellow's wife*), although, to be sure, the prohibitions are given as case laws in Lev. 20 and not as apodictic prohibitions.[62] The apodictic prohibitions are given in Lev. 18 with *2MSg* as the addressee.[63] The marriage laws are stricter for *Aaron*, who is obliged to marry a *virgin* of his own kin (21.13, 14). *Aaron's sons* are not explicitly commanded to marry a *virgin* of their own kin, but are prohibited from marrying prostituted, defiled, or divorced women (21.7). The overall concern of the incestual laws and marriage laws is the threat of defilement related to these illicit interactions. Defilement compromises the relationship between YHWH and the *Israelites*, as explicitly stated in the opening and final verses of Lev. 18 (1–5, 24–30). For this reason, there is capital punishment for transgressing the incestual laws. Both

---

[62] 20.10 (×2), 11 (×2), 12, 14, 17 (×2), 18 (×2), 20 (×2), 21 (×2).
[63] 18.7 (×2), 8, 9, 10, 11, 12, 13, 14 (×2), 15 (×2), 16, 17 (×3), 18 (×2), 19 (×2), 20; 20.19.

male and female perpetrators are put to death, either by the *Israelites* (20.14, 27) or, in one case, by *2MSg* (20.16). The threat of defilement also affects other interactions. Firstly, *2MSg* may not defile his *daughter* by making her a prostitute (19.29). A similar law is given with regard to the *daughter* of a priest, who may not defile her father by becoming a prostitute (21.9). Secondly, the *priests* may not defile themselves by coming close to a dead relative (21.1–3, 11), except that *Aaron's sons* may undergo defilement for a virgin sister, because she has no husband (21.3). The *mother* stands out in the group of *women*. She is the only woman explicitly to be feared, or revered, by the *Israelites* (19.3). Moreover, if *an Israelite* or a *sojourner* curses his *mother* (or his *father*), he will be put to death (20.9). Finally, the *Israelites* are allowed to buy *handmaids*, as well as male slaves, from the surrounding nations (25.44).

In sum, in light of the SNA, the purpose of the text is not so much to list the legal rights of the *women*, nor to objectivise the *women* as male property. Rather, it is the interactions themselves that are relevant, insofar as incestual relationships (as well as homoerotic and bestial acts) compromise the ritual and moral purity of the people and thereby the covenantal relationship with YHWH. Therefore, to preserve the ritual purity of the people, the interactions between men and women are constrained. If they deliberately incur defilement, both women and men are held accountable and are most often punished by death. In this respect, the text is not so much concerned with the rights and obligations of the *women*, but rather the obligations of the Israelite addressees, because the interactions between men and women have critical implications for the relationship with YHWH.

### 5.3.2. The *Father*

The *father* occurs a few times in the network, only in relation to core participants, namely, *an Israelite*, the *sojourner*, *2MSg*, *Aaron*, and the *Israelites*. His mean agency is low, as illustrated in Figure 35.

Figure 35: Mean agency invested by the *father*

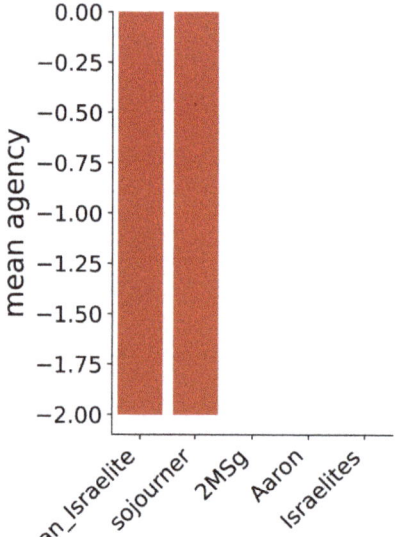

The intention of the discourse appears to be to protect the status and rights of the *father*. *An Israelite* is prohibited from cursing his *father* (as well as his *mother*), although indirectly, by means of a case law (20.9). The same law applies to the *sojourner*. Moreover, by prohibiting *2MSg* from having intercourse with his *mother*, whose 'nakedness' is said to be the 'nakedness' of the *father*, the *father's* rights are protected (18.7). Rather than dishonouring their *father*, the *Israelites* are commanded to fear, or revere, their *father* as well as their *mother* (19.3). The only recorded exception to this call for reverence regards *Aaron*, who is prohibited from coming near his deceased *father* (21.11), most likely as part of a mourning rite (Wenham 1979, 291).

In sum, the *father* plays a peripheral role in the network and is never active. Nevertheless, the *father* is important in terms of delineating the domain of the Israelites (including *2MSg*, the *Israelites*, and *an Israelite*) and the *sojourner*. Their roles and social space are limited by their obligations to the *father*.

### 5.3.3. The *Deaf, Blind, Poor,* and *Elderly*

A certain group of peripheral participants are particularly vulnerable. To this group belong the *deaf*, the *blind*, the *poor*, and the *elderly*. Never active in the network, these participants are only connected with the individual Israelite (*2MSg*). Apparently, their function is to demarcate the domain of *2MSg* and illustrate his social obligations to vulnerable members of the community. Accordingly, *2MSg* may not curse the *deaf* (19.14), nor put stumbling blocks in front of the *blind* (19.14). In other words, *2MSg* is prohibited from taking advantage of the disabled—just as he is prohibited from taking advantage of his debt-burdened *brother* (see §5.2.2). His interaction with the *poor*, however, shows that there must be a limit to his generosity. On the one hand, he is obliged to leave the leftovers of the harvest for the *poor* (19.10; 23.22). On the other hand, he is not allowed to "lift the face of the poor" (19.15), that is, he is not to favour the *poor* in legal cases, just as he is not allowed to favour the *rich* (19.15). Even if he sympathises with the *poor* in his legal struggle, *2MSg* is not allowed to bend the law. Finally, *2MSg* is to "honour the faces of the old" and to "arise before the aged" (19.32). Although the *elderly* may very well enjoy the respect that follows from a long life, the command to honour him presupposes a tendency to the opposite. Just as the *father* may be dishonoured (see above), the status of the *elderly* may be violated by the potentially presumptuous *2MSg*. Thus, the aim of the law is to preserve the respect deserved by the *elderly*, as well as the dignity of disabled people, as represented by the *deaf* and the *blind*.

## 6.0. Holiness and the Social Network

The detailed explorations of the participant roles in the Holiness Code network support the initial statistical analysis. That is, the participants can reasonably be divided into three groups based on frequency, connectivity, and agency. The most complex relationships revolve around the core members: Y*HWH*, the *Israelites*, *2MSg, an Israelite*, the *sojourner*, and the *priests*. This is not unexpected, since the text is composed of divine speeches to the *Israelites* and, indirectly, to *2MSg*. Most other participants are presented in relation to the *Israelites* and *2MSg*. *Moses* has the role of a mediator by whom the divine law is revealed to the people. The *priests* are facilitators of the ongoing relationship between Y*HWH* and the people through their special obligations concerning purity. The *sojourner* represents the border of the covenantal community, while the *blasphemer* is the paradigmatic rebel who curses YHWH from within the covenantal community. The peripheral participants, the *women*, the *father*, the *deaf*, the *blind*, the *poor*, and the *elderly*, serve to demarcate the domain or agency of the addressees. Notably, therefore, the social network derived from the Holiness Code is not a neutral representation of an ancient Israelite society, but rather the author's depiction of a community with specific emphasis on the relationship between YHWH and the *Israelites*. The text appears to presuppose a tendency for *2MSg*, in particular, to extend his domain—in terms of wealth and power—at the expense of vulnerable members of his family and society. The purpose of the text, then, is to counter this tendency by commanding the addressees to view vulnerable members of the society as equals and persons with equal legal rights.

What, then, is the relationship between social domains, values of equality, and holiness? The Holiness Code is not merely a civil law, but a religious law composed of divine speeches and centred around the command to be holy (Lev. 19.2). How does the social network analysis relate to the religious perspective of the text? To begin with, religion is not only a partial concern of the law, in addition to social concerns. What makes the Holiness Code so interesting is that it integrates society and cult. Lev. 19 is a prime example, with its mix of cultic and social prescriptions. Holiness has to do with order and distinctions, the most important separation being that between the holy and profane. The Holiness Code claims that Israel is holy because it has been "separated" from the nations (Lev. 20.25), and therefore the people have to separate the clean from the unclean to protect their holiness (Lev. 20.24, 26).[64] Within the priestly worldview, different degrees of holiness pertain to the spatial, temporal, and social spheres (Jenson 1992). These gradations of holiness, however, do not correspond to the social clusters of the social network analysis. On the contrary, the legal obligations of the Holiness Code run across spheres of holiness, in order to advance a social order within a covenantal community inhabited by both the holy and the profane. More concretely, holiness interferes with the social network in at least three domains. Firstly, the aim of the Holiness Code is to advance equality among equals, that is, among the members of the covenantal community. The repeated references to the shared exodus story and the frequent designation of the fellow as *brother* accentuate the laws' concern that one's fellow be viewed as an equal despite social differences (see Højgaard 2023). In a sense, therefore, the laws are unequal, in that they benefit the *brother* more than the addressees. This tendency to benefit some participants more than others was already shown in the reciprocity analysis, where only a minority of the stipulations of the law were found to be mutual (§3.3). Yet, the inequality of the law is meant to counter the assumed inequality of society, so that the poor *brother* should not remain poor.

---

[64] Thus, while Deuteronomy anchors the holiness of Israel firmly in the election of the people, and the priestly laws restrict holiness to the cult, the Holiness Code blurs or merges this discrepancy. Holiness is both anchored in the election of Israel *and* something to be continually attained by the whole people. In other words, for the Holiness Code, holiness is dynamic (Milgrom 2000, 1398).

Secondly, while the poor *brother* is a hypothetical person in the Holiness Code, ideally non-existent in the expected equal society, the *sojourner* is a real category. For the Holiness Code, the sojourner remains a legal and social concern insofar as he is, unlike the *brother*, outside the covenantal community. The Holiness Code does not aim to integrate *sojourners* and make them natives, in contrast to the aim of restoring the poor *brother* to the status of a real equal of the addressee. In other words, equality does not extend beyond the borders of the covenantal community. The *sojourner*, rather, demarcates the domain of the community, by being a foreigner who has settled (temporarily) in the society.

Thirdly, even within the equal covenantal community expected by the author of the Holiness Code, inequality persists. Despite its communal view of holiness, the Holiness Code does not abandon the strict cultic hierarchy established in P. The *priests* continue to enjoy a somewhat privileged role, and *Moses* continues to be the mediator of divine revelation. The author most likely agrees with the phrase מַמְלֶכֶת כֹּהֲנִים "a kingdom of priests" (Exod. 19.6) as a designation of the covenantal people, but certainly not at the expense of the Aaronide priesthood (see Otto 2009, 140). In other words, equality does not negate the existence of different roles. The *priests* do have certain exclusive privileges, but they are also constrained by exclusive restrictions in order to fulfil their particular role for the good of the community in its covenant with YHWH.

# 8. CONCLUSION: THE SOCIAL NETWORK OF LEVITICUS 17–26

## 1.0. Summary of Research

The aim of this study has been to develop and discuss a social network model for capturing the roles of the participants in the Holiness Code. The law text contains 59 human/divine participants related to one another in a variety of ways. The participants thus form a network of interaction closely related to the content matter of the law. It is the claim of this study that the ethical values of the law text are related to the participants and their internal relationships—in other words, their roles. The methodology developed in this thesis contrasts with traditional approaches to the characterisation of literary participants in significant ways. Within Biblical studies, it has been common to focus on one participant or a small set of participants and to employ literary, linguistic, and historical insights to interpret the role of the participant(s). An obvious advantage of this approach is a multifaceted characterisation not limited to certain features of a text. The downside is the often narrow focus on one participant, at the cost of viewing said participant in light of the other participants in the text. In particular, there is a risk that the role of a participant is over- or underemphasised, or even misunderstood, because its embeddedness in a network of interacting participants is not taken seriously. Chapter 2 illustrated this methodological issue by reviewing previous research on the participants of H. It was shown that previous interpretations have led to rather diverse characterisations of the participants and their roles, and it was contended that a social network approach better accounts for the participants' roles within the text at large. Consequently, a sociological framework was outlined and integrated with a literary approach to H. In particular, recent narratological and rhetorical readings of Biblical law were invoked to argue that H is not an arbitrary collection of laws, but a carefully written document that lends itself to literary analysis, even though it may not meet the literary criteria of modern critics. In light of this framework, it was further argued that the participants should not be treated as discrete entities but as members of a social community implied by the text. Accordingly, the participants were claimed to form a social network connected by physical, perceptional, and emotional exchanges. By implication, the role of each participant can be explained in light of the entire network. The social network model necessitated a structured harvesting of data to ensure a consistent and transparent mapping of the participants. The two datatypes required were participant tracking data and some abstract measures of interaction between the participants. Both data types demanded careful investigation, and four chapters were dedicated to that task.

Chapter 3 explained the participant-tracking strategy developed by Eep Talstra and pursued in this study. The methodology is essentially a bottom-up linking of linguistic entities to textual participants. Talstra developed his methodology primarily on the basis of narrative and prophetic texts, and it was the aim of this chapter to review the tracking procedure on the basis of a concrete dataset of the participant references in H. Three important insights were yielded by the research.

Firstly, as a law text, H offers its own complications in terms of participant tracking. Most significantly, the usage of אִישׁ 'a man/anyone' is a literary convention in Biblical law to introduce an indefinite, hypothetical participant. The participant is commonly disambiguated by means of adding complex phrases, relative clauses, or temporal/circumstantial clauses. In order for a computational algorithm to account better for legal texts, these linguistic devices for disambiguating participants need to be taken into consideration. Furthermore, the algorithm did not always handle nominal clauses well. For a participant-tracking analysis, it is crucial to discern whether the non-verbal predicate of a nominal clause identifies or classifies the subject, since an identifying clause involves one participant and a classifying clause two. A two-step procedure was proposed to discern 1) the phrase functions (predicate and subject) and 2) the overall semantics of the clause on the basis of definiteness.

Secondly, the dataset under consideration also exhibited some abnormalities, including the frequent first-person references to YHWH in Moses' speeches and the alternation between plural and singular references to the addressees. It was argued that both types of participant shifts were rhetorical devices outside the scope of participant tracking. Nevertheless, a computational analysis has the merit of revealing abnormalities, because, unlike human interpreters, it is not prone to harmonising or ignoring tensions. Thus, a formalised participant-tracking procedure shows both the internal coherence of the text, due to its ability to link participant references across the span of a text, and also the 'knots' and 'gaps' of the text, whether they are intentional or not.

Finally, it was shown that participants are not always entirely distinct entities. Often, they overlap in terms of group membership, that is, a participant can be referred to individually or as a member of a group. In other words, the participants form a hierarchy, and this hierarchy must be respected in a participant analysis (SNA included), because references and events ascribed to an individual participant cannot necessarily be ascribed to other members of the same group.

Chapter 4 developed a framework for capturing semantic roles of verbal events. In light of the present project at large, the major aim was to define a feature that could be quantified across any given verbal event so that it could function in a social network analysis. Agency was found to be one such feature, because any event involves some degree of agency. Agency is a compositional entity and involves notions of volition, sentience, causation, and dynamicity. As an example, a volitional participant is generally considered more agentive than a non-volitional participant. In turn, by analysing verbal events in terms of agency, it would be possible to rank semantic roles and thereby deduce how much agency participants of the Holiness Code invested in concrete events. Apart from the internal aspect of the verb (also known as *Aktionsart*), agency is also affected by the relational properties of the arguments of the verb and the pragmatic context of the clause. A multifaceted analysis was therefore required to capture the degree of agency entailed by a verbal event. The chapter prioritised the verbal properties of dynamicity and causation, arguably the most significant verbal features with respect to agency. The Role and Reference Grammar approach to lexical decomposition of verbs proved useful, because it offers a strict procedure to follow from determination of *Aktionsart* to indexing of semantic roles. In particular, verbs index their semantic roles according to dynamicity (states vs activities) and causation. Since Biblical Hebrew is an ancient language, however, the determination of *Aktionsart* is more complicated than for modern languages. Canonical RRG has incorporated Dowty's test-questions to 'interrogate' the verbs, but these test-questions assume an intuition about the language that we can hardly possess for ancient languages, including BH. It was therefore argued that statistical approaches are needed alongside traditional ones insofar as they take seriously the frequencies of actual attestations in the corpus.

Chapter 5 was dedicated to the analysis of dynamicity. To identify dynamic verbs, a collostructional analysis was applied, whereby the reliance of BH verbs on selected adverbials was investigated. The analysis showed a clear distinction between verbs which are attracted by directional adverbials and verbs which are not. Thus, the analysis provided a statistical basis for distinguishing states and activities. More generally, the research illustrated the benefits of applying quantitative methods to the analysis of BH. In future research on BH *Aktionsart*, other adverbials and constructions should preferably be considered, in order to substantiate the findings of the present study.

The other major feature contributing to agency, causation, was analysed in chapter 6. Biblical Hebrew has two morphological causative stems, *hifʿil* and *piʿel*. The *hifʿil* is generally acknowledged as a 'real' causative, while the *piʿel* is more likely factitive. Not all verbs occurring in these stems, however, appear to be causative or factitive. It was therefore investigated whether morphological causatives can be identified on the basis of the ratio by which they increase in transitivity when they alternate from the non-causative stem, the *qal*, to the *hifʿil* or the *piʿel*. The statistical analysis showed clearly that prototypical morphological causatives have a high tendency towards adding an external causer in the *hifʿil* and the *piʿel*, while ambiguous and true negative cases have a lower or even negative tendency towards transitivity increase. Apart from a statistical analysis, each stem was conceptualised with RRG logical structures, and it was shown that the two stems in fact express finer causative distinctions, namely factitive (*piʿel*) and 'real' causative (*hifʿil*). Importantly, when a verb is attested in both the *hifʿil* and the *piʿel*, it often indexes different semantic roles according to the causative type of the stem. The analysis was primarily restricted to verbs attested in Lev. 17–26, so further research into the remaining verbs of the HB is required to validate this hypothesis.

Lexical causatives proved harder to decompose, since there are no syntactic clues to distinguish non-causatives and causatives, apart from transitivity, insofar as intransitive verbs cannot be causative. There is some correlation between causation and

8. Conclusion 367

the semantic transitivity hypothesis proposed by Hopper and Thompson (1980), since causatives are likely to involve an instigating causer and a fully affected undergoer. The correspondence was tested on BH verbs using Næss' (2007) semantic transitivity parameters: instigation, volition, and affectedness. Some correlation was noted, but since causation is a multifaceted concept (see Talmy 2000) and includes, e.g., permission, non-intervention, and hindrance—in addition to the prototypical direct causation—one cannot escape a logical, lexical decomposition of the verb itself, despite the obvious challenges presented by an ancient language. The chapter concluded with the proposal of a hierarchy of semantic roles, arranged according to dynamicity and causation, as well as clausal properties. The hierarchy provides a useful means of ranking participants according to their roles in concrete verbal events. Thus, although Lev. 17–26 contains 181 different verbal predicates denoting a wide range of events, the agency hierarchy allows for comparing 'apples and oranges', so to speak.

Chapter 7 combined the results of the participant tracking and the semantic role analysis in order to investigate the roles of the participants within the social network of Lev. 17–26. The participants were conceptualised as network nodes and the verbs and agency scores as edges connecting the nodes. Although SNA has previously been applied to the study of literature, the present approach differed in several respects. Firstly, it was the first time that the social network implied by a single law text has been analysed. Secondly, the conceptualisation of agency as network edges is unique, and particularly apt for a law text in which agency plays a significant role. Thirdly, it was the first time that the syntactic structure of the text was incorporated into SNA as a third dimension alongside participants and agency. The 'control network' derived from the syntactic structure of the text proved useful in explaining the role of *Moses*. In the ordinary social network, *Moses* was found to have a limited role, because many participants have direct interactions with YHWH besides *Moses'* mediation of divine revelation. However, the control network 'restored' his role, because he was shown to be the second-most 'controlling' participant next to YHWH, due to the fact that the vast majority of interactions recorded are part of *Moses'* direct speeches. Hence, the syntactic structure is a crucial component in capturing the roles of the participants, and an SNA risks misrepresenting the participants if this component is not considered.

More generally, three clusters of participants were identified using the node2vec algorithm for structural role detection. One cluster consisted of core participants: YHWH; the *Israelites* (2MPl); an individual, directly addressed Israelite (2MSg); a third-person *Israelite*; the *sojourner*; *Aaron*; and *Aaron's sons*. Another cluster consisted of intermediate participants, less frequently attested, but with connections to multiple core participants. This group included *Moses*, the *blasphemer* of Lev. 24.10–23, and the *brother*, among others. The last cluster consisted of peripheral participants that occur very infrequently in the network and often with low agency invested (i.e., the participants are more often undergoers of an event than actors). Most women of the text belong to this group, as well as the *father*, among others.

## 8. Conclusion

Selected participants of each cluster were closely inspected with an eye to their structural importance and the degree of agency invested by them in interactions with other participants. The most important participant is YHWH, who controls most of the network and has the most connections with the most important participants. It is therefore safe to conclude that the Holiness Code is YHWH's law. Not only does it originate with YHWH as divine speeches, it is also orientated towards him. Although H is commonly viewed as community-orientated, in contrast to the cult-oriented P, YHWH is the organising principle of the community implied by the text. The *Israelites*, who are the primary addressees of *Moses'* speeches, are the second most important participants. Most other participants are referred to in relation to the *Israelites* or the individually addressed *2MSg*, e.g., 'your (Sg) brother', 'your (Pl) enemies', and 'the sojourner who dwells among you (Pl)'. The particular perspective of the author on the society implied by the text is thus that it is the covenantal community formed by YHWH and the people of Israel. The roles of the participants are derived from this perspective. Like any other law text, H presupposes and reacts against violations of the social order. In this particular law text, the covenantal relationship with YHWH is at stake, and the members and outsiders of the community are presumed to be willing to violate the order of society by reaching out for more wealth, power, and privileges at the expense of others. The covenantal community thus finds itself under constant threat of injustice and disentanglement. It is threatened by the greedy individual Israelite (*2MSg*), the transitional *brother* who drifts away from his family and the community because of poverty and oppression, and the rebellious *blasphemer* who attacks the community and curses its god. The purpose of the law, then, is to constrain the behaviour of the members of the community for the purpose of preserving order and holiness.

In sum, the SNA provides a multifaceted picture of the participants and the network of the Holiness Code. More than that, the participant roles derived from the SNA shed light upon the ethical and theological 'expectancies' pertaining to the social community. The social community implied by the author may not be an ideal community. After all, there is always the threat of internal disentanglement and ritual impurity, as well as attacks from outsiders. Nevertheless, while the society implied by the author may not be an ideal society, the participant roles reveal how the lawgiver expects his addressees to act in this particular society under certain circumstances. More than anything, the lawgiver values the covenantal community between YHWH and the *Israelites*, and this community can only be upheld if the people fulfil certain roles, e.g., if the *priests* respectfully facilitate the sacrifices offered by the *Israelites*, and if the individual Israelites sustain and care for their poor fellows. In other words, if holiness is the unifying theme of the Holiness Code, as often argued, the expected participant roles are the manifestations of the author's view on holiness. Holiness is manifested and maintained through social interaction.

## 2.0. Recommendations for Further Research

Finally, I want to indicate some trajectories for further research along the lines of the present study. First, as was pointed out in the participant tracking of H (chapter 3), participant references cannot easily be resolved into clearly delineated participants. In general, participants fluctuate between group membership references and individual references, and they can be referred to by a variety of synonyms. In fact, quite distinct participants can be referred to by the same references. The most curious phenomenon is the reference גֵּר 'sojourner', which typically refers to non-Israelite residents but is also used to designate the status of the Israelites (25.23). This change of reference evidently introduces a play on identity, because the Israelites, who are clearly set apart from non-Israelite sojourners, are in some sense sojourners themselves. In other words, the text consciously blurs the referential boundaries of the participants for ideological reasons. The task of participant tracking has to deal with such phenomena, and the present study has discussed how participants should be thought of as semantically overlapping. Still, further research is required in order to be able to retrieve hierarchies or networks of overlapping or fluctuating participants. More concretely, it was suggested that additional linguistic parameters should be included in the disambiguation of participants, because the text frequently employs complex phrases or relative clauses to specify the identity of the participants. Further, nominal clauses deserve more attention, in order to further validate the two-step approach suggested in this book for tracking the participants of these particular clauses.

Second, along with participant tracking, the analysis of semantic roles (chapter 4–6) formed the backbone of the SNA of H. It was the goal of this study to propose ways of linguistically determining semantic roles given the inherent aspect (*Aktionsart*) of the verb. In particular, quantitative methods were applied to explore dynamicity on the basis of collostructions of verbs and selected adverbials, as well as to explore morphological causatives on the basis of transitivity alternation between non-causative and causative stems. As for the collostruction analysis, much more research is surely needed to confirm or reject the conclusions of this study. Additional collostructions should be explored, not least collostructions of verbs and temporal modifiers, in order to further scrutinise the inherent aspect of Biblical verbs. Also, the study of morphological causatives was limited primarily to those attested in H, but the transitivity alternation model should preferably be expanded to the entire Biblical corpus, in order to validate the approach and explore morphological causatives further.

Third, while most Biblical studies are oriented towards the historical context of Biblical texts, in order to understand the *Sitz im Leben* of the text, the present study has deliberately refrained from historical questions. This choice is legitimate insofar as the object under consideration was not the historical setting of the Israelite community depicted in H, but the author's portrayal of and ethical stance towards the community. Nevertheless, texts are products of historical authors and reflect historical contexts in one way or another. It is therefore relevant to relate the observations made here about the implied society and the expected social roles to more general considerations of the historical context of H. Given the claim that the author does not stipulate how the society should look, but rather how different participants are to act within a given society, it is reasonable to expect the implied society to reflect a historical one. In particular, due to the lack of external evidence, the question of authorship has often focused on indirect evidence, that is, which social group can be said to benefit more from the legislation. I have argued that the Holiness Code does not benefit the priestly class in any significant way. This conclusion was based on the role the priests fulfil in the social network. Hence, SNA can inform the ongoing debate on authorship attribution.

Fourth, the methodology developed in this project can be applied to other legal collections, most importantly the Covenant Code (Exod. 20.22–23.33) and the Deuteronomic Code (Deut 12–26), in order to characterise the participants of those texts. As a matter of fact, SNA is more efficient when similar social networks are compared and contrasted. For example, does YHWH have a more prominent role in H than in the other law texts? And is the sojourner characterised differently in H to in the other codes, as often suggested? It is my contention that valuable insights on Biblical law and ethical roles could be gleaned by applying SNA to these texts as well. Importantly, SNA need not be limited to Biblical corpora. In fact, SNA has already been applied to the study of cuneiform archives as a method for mapping tablets and the participants mentioned in those tablets (see the summary of Mesopotamian research in chapter 7, §2.3). However, along the lines of the present study, SNA could also be applied to individual

Mesopotamian and Egyptian law texts in order to map the ethical and social roles of the participants involved. The Code of Hammurabi, for example, has often been compared to the Biblical laws. A similar SNA of the Code of Hammurabi would qualify the comparisons even further.

Fifth, the methodology developed here can be applied to other genres of the Hebrew Bible. Although SNA has already been used for narratives (e.g., Che 2017), the present methodology captures interactions in a unique way by including all types of interactions and by quantifying the interactions by means of agency. It is reasonable to believe that narratives form small social networks with core and peripheral participants. The social network methodology developed here provides statistical tools for measuring the structural prominence of participants, and quantifying their interactions according to agency. The drawback of the methodology is its reliance upon advanced semantic data that cannot automatically be extracted from the text. On the other hand, the demanding work of participant tracking and semantic role annotation can itself uncover important structural and literary features relevant for the interpretation of participant roles. Hopefully, the research documented here has broken new ground for further studies into BH semantics.

Sixth, it is my contention that more general studies of Biblical ethics would benefit from a network analysis of Biblical law. As shown, the laws of the Holiness Code are addressed to concrete participants in concrete situations. By implication, a particular law does not necessarily apply to everyone (although some

## 8. Conclusion

laws might in fact do). Thus, in my opinion, it is much more fruitful to observe how the Israelites should act in specific contexts with respect to specific participants, rather than deriving abstract ethical principles divorced from their situational contexts. For example, while H is indeed concerned with social order and equality, this concern is embedded in a holiness framework, and this framework determines how the individual social laws should be interpreted and evaluated. Accordingly, I have argued that the purpose of the anti-incest laws in Lev. 18 and 20 is not to protect the property of males, nor to protect the legal rights of women, but to preserve the purity and sanctity of the people by prohibiting certain sexual interactions. Thus, to rightly interpret Biblical law from an ethical point of view, the laws need to be related to the participants, the specific situation (if stated), and the roles of the participants in their social setting. The present study has laid the foundation for exploring the ethical potential and scope of Biblical law by taking seriously the network roles of the participants and their concrete relationships with other participants. Having done this detailed research, I believe that the theological and ethical values of the law can be more adequately evaluated and related to modern ethics through SNA.

# BIBLIOGRAPHY

Achenbach, Reinhard. 2008. 'Das Heiligkeitsgesetz und die sakralen Ordnungen des Numeribuches im Horizont der Pentateuchredaktion'. In *The Books of Leviticus and Numbers*, edited by Thomas Römer, 145–75. Bibliotheca Ephemeridum Theologicarum Lovaniensium 215. Leuven: Peeters.

———. 2011. 'Gêr–Nåkhrî–Tôshav–Zâr: Legal and Sacral Distinctions Regarding Foreigners in the Pentateuch'. In *The Foreigner and the Law: Perspectives from the Hebrew Bible and the Ancient Near East*, edited by Reinhard Achenbach, Rainer Albertz, and Jakob Wöhrle, 29–51. Beihefte zur Zeitschrift für Altorientalische und Biblische Rechtsgeschichte 16. Wiesbaden: Harrassowitz.

Agarwal, Apoorv, Augusto Corvalan, Jacob Jensen, and Owen Rambow. 2012. 'Social Network Analysis of Alice in Wonderland'. In *Proceedings of the NAACL-HLT 2012 Workshop on Computational Linguistics for Literature*, edited by David Elson, Anna Kazantseva, Rada Mihalcea, and Stan Szpakowicz, 88–96. Montréal: Association for Computational Linguistics.

Aissen, Judith. 1979. *The Syntax of Causative Constructions*. New York: Garland.

Albertz, Rainer. 1994. *A History of Israelite Religion in the Old Testament Period*. Vol. 2, *From the Exile to the Maccabees*. Translated by John Bowden. Old Testament Library. Louisville, KY: Westminster John Knox.

———. 2011. 'From Aliens to Proselytes: Non-Priestly and Priestly Legislation Concerning Strangers'. In *The Foreigner and the Law: Perspectives from the Hebrew Bible and the Ancient Near East*, edited by Reinhard Achenbach, Rainer Albertz, and Jakob Wöhrle, 53–69. Beihefte zur Zeitschrift für Altorientalische und Biblische Rechtsgeschichte 16. Wiesbaden: Harrassowitz.

———. 2012. *Exodus 1–18*. Zürcher Bibelkommentare, Altes Testament 2.1. Zürich: Theologischer Verlag.

———. 2015. *Exodus 19–40*. Zürcher Bibelkommentare, Altes Testament 2.2. Zürich: Theologischer Verlag.

Alstola, Tero. 2017. 'Judean Merchants in Babylonia and Their Participation in Long-Distance Trade'. *Welt des Orients* 47 (1): 25–51. https://doi.org/10.13109/wdor.2017.47.1.25.

Alt, Albrecht. 1967. *Essays on Old Testament History and Religion*. Translated by R. A. Wilson. Garden City, NY: Doubleday.

Al-Taie, Mohammed Z., and Seifedine Kadry. 2017. *Python for Graph and Network Analysis*. Advanced Information and Knowledge Processing (AI&KP). Cham: Springer. https://doi.org/10.1007/978-3-319-53004-8.

Andersen, Francis I. 1970. *The Hebrew Verbless Clause in the Pentateuch*. Journal of Biblical Literature Monograph Series 14. Nashville, TN: Abingdon.

Arnold, Bill T. 2009. *Genesis*. New Cambridge Bible Commentary. Cambridge: Cambridge University Press.

———. 2017. 'Number Switching in Deuteronomy 12–26 and the Quest for Urdeuteronomium'. *Zeitschrift für Altorientalische und Biblische Rechtsgeschichte* 23: 163–80.

Audenaert, Pieter, Didier Colle, and Mario Pickavet. 2019. 'Regular Equivalence for Social Networks'. *Applied Sciences* 9 (1): 117. https://doi.org/10.3390/app9010117.

Averbeck, Richard E. 1996. 'Leviticus: Theology of'. In *New International Dictionary of Old Testament Theology and Exegesis*, edited by Willem A. VanGemeren, 4:907–23. Grand Rapids, MI: Zondervan.

Baasten, Martinus F. J. 2006. 'The Non-Verbal Clause in Qumran Hebrew'. PhD dissertation, Leiden University.

Baentsch, Bruno. 1893. *Das Heiligkeits-Gesetz, Lev. XVII–XXVI: Eine historisch-kritische Untersuchung*. Erfurt: Verlag von Hugo Güther.

Barabási, Albert-László, and Réka Albert. 1999. 'Emergence of Scaling in Random Networks'. *Science* 286: 509–12. https://doi.org/10.1515/9781400841356.349.

Barbiero, Gianni. 1991. *L'asino del nemico: Rinuncia alla vendetta e amore del nemico nella legislazione dell'Antico Testamento (Es 23,4–5; Dt 22,1–4; Lv 19,17–18)*. Analecta Biblica 128. Rome: Pontifical Biblical Institute.

———. 2002. *Studien zu Alttestamentlichen Texten*. Stuttgarter Biblische Aufsatzbände, Altes Testament 34. Stuttgart: Verlag Katholisches Bibelwerk.

Bartor, Assnat. 2010. *Reading Law as Narrative: A Study in the Casuistic Laws of the Pentateuch*. Ancient Israel and Its Literature 5. Atlanta, GA: Society of Biblical Literature.

Beavers, John. 2011. 'On Affectedness'. *Natural Language and Linguistic Theory* 29: 335–70. https://doi.org/10.1007/s11049-011-9124-6.

Beckman, John C. 2015. 'Toward the Meaning of the Biblical Hebrew Piel Stem'. PhD dissertation, Harvard University.

Bergland, Kenneth. 2020. 'Memorized Covenantal Instruction and Legal Reuse in Torah'. In *Exploring the Composition of the Pentateuch*, edited by L. S. Baker, Jr., Kenneth Bergland, Felipe A. Masotti, and A. Rahel Wells, 95–112. Bulletin for Biblical Research Supplement 27. University Park, PA: Eisenbrauns. https://doi.org/10.5325/j.ctv1c5cshm.11.

Berman, Joshua. 2017. *Inconsistency in the Torah: Ancient Literary Convention and the Limits of Source Criticism*. New York: Oxford University Press. https://doi.org/10.1093/acprof:oso/9780190658809.001.0001.

Bertholet, Alfred. 1896. *Die Stellung der Israeliten und der Juden zu den Fremden*. Freiburg and Leipzig: J. C. B. Mohr (Paul Siebeck).

Beveridge, Andrew, and Jie Shan. 2016. 'Network of Thrones'. *Math Horizons* 23 (4): 18–22. https://doi.org/10.4169/mathhorizons.23.4.18.

Bibb, Bryan D. 2009. *Ritual Words and Narrative Worlds in the Book of Leviticus*. The Library of Hebrew Bible/Old Testament Studies 480. New York: T&T Clark International.

Blenkinsopp, Joseph. 1992. *The Pentateuch: An Introduction to the First Five Books of the Bible*. The Anchor Bible Reference Library. New York: Doubleday.

Blum, Erhard. 1990. *Studien zur Komposition des Pentateuch*. Beihefte zur Zeitschrift für die alttestamentliche Wissenschaft 189. Berlin: De Gruyter.

Borgatti, Stephen P., and Martin G. Everett. 1992. 'Notions of Position in Social Network Analysis'. *Sociological Methodology* 22: 1–35. https://doi.org/10.2307/270991.

———. 1993. 'Two Algorithms for Computing Regular Equivalence'. *Social Networks* 15: 361–76. https://doi.org/10.1016/0378-8733(93)90012-a.

Borgatti, Stephen P., Martin G. Everett, and Jeffrey C. Johnson. 2018. *Analyzing Social Networks*. 2nd ed. New York: SAGE.

Borgatti, Stephen P., Ajay Mehra, Daniel J. Brass, and Giuseppe Labianca. 2009. 'Network Analysis in the Social Sciences'. *Science* 323: 892–95. https://doi.org/10.1126/science.1165821.

Bosman, Hendrik J. 2019. 'Syntax and Stylistics: In Search for Syntactical Parameters for the Textual Hierarchy of Prophetic Texts'. PhD dissertation, Vrije Universiteit Amsterdam.

Brandes, Ulrik, and Thomas Erlebach (eds). 2005. *Network Analysis: Methodological Foundations*. Lecture Notes in Computer Science. Berlin: Springer. https://doi.org/10.1007/b106453.

Brass, Daniel J. 1984. 'Being in the Right Place: A Structural Analysis of Individual Influence in an Organization'. *Administrative Science Quarterly* 29 (4): 518–39. https://doi.org/10.2307/2392937.

Britt, Brian, and Patrick Creehan. 2000. 'Chiasmus in Leviticus 16,29–17,11'. *Zeitschrift für die alttestamentliche Wissenschaft* 112: 398–400.

Bultmann, Christoph. 1992. *Der Fremde im Antiken Juda: Eine Untersuchung zum sozialen Typenbegriff 'Ger' und seinem Bedeutungswandel in der Alttestamentlichen Gesetzgebung.* Forschungen zur Religion und Literatur des Alten und Neuen Testaments 153. Göttingen: Vandenhoeck & Ruprecht.

Carron, Pádraig Mac, and Ralph Kenna. 2012. 'Universal Properties of Mythological Networks'. *Europhysics Letters* 99 (2): 28002. https://doi.org/10.1209/0295-5075/99/28002.

Castaldi, Maria R. 2013. 'Causative Verb: Biblical Hebrew'. In *Encyclopedia of Hebrew Language and Linguistics*, online edition, edited by Geoffrey Khan. Leiden: Brill. http://dx.doi.org/10.1163/2212-4241_ehll_EHLL_COM_00000413.

Che, Chebineh. 2017. 'Participants, Characters and Roles. A Text-Syntactic, Literary and Socioscientific Reading of Genesis 27–28'. PhD dissertation, Vrije Universiteit Amsterdam.

Cholewiński, Alfred. 1976. *Heiligkeitsgesetz und Deuteronomium: Eine vergleichende Studie.* Analecta Biblica 66. Rome: Biblical Institute Press.

Christian, Mark A. 2011. 'Levites and the Plenary Reception of Revelation'. PhD dissertation, Vanderbilt University.

Clines, David J. A. 1978. *The Theme of the Pentateuch.* Journal for the Study of the Old Testament Supplement Series 10. Sheffield: JSOT Press.

Cohen, Matty. 1990. 'Le « ger » biblique et son statut socio-religieux'. *Revue de l'Histoire des Religions* 207 (2): 131–58. https://doi.org/10.3406/rhr.1990.1736.

Comrie, Bernard. 1976. *Aspect: An Introduction to the Study of Verbal Aspect and Related Problems*. Cambridge: Cambridge University Press.

Comrie, Bernard, and Maria Polinsky (eds). 1993. *Causatives and Transitivity*. Studies in Language Companion Series 23. Amsterdam: John Benjamins. https://doi.org/10.1075/slcs.23.

Cook, John A. 2002. 'The Biblical Hebrew Verbal System: A Grammaticalization Approach'. PhD dissertation, University of Wisconsin-Madison.

Copley, Bridget, and Fabienne Martin, (eds). 2014. *Causation in Grammatical Structures*. Oxford Studies in Theoretical Linguistics 52. Oxford: Oxford University Press. https://doi.org/10.1093/acprof:oso/9780199672073.001.0001.

Creason, Stuart A. 1995. 'Semantic Classes of Hebrew Verbs: A Study of Aktionsart in the Hebrew Verbal System'. PhD dissertation, University of Chicago.

Croft, William. 2012. *Verbs: Aspect and Causal Structure*. Oxford Linguistics. Oxford: Oxford University Press. https://doi.org/10.1093/acprof:oso/9780199248582.001.0001.

Crüsemann, Frank. 1992. *Die Tora: Theologie und Sozialgeschichte des alttestamentlichen Gesetzes*. Munich: Chr. Kaiser.

Dahl, Östen. 1985. *Tense and Aspect Systems*. Oxford: Basil Blackwell.

Dan, Barak. 2013. 'Binyanim: Biblical Hebrew'. In *Encyclopedia of Hebrew Language and Linguistics*, online edition, edited by Geoffrey Khan. Leiden: Brill. https://doi.org/10.1163/2212-4241_ehll_EHLL_COM_00000210.

Delancey, Scott. 1984. 'Notes on Agentivity and Causation'. *Studies in Languages* 8 (2): 181–213. https://doi.org/10.1075/sl.8.2.05del.

Dépelteau, François. 2018. 'Relational Thinking in Sociology: Relevance, Concurrence and Dissonance'. In *The Palgrave Handbook of Relational Sociology*, edited by François Dépelteau, 3–33. Cham: Palgrave Macmillan. https://doi.org/10.1007/978-3-319-66005-9_1.

de Regt, Lénart J. 1999a. 'Macrosyntactic Functions of Nominal Clauses Referring to Participants'. In *The Verbless Clause in Biblical Hebrew: Linguistic Approaches*, edited by Cynthia L. Miller, 273–96. Linguistic Studies in Ancient West Semitic 1. Winona Lake, IN: Eisenbrauns. https://doi.org/10.5325/j.ctv1bxh3hg.15.

———. 1999b. *Participants in Old Testament Texts and the Translator: Reference Devices and Their Rhetorical Impact*. Studia Semitica Neerlandica 39. Assen: Van Gorcum. https://doi.org/10.1163/9789004358690.

———. 2001. 'Person Shift in Prophetic Texts: Its Function and Its Rendering in Ancient and Modern Translations'. In *The Elusive Prophet: The Prophet as a Historical Person, Literary Character and Anonymous Artist*, edited by Johannes C. de Moor, 214–31. Old Testament Studies 45. Leiden: Brill. https://doi.org/10.1163/9789004496255_015.

———. 2019. *Linguistic Coherence in Biblical Hebrew Texts: Arrangement of Information, Participant Reference Devices, Verb Forms, and Their Contribution to Textual Segmentation and Coherence*. Rev. and extended ed. Perspectives on Hebrew

Scriptures and Its Contexts 28. Piscataway, NJ: Gorgias. https://doi.org/10.31826/9781463240684.

Diedrichsen, Elke. 2015. 'Degrees of Causativity in German Lassen Causative Constructions'. In *Causation, Permission, and Transfer: Argument Realisation in GET, TAKE, PUT, GIVE and LET Verbs*, edited by Brian Nolan, Gudrun Rawoens, and Elke Diedrichsen, 53–105. Studies in Language Companion Series 167. Amsterdam: John Benjamins. https://doi.org/10.1075/slcs.167.001int.

Dixon, Robert M. W. 2000. 'A Typology of Causatives: Form, Syntax and Meaning'. In *Changing Valency: Case Studies in Transitivity*, edited by Robert M. W. Dixon and Alexandra Y. Aikhenvald, 30–83. Cambridge: Cambridge University Press. https://doi.org/10.1017/cbo9780511627750.003.

Dobbs-Allsopp, F. W. 2000. 'Biblical Hebrew Statives and Situation Aspect'. *Journal of Semitic Studies* 45 (1): 21–53. https://doi.org/10.1093/jss/XLV.1.21.

Donati, Pierpaolo. 2011. *Relational Sociology: A New Paradigm for the Social Sciences*. London: Routledge. https://doi.org/10.4324/9780203860281.

———. 2017. 'Relational versus Relationist Sociology: A New Paradigm in the Social Sciences'. *Stan Rzeczy* 12: 15–66. https://doi.org/10.51196/srz.12.2.

Doron, Edit. 2020. 'From a Collective to a Free Choice Determiner in Biblical Hebrew'. In *Quantification and Scales in Change*, edited by Remus Gergel and Jonathan Watkins, 1–31. Berlin: Language Science Press.

Douglas, Mary. 1993. 'The Forbidden Animals in Leviticus'. *Journal for the Study of the Old Testament* 18 (59): 3–23. https://doi.org/10.1177/030908929301805901.

———. 1994. 'The Stranger in the Bible'. *European Journal of Sociology / Archives Européennes de Sociologie* 35 (2): 283–98. https://doi.org/10.1017/s0003975600006871.

———. 1995. 'Poetic Structure in Leviticus'. In *Pomegranates and Golden Bells: Studies in Biblical, Jewish, and Near Eastern Ritual, Law, and Literature in Honor of Jacob Milgrom*, edited by David P. Wright, David N. Freedman, and Avi Hurvitz, 239–56. Winona Lake, IN: Eisenbrauns.

———. 1999. *Leviticus as Literature*. Oxford: Oxford University Press. https://doi.org/10.1093/0199244197.001.0001.

Dowty, David R. 1979. *Word Meaning and Montague Grammar: The Semantics of Verbs and Times in Generative Semantics and in Montague's PTQ*. Dordrecht: Reidel. https://doi.org/10.1007/978-94-009-9473-7.

———. 1991. 'Thematic Proto-Roles and Argument Selection'. *Language* 67 (3): 547–619. https://doi.org/10.2307/415037.

Driver, G. R. 1936. *Problems of the Hebrew Verbal System*. Edinburgh: T&T Clark.

Dupont, Joanne M. 1989. 'Women and the Concept of Holiness in the "Holiness Code" (Leviticus 17–26): Literary, Theological and Historical Context'. PhD dissertation, Marquette University.

Dyk, Janet W. 2014. 'Traces of Valence Shift in Classical Hebrew'. In *Discourse, Dialogue & Debate in the Bible: Essays in Honour of Frank H. Polak*, edited by Athalya Brenner-Idan, 48–65.

Hebrew Bible Monographs 63. Sheffield: Sheffield Phoenix Press.

Dyk, Janet W., Oliver Glanz, and Reinoud Oosting. 2014. 'Analysing Valence Patterns in Biblical Hebrew: Theoretical Questions and Analytic Frameworks'. *Journal of Northwest Semitic Languages* 40 (1): 1–20.

Dyk, Janet W., and Eep Talstra. 1999. 'Paradigmatic and Syntagmatic Features in Identifying Subject and Predicate in Nominal Clauses'. In *The Verbless Clause in Biblical Hebrew: Linguistic Approaches*, edited by Cynthia L. Miller, 133–85. Linguistic Studies in Ancient West Semitic 1. Winona Lake, IN: Eisenbrauns. https://doi.org/10.1515/9781575065175-009.

Eerdmans, B. D. 1912. *Alttestamentliche Studien*. Vol. 4, *Das Buch Leviticus*. Gießen: Alfred Töpelmann.

Ellens, Deborah L. 2008. *Women in the Sex Texts of Leviticus and Deuteronomy: A Comparative Conceptual Analysis*. The Library of Hebrew Bible/Old Testament Studies 458. New York: T&T Clark International.

Elliger, Karl. 1966. *Leviticus*. Handbuch zum Alten Testament 4. Tübingen: J. C. B. Mohr (Paul Siebeck).

Elliott-Binns, L. E. 1955. 'Some Problems of the Holiness Code'. *Zeitschrift für die alttestamentliche Wissenschaft* 67: 26–40. https://doi.org/10.1515/zatw.1955.67.1.26.

Ellis, Nick C. 2006. 'Language Acquisition as Rational Contingency Learning'. *Applied Linguistics* 27 (1): 1–24. https://doi.org/10.1093/applin/ami038.

Ellis, Nick C., and Fernando Ferreira-Junior. 2009. 'Construction Learning as a Function of Frequency, Frequency Distribution, and Function'. *The Modern Language Journal* 93 (3): 370–85. https://doi.org/10.1111/j.1540-4781.2009.00896.x.

Emirbayer, Mustafa. 1997. 'Manifesto for a Relational Sociology'. *American Journal of Sociology* 103 (2): 281–317. https://doi.org/10.1086/231209.

Erwich, Christiaan M. 2020. 'Who Is Who in the Psalms? Coreference Resolution as Exegetical Tool for Participant Analysis in Biblical Texts'. PhD dissertation, Vrije Universiteit Amsterdam.

Escamilla, Ramón M., Jr. 2012. 'An Updated Typology of Causative Constructions: Form-Function Mappings in Hupa (California Athabaskan), Chungli Ao (Tibeto-Burman) and Beyond'. PhD dissertation, University of California.

Evert, Stefan. 2004. 'The Statistics of Word Cooccurrences: Word Pairs and Collocations'. PhD dissertation, Universität Stuttgart.

———. 2008. 'Corpora and Collocations'. In *Corpus Linguistics: An International Handbook*, edited by Anke Lüdeling and Merja Kytö, 2:1212–48. Berlin: De Gruyter. https://doi.org/10.1515/9783110213881.2.1212.

Ewald, Heinrich. 1864. *Einleitung in die Geschichte des Volkes Israel*. 3rd ed. Vol. 1. Göttingen: Dieterichschen Buchhandlung.

Fellbaum, Christiane, Joachim Grabowski, and Shari Landes. 1998. 'Performance and Confidence in a Semantic Annotation Task'. In *WordNet: An Electronic Lexical Database and*

*Some of Its Applications*, edited by Christiane Fellbaum, 217–37. Cambridge, MA: MIT Press. https://doi.org/10.7551/mitpress/7287.003.0016.

Feucht, Christian. 1964. *Untersuchungen zum Heiligkeitsgesetz*. Theologische Arbeiten 20. Berlin: Evangelische Verlagsanstalt.

Fillmore, Charles J. 1968. 'The Case for Case'. In *Universals in Linguistic Theory*, edited by Emmon Bach and Robert T. Harms, 1–90. New York: Holt, Rinehart and Winston.

———. 1988. 'The Mechanisms of "Construction Grammar"'. In *Proceedings of the Fourteenth Annual Meeting of the Berkeley Linguistics Society*, edited by Shelley Axmaker, Annie Jaisser, and Helen Singmaster, 35–55. Berkeley, CA: Berkeley Linguistics Society. https://doi.org/10.3765/bls.v14i0.1794.

———. 2003. *Form and Meaning in Language*. Center for the Study of Language and Information Lecture Notes 121. Stanford, CA: CSLI Publications.

Foley, William A., and Robert D. Van Valin, Jr. 1984. *Functional Syntax and Universal Grammar*. Cambridge Studies in Linguistics 38. Cambridge: Cambridge University Press.

Frajzyngier, Zygmunt, and Erin Shay. 2016. *The Role of Functions in Syntax: A Unified Approach to Language Theory, Description, and Typology*. Typological Studies in Language 111. Amsterdam: John Benjamins. https://doi.org/10.1075/tsl.111.

Franzosi, Roberto. 1997. 'Mobilization and Counter-Mobilization Processes: From the "Red Years" (1919–20) to the "Black

Years" (1921–22) in Italy—A New Methodological Approach to the Study of Narrative Data'. *Theory and Society* 26: 275–304.

Freeman, Linton C. 1978. 'Centrality in Social Networks: Conceptual Clarification'. *Social Networks* 1: 215–39. https://doi.org/10.1016/0378-8733(78)90021-7.

———. 2004. *The Development of Social Network Analysis: A Study in the Sociology of Science*. Vancouver: Empirical Press.

———. 2014. 'The Development of Social Network Analysis—with an Emphasis on Recent Events'. In *The SAGE Handbook of Social Network Analysis*, edited by John Scott and Peter J. Carrington, 26–39. London: SAGE Publications. https://doi.org/10.4135/9781446294413.n3.

Fuhse, Jan A. 2009. 'The Meaning Structure of Social Networks'. *Sociological Theory* 27 (1): 51–73. https://doi.org/10.1111/j.1467-9558.2009.00338.x.

Fuller, Lon L. 1969. 'Human Interaction and the Law'. *The American Journal of Jurisprudence* 14 (1): 1–36. https://doi.org/10.1093/ajj/14.1.1.

Gane, Roy E. 2015. 'Didactic Logic and the Authorship of Leviticus'. In *Current Issues in Priestly and Related Literature: The Legacy of Jacob Milgrom and Beyond*, edited by Roy E. Gane and Ada Taggar-Cohen, 197–221. Atlanta, GA: Society of Biblical Literature. https://doi.org/10.2307/j.ctt18z4h0x.14.

———. 2017. *Old Testament Law for Christians: Original Context and Enduring Application*. Grand Rapids, MI: Baker Academic.

Gerleman, G. 1984. 'Mūt Sterben'. In *Theologisches Handwörterbuch zum Alten Testament*, edited by Ernst Jenni, 1:893–97. Munich; Zürich: Chr. Kaiser; Theologischer Verlag.

Gerstenberger, Erhard S. 1996. *Leviticus: A Commentary*. Old Testament Library. Louisville, KY: Westminster John Knox.

———. 2009. *Wesen und Herkunft des Apodiktischen Rechts*. Eugene, OR: Wipf and Stock.

Gibson, D. 2005. 'Taking Turns and Talking Ties: Networks and Conversational Interaction'. *American Journal of Sociology* 110 (6): 1561–97. https://doi.org/10.1086/428689.

Givón, T. 2001. *Syntax: An Introduction*. Rev. ed. 2 vols. Amsterdam: John Benjamins. https://doi.org/10.1075/z.syn1 (vol. 1); https://doi.org/10.1075/z.syn2. (vol. 2).

Glanz, Oliver. 2013. *Understanding Participant-Reference Shifts in the Book of Jeremiah: A Study of Exegetical Method and Its Consequences for the Interpretation of Referential Incoherence*. Studia Semitica Neerlandica 60. Leiden: Brill. https://doi.org/10.1163/9789004242180.

Glanz, Oliver, Reinoud Oosting, and Janet W. Dyk. 2015. 'Valence Patterns in Biblical Hebrew: Classical Philology and Linguistic Patterns'. *Journal of Northwest Semitic Languages* 41 (2): 31–55.

Glynn, Dylan. 2010. 'Testing the Hypothesis: Objectivity and Verification in Usage-Based Cognitive Semantics'. In *Quantitative Methods in Cognitive Semantics: Corpus-Driven Approaches*, edited by Dylan Glynn and Kerstin Fischer, 239–69. Cognitive Linguistics Research 46. Berlin: De Gruyter Mouton. https://doi.org/10.1515/9783110226423.239.

Goetze, Albrecht. 1942. 'The So-Called Intensive of the Semitic Languages'. *Journal of the American Oriental Society* 62: 1–8. https://doi.org/10.2307/594095.

Goldberg, Adele E. 1995. *Constructions: A Construction Grammar Approach to Argument Structure*. Chicago, IL: University of Chicago Press.

Goldfajn, Tal. 1998. *Word Order and Time in Biblical Hebrew Narrative*. Oxford Theological Monographs. Oxford: Clarendon. https://doi.org/10.1093/acprof:oso/9780198269533.001.0001.

Graf, Karl H. 1866. *Die geschichtlichen Bücher des Alten Testaments: zwei historisch-kritische Untersuchungen*. Leipzig: T. O. Weigel.

Greenberg, Moshe. 1984. 'The Design and Themes of Ezekiel's Program of Restoration'. *Interpretation* 38 (2): 181–208. https://doi.org/10.1177/002096438403800206.

Gries, Stefan Th., and Anatol Stefanowitsch. 2004. 'Covarying Collexemes in the Into-Causative'. In *Language, Culture, and Mind*, edited by Michel Achard and Suzanne Kemmer, 225–36. Stanford, CA: CSLI Publications.

Groenewegen, Peter, Julie E. Ferguson, Christine Moser, John W. Mohr, and Stephen P. Borgatti (eds). 2017. *Structure, Content and Meaning of Organizational Networks: Extending Network Thinking*. Research in the Sociology of Organizations 53. Bingley: Emerald Publishing. https://doi.org/10.1108/s0733-558x201753.

Gross, Walter. 1980. 'Syntaktische Erscheinungen am Anfang althebräischer Erzählungen: Hintergrund und Vordergrund'. In *Congress Volume Vienne 1980*, edited by J. A. Emerton, 131–45. Leiden: Brill. https://doi.org/10.1163/9789004275553_009.

Grover, Aditya, and Jure Leskovec. 2016. 'Node2vec: Scalable Feature Learning for Networks'. In *Proceedings of the 22nd ACM SIGKDD International Conference on Knowledge Discovery and Data Mining*, 855–64. New York: Association for Computing Machinery. https://doi.org/10.1145/2939672.2939754.

Grünwaldt, Klaus. 1999. *Das Heiligkeitsgesetz Leviticus 17–26: Ursprüngliche Gestalt, Tradition und Theologie*. Beihefte zur Zeitschrift für die alttestamentliche Wissenschaft 271. Berlin: De Gruyter. https://doi.org/10.1515/9783110800777.

———. 2003. 'Amt und Gemeinde im Heiligkeitsgesetz'. In *Textarbeit: Studien zu Texten und ihrer Rezeption aus dem Alten Testament und der Umwelt Israels—Festschrift für Peter Weimar*, edited by Klaus Kiesow and Thomas Meurer, 227–44. Alter Orient und Altes Testament 294. Münster: Ugarit-Verlag.

Guillaume, Philippe. 2009. *Land and Calendar: The Priestly Document from Genesis 1 to Joshua 18*. The Library of Hebrew Bible/Old Testament Studies 391. New York: T&T Clark International.

Halliday, M. A. K. 1967. 'Notes on Transitivity and Theme in English: Part 2'. *Journal of Linguistics* 3 (2): 199–244. https://doi.org/10.1017/s0022226700016613.

———. 1970. 'Language Structure and Language Function'. In *New Horizons in Linguistics,* edited by John Lyons, 140–65. Harmondsworth: Penguin.

Harper, G. Geoffrey. 2018. *'I Will Walk Among You': The Rhetorical Function of Allusion to Genesis 1–3 in the Book of Leviticus.* Bulletin for Biblical Research Supplement 21. University Park, PA: Eisenbrauns. https://doi.org/10.5325/j.ctv14gp60r.

Harrington, Hannah K. 2012. 'Leviticus'. In *Women's Bible Commentary,* edited by Carol A. Newsom, Sharon H. Ringe, and Jacqueline E. Lapsley, 3rd ed., twentieth anniversary ed., 70–78. Louisville, KY: Westminster John Knox.

Hartley, John E. 1992. *Leviticus.* Word Biblical Commentary 4. Dallas, TX: Word, Incorporated.

Hasegawa, Yoko. 1996. *A Study of Japanese Clause Linkage: The Connective TE in Japanese.* Studies in Japanese Linguistics 5. Stanford, CA: CSLI Publications.

Haspelmath, Martin. 1994. 'Passive Participles across Languages'. In *Voice: Form and Function,* edited by Barbara Fox and Paul J. Hopper, 151–77. Amsterdam: John Benjamins. https://doi.org/10.1075/tsl.27.08has.

Hendel, Ronald. 1996. 'In the Margins of the Hebrew Verbal System: Situation, Tense, Aspect, Mood'. *Zeitschrift für Althebraistik* 9: 152–81.

Hendel, Ronald, and Jan Joosten. 2018. *How Old Is the Hebrew Bible? A Linguistic, Textual, and Historical Study.* New Haven, CT: Yale University Press. https://doi.org/10.12987/9780300240382.

Hermansen, Anders, Bjarke T. Carstens, Mads R. Jensen, and Mathias F. Spaniel. 2017. 'Vertex Similarity in Graphs Using Feature Learning'. MA thesis, Aalborg University.

Hieke, Thomas. 2014. *Levitikus 16–27*. Herders Theologischer Kommentar zum Alten Testament. Freiburg: Herder.

Hoffmann, David. 1906. *Das Buch Leviticus*. Vol. 2. Berlin: M. Poppelauer.

Hoffmann, Thomas, and Graeme Trousdale (eds). 2013. *The Oxford Handbook of Construction Grammar*. Oxford: Oxford University Press. https://doi.org/10.1093/oxfordhb/9780195396683.001.0001.

Hoftijzer, J. 1973. 'Review: The Nominal Clause Reconsidered'. *Vetus Testamentum* 23: 446–510. https://doi.org/10.1163/156853373x00342.

Holguín, Julián A. G. 2015. 'Leviticus 24:10–23: An Outsider Perspective'. *Hebrew Studies* 56: 89–102. https://doi.org/10.1353/hbr.2015.0002.

Holisky, Dee A. 1987. 'The Case of the Intransitive Subject in Tsova-Tush (Batsbi)'. *Lingua* 71: 103–32. https://doi.org/10.1016/0024-3841(87)90069-6.

Hopper, Paul J. 1986. 'Causes and Affects'. In *Causatives and Agentivity: Papers of the Parasession on Agency and Causativity of the 21st Annual Meeting of the Chicago Linguistic Society*, edited by W. H. Eilfort, P. Kroeber, and K. L. Peterson, 67–88. Chicago, IL: CLS.

Hopper, Paul J., and Sandra A. Thompson. 1980. 'Transitivity in Grammar and Discourse'. *Language* 56 (2): 251–99. https://doi.org/10.2307/413757.

Hornkohl, Aaron. 2013. 'Biblical Hebrew: Periodization'. In *Encyclopedia of Hebrew Language and Linguistics*, online edition, edited by Geoffrey Khan. Leiden: Brill. https://doi.org/10.1163/2212-4241_ehll_ehll_com_00000390.

Huddleston, Rodney, and Geoffrey K. Pullum. 2002. *The Cambridge Grammar of the English Language*. Cambridge: Cambridge University Press. https://doi.org/10.1017/9781316423530.

Hutton, Rodney R. 1999. 'The Case of the Blasphemer Revisited (Lev. XXIV 10–23)'. *Vetus Testamentum* 49 (4): 532–41. https://doi.org/10.1163/156853399323228434.

Højgaard, Christian C. 2023. 'Rational Actors and the Ancient Israelite Jubilee Legislation'. In *Modern Economics and the Ancient World: Were the Ancients Rational Actors?—Selected Papers from the Online Conference, 29–31 July 2021*, edited by Sven Günther, 91–109. Muziris 2. Münster: Zaphon.

Jackendoff, Ray. 1990. *Semantic Structures*. Current Studies in Linguistics 18. Cambridge, MA: MIT Press.

———. 2002. *Foundations of Language: Brain, Meaning, Grammar, Evolution*. Oxford: Oxford University Press. https://doi.org/10.1093/acprof:oso/9780198270126.001.0001.

Jackson, Matthew O. 2011. 'An Overview of Social Networks and Economic Applications'. In *Handbook of Social Economics*, edited by Jess Benhabib, Alberto Bisin, and Matthew O. Jackson, 1:511–85. San Diego, CA: North-Holland. https://doi.org/10.1016/b978-0-444-53187-2.00012-7.

Janowski, Bernd. 2017. 'Persönlichkeitszeichen: Ein Beitrag zum Personverständnis des Alten Testaments'. In *Individualität und Selbstreflexion in den Literaturen des Alten Testaments*, edited by Andreas Wagner and Jürgen van Oorschot, 315–40. Veröffentlichungen der Wissenschaftlichen Gesellschaft für Theologie 48. Leipzig: Evangelische Verlagsanstalt.

Jenni, Ernst. 1967. 'Faktitiv und Kausativ von אבד "Zugrunde Gehen"'. In *Hebräische Wortforschung: Festschrift zum 80. Geburtstag von Walter Baumgartner*, 143–57. Supplements to Vetus Testamentum 16. Leiden: Brill. https://doi.org/10.1163/9789004275393_016.

———. 1968. *Das hebräische Piʾel: Syntaktisch-semasiologische Untersuchung einer Verbalform im Alten Testament*. Zürich: EVZ-Verlag.

Jensen, Christian H. 2016. 'Participant-Reference Shifts in Zech. 1:1–6: An Assessment of Diachronic and Synchronic Approaches'. *HIPHIL Novum* 3 (1): 25–46.

———. 2017. 'A Rhetorical-Structural Reading of Zechariah's Night Visions'. MA thesis, University of Copenhagen.

———. 2019. 'Kollektiv identitet og individuelt ansvar: Et retorisk studium af referenceskift i Lev 18–20 og 25–26'. *Dansk Tidsskrift for Teologi og Kirke* 46 (1): 21–37.

Jenson, Philip P. 1992. *Graded Holiness: A Key to the Priestly Conception of the World*. Journal for the Study of the Old Testament Supplement Series 106. Sheffield: Sheffield Academic Press.

Jero, Christopher. 2008. 'The Verbal System of Biblical Hebrew Poetry: The Morphosyntactic Role of Internal Aspect (Aktionsart)'. PhD dissertation: Hebrew Union College, Cincinnati.

Jolliffe, I. T. 2002. *Principal Component Analysis*. 2nd ed. Springer Series in Statistics. New York: Springer. https://doi.org/10.1007/b98835.

Joosten, Jan. 1996. *People and Land in the Holiness Code: An Exegetical Study of the Ideational Framework of the Law in Leviticus 17–26*. Supplements to Vetus Testamentum 67. Leiden: Brill. https://doi.org/10.1163/9789004275911.

———. 1997. '«Tu» et «vous» dans le Code de Sainteté (Lév. 17–26)'. *Revue des sciences religieuses* 71 (1): 3–8. https://doi.org/10.3406/rscir.1997.3385.

———. 2010. 'La persuasion coopérative dans le discours sur la loi: Pour une analyse de la rhétorique du Code de Sainteté'. In *Congress Volume Ljubljana 2007*, edited by André Lemaire, 381–98. Supplements to Vetus Testamentum 133. Leiden: Brill. https://doi.org/10.1163/ej.9789004179776.i-640.94.

———. 2012. *The Verbal System of Biblical Hebrew. A New Synthesis Elaborated on the Basis of Classical Prose*. Jerusalem Biblical Studies 10. Jerusalem: Simor.

Joüon, Paul, and Takamitsu Muraoka. 1993. *A Grammar of Biblical Hebrew*. Repr. of 1st ed., with corrections. 2 vols. Subsidia Biblica 14. Rome: Pontifical Biblical Institute.

Jürgens, Benedikt. 2001. *Heiligkeit und Versöhnung: Levitikus 16 in seinem literarischen Kontext*. Herders biblische Studien 28. Freiburg: Herder.

Kalkman, Gino J. 2015. 'Verbal Forms in Biblical Hebrew Poetry: Poetic Freedom or Linguistic System?' PhD dissertation, Vrije Universiteit Amsterdam.

Kayser, August. 1874. *Das vorexilische Buch der Urgeschichte Israels und seine Erweiterungen: Ein Beitrag zur Pentateuchkritik*. Strassburg: C. F. Schmidt's Universitäts-Buchhandlung.

Kellermann, Diether. 1977. 'גּוּר Gûr'. In *Theological Dictionary of the Old Testament*, edited by G. Johannes Botterweck and Helmer Ringgren, translated by John T. Willis, rev. ed., 2:439–49. Grand Rapids, MI: Eerdmans.

Kemmer, Suzanne, and Arie Verhagen. 1994. 'The Grammar of Causatives and the Conceptual Structure of Events'. *Cognitive Linguistics* 5 (2): 115–56. https://doi.org/10.1515/cogl.1994.5.2.115.

Khan, Geoffrey. 1988. *Studies in Semitic Syntax*. London Oriental Series 38. Oxford: Oxford University Press.

Kilchör, Benjamin. 2015. *Mosetora und Jahwetora: Das Verhältnis von Deuteronomium 12–26 zu Exodus, Levitikus und Numeri*. Beihefte zur Zeitschrift für Altorientalische und Biblische Rechtsgeschichte 21. Wiesbaden: Harrassowitz. https://doi.org/10.2307/j.ctvc2rmx0.

Kilian, Rudolf. 1963. *Literarkritische und formgeschichtliche Untersuchungen des Heiligkeitsgesetzes*. Bonner Biblische Beiträge 19. Bonn: Peter Hanstein.

King, Thomas J. 2009. *The Realignment of the Priestly Literature: The Priestly Narrative in Genesis and Its Relation to Priestly Legislation and the Holiness School*. Princeton Theological Monograph Series 102. Eugene, OR: Pickwick Publications.

Kingham, Cody. 2018. 'Data Creation'. http://www.etcbc.nl/datacreation/, accessed 11 January 2024.

Kline, Moshe. 2005. 'The Literary Structure of Leviticus'. *The Biblical Historian* 2 (1): 11–28.

———. 2008. '"The Editor Was Nodding": A Reading of Leviticus 19 in Memory of Mary Douglas'. *Journal of Hebrew Scriptures* 8. 58 pages. https://doi.org/10.5508/jhs.2008.v8.a17.

———. 2015. 'Structure Is Theology: The Composition of Leviticus'. In *Current Issues in Priestly and Related Literature: The Legacy of Jacob Milgrom and Beyond*, edited by Roy E. Gane and Ada Taggar-Cohen, 225–64. Atlanta, GA: Society of Biblical Literature. https://doi.org/10.2307/j.ctt18z4h0x.15.

Klostermann, August. 1893. *Der Pentateuch: Beiträge zu seinem Verständnis und seiner Entstehungsgeschichte*. Leipzig: Deichert.

Knohl, Israel. 1987. 'The Priestly Torah Versus the Holiness School: Sabbath and the Festivals'. *Hebrew Union College Annual* 58: 65–117.

———. 1988. 'The Conception of God and Cult in the Priestly Torah and in the Holiness School'. PhD dissertation, Hebrew University of Jerusalem.

———. 2007. *The Sanctuary of Silence: The Priestly Torah and the Holiness School*. Winona Lake, IN: Eisenbrauns.

Koenig, Jean-Pierre, and Anthony R. Davis. 2001. 'Sublexical Modality And The Structure Of Lexical Semantic Representations'. *Linguistics and Philosophy* 24: 71–124.

Köhler, Ludwig, Walter Baumgartner, M. E. J. Richardson, and Johann J. Stamm. 1994. *The Hebrew and Aramaic Lexicon of the Old Testament*. Leiden: Brill.

Koorevaar, Hendrik J. 2008. 'The Books of Exodus, Leviticus and Numbers, and the Macro-Structural Problem of the Pentateuch'. In *The Books of Leviticus and Numbers*, edited by Thomas Römer, 423–53. Bibliotheca Ephemeridum Theologicarum Lovaniensium 215. Leuven: Peeters.

Kornfeld, Walter. 1952. *Studien zum Heiligkeitsgesetz (Lev 17–26)*. Vienna: Herder.

Koschützki, Dirk, Katharina A. Lehmann, Leon Peeters, Stefan Richter, Dagmar Tenfelde-Podehl, and Oliver Zlotowski. 2005. 'Centrality Indices'. In *Network Analysis: Methodological Foundations*, edited by Ulrik Brandes and Thomas Erlebach, 16–61. Lecture Notes in Computer Science 3418. Berlin: Springer. https://doi.org/10.1007/978-3-540-31955-9_3.

Kouwenberg, N. J. C. 1997. *Gemination in the Akkadian Verb*. Studia Semitica Neerlandica 33. Assen: Van Gorcum. https://doi.org/10.1163/9789004358638.

———. 2010. *The Akkadian Verb and Its Semitic Background*. Languages of the Ancient Near East 2. Winona Lake, IN: Eisenbrauns. https://doi.org/10.1515/9781575066240.

Küchler, Siegfried. 1929. *Das Heiligkeitsgesetz: Lev. 17–26—Eine literar-kritische Untersuchung*. Königsberg: Kümmel.

Kugler, Robert A. 1997. 'Holiness, Purity, the Body, and Society: The Evidence for Theological Conflicts in Leviticus'. *Journal for the Study of the Old Testament* 22 (76): 3–27. https://doi.org/10.1177/030908929702207601.

Kühlewein, J. 1984. 'Jld Gebären'. In *Theologisches Handwörterbuch zum Alten Testament*, edited by Ernst Jenni, 1:732–36. Munich; Zürich: Chr. Kaiser; Theologischer Verlag.

Kulikov, Leonid I. 2001. 'Causatives'. In *Language Typology and Language Universals: An International Handbook*, edited by Martin Haspelmath, Ekkehard König, Wulf Oesterreicher, and Wolfgang Raible, 2:886–98. Berlin: De Gruyter. https://doi.org/10.1515/9783110194265-003.

Labov, William, and Joshua Waletsky. 1967. 'Narrative Analysis'. In *Essays on the Verbal and Visual Arts: Proceedings of the 1966 Annual Spring Meeting of the American Ethnological Society*, edited by June Helm, 12–44. Seattle, WA: University of Washington Press.

Lambrecht, Knud. 1994. *Information Structure and Sentence Form: Topic, Focus, and the Mental Representations of Discourse Referents*. Cambridge: Cambridge University Press. https://doi.org/10.1017/cbo9780511620607.

Lerner, Jürgen. 2005. 'Role Assignments'. In *Network Analysis: Methodological Foundations*, edited by Ulrik Brandes and Thomas Erlebach, 216–52. Lecture Notes in Computer Science 3418. Berlin: Springer. https://doi.org/10.1007/978-3-540-31955-9_9.

Levine, Baruch A. 1989. *Leviticus: The Traditional Hebrew Text with the New JPS Translation*. The JPS Torah Commentary. Philadelphia, PA: Jewish Publication Society of America.

Levinson, Bernard M. 2006. 'The "Effected Object" in Contractual Legal Language: The Semantics of "If You Purchase a Hebrew Slave" (Exod. XXI 2)'. *Vetus Testamentum* 56 (4): 485–504. https://doi.org/10.1163/156853306778941737.

Levshina, Natalia. 2015. *How to Do Linguistics with R: Data Exploration and Statistical Analysis*. Amsterdam: John Benjamins. https://doi.org/10.1075/z.195.

Liedke, G. 1984. 'Špṭ Richten'. In *Theologisches Handwörterbuch zum Alten Testament*, edited by Ernst Jenni, 2:999–1009. Munich; Zürich: Chr. Kaiser; Theologischer Verlag.

Lohfink, Norbert. 1963. *Das Hauptgebot: Eine Untersuchung literarischer Einleitungsfragen zu Dtn 5–11*. Analecta Biblica 20. Rome: Pontifical Biblical Institute.

Longacre, Robert E. 2003. *Joseph: A Story of Divine Providence—A Text Theoretical and Textlinguistic Analysis of Genesis 37 and 39–48*. 2nd ed. Winona Lake, IN: Eisenbrauns.

Lorrain, François, and Harrison C. White. 1971. 'Structural Equivalence of Individuals in Social Networks'. *The Journal of Mathematical Sociology* 1 (1): 49–80. https://doi.org/10.1080/0022250X.1971.9989788.

Luczkovich, Joseph J., Stephen P. Borgatti, Jeffrey C. Johnson, and Martin G. Everett. 2003. 'Defining and Measuring Trophic Role Similarity in Food Webs Using Regular Equivalence'. *Journal of Theoretical Biology* 220 (3): 303–21. https://doi.org/10.1006/jtbi.2003.3147.

Magonet, Jonathan. 1983. 'The Structure and Meaning of Leviticus 19'. *Hebrew Annual Review* 7: 151–67.

Mann, Thomas W. 1988. *The Book of the Torah: The Narrative Integrity of the Pentateuch*. Louisville, KY: Westminster John Knox.

Massey, Steven E. 2016. 'Social Network Analysis of the Biblical Moses'. *Applied Network Science* 1: 13. https://doi.org/10.1007/s41109-016-0012-1.

Mathys, Hans-Peter. 1986. *Liebe deinen Nächsten wie dich selbst: Untersuchungen zum alttestamentlichen Gebot der Nächstenliebe (Lev 19,18)*. Orbis Biblicus et Orientalis 71. Freiburg: Universitätsverlag.

McCawley, James D. 1968. 'Lexical Insertion in a Transformational Grammar without Deep Structure'. In *Papers from the Fourth Regional Meeting of the Chicago Linguistic Society*, edited by Bill J. Darden, Charles-James N. Bailey, and Alice Davison, 71–80. Chicago, IL: University of Chicago Press.

McClenney-Sadler, Madeline G. 2007. *Recovering the Daughter's Nakedness: A Formal Analysis of Israelite Kinship Terminology and the Internal Logic of Leviticus 18*. The Library of Hebrew Bible/Old Testament Studies 476. New York: T&T Clark International.

McConville, J. G. 2007. '"Fellow Citizens": Israel and Humanity in Leviticus'. In *Reading the Law: Studies in Honour of Gordon J. Wenham*, edited by J. G. McConville and Karl Möller, 10–32. The Library of Hebrew Bible/Old Testament Studies 461. New York: T&T Clark International.

McLean, Paul. 2017. *Culture in Networks*. Cultural Sociology. Cambridge: Polity Press.

Menéndez-Benito, Paula. 2010. 'On Universal Free Choice Items'. *Natural Language Semantics* 18 (1): 33–64. https://doi.org/10.1007/s11050-009-9050-x.

Meyer, Esias E. 2005. *The Jubilee in Leviticus 25: A Theological Ethical Interpretation from a South African Perspective*. Exegese in Unserer Zeit 15. Münster: Lit.

———. 2015a. 'Leviticus 17, Where P, H, and D Meet: Priorities and Presuppositions of Jacob Milgrom and Eckart Otto'. In *Current Issues in Priestly and Related Literature: The Legacy of Jacob Milgrom and Beyond*, edited by Roy E. Gane and Ada Taggar-Cohen, 349–67. Atlanta, GA: Society of Biblical Literature. https://doi.org/10.2307/j.ctt18z4h0x.19.

———. 2015b. 'People and Land in the Holiness Code: Who Is YHWH's Favourite?' *Old Testament Essays* 28 (2): 433–50.

Milgrom, Jacob. 1991. *Leviticus 1–16: A New Translation with Introduction and Commentary*. Anchor Bible 3. New York: Doubleday. https://doi.org/10.5040/9780300261110.

———. 2000. *Leviticus 17–22: A New Translation with Introduction and Commentary*. Anchor Bible 3A. New York: Doubleday. https://doi.org/10.5040/9780300262001.

———. 2001. *Leviticus 23–27: A New Translation with Introduction and Commentary*. Anchor Bible 3B. New York: Doubleday. https://doi.org/10.5040/9780300261127.

———. 2003. 'HR in Leviticus and Elsewhere in the Torah'. In *The Book of Leviticus: Composition and Reception*, edited by Rolf Rendtorff and Robert A. Kugler, 24–40. Leiden: Brill. https://doi.org/10.1163/9789047401643_004.

Miller, Cynthia L. (ed.). 1999. *The Verbless Clause in Biblical Hebrew: Linguistic Approaches*. Linguistic Studies in Ancient West Semitic 1. Winona Lake, IN: Eisenbrauns. https://doi.org/10.1515/9781575065175.

Mische, Ann. 2014. 'Relational Sociology, Culture, and Agency'. In *The SAGE Handbook of Social Network Analysis*, edited by John Scott and Peter J. Carrington, 80–98. London: SAGE Publications. https://doi.org/10.4135/9781446294413.n7.

Moenikes, Ansgar. 2012. 'Liebe / Liebesgebot (AT)'. In *Das wissenschaftliche Bibellexikon im Internet*. https://www.bibelwissenschaft.de/stichwort/24991/, accessed 11 January 2024.

Morales, L. Michael. 2015. *Who Shall Ascend the Mountain of the Lord? A Biblical Theology of the Book of Leviticus*. New Studies in Biblical Theology 37. Downers Grove, IL: IVP Academic.

Moretti, Franco. 2011. 'Network Theory, Plot Analysis'. *New Left Review* 68: 80–102.

———. 2014. '"Operationalizing"; or, the Function of Measurement in Literary Theory'. *English Language and Literature* 60 (1): 3–19. https://doi.org/10.15794/jell.2014.60.1.001.

Morrow, William S. 2017. *An Introduction to Biblical Law*. Grand Rapids, MI: Eerdmans.

Müller, H.-P. 1984. 'Qdš Heilig'. In *Theologisches Handwörterbuch zum Alten Testament*, edited by Ernst Jenni, 2:589–609. Munich; Zürich: Chr. Kaiser; Theologischer Verlag.

Müller, Reinhard. 2015. 'The Sanctifying Divine Voice: Observations on the אני יהוה-Formula in the Holiness Code'. In *Text, Time, and Temple: Literary, Historical and Ritual Studies in Leviticus*, edited by Francis Landy, Leigh M. Trevaskis, and Bryan D. Bibb, 70–84. Hebrew Bible Monographs 64. Sheffield: Sheffield Phoenix Press.

Næss, Åshild. 2007. *Prototypical Transitivity*. Typological Studies in Language 72. Amsterdam: John Benjamins. https://doi.org/10.1075/tsl.72.

Naudé, Jacobus A. 2011. 'The Interpretation and Translation of the Biblical Hebrew Quantifier Kol'. *Journal for Semitics* 20 (2): 408–21.

Neudecker, Reinhard. 1992. '"And You Shall Love Your Neighbor as Yourself—I Am the Lord" (Lev 19,18) in Jewish Interpretation'. *Biblica* 73 (4): 496–517.

Newman, M. E. J. 2010. *Networks: An Introduction*. Oxford: Oxford University Press. https://doi.org/10.1093/acprof:oso/9780199206650.001.0001.

Newman, M. E. J., and Michelle Girvan. 2004. 'Finding and Evaluating Community Structure in Networks'. *Physical Review E* 69 (2): 026113. https://doi.org/10.1103/physreve.69.026113.

Niccacci, Alviero. 1999. 'Types and Functions of the Nominal Sentence'. In *The Verbless Clause in Biblical Hebrew: Linguistic Approaches*, edited by Cynthia L. Miller, 215–48. Linguistic Studies in Ancient West Semitic 1. Winona Lake, IN: Eisenbrauns. https://doi.org/10.1515/9781575065175-011.

Nihan, Christophe. 2007. *From Priestly Torah to Pentateuch: A Study in the Composition of the Book of Leviticus*. Forschungen zum Alten Testament, 2. Reihe 25. Tübingen: Mohr Siebeck. https://doi.org/10.1628/978-3-16-151123-3.

———. 2011. 'Resident Aliens and Natives in the Holiness Legislation'. In *The Foreigner and the Law: Perspectives from the Hebrew Bible and the Ancient Near East*, edited by Reinhard

Achenbach, Rainer Albertz, and Jakob Wöhrle, 111–34. Beihefte zur Zeitschrift für Altorientalische und Biblische Rechtsgeschichte 16. Wiesbaden: Harrassowitz.

Nolan, Brian, Gudrun Rawoens, and Elke Diedrichsen (eds). 2015. *Causation, Permission, and Transfer: Argument Realisation in GET, TAKE, PUT, GIVE and LET Verbs*. Studies in Language Companion Series 167. Amsterdam: John Benjamins. https://doi.org/10.1075/slcs.167.

Noth, Martin. 1977. *Leviticus: A Commentary*. Translated by J. E. Anderson. 2nd ed. Old Testament Library. London: SCM Press.

O'Banion, John D. 1992. *Reorienting Rhetoric: The Dialectic of List and Story*. University Park, PA: Pennsylvania State University Press.

Olsen, Mari B. 1997. *A Semantic and Pragmatic Model of Lexical and Grammatical Aspect*. Outstanding Dissertations in Linguistics. New York: Garland.

Oosting, Reinoud. 2013. *The Role of Zion/Jerusalem in Isaiah 40–55: A Corpus-Linguistic Approach*. Studia Semitica Neerlandica 59. Leiden: Brill. https://doi.org/10.1163/9789004241480.

Oosting, Reinoud, and Janet W. Dyk. 2017. 'Valence Patterns of Motion Verbs: Syntax, Semantics, and Linguistic Variation'. *Journal of Northwest Semitic Languages* 43 (1): 63–85.

Otto, Eckart. 1994a. 'Das Heiligkeitsgesetz Leviticus 17–26 in der Pentateuchredaktion'. In *Altes Testament: Forschung und Wirkung—Festschrift für Henning Graf Reventlow*, edited by Peter Mommer and Winfried Thiel, 65–80. Frankfurt am Main: Peter Lang.

———. 1994b. *Theologische Ethik des Alten Testaments*. Theologische Wissenschaft 3.2. Stuttgart: Kohlhammer.

———. 1999. 'Innerbiblische Exegese im Heiligkeitsgesetz Leviticus 17–26'. In *Levitikus als Buch*, edited by Heinz-Josef Fabry and Hans-Winfried Jüngling, 125–96. Bonner Biblische Beiträge 119. Berlin: Philo.

———. 2008. 'Das Buch Levitikus zwischen Priesterschrift und Pentateuch'. *Zeitschrift für Altorientalische und Biblische Rechtsgeschichte* 14: 365–407.

———. 2009. 'The Holiness Code in Diachrony and Synchrony in the Legal Hermeneutics of the Pentateuch'. In *The Strata of the Priestly Writings: Contemporary Debate and Future Directions*, edited by Sarah Shectman and Joel S. Baden, 135–56. Abhandlungen zur Theologie des Alten und Neuen Testaments 95. Zürich: Theologischer Verlag Zürich.

———. 2015. 'Priesterschrift und Deuteronomium im Buch Leviticus: Zur Integration des Deuteronomiums in den Pentateuch'. In *Abschied von der Priesterschrift? Zum Stand der Pentateuchdebatte*, edited by Friedhelm Hartenstein and Konrad Schmid, 161–85. Veröffentlichungen der Wissenschaftlichen Gesellschaft für Theologie 40. Leipzig: Evangelische Verlagsanstalt.

Padgett, John F., and Christopher K. Ansell. 1993. 'Robust Action and the Rise of the Medici, 1400–1434'. *American Journal of Sociology* 98 (6): 1259–1319. https://doi.org/10.1086/230190.

Page, Lawrence, Sergey Brin, Rajeev Motwani, and Terry Winograd. 1998. 'The PageRank Citation Ranking: Bringing Order to the Web'. Stanford Digital Library working paper SIDL-WP-1999-0120.

Parsons, Terence. 1979. 'Type Theory and Ordinary Language'. In *Linguistics, Philosophy, and Montague Grammar*, edited by Steven Davis and Marianne Mithun, 127–51. Austin: University of Texas Press. https://doi.org/10.7560/746251-006.

Pavey, Emma L. 2010. *The Structure of Language: An Introduction to Grammatical Analysis*. Cambridge: Cambridge University Press. https://doi.org/10.1017/cbo9780511777929.

Perozzi, Bryan, Rami Al-Rfou, and Steven Skiena. 2014. 'DeepWalk: Online Learning of Social Representations'. In *Proceedings of the 20th ACM SIGKDD International Conference on Knowledge Discovery and Data Mining*, 701–10. New York: Association for Computing Machinery. https://doi.org/10.1145/2623330.2623732.

Petersson, Lina. 2017. 'The Syntactic Pattern: Qtol → Wəyiqtol and the Expression of Indirect Command in Biblical Hebrew'. In *Advances in Biblical Hebrew Linguistics: Data, Methods, and Analyses*, edited by Adina Moshavi and Tania Notarius, 271–95. Linguistic Studies in Ancient West Semitic 12. Winona Lake, IN: Eisenbrauns.

Podlesskaya, Vera I. 1993. 'Causatives and Causality: Towards a Semantic Typology of Causal Relations'. In *Causatives and Transitivity*, edited by Bernard Comrie and Maria Polinsky,

165–76. Studies in Language Companion Series 23. Amsterdam: John Benjamins. https://doi.org/10.1075/slcs.23.08pod.

Preuß, Horst D. 1985. 'Heilligkeitsgesetz'. In *Theologische Realencyklopädie*, 14:713–18. Berlin: De Gruyter. https://doi.org/10.1515/9783110867961-121.

Raj P. M., Krishna, Ankith Mohan, and K. G. Srinivasa. 2018. *Practical Social Network Analysis with Python*. Computer Communications and Networks. Cham: Springer. https://doi.org/10.1007/978-3-319-96746-2.

Ramírez Kidd, José E. 1999. *Alterity and Identity in Israel: The גר in the Old Testament*. Beihefte zur Zeitschrift für die alttestamentliche Wissenschaft 283. Berlin: De Gruyter. https://doi.org/10.1515/9783110802221.

Rappaport Hovav, Malka. 2008. 'Lexicalized Meaning and the Internal Temporal Structure of Events'. In *Theoretical and Crosslinguistic Approaches to the Semantics of Aspect*, edited by Susan D. Rothstein, 13–42. Linguistik Aktuell/Linguistics Today 110. Amsterdam: John Benjamins. https://doi.org/10.1075/la.110.03hov.

Rayson, Paul, and Mark Stevensen. 2008. 'Sense and Semantic Tagging'. In *Corpus Linguistics: An International Handbook*, edited by Anke Lüdeling and Merja Kytö, 1:564–79. Berlin: De Gruyter.

Rendtorff, Rolf. 1996. 'The Gēr in the Priestly Laws of the Pentateuch'. In *Ethnicity and the Bible*, edited by Mark G. Brett, 77–87. Leiden: Brill. https://doi.org/10.1163/9789004493544_007.

Renkema, Jan. 2009. *The Texture of Discourse: Towards an Outline of Connectivity Theory*. Amsterdam: John Benjamins. https://doi.org/10.1075/z.151.

Reventlow, Henning G. 1961. *Das Heiligkeitsgesetz: Formgeschichtlich Untersucht*. Wissenschaftliche Monographien zum Alten und Neuen Testament 6. Neukirchen: Neukirchener.

Rezetko, Robert, and Ian Young. 2019. 'Currents in the Historical Linguistics and Linguistic Dating of the Hebrew Bible: Report on the State of Research as Reflected in Recent Major Publications'. *HIPHIL Novum* 5 (1): 3–95.

Richter, Wolfgang. 1980. *Grundlagen einer althebräischen Grammatik*. Vol. B, *Die Beschreibungsebenen*. Vol. 3, *Der Satz (Satztheorie)*. Arbeiten zu Text und Sprache im Alten Testament 13. St Ottilien: EOS.

Rogland, Max. 2003. *Alleged Non-Past Uses of Qatal in Classical Hebrew*. Studia Semitica Neerlandica 44. Assen: Royal Van Gorcum. https://doi.org/10.1163/9789004358744.

Rooke, Deborah W. 2015. 'The Blasphemer (Leviticus 24): Gender, Identity and Boundary Construction'. In *Text, Time, and Temple: Literary, Historical and Ritual Studies in Leviticus*, edited by Francis Landy, Leigh M. Trevaskis, and Bryan D. Bibb, 153–67. Hebrew Bible Monographs 64. Sheffield: Sheffield Phoenix Press.

Roorda, Dirk, Cody Kingham, Christiaan Erwich, and W. T. van Peursen. 2019. 'ETCBC/BHSA'. Zenodo. https://doi.org/10.5281/ZENODO.2554324.

Roorda, Dirk, Cody Kingham, and Camil Staps. 2020. 'Text-Fabric'. Zenodo. https://doi.org/10.5281/ZENODO.592193.

Rossi, Ryan A., and Nesreen K. Ahmed. 2015. 'Role Discovery in Networks'. *IEEE Transactions on Knowledge and Data Engineering* 27 (4): 1112–31. https://doi.org/10.1109/tkde.2014.2349913.

Runge, S. E. 2007. 'A Discourse-Functional Description of Participant Reference in Biblical Hebrew Narrative'. DLitt thesis, University of Stellenbosch. http://scholar.sun.ac.za/handle/10019.1/1212, accessed 11 January 2024.

Ruwe, Andreas. 1999. *'Heiligkeitsgesetz' und 'Priesterschrift': Literaturgeschichtliche und rechtssystematische Untersuchungen zu Leviticus 17,1–26,2*. Forschungen zum Alten Testament 26. Tübingen: Mohr Siebeck.

———. 2003. 'The Structure of the Book of Leviticus in the Narrative Outline of the Priestly Sinai Story (Exod 19:1–Num 10:10*)'. In *The Book of Leviticus: Composition and Reception*, edited by Rolf Rendtorff and Robert A. Kugler, 55–78. Leiden: Brill. https://doi.org/10.1163/9789047401643_006.

Rydberg-Cox, Jeff. 2011. 'Social Networks and the Language of Greek Tragedy'. *Journal of the Chicago Colloquium on Digital Humanities and Computer Science* 1 (3): 1–11.

Sailhamer, John. 1992. *The Pentateuch as Narrative: A Biblical-Theological Commentary*. Library of Biblical Interpretation. Grand Rapids, MI: Zondervan.

Sawyer, John F. A. (ed.). 1996. *Reading Leviticus: A Conversation with Mary Douglas*. Journal for the Study of the Old Testament Supplement Series 227. Sheffield: Sheffield Academic Press.

Schellenberg, Annette. 2017. 'Der Einzelne und die Gemeinschaft nach den Rechtstexten des Alten Testaments'. In *Individualität und Selbstreflexion in den Literaturen des Alten Testaments*, edited by Andreas Wagner and Jürgen van Oorschot, 373–98. Veröffentlichungen der Wissenschaftlichen Gesellschaft für Theologie 48. Leipzig: Evangelische Verlagsanstalt.

Schenker, Adrian. 2012. 'Das Gebot der Nächstenliebe in seinem Kontext (Lev 19,17–18): Lieben ohne Falschheit'. *Zeitschrift für die Alttestamentliche Wissenschaft* 124 (2): 244–48. https://doi.org/10.1515/zaw-2012-0018.

Schipper, Jeremy, and Jeffrey Stackert. 2013. 'Blemishes, Camouflage, and Sanctuary Service: The Priestly Deity and His Attendants'. *Hebrew Bible and Ancient Israel* 2 (4): 458–78. https://doi.org/10.1628/219222713x13933396528289.

Schmid, Hans-Jörg. 2000. *English Abstract Nouns as Conceptual Shells: From Corpus to Cognition*. Topics in English Linguistics 34. Berlin: De Gruyter Mouton. https://doi.org/10.1515/9783110808704.

———. 2010. 'Does Frequency in Text Instantiate Entrenchment in the Cognitive System?' In *Quantitative Methods in Cognitive Semantics: Corpus-Driven Approaches*, edited by Dylan Glynn and Kerstin Fischer, 101–33. Cognitive Linguistics Research 46. Berlin: De Gruyter Mouton. https://doi.org/10.1515/9783110226423.101.

Schmid, Hans-Jörg, and Helmut Küchenhoff. 2013. 'Collostructional Analysis and Other Ways of Measuring Lexicogrammatical Attraction: Theoretical Premises, Practical Problems and Cognitive Underpinnings'. *Cognitive Linguistics* 24 (3): 531–77. https://doi.org/10.1515/cog-2013-0018.

Schwartz, Baruch J. 2009. 'Introduction: The Strata of the Priestly Writings and the Revised Relative Dating of P and H'. In *The Strata of the Priestly Writings: Contemporary Debate and Future Directions*, edited by Sarah Shectman and Joel S. Baden, 1–12. Abhandlungen zur Theologie des Alten und Neuen Testaments 95. Zürich: Theologischer Verlag Zürich.

Scott, John. 2017. *Social Network Analysis*. 4th ed. London: SAGE Publications. https://doi.org/10.4135/9781529716597.

Shibatani, Masayoshi (ed.). 1976a. *The Grammar of Causative Constructions*. Syntax and Semantics 6. New York: Academic Press. https://doi.org/10.1163/9789004368842.

———. 1976b. 'The Grammar of Causative Constructions: A Conspectus'. In *The Grammar of Causative Constructions*, edited by Masayoshi Shibatani, 1–40. Syntax and Semantics 6. New York: Academic Press. https://doi.org/10.1163/9789004368842_002.

Siegismund, Kasper. 2018. 'Studies in the Hebrew Verbal System: Hebrew as a System of Relative Tense and the Origins and Development of the Classical Consecutive Forms'. PhD dissertation, University of Copenhagen.

Ska, Jean L. 2001. 'La structure du Pentateuque dans sa forme canonique'. *Zeitschrift für die Alttestamentliche Wissenschaft* 113 (3): 331–52.

Smith, Carlota S. 1991. *The Parameter of Aspect*. Studies in Linguistics and Philosophy 43. Dordrecht: Kluwer Academic Publishers. https://doi.org/10.1007/978-94-015-7911-7.

Smith, Christopher R. 1996. 'The Literary Structure of Leviticus'. *Journal for the Study of the Old Testament* 21 (70): 17–32. https://doi.org/10.1177/030908929602107002.

Song, Jae J. 1996. *Causatives and Causation: A Universal-Typological Perspective*. Longman Linguistics Library. New York: Longman.

Stackert, Jeffrey. 2007. *Rewriting the Torah: Literary Revision in Deuteronomy and the Holiness Legislation*. Forschungen zum Alten Testament 52. Tübingen: Mohr Siebeck. https://doi.org/10.1628/978-3-16-151093-9.

———. 2009. 'The Holiness Legislation and Its Pentateuchal Sources: Revision, Supplementation, and Replacement'. In *The Strata to the Priestly Writings: Contemporary Debate and Future Directions*, edited by Sarah Shectman and Joel S. Baden, 187–204. Abhandlungen zur Theologie des Alten und Neuen Testaments 95. Zürich: Theologischer Verlag Zürich.

———. 2011. 'The Sabbath of the Land in the Holiness Legislation: Combining Priestly and Non-Priestly Perspectives'. *The Catholic Biblical Quarterly* 73 (2): 239–50.

Stefanowitsch, Anatol, and Stefan Th. Gries. 2003. 'Collostructions: Investigating the Interaction of Words and Constructions'. *International Journal of Corpus Linguistics* 8 (2): 209–43. https://doi.org/10.1075/ijcl.8.2.03ste.

———. 2005. 'Covarying Collexemes'. *Corpus Linguistics and Linguistic Theory* 1 (1): 1–43. https://doi.org/10.1515/cllt.2005.1.1.1.

Still, Bastian. 2019. *The Social World of the Babylonian Priest*. Culture and History of the Ancient Near East 103. Leiden: Brill. https://doi.org/10.1163/9789004399969.

Sun, Henry T. C. 1990. 'An Investigation into the Compositional Integrity of the So-Called Holiness Code (Leviticus 17–26)'. PhD dissertation, Claremont Graduate School.

Talmy, Leonard. 1976. 'Semantic Causative Types'. In *The Grammar of Causative Constructions*, edited by Masayoshi Shibatani, 43–116. Syntax and Semantics 6. New York: Academic Press. https://doi.org/10.1163/9789004368842_003.

———. 1985. 'Lexicalization Patterns: Semantic Structure in Lexical Forms'. In *Language Typology and Syntactic Description*, vol. 3, *Grammatical Categories and the Lexicon*, edited by Timothy Shopen, 57–149. Cambridge: Cambridge University Press.

———. 1988. 'Force Dynamics in Language and Cognition'. *Cognitive Science* 12 (1): 49–100. https://doi.org/10.1207/s15516709cog1201_2.

———. 2000. *Toward a Cognitive Semantics*. Vol. 1. Language, Speech, and Communication. Cambridge, MA: MIT Press. https://doi.org/10.7551/mitpress/6847.001.0001.

Talstra, Eep. 2003. 'Text Segmentation and Linguistic Levels: Preparing Data for SESB'. Unpublished manuscript. 41 pages.

———. 2004. 'Text Segmentation and Linguistic Levels: Preparing Data for SESB'. In *Handbuch/Instruction Manual SESB*

*(Stuttgart Elektronic Study Bible)*, edited by Christof Hardmeier, Eep Talstra, and Bertram Salzmann, 23–31. Stuttgart: Deutsche Bibelgesellschaft; Haarlem: Nederlands Bijbelgenootschap.

———. 2014. 'The Bible as Data and as Literature: The Example of Exod 16'. In *A Pillar of Cloud to Guide: Text-Critical, Redactional, and Linguistic Perspectives on the Old Testament in Honour of Marc Vervenne*, edited by Hans Ausloos and Bénédicte Lemmelijn, 549–67. Bibliotheca Ephemeridum Theologicarum Lovaniensium 269. Leuven: Peeters.

———. 2016a. 'Data, Knowledge and Tradition: Biblical Scholarship and the Humanities 2.0: Exodus 19 as a Laboratory Text'. In *The Present State of Old Testament Studies in the Low Countries: A Collection of Old Testament Studies Published on the Occasion of the Seventy-Fifth Anniversary of the Oudtestamentisch Werkgezelschap*, edited by Klaas Spronk, 228–47. Old Testament Studies 69. Leiden: Brill. https://doi.org/10.1163/9789004326255_014.

———. 2016b. 'Approaching the Mountain of Exodus 19: Thou Shalt Explore Syntax First'. *HIPHIL Novum* 3 (1): 2–24.

———. 2018a. 'Who Is Who in Zechariah 1:1–6? Text Linguistics, Participant Tracking and the Reading of Biblical Texts'. In *Reading and Listening: Meeting One God in Many Texts—Festschrift for Eric Peels on the Occasion of His 25th Jubilee as Professor of Old Testament Studies*, edited by Jaap Dekker and Gert Kwakkel, 151–58. Amsterdamse Cahiers Supplement Series 16. Bergambacht: 2VM.

———. 2018b. 'Participant Tracking Dataset of Leviticus 17–26'. Zenodo. https://doi.org/10.5281/zenodo.1479491.

Talstra, Eep, and Constantijn J. Sikkel. 2000. 'Genese und Kategorienentwicklung der WIVU-Datenbank; oder, Ein Versuch, dem Computer Hebräisch beizubringen'. In *Ad Fontes! Quellen Erfassen–Lesen–Deuten: Was ist Computerphilologie? Ansatzpunkte und Methodologie–Instrumente und Praxis*, edited by Christof Hardmeier, Wolf-Dieter Syring, Jochen D. Range, and Eep Talstra, 33–68. Applicatio 15. Amsterdam: VU University Press.

Tampubolon, D. P. 1983. *Verbal Affixations in Indonesian: A Semantic Exploration*. Canberra: Pacific Linguistics.

Tang, Jie. 2017. 'Computational Models for Social Network Analysis: A Brief Survey'. In *Proceedings of the 26th International Conference on World Wide Web Companion*, 921–25. Perth, Australia: ACM Press. https://doi.org/10.1145/3041021.3051101.

Thiel, Winfried. 1969. 'Erwägungen zum Alter des Heiligkeitsgesetzes'. *Zeitschrift für die alttestamentliche Wissenschaft* 81 (1): 40–73. https://doi.org/10.1515/zatw.1969.81.1.40.

Tilly, Charles. 1997. 'Parliamentarization of Popular Contention in Great Britain, 1758–1834'. *Theory and Society* 26: 245–73.

———. 2008. *Contentious Performances*. Cambridge Studies in Contentious Politics. Cambridge: Cambridge University Press. https://doi.org/10.1017/cbo9780511804366.

Tucker, Paavo N. 2017. *The Holiness Composition in the Book of Exodus*. Forschungen zum Alten Testament 2. Reihe 98. Tübingen: Mohr Siebeck. https://doi.org/10.1628/978-3-16-155547-3.

van der Merwe, Christo H. J., Jacobus A. Naudé, and Jan H. Kroeze. 2017. *A Biblical Hebrew Reference Grammar*. 2nd ed. London: Bloomsbury T&T Clark.

van Houten, Christiana. 1991. *The Alien in Israelite Law*. Journal for the Study of the Old Testament Supplement Series 107. Sheffield: Sheffield Academic Press.

van Peursen, Willem Th. 2004. *The Verbal System in the Hebrew Text of Ben Sira*. Leiden: Brill. https://doi.org/10.1163/9789047412304.

———. 2017. 'New Directions in Computational Analysis of Biblical Poetry'. In *Congress Volume Stellenbosch 2016*, edited by Louis Jonker, Gideon R. Kotzé, and Christl M. Maier, 378–94. Vetus Testamentum Supplements 177. Leiden: Brill. https://doi.org/10.1163/9789004353893_016.

Van Valin, Robert D., Jr. 2005. *Exploring the Syntax-Semantics Interface*. Cambridge: Cambridge University Press. https://doi.org/10.1017/cbo9780511610578.

———. 2015. 'Role and Reference Grammar as a Framework for Linguistic Analysis'. In *The Oxford Handbook of Linguistic Analysis*, edited by Bernd Heine and Heiko Narrog, 2nd ed., 707–42. Oxford: Oxford University Press. https://doi.org/10.1093/oxfordhb/9780199677078.013.0028.

———. 2018. 'Some Issues Regarding (Active) Accomplishments'. In *Applying and Expanding Role and Reference Grammar*, edited by Rolf Kailuweit, Lisann Künkel, and Eva Staudinger, 71–93. Freiburg: Freiburg Institute for Advanced Studies, Albert-Ludwigs-Universität Freiburg.

Van Valin, Robert D., Jr, and Randy J. LaPolla. 1997. *Syntax: Structure, Meaning, and Function*. Cambridge Textbooks in Linguistics. Cambridge: Cambridge University Press. https://doi.org/10.1017/cbo9781139166799.

Van Valin, Robert D., Jr, and David P. Wilkins. 1996. 'The Case for "Effector": Case Roles, Agents and Agency Revisited'. In *Grammatical Constructions: Their Form and Meaning*, edited by Masayoshi Shibatani and Sandra A. Thompson, 289–322. Oxford: Oxford University Press.

van Wolde, Ellen. 1999. 'The Verbless Clause and Its Textual Function'. In *The Verbless Clause in Biblical Hebrew: Linguistic Approaches*, edited by Cynthia L. Miller, 321–36. Linguistic Studies in Ancient West Semitic 1. Winona Lake, IN: Eisenbrauns. https://doi.org/10.5325/j.ctv1bxh3hg.17.

Vendler, Zeno. 1957. 'Verbs and Times'. *The Philosophical Review* 66 (2): 143–60. https://doi.org/10.2307/2182371.

Verhagen, Arie, and Suzanne Kemmer. 1997. 'Interaction and Causation: Causative Constructions in Modern Standard Dutch'. *Journal of Pragmatics* 27: 61–82. https://doi.org/10.1016/s0378-2166(96)00003-3.

Verheij, A. J. C. 2000. *Bits, Bytes, and Binyanim: A Quantitative Study of Verbal Lexeme Formations in the Hebrew Bible*. Orientalia Lovaniensia Analecta 93. Leuven: Peeters.

Verkuyl, Henk J. 1972. *On the Compositional Nature of the Aspects*. Foundations of Language Supplementary Series 15. Dordrecht: Reidel. https://doi.org/10.1007/978-94-017-2478-4.

Vieweger, Dieter. 1995. 'Vom "Fremdling" zum "Proselyt": Zur sakralrechtlichen Definition des גר im späten 5. Jahrhundert v. Chr.' In *Von Gott reden: Beiträge zur Theologie und Exegese des Alten Testaments—Festschrift für Siegfried Wagner zum 65. Geburtstag*, edited by Dieter Vieweger and Ernst-Joachim Waschke, 271–84. Neukirchen-Vluyn: Neukirchener.

von Rad, Gerhard. 1953. *Studies in Deuteronomy*. Studies in Biblical Theology 9. London: SCM Press.

Waerzeggers, Caroline. 2014a. 'Locating Contact in the Babylonian Exile: Some Reflections on Tracing Judean-Babylonian Encounters in Cuneiform Texts'. In *Encounters by the Rivers of Babylon: Scholarly Conversations Between Jews, Iranians and Babylonians in Antiquity*, edited by Uri Gabbay and Shai Secunda, 131–46. Tübingen: Mohr Siebeck.

———. 2014b. 'Social Network Analysis of Cuneiform Archives: A New Approach'. In *Documentary Sources in Ancient Near Eastern and Greco-Roman Economic History: Methodology and Practice*, edited by Heather D. Baker and Michael Jursa, 207–33. Oxford: Oxbow Books. https://doi.org/10.2307/j.ctvh1dn9m.14.

Wagner, Allon, Yuval Levavi, Sivan Kedar, Kathleen Abraham, Yoram Cohen, and Ran Zadok. 2013. 'Quantitative Social

Network Analysis (SNA) and the Study of Cuneiform Archives: A Test-Case Based on the Murašû Archive'. *Akkadica* 134: 117–34.

Wagner, Andreas, and Jürgen van Oorschot (eds). 2017. *Individualität und Selbstreflexion in den Literaturen des Alten Testaments*. Veröffentlichungen der Wissenschaftlichen Gesellschaft für Theologie 48. Leipzig: Evangelische Verlagsanstalt.

Wagner, Volker. 1974. 'Zur Existenz des Sogenannten "Heiligkeitsgesetzes"'. *Zeitschrift für die alttestamentliche Wissenschaft* 86 (3): 307–16. https://doi.org/10.1515/zatw.1974.86.3.307.

Waltke, Bruce K., and Michael Patrick O'Connor. 1990. *An Introduction to Biblical Hebrew Syntax*. Winona Lake, IN: Eisenbrauns.

Warner, Megan. 2012. 'And I Will Remember My Covenant with Abraham: The Holiness School in Genesis'. PhD dissertation, Melbourne College of Divinity.

———. 2015. 'The Holiness School in Genesis?' In *Current Issues in Priestly and Related Literature: The Legacy of Jacob Milgrom and Beyond*, edited by Roy E. Gane and Ada Taggar-Cohen, 155–74. Atlanta, GA: Society of Biblical Literature. https://doi.org/10.2307/j.ctt18z4h0x.12.

———. 2018. *Re-Imagining Abraham: A Re-Assessment of the Influence of Deuteronomism in Genesis*. Old Testament Studies 72. Leiden: Brill. https://doi.org/10.1163/9789004355897.

Warning, Wilfried. 1999. *Literary Artistry in Leviticus*. Leiden: Brill. https://doi.org/10.1163/9789004497153.

Watts, Duncan J., and Steven H. Strogatz. 1998. 'Collective Dynamics of "Small-World" Networks'. *Nature*, 4 June 1998.

Watts, James W. 1999. *Reading Law: The Rhetorical Shaping of the Pentateuch*. Biblical Seminar 59. Sheffield: Sheffield Academic Press.

———. 2007. *Ritual and Rhetoric in Leviticus: From Sacrifice to Scripture*. Cambridge: Cambridge University Press. https://doi.org/10.1017/CBO9780511499159.

———. 2013. *Leviticus 1–10*. Historical Commentary on the Old Testament. Leuven: Peeters.

Waumans, Michaël C., Thibaut Nicodème, and Hugues Bersini. 2015. 'Topology Analysis of Social Networks Extracted from Literature'. *PLoS ONE* 10 (6): e0126470. https://doi.org/10.1371/journal.pone.0126470.

Wegner, Judith R. 1988. *Chattel or Person? The Status of Women in the Mishnah*. New York: Oxford University Press.

———. 1998. 'Leviticus'. In *Women's Bible Commentary*, edited by Carol A. Newsom and Sharon H. Ringe, expanded ed., 40–48. Louisville, KY: Westminster John Knox.

Weinfeld, Moshe. 1972. *Deuteronomy and the Deuteronomic School*. Oxford: Oxford University Press.

———. 1991. *Deuteronomy 1–11: A New Translation with Introduction and Commentary*. Anchor Bible 5. New York: Doubleday.

———. 2004. *The Place of the Law in the Religion of Ancient Israel*. Supplements to Vetus Testamentum 100. Leiden: Brill. https://doi.org/10.1163/9789047402954.

Wellhausen, Julius. 1927. *Prolegomena zur Geschichte Israels*. 6th ed. Berlin: De Gruyter.

Wenham, Gordon J. 1979. *The Book of Leviticus*. New International Commentary on the Old Testament. Grand Rapids, MI: Eerdmans.

———. 2000. *Story as Torah: Reading the Old Testament Ethically*. Edinburgh: T&T Clark.

Westaby, James D., Danielle L. Pfaff, and Nicholas Redding. 2014. 'Psychology and Social Networks: A Dynamic Network Theory Perspective.' *American Psychologist* 69 (3): 269–84. https://doi.org/10.1037/a0036106.

Westbury, Joshua R. 2014. 'Left Dislocation in Biblical Hebrew: A Cognitive Linguistic Account'. PhD dissertation, University of Stellenbosch.

White, Douglas R., and Karl P. Reitz. 1983. 'Graph and Semigroup Homomorphisms on Networks of Relations'. *Social Networks* 5 (2): 193–234. https://doi.org/10.1016/0378-8733(83)90025-4.

White, Harrison C. 1992. *Identity and Control: A Structural Theory of Social Action*. Princeton, NJ: Princeton University Press.

———. 2008. *Identity and Control: How Social Formations Emerge*. 2nd ed. Princeton, NJ: Princeton University Press.

Winther-Nielsen, Nicolai. 1995. *A Functional Discourse Grammar of Joshua: A Computer-Assisted Rhetorical Structure Analysis*. Coniectanea Biblica. Old Testament Series 40. Stockholm: Almqvist & Wiksell International.

———. 2008. 'A Role-Lexical Module (RLM) for Biblical Hebrew: A Mapping Tool for RRG and WordNet'. In *Investigations of the Syntax-Semantics-Pragmatics Interface*, edited by Robert D. Van Valin, Jr., 455–78. Studies in Language Companion Series 105. Amsterdam: John Benjamins. https://doi.org/10.1075/slcs.105.31win.

———. 2009. 'Biblical Hebrew Parsing on Display: The Role-Lexical Module (RLM) as a Tool for Role and Reference Grammar'. *SEE-J Hiphil* 6: 1–51.

———. 2012. 'Stones on Display in Joshua 6: The Linguistic Tree Constructor as a "PLOT" Tool'. *Journal of Hebrew Scriptures* 12 (17). 29 pages. https://doi.org/10.5508/jhs.2012.v12.a17.

———. 2016. 'How to Classify Hebrew Verbs: Plotting Verb-Specific Roles'. In *Contemporary Examinations of Classical Languages (Hebrew, Aramaic, Syriac, and Greek): Valency, Lexicography, Grammar, and Manuscripts*, edited by Timothy M. Lewis, Alison G. Salvesen, and Beryl Turner, 67–94. Perspectives on Linguistics and Ancient Languages 8. Piscataway, NJ: Gorgias. https://doi.org/10.31826/9781463237332-011.

———. 2017. 'Corpus-Driven Valence: Give and the Meaning of נתן, Nātan, in Genesis'. In *Advances in Biblical Hebrew Linguistics: Data, Methods, and Analyses*, edited by Adina Moshavi and Tania Notarius, 363–85. Linguistic Studies in Ancient West Semitic 12. Winona Lake, IN: Eisenbrauns.

———. 2021. 'Why Eve Shouldn't Eat the Snake: An Intelligent Answer from Corpus-Driven Information Structure and Reference Tracking in Biblical Hebrew'. In *Challenges at the Syntax–Semantics–Pragmatics Interface: A Role and Reference Grammar Perspective*, edited by Robert D. Van Valin, Jr.,

285–307. Newcastle upon Tyne: Cambridge Scholars Publishing.

Winther-Nielsen, Nicolai, Claus Tøndering, and Chris Wilson. 2009. 'Transliteration of Biblical Hebrew for the Role-Lexical Module'. *Hiphil* 6: 1–17.

Wolff, Phillip. 2007. 'Representing Causation'. *Journal of Experimental Psychology: General* 136 (1): 82–111. https://doi.org/10.1037/0096-3445.136.1.82.

———. 2014. 'Causal Pluralism and Force Dynamics'. In *Causation in Grammatical Structures*, edited by Bridget Copley and Fabienne Martin, 100–119. Oxford Studies in Theoretical Linguistics 52. Oxford: Oxford University Press. https://doi.org/10.1093/acprof:oso/9780199672073.003.0005.

Wolff, Phillip, Aron K. Barbey, and Matthew Hausknecht. 2010. 'For Want of a Nail: How Absences Cause Events'. *Journal of Experimental Psychology: General* 139 (2): 191–221. https://doi.org/10.1037/a0018129.

Wolff, Phillip, and Grace Song. 2003. 'Models of Causation and the Semantics of Causal Verbs'. *Cognitive Psychology* 47 (3): 276–332. https://doi.org/10.1016/s0010-0285(03)00036-7.

Wright, David P. 1999. 'Holiness in Leviticus and Beyond: Differing Perspectives'. *Interpretation: A Journal of Bible and Theology* 53 (4): 351–64. https://doi.org/10.1177/002096439905300404.

———. 2012. 'Ritual Theory, Ritual Texts, and the Priestly-Holiness Writings of the Pentateuch'. In *Social Theory and the Study of Israelite Religion: Essays in Retrospect and Prospect*, edited by Saul M. Olyan, 195–216. Atlanta, GA: Society of Biblical Literature. https://doi.org/10.2307/j.ctt32bz5t.14.

Wu, Zonghan, Shirui Pan, Fengwen Chen, Guodong Long, Chengqi Zhang, and Philip S. Yu. 2021. 'A Comprehensive Survey on Graph Neural Networks'. *IEEE Transactions on Neural Networks and Learning Systems*, 32 (1): 4–24. https://doi.org/10.1109/TNNLS.2020.2978386.

Wuench, Hans-Georg. 2014. 'The Stranger in God's Land—Foreigner, Stranger, Guest: What Can We Learn from Israel's Attitude Towards Strangers?' *Old Testament Essays* 27 (3): 1129–54.

Wurster, Paul. 1884. 'Zur Charakteristik und Geschichte des Priestercodex und Heiligkeitsgesetzes'. *Zeitschrift für die alttestamentliche Wissenschaft* 4: 112–33. https://doi.org/10.1515/zatw.1884.4.1.112.

Young, Ian, Robert Rezetko, and Martin Ehrensvärd. 2008. *Linguistic Dating of Biblical Texts*. Vol. 1. *An Introduction to Approaches and Problems*; Vol. 2. *A Survey of Scholarship, a New Synthesis and a Comprehensive Bibliography*. BibleWorld. London: Equinox.

Zehnder, Markus. 2005. *Umgang mit Fremden in Israel und Assyrien: Ein Beitrag zur Anthropologie des 'Fremden' im Licht antiker Quellen*. Beiträge zur Wissenschaft vom Alten und Neuen Testament 168. Stuttgart: Kohlhammer.

Zenger, Erich. 1996a. 'Die Entstehung des Pentateuch'. In *Einleitung in das Alte Testament*, edited by Erich Zenger, Georg Braulik, Herbert Niehr, Georg Steins, and Helmut Engel,

2nd rev. and expanded ed., 46–75. Kohlhammer-Studienbücher Theologie 1.1. Stuttgart: Kohlhammer.

———. 1996b. 'Die Tora/der Pentateuch als Ganzes'. In *Einleitung in das Alte Testament*, edited by Erich Zenger, Georg Braulik, Herbert Niehr, Georg Steins, and Helmut Engel, 2nd rev. and expanded ed., 34–46. Kohlhammer-Studienbücher Theologie 1.1. Stuttgart: Kohlhammer.

———. 1999. 'Das Buch Levitikus als Teiltext der Tora/des Pentateuch: Eine synchrone Lektüre mit kanonischer Perspektive'. In *Levitikus als Buch*, edited by Heinz-Josef Fabry and Hans-Winfried Jüngling, 47–83. Bonner Biblische Beiträge 119. Berlin: Philo.

Zhang, Si, Hanghang Tong, Jiejun Xu, and Ross Maciejewski. 2019. 'Graph Convolutional Networks: A Comprehensive Review'. *Computational Social Networks* 6 (1): 11. https://doi.org/10.1186/s40649-019-0069-y.

Zimmerli, Walther. 1963. 'Ich bin Jahwe'. In *Gottes Offenbarung: Gesammelte Aufsätze*, 2nd ed., 11–40. Munich: Chr. Kaiser.

# INDICES

## General Index

אִישׁ, 43, 64, 97–100, 115–17, 120–23, 126, 363
כֹּל, 85–86, 97, 122, 126, 255–56
actor, 36, 79–81, 96–97, 114, 117, 120, 142–43, 162, 230, 232, 242, 245, 247–48, 250–51, 256–58, 262–63, 266–67, 270, 280, 285, 288, 290, 293, 298–99, 304, 319–20, 351, 368
adverbials, 146, 148–49, 153, 158, 172–73, 189–90, 192, 365, 372
adverbs, 148–49
affectedness, 140, 144, 201, 202 n. 7, 225, 243–46, **253–63**, 265, 267, 367
  affectee, 200
  materiality, 254–55, 263–64
agency, 6, 35, 67, **131–54**, 161–62, 193–95, 199–200, 202, 243–44, 265–73, 284, 286–88, 302, 305 n. 21, 306–8, 312, 315, 318–19, 322–24, 330, 335, 344–45, 347–48, 351–52, 354, 356–57, 364–69, 374

hierarchy of agency, **265–71**, 306–7, 367
*Aktionsart*, 5, 134, 145–46, 148, 150–52, 155–56, 161 n. 4, 167, 169, 171, 242, 263, 364–65, 372
alternation hypothesis, 153, 206, **208–12**, 215, 218–19, 222, 227–29, 233–34, 236–40, 372
animacy, 66, 135 n. 3, 139, 141, 143, 162, 200, 202, 213, 247, 249, 259
anti-incestual laws, 48–50, 123–24, 238–39, 268–69, 322, 330, 352, 375
argument-indexing, 131–32, 137–39, 143
association strength, 174–76, 180–82, 365
  Fisher-Yates Exact, 176, 180–82
  $\Delta P$, 176, 180–82, 185
authorship, 10–11, 16, 18, 20, 26 n. 30, 337, 359, 373
Case Grammar, 135–38, 141, 266
causation, 5, 23, 131–32, 138, 145, 150–54, 171, **193–273**,

287, 316, 326, 336, 364–67, 372
causee, 152, 199–201, 202 n. 7, 213, 249
causer, 152–53, 195, 201, 203–4, 206, 214, 218–19, 222–23, 227, 229–30, 232, 236, 238, 240, 243, 250–51, 258, 264, 321, 366–67
circumstantial clause, 100, 363
Classic Biblical Hebrew, **156–57 n. 1**, 163, 177–78, 205–6, 211, 228, 241 n. 33
clause atom, 80, 80–81 n. 6
collostructional analysis, **171–92**, 365, 372
communication pattern, 75, 78–79, **102–14**
complex phrase, 55, 77, **82–86**, 100, 363, 371
computational methods, 73, 76 n. 4, 81, 96, 101, 110, 113–14, 120, 129, 275–77, 280, 289 n. 10, 303, 309–10
  multidimensional scaling, 307–8, 312
  principal component analysis, 182, 185, 188, 191
construct chain, 82, 85–86, 92–93
Construction Grammar, 173
culture, 36 n. 37, 39, 41, 49

definiteness, 43, 89–95, 97–98, 123, 141, 233, 244 n. 35, 254–55, 263, 363
democratisation, 60, 358–59
demonstrative pronoun, 77, 90, 91 n. 17, 93
directional ה, 173, 177–78, 181–83
directionality, 186, 191–92
disambiguation, 78, 100, 124–25, 371
discourse structure, 77 n. 5, 96–97, 284, 289, **296–301**, 342–43
discourse-pragmatics, 26, 46, 65–66, 74, 93 n. 19, 105, 107, 132, 141 n. 8, 144, 196, 198, 206 n. 12, 349, 354
Dowty's test questions, 148–49, 365
elimination test, **316–17**, 328–29, 334, 340
equality, 35, 53–54 n. 55, 55 n. 57, 56, 292, 345–46, **357–59**, 375
ETCBC database, 6–7, 80 n. 6, 165, 206–7 n. 12, 284, 299
ethics, 3, 6, 25, 40, 41–42 n. 39, 119, 123, 273, 315–16, 327, 333, 361, 370, 372–75
ethnicity, 55 n. 57, 59
exhortations, 9–10, 15 n. 15, 17, 24, 26, 32, 38, 44–45 n. 41, 46, 325

paraenetic frames, 9
factivity, 204, 239
falsification, 158, 169, 172, 192
force dynamics, 155, **195–203**
  hindrance, 218, 264, 269, 367
  non-intervention, 202, 248–49, 367
gender, 49, 64 n. 69, 75–77, 100, 111, 293 n. 15, 347
genre, 17, 24, 27, 32, 41–42, 97, 156, 157–58 n. 2, 374
holiness, 19, 21, 28, 38, 43, 50, 57, 60–62, 101, **229–32**, 285, **356–59**, 370, 375
Holiness Code, 3, **9–19**, 38, 42, 49 n. 46, 50, 79–81, 104–5, 117, 125–28, 192, 211–12, 216–18, 221, 229, 237, 241, 247, 258, 272, 283, 285, 288–89, 298–300, 315, 337, 356–59, 369–70
  Holiness School, 12–15, 19, 61 n. 64
homogeneity, 293, 304, 311
impurity, 1, 14 n. 14, 16 n. 17, 232, 285, 288, 291, 319, 327, 331, 335–37, 352–53, 370
inherent aspect. See *Aktionsart*
instigation, 64, 123, 140–41, 202, **244–51**, 262–63, 265, 267, 301, 367
intentionality. See volition

law, 1–4, 9, 12, 14–17, 24–32, 34 n. 36, 38–42, 44 n. 40, 54–57, 60, 84, 97–100, 107–8, 110, 117, 121–24, 131, 213–14 n. 15, 269, 273–74, 283, 291–92, 299, 315–16, 328, 338 n. 48, 348 n. 60, 349, 352–54, 356–58, 361–63, 367, 369–70, 373–75
  apodictic law, 29 n. 32, 32, 45 n. 41, 214 n. 15
  casuistic law, 29, 32, 48, 98–100, 117, 120–23, 214 n. 15, 299, 352, 354
  common law, 41–42, 283
lexical aspect. See *Aktionsart*
lexical decomposition, 133–34, 141, **144–50**, 156–58, 171, 193, 217 n. 18, 264, 365–67
lexical identity, 77–79, 97–100, 114
marginalisation, 50, 53–54, 56, 58, 67, 69, 313, 328, 346, 348
mimesis, 30
mood, 160, 164, 198
narrative criticism, 20 n. 25, 21–22, 24–25, 29, 31, 32–33, 74, 362
negation, 141, 146–47, 245, 269 n. 51
nominal clause, 77, **86–94**, 363, 371

part-whole relationships, 80, 84–85, 118, **120–24**
participant-reference shifts, 75, 78, **102–114**, 157 n. 2
*Numeruswechsel*, 44–48, 110–14
participants, 2–6, 29–30, 32–41, **43–69**, 127–28, 198–202, 225, 242–46, 264–65, 267, 272, **273–359**, 361–64, 367–71, 373–75
  Aaron, high priest, 28 n. 31, 44, 49 n. 46, 60, 62 n. 67, 83–84, 94–95, 97, 106, 110 n. 34, 118, 120, 127, 270, 272, 293–96, 306–8, 313, 315, 321, 326, **334–37**, 338 n. 49, 339, 340 n. 54, 341, 351–55, 368
  blasphemer, 39–40, 48–49, **63–65**, 67–69, 95, 128, 301, 314, 318–19, 326, 338–39, 341, **347–49**, 356, 368, 370
  brother, **51–52**, 53 n. 54, 55, 69, 113 n. 38, 119, 128, 270, 272, 294, 308, 314, 323, 325, 328, 333, 338, **344–47**, 350, 355, 358–59, 368–70
  disabled people, 355–56
  father, 2, 47, 49 n. 48, 50, 128, 252, 288, 294, 323, 327, 335, 350, 353, **354–55**, 356–57, 368
  foreign nations, 118–19, 272, 288, 292, 306, 318, 320, 322, 326, 338
  Moses, 42–43, 49, 55, 62 n. 67, 65, 72, 81, 95, 97, 101–4, 106–10, 118, 127, 129, 207 n. 12, 262, 270, 272, 280, 288, 291, 296–97, **299–301**, 306, 314, 318, 321, 326, 334, 336–38, **339–43**, 347, 356, 359, 363, 368–69
  priests, 26 n. 30, 28, 42–44, **59–63**, 69, 84, 101–2, 108 n. 32, 249 n. 39, 293–96, 306–8, 321, 323–24, **334–38**, 341, 343, 350–53, 356, 359, 370, 373
  sojourner, 47, 51, **52–59**, 63–64, 67–69, 88, 95, 98, 100, 115–18, 121–22, 125 n. 45, 128–30, 249, 254, 268, 272, 288, 291, 293–95, 301, 306, 308, 313–15, 317, 319, 322–24, 326 n. 35, **328–33**, 341, 344, 346, 349, 351–56, 359, 368–69, 371, 373
  women, 2, **48–51**, 59, 65, 67–69, 95, 125, 127–28, 252, 255, 294, 314, 323, 325 n. 32, 327, 330, 333, 335, 347–48, **350–54**, 355, 357, 368, 375
  Yhwh, 25–26, 30, 43 n. 40, 62, 65–66, 69, 72, 79–81,

95, **102–10**, 116, 118, 127, 129, 248, 268–72, 280, 290, 293–97, **299–300**, 306, 308, 313, 315, **316–21**, 323, 325–28, 331–34, 336–43, 347–48, 351–54, 356–57, 359, 363, 368–70, 373

personification, 65–67, 268 n. 50

poverty, 34, 51, 53–55, 95, 127, 130, 249, 306, 325 n. 32, 345, 350, **355–56**, 357–59, 370

power, 3, 34–35, 113, 280, 346, 357, 369

pragmatic implicature, 143, 146, 247

predicative NP, 236

prepositional phrase, 82, 87 n. 9, 90, 135, 146, 175, 177, 221 n. 20

priestly document, 10 n. 3, 11–13, 15–16, 18, 25–26, 57, 61

profiling. See role discovery

proto-roles, 137–38

quantitative analysis, 162 n. 6, 171–73, 179

redaction criticism, 3, 12–15, 18–19, 38 n. 38, 44–47, 57 n. 59, 110

referentiality, 95, 141

relational sociology, **32–37**, 39, 41, 273

expectancy, 36–37, 39–41, 283, 315–16, 332, 346, 359, 370, 372

reliance. See association strength

rhetorical criticism, 1, 3, 16, 20, 22 n. 26, **24–32**, 43–44, 46–47, 66–67, 71–72, 79, 103, 105, 107–13, 116, 133 n. 2, 214 n. 15, 315, 322, 362–63

Role and Reference Grammar, 5, 92 n. 18, **132–34**, 144–45, 148, 155, 167 n. 8, 171, 193–95, 230, 240, 247–48, 264–67, 365

  logical structures, 134, 142, 144, **150–53**, 170 n. 9, 173, 211, 214, 227, 229–30, 251, 256, 261, 265, 366

  operators, 150, 153, 155, 167 n. 8, 193, 264

role discovery, 68, 276, 281, **302–14**, 368

  DeepWalk, 312 n. 25

  feature-based, 303, **310–14**

  graph-based, **303–10**

  hierarchical clustering, 305–6, 308, 312

  k-means, 312–13

  node2vec, 303, 310–13, 368

  regular equivalence, 309, 311

structural equivalence, 303–9
*Selbstvorstellungsformel*, 9, 15, 103–5, 108
semantic annotation, 179
semantic roles, 5–6, **131–54**, 171, 179, 230–31, 252, 263, **265–73**, 306–7, 364–67, 372
  affected agent, 257, **268–69**, 288
  agent, 50, 56 n. 58, 65–66, 69, **134–44**, 148, 225 n. 22, 242, 244–49, 256–57, 262 n. 48, **266–69**, 271, 288, 345
  beneficiary, 105–6, 137 n. 6, 178–79, 187–88, 249, 252, 266, 269, 286, 294, 319, 341
  effector, 142–44, 194, 259
  experiencer, 141–42, 187, 251–52, 266, 269–70
  force, 139, **268–69**, 272
  frustrative, **268–69**, 271–72, 288
  goal, 137 n. 6, 152, 179, 183, 188–89, 191, 266, 269
  instrument, 69, 136, 139–41, 152, 178–79, 247, 259, 266, **268–69**
  locative, 136, 137 n. 6, 178, 183, 191
  neutral, 136 n. 4, **268–70**, 288
  patient, 69, **134–41**, 225 n. 22, 231, 242, 244–45, 253, 256, 257 n. 45, **266–68**, 270, 272, 288, 319, 321
  recipient, 178, 230–31, 252–53, 269, 286, 291, 292 n. 14, 294, 296, 314, 319, 321, 336, 341
  source, 137 n. 6, 178–79, 183, 188–89, 191, 266, 269
  volitional undergoer, **268–70**, 288, 319
semantic transitivity, 225–27, 233, **242–65**, 367
sentience. See volition
social capital, 3
social domain, 57, 113–14, 297–300, 337, 349, 355, 357–59
social network analysis, 3–6, 32–33, **38–42**, 48, 51, 59, 68–69, 114, 123, 125, 131, 265, 271, 273, **274–84**, 289 n. 10, 296, 331, 340, 343, 357–58, 364, 367–70, 372–75
  betweenness, 294–95
  centrality measure, 283, 293–96, 301
  cohesion, 288, **289–91**, 316, 318, 341–43
  connectivity, 278–79, 280–1, 289–91, 293, 295–96, 302, 312 n. 25, 314, 317, 356
  core, 69, 293, 314, **315–39**, 350–52, 354, 356, 368, 374

degree, **277–78**, 280–81, 290–91, 293–94, 296, 300–1, 317, 349

density, 290 n. 11, 316–17, 328–29, 340

PageRank, 294–95

periphery, 49–50, 273, 291, 293, 296, 313–14, 316, 318, 333, 338–39, **350–56**, 368, 374

reciprocity, 289, **291–92**, 358

semantic triplet, 280, 285, 287–88

social network roles
broker, 339, 341–43
facilitator, 337, 356, 370
mediator, 42, 62 n. 67, 339, 341–43, 356, 359, 368
outsider, 31 n. 34, 42, 56, 58 n. 61, 64, 322, 326, 347–49, 359, 369–70

subphrase, 83, 86, 94

substantialism, 34

synonyms, 51 n. 52, 73, 75, 79–80, **114–20**, 126, 371

syntactic transitivity, 139–140, 146, 161–62, 169, 171, 188 n. 30, 199, 201, **206–12**, 215, 218–25, 227–29, 232–33, 236–38, 240–42, 256 n. 43, 366, 372

textual domain, **77–79**, 86, 102, 297–300

thematic roles, 136–37, 139–44

undergoer, 123, 142 n. 9, 195, 213–15, 224, 229–32, 234–35, 237, 242–43, 245, 247, 250–52, 253 n. 41, 255–64, 267, 270, 280, 285, 288, 290, 294, 313, 330, 339, 351, 367–68

valency, 169–70, 172, 206 n. 12

verbal ambiguity, 158, 167–68, 189, 222, 366

verbal aspect, 5, 141, 145–53, 155, 158, 160–61, 163–64, 166–69, 172, 243–44, 264, 364, 372
causative. See causation
durative, 146–47, 164–67
dynamic, 5, 131, 143, 146–52, **155–93**, 195–99, 201–4, 216, 237–38, 250, 255, 256 n. 43, 261–62, 265, 364–65, 367, 372
punctual, 145–47, 150–152, 155, 164, 166–68, 229, 232, 235, 243–44, 256
resultative, 150, 163, 204, 223–24, 227, 233, 236 n. 30, 237, 239, 256 n. 43
stage-level predicate, 214–15,
stative, 136 n. 4, 138, 145–46, 148–53, 155, 159–61, 163, 167–69, 172, 179, 181,

183–86, 189–91, 193–95,
198–99, 201–3, 212–15, 217,
224–25, 229–32, 234, 236,
246–47, 253, 257, 259, 365
  telic, 146–47, 161–62, 167,
  204, 244
verbal complement, 147, 168,
  173, 175, 177–79, 184, 207
  n. 12, 230, 265
verbal stem, 161–62, 203
  hifʿil, 161, 195, 202–4, **205–23**, 229–31, 253 n. 41, 366
  hitpaʿel, 258
  nifʿal, 248

piʿel, 161, 195, 202–4, 212–15, **223–40**, 366
qal, 155, 162, 166, 173, 203–12, 215–29, 232–40, 366
verbal tenses,
  participle, 87 n. 9, 115, 164–67, 206 n. 11, 211 n. 14, 228 n. 23, 234, 256–57
  qātal, 159–61, 164, 205, 223
  yiqtōl, 159–61, 164, 205, 223
volition, 131, 134, 138–40, 143–44, 199 n. 5, 200–201, 243–46, 247 n. 36, **250–53**, 262–65, 267–70, 364, 367

## Index of Hebrew Verbs

אבד, 109, 212–13, 287
אבה, 241
אהב, 248
אזן, 205
איב, 166
אכל, 86, 115, 190, 254–55
אמר, 62, 81, 165, 173, 175, 180, 190, 207, 233
אסף, 248, 258
אפה, 255
אקץ, 288
בוא, 180, 182, 190, 216, 259
בין, 166
בער, 207

בצר, 258
ברח, 189
גאל, 248
גור, 215, 241
גלה, 238–39, 352
גלח, 260–61
געל, 238
דבק, 181, 184
דבר, 81, 207, 224, 226, 288
היה, 87, 88, 241
הלך, 162, 182, 190, 209–11, 216
הרג, 194, 217, 259
זבח, 186, 226, 260

זוב, 166
זמר, 261
זנה, 165, 166
זעק, 180
חוה, 241, 248
חזק, 183, 220–221, 223, 229
חטא, 229
חלל, 288
חנה, 184
חסר, 236
חפץ, 181
חפש, 241
חרף, 241
חשב, 237
חתן, 166
טהר, 229

טמא, 168, 228, 232, 251
ידע, 161, 187
יטב, 184
ילד, 165, 187, 209–11, 218–19, 222
יסף, 221–22
יסר, 248
יצא, 189, 190, 204, 205, 216, 235, 252–53, 349
יצק, 18
ירא, 183, 189, 191, 288
ירד, 173, 182, 189
ישב, 159, 165, 181, 184, 190, 214–15
כבד, 229
כחש, 241
כלה, 237–38, 240
כרת, 222, 321
כשל, 241
כתב, 165
לבש, 160, 236, 257
לין, 215, 241
למד, 207, 229
לקח, 165, 189, 235, 258, 260, 352
לקט, 232–33, 239

מוט, 241
מוך, 241
מות, 123, 216–17, 235, 252, 259
מכר, 258
מלא, 207, 236–37, 240
מלך, 173
מקק, 241
משח, 204
משל, 181
נאף, 352
נבט, 164
נגע, 165, 181, 184, 191, 204, 231
נגש, 180, 190
נוס, 182, 189, 190
נחל, 258
נחש, 241
נכה, 217, 259–260
נסע, 189
נפל, 166, 182, 189
נצה, 241, 248
נקב, 64
נקף, 261
נשא, 190
נשק, 187, 188
נתן, 170–71, 230, 259, 352
סור, 189
סלח, 241

עבר, 182, 190, 216
עזב, 249
עלה, 182, 190, 216, 222
עלל, 258
עמד, 159, 190, 215
ענה, 248
ערך, 258
עשה, 170, 187–88, 190
פגע, 181
פנה, 180, 182
פקד, 220
פרע, 249
פרש, 241
פשה, 181, 184
פשט, 236
צוה, 224, 260, 262
צעק, 180
צרע, 241
צרר, 183, 186–187
קדש, 61, 100–1, 204, 207, 228, 229–31, 232, 258
קום, 190, 205, 215–216
קוץ, 241
קלל, 63, 234–35, 252, 347
קנה, 258

קצף, 183
קצר, 258
קרא, 190, 216, 236
קרב, 160, 180, 190, 216, 288, 352
ראה, 164, 184, 190, 352
רגם, 259
רדף, 259
רום, 166
רחץ, 181, 184, 191
רמשׂ, 241
רעע, 181, 184
רצח, 166
שׂבע, 236
שׂים, 190–91, 258
שׂרף, 260
שׁבע, 248
שׁבת, 217–18, 222
שׁוב, 180, 182, 190, 216
שׁחט, 235, 259–60
שׁחת, 261
שׁכב, 182, 184, 190, 215, 352
שׂכל, 236
שׁכן, 184, 215
שׁלח, 180, 235
שׁמם, 166
שׁמע, 180, 190, 205
שׁמר, 254
שׁפט, 260–61
שׁקר, 241
תקע, 181, 184–85

## Scripture Index

**Genesis**, 13, 21, 26
1   18
1–11   22
1.1   177
2.22   189
2.24   184
3.1   173
3.3   184
3.6   189
4.18   219
5   219
6.4   187
8.12   235
8.20   189, 216
9.24   187
11   219
11.12   168
12.3   234
12.10   173
14.2   89
14.23   189
15.6   237
16.1   187
16.5   234
16.6   187
17.12   58
17.21   187
19.1   216
19.8   187
19.14   234
21.1   187
21.3   187
21.9   187
21.15   238
21.18   221
22.2   216
22.10   235
22.13   216
23.13   189
24.24   187
24.47   187
25.12   187
27.26   187
27.27   187
27.45   187, 236
28.11   189
29.11   187
30.1   187
30.30   187
31.46   233
34.1   187
31.25   185
32.8   186
32.26   184
32.33   184
34.3   184

| | | |
|---|---|---|
| 37.23 236 | 13.2 230 | 32.8 186 |
| 39.19 187 | 14.11 104 | 33.1 104 |
| 41.50 187 | 15 104 | 34.15 186 |
| 42.25 187 | 15.22 204 | 34.34 107 |
| 43.11 189 | 16 103–4 | 35–40 14 |
| 46.15 187 | 16.12 236 | 40.23 107 |
| 46.20 187 | 18.7 187 | 40.25 107, 216 |
| 48.10 187 | 19 120 | 40.29 216 |
| 48.22 189 | 19–40 21 | |
| 50.1 187 | 19.6 359 | **Leviticus**, 1–2, 9–10, 14, 16–24, 26–32, 38–41, 62, 103, 177, 331, 337–38 |
| 50.12 187 | 19.7 82 | |
| | 19.12 184 | |
| **Exodus**, 13, 20, 21, 26 | 19.13 184 | |
| | 19.14 207 | |
| 1.15 165 | 20.19 339 | |
| 3.3 207 | 20.22–26 10 | 1–7 16, 17, 23 |
| 3.11 204 | 21.17 234, 235 | 1–10 14, 16 |
| 3.18 186 | 23.10–11 45, 46 | 1–16 28 |
| 4.27 187 | 23.20–33 10 | 1.3 107 |
| 5.3 186 | 24.2 339 | 1.5 107 |
| 5.5 218 | 24.5 216 | 1.11 107 |
| 5.8 186 | 25–31 16 | 2.1 18 |
| 5.15 187 | 25–40 1, 9 | 2.6 18 |
| 5.17 186 | 25.37 216 | 2.13 218 |
| 6.2–8 13, 15 | 27.20 216 | 3.1 107 |
| 8.4 186 | 27.21 107 | 3.7 107 |
| 8.21 186 | 28.35 107 | 3.12 107 |
| 8.22 186 | 29.21 189 | 4.4 107 |
| 8.23 186 | 29.37 204, 231 | 4.6 107 |
| 8.24 186 | 29.43–46 13 | 4.7 107 |
| 8.25 186 | 30.8 107 | 4.27 331 |
| 9.30 189 | 30.9 216 | 5.2 184 |
| 10.5 255 | 31.12–17 13 | 5.3 184 |
| 12.12 15 | 32.7 104 | 6.11 184 |
| 12.15 218 | | 6.20 184 |

7.19  184
7.21  184
8–9  14, 26
8–10  17
8–12  23
8.12  18, 204
8.15  18
9.9  18
9.23–24  21
10.8–11  62
10.11  338
11–15  14, 16, 17
11–22  16
11–27  16
11.8  184
11.44  9, 62
11.44–45  15
11.45  9
12.4  184
13.3  232
13.5  184
13.6  184
13.7  184
13.8  184
13.34  184
13.35  184
13.36  89, 184
13.51  184
13.53  184
14.8  184
14.9  261
14.15  18
14.20  216

14.26  18
14.39  184
14.44  184
14.48  184
15.5  184
15.6  184
15.7  184
15.8  184
15.10  184
15.11  184
15.12  184
15.18  50, 184
15.21  184
15.22  184
15.24  50
15.27  184
15.33  50
16  16, 17
16–17  16–17
16–18  23
16–26  15
16.2  21
16.24  236
16.29  56
16.30–17.11  17
17  10, 11, 17, 54, 60, 98, 100, 118
17–24  16
17.1  207, 298, 339
17.1–2  81
17.1–24.9  17

17.2  44, 60, 83–86, 94, 120, 298, 336, 339
17.3  84, 85, 98, 120–122
17.3–7  57, 98, 298
17.4  104, 105, 106, 117, 338
17.5  60, 85, 104, 105, 319, 323, 331, 336
17.6  104, 105, 106
17.7  103, 126, 323
17.8  52, 85, 98, 120–122, 216, 298, 339
17.8–9  98
17.8–11  298
17.9  104, 105, 331, 338
17.10  30, 85, 86, 98, 103, 107, 115, 117, 120–122, 222, 254, 319, 332, 333, 338
17.10–12  98
17.11  108, 320, 332

17.12  85, 86, 108, 268, 298, 320, 332
17.12–14  298
17.13  85, 98, 120–122
17.13–14  98
17.14  85, 86, 97, 108, 320, 332
17.14–16  298
17.15  57, 86, 96, 97, 98, 122, 184, 232
17.15–16  98
18  9, 48, 49, 50, 96, 111, 238, 352, 375
18–20  17, 23, 84
18.1  297, 298, 339
18.1–2  297
18.1–5  9, 46, 352
18.2  9, 44, 104, 297, 298, 299, 339
18.2–24  298
18.3  119, 190, 320, 332, 342
18.4  104, 108
18.5  97, 104, 108
18.6  49, 87, 104, 124, 125, 322
18.7  49, 50, 239, 352, 355
18.7–11  49
18.7–15  124
18.7–23  46
18.8  352
18.9  352
18.10  352
18.11  352
18.12  352
18.13  352
18.14  352
18.15  352
18.16  352
18.17  352
18.18  352
18.19  352
18.20  352
18.21  126, 319, 323, 331
18.24  119, 320, 332
18.24–30  9, 46, 66, 352
18.25  65, 107, 119, 167–168, 268, 298
18.26  54, 57, 95, 108, 328
18.26–27  298
18.27  65, 119, 298
18.28  65
18.28–30  298
18.29  338
18.30  108, 251
19  21, 23, 44–45, 53, 104
19.1  102, 298, 339
19.1–4  9
19.2  28, 44, 57, 102–103, 298, 339, 357
19.2–3  323
19.2–37  298
19.3  2, 108, 288, 323, 353, 355
19.3–4  9
19.4  126, 323
19.5  103, 105, 319, 331, 341
19.8  103, 106, 338
19.9  233, 238
19.9–10  44, 53
19.10  54, 95, 233, 249, 324, 329, 355
19.11  112
19.11–12  44
19.12  248, 319, 331

19.13  59, 325
19.14  189, 319, 331, 355
19.15  260–261, 325, 345, 355, 356
19.16  325, 345
19.17  325, 345
19.17–18  344
19.18  51, 54, 119, 243, 248, 268, 325, 345
19.19  108
19.20  352
19.20–22  48, 50
19.21  105
19.22  105, 336
19.24  105
19.25  222
19.27  46, 261
19.29  65, 237, 353
19.30  108
19.31  126, 323
19.32  112, 189, 319, 331, 356
19.33  95, 324–325, 329
19.34  51, 54, 88, 96, 248, 324, 329
19.36  9, 30, 108, 243, 252, 268, 320, 332, 333, 342, 347
19.36–37  9
19.37  108
20  48, 49, 238, 352, 375
20.1  298, 339
20.1–22.25  23
20.2  44, 259, 268, 298, 325, 326, 329, 330, 339
20.2-2  298
20.3  30, 107, 319, 331, 332, 333, 338
20.4  217, 326, 329, 330
20.4–5  299
20.5  107, 191, 319, 332, 333, 338
20.5–6  30
20.6  107, 319, 332, 333, 338
20.7  258
20.7–8  9
20.8  108, 320, 332, 333
20.9  126, 252, 354
20.10  352
20.10–21  50
20.11  123, 352
20.12  95, 352
20.14  325, 326, 329, 330, 352, 353
20.16  353
20.17  268–269, 352
20.18  338, 352
20.19  352
20.20  217, 352
20.21  352
20.22  108, 320, 332, 342
20.22–27  9
20.23  320, 332
20.23–24  298
20.24  62, 108, 298, 320, 332, 333, 342, 358
20.24–26  298
20.25  108, 320, 332, 357
20.26  298, 320, 332, 333, 358
20.27  9, 97, 298, 353
21–22  14, 17, 48
21.1  44, 60, 101, 298, 336, 339
21.1–3  353
21.1–7  336
21.1–9  60

21.1–15  298
21.3  353
21.5  260
21.6  106, 321
21.7  28, 165, 352
21.8  61, 100–101, 231, 324
21.9  50, 353
21.10  18, 236, 249
21.10–23  60
21.11  353, 355
21.13  352
21.13–15  28
21.14  352
21.15  231, 321, 336, 338
21.16  298, 339
21.16–24  60
21.17  44, 298, 336, 339
21.17–2  298
21.21  106
21.23  108, 321, 336
21.24  61, 101, 298, 336, 339
22  341
22.1  298, 339
22.1–2  106
22.1–9  28
22.1–16  96

22.2  44, 60, 106–107, 110, 319, 331, 336, 339, 341
22.2–3  84, 298
22.3  105, 107, 231, 298, 319, 321, 331, 336, 337, 339, 341
22.4–16  298
22.5  184, 335
22.6  184
22.8  9
22.9  108, 321, 336
22.10  59
22.10–13  58
22.14  221, 336
22.15  105, 319, 331, 341
22.16  321, 326, 336
22.17  298, 339
22.17–25  96
22.18  52, 105, 298, 331, 336, 339
22.18–25  298
22.21  105, 319
22.22  105, 319, 321, 341
22.24  105, 319, 321, 341
22.25  58

22.26  298, 339
22.26–33  96
22.26–24.23  23
22.27  105
22.27–33  298
22.29  105, 319, 321, 336, 341
22.30  268
22.31  108
22.31–33  9
22.32  320, 321, 332, 333, 336
22.32–33  62
22.33  9, 30, 95, 320, 321, 332, 333, 342, 347
23  18, 60, 331
23–25  16
23–26  17
23.1  298, 339
23.2  92, 106, 108, 233, 298, 339
23.2–8  298
23.3  105
23.4  106
23.5  105
23.6  105
23.8  105, 319, 331, 341
23.9  298, 339
23.10  96, 298, 320, 323, 332, 336, 339, 342

23.10–22  298
23.11  60, 105, 321, 336
23.12  105
23.13  92, 105
23.16  105, 319, 331, 341
23.17  105
23.18  105
23.20  105, 321, 336
23.22  96, 249, 324, 329, 355
23.23  298, 339
23.24  93, 298, 339
23.24–25  298
23.25  105, 319, 331, 341
23.26  298, 339
23.27  92, 105, 319, 331, 341
23.27–32  298
23.28  105
23.28–30  109
23.29  248, 338
23.30  30, 107, 213, 287, 319, 332, 338
23.32  217
23.33  298, 339
23.34  105, 298, 339
23.34–43  298

23.36  105, 319, 331, 341
23.37  105, 106, 319, 331, 341
23.38  105, 319, 331, 341
23.39  106
23.40  105, 319, 331
23.41  105
23.42  96, 215, 331–332
23.43  9, 30, 108, 215, 320, 332, 333, 342, 347
23.44  106, 298, 339
24.1  298, 339
24.2  216, 260, 262, 339
24.2–4  107
24.2–9  298
24.3  105, 321, 336
24.4  105
24.6  105
24.7  105
24.8  105, 321, 336
24.9  106
24.10  248, 349
24.10–11  48
24.10–13  298

24.10–23  17, 39, 63–65, 95, 347–349, 368
24.11  95, 234, 319, 326, 339, 347
24.11–12  347
24.13  339
24.14  63, 234–235, 326, 339, 347–348
24.14–15  298
24.15  234, 331, 339
24.15–21  298
24.15–22  260
24.16  96, 106, 325, 326, 329, 330, 331, 349
24.17  259
24.22  54, 96, 298, 328, 349
24.23  63, 234, 298, 326, 339, 347–348
25  18, 46, 58, 63, 111
25–26  96
25–27  16, 17, 23
25.1  298, 339
25.1–2  72
25.2  65, 96, 105, 217, 259,

298, 320, 332,
   339, 342
25.2–7   45
25.2–20   298
25.3   261
25.4   105, 261
25.5   67
25.6   48, 59
25.7–9   112–113
25.10   99–100
25.13   99–100
25.13–17   46
25.14   99–100,
   287, 325, 345
25.15   325
25.17   72, 99,
   189, 319, 331
25.18   108
25.18–19   9
25.19   65
25.20   298
25.21   108, 262,
   320, 332
25.21–55   298
25.23   55, 66,
   129, 345, 371
25.25   52
25.26   99–100,
   285
25.27   99–100,
   237
25.29   99–100

25.35   55, 56,
   130, 220, 325,
   345
25.36   189, 319,
   325, 331
25.36–37   345
25.37   325
25.38   9, 30,
   108, 320, 332,
   333, 342, 347
25.39   325, 345
25.40   59
25.41   345
25.42   9, 30,
   108, 320, 332,
   333, 342, 347
25.43   189, 319,
   325, 331, 345
25.44   48, 326,
   353
25.44–45   55
25.45   54, 55,
   326
25.45–46   55
25.46   258, 325,
   326, 327
25.47   54
25.47–54   51
25.48   345
25.48–49   52
25.49   248, 345
25.50   59, 237
25.52   237
25.53   59, 346

25.55   9, 30,
   108, 320, 332,
   333, 342, 347
26   10, 25, 26,
   306, 321
26.1   96, 216,
   248
26.1–2   9
26.1–13   298
26.2   108
26.3   108, 254
26.4   65, 66
26.6   218
26.7   326
26.8   259, 326
26.9   108, 320,
   332
26.11   108, 320,
   331, 332
26.12   21, 320,
   332
26.13   9, 30,
   108, 298, 320,
   332, 333, 342,
   347
26.14   319, 331,
   332
26.14–45   298
26.15   108
26.16   220, 268,
   320, 332
26.17   326, 327,
   332

| | | |
|---|---|---|
| 26.18 221, 319, 320, 331, 332 | 27 17 | 10.20 184 |
| 26.20 65 | 27.9 230 | 11.22 184 |
| 26.21 221, 319, 320, 331, 332 | 27.14 230 | 12 98 |
| 26.22 320, 332 | 27.16 230 | 12.1–14.21 10 |
| 26.23 248, 319, 331, 332 | 27.22 230 | 12.3 214 |
| 26.24 260, 320, 332 | **Numbers** | 13.5 184 |
| 26.25 248, 320, 326, 332 | 1–10 20 | 13.18 184 |
| 26.26 48, 255, 320, 332 | 5.3 232 | 14.8 184 |
| 26.27 319, 331, 332 | 6.9 261 | 16.2 186 |
| 26.28 320, 332 | 6.18 261 | 16.6 215 |
| 26.29 48, 327 | 10.3 185 | 20.1 189 |
| 26.30 331 | 10.4 185 | 21.12 261 |
| 26.33 320, 332 | 10.8 185 | 23.12 184 |
| 26.34 65, 218 | 10.10 185 | 27–28 10 |
| 26.35 65, 217 | 16.26 184 | 28.10 189 |
| 26.36 327 | 19.16 184 | 28.60 184 |
| 26.38 65, 212, 326 | 19.19 184 | 30.20 184 |
| 26.39 327 | 19.22 184 | 31.19 207 |
| 26.40–41 320 | 22.31 239 | 32.17 186 |
| 26.42 108 | 33.52 213 | 32.26 218 |
| 26.42–45 26 | 36.7 184 | **Joshua** |
| 26.43 65, 108 | 36.9 184 | 5 18 |
| 26.44 108, 238 | **Deuteronomy**, 1, 25, 26, 45–46, 52–55, 98, 358 | 6.4 185 |
| 26.45 9, 30–31, 108 | 1.29 189 | 6.8 185 |
| 26.46 298, 332 | 2.4 189 | 6.9 185 |
| | 2.7 236 | 6.13 185 |
| | 5–11 112 | 6.16 185 |
| | 5.5 189 | 6.20 185 |
| | 5.25–27 339 | 9.19 184 |
| | 7.18 189 | 10.8 189 |
| | 7.24 214 | 10.26 217 |
| | | 11.6 189 |
| | | 11.17 217 |
| | | 17.13 220 |

22.5   184
23.8   184
23.12   184

**Judges**
2.5   186
2.15   186
3.27   185
6.21   184
6.34   185
7.18   185
7.19   185
7.20   185, 221
9.48   222
10.9   186
11.7   186
16.14   185

**1 Samuel**
1.3   186
3.13   234
6.9   184
7.7   189
8.7–9   255
8.10   255
9.15   239
10.26   184
13.3   185
13.6   186
15.15   186
15.21   186
16.2   186
16.5   186
17.5   257
18.12   189

18.29   189
21.13   189
26.3   165
28.15   186
28.20   189
30.6   186

**2 Samuel**
1.26   186
2.28   185
4.7   217
5.8   184
11.25   220
12.15   187
13.2   186
14.26   261
14.33   187
15.5   187
16.5   234
16.7   234
18.15   217
18.16   185
19.40   187
20.1   185
20.2   184
20.9   187
20.22   185
21.8   187
21.17   217
24.14   186

**1 Kings**
1.34   185
1.39   185
1.50   189

3.28   189
6.38   238
8.63   186
11.2   184
16.10   217
16.23   173
18.7   91
18.34   236–237
19.18   187
19.20   187
22.10   257

**2 Kings**
1.15   189
5.10   184
5.12   184
5.27   184
9.13   185
15.10   217
15.30   217
17.35   186
17.36   186
18.6   184
19.6   189
23.5   218
23.11   218
25.21   238
25.24   189
25.26   189

**Isaiah**
1.2   205
1.11   236
32.6   236

**Jeremiah**, 104–5
11.21  207
15.10  234
29.7  105

**Ezekiel**, 11

**Zechariah**
1.2  102

**Malachi**
3.11  236

**Psalms**
62.5  234

**Proverbs**
20.20  234

**Ecclesiastes**
7.21  234

**Ezra**
3.10  257

**1 Chronicles**
8.9  219

**2 Chronicles**
5.12  257
18.9  257

# About the Team

Alessandra Tosi was the managing editor for this book and provided quality control.

Anne Burberry performed the copyediting of the book in Word. The fonts used in this volume are Charis SIL, SBL Hebrew, and SBL Greek.

Cameron Craig created all of the editions — paperback, hardback, and PDF. Conversion was performed with open source software freely available on our GitHub page at https://github.com/OpenBookPublishers.

Jeevanjot Kaur Nagpal designed the cover of this book. The cover was produced in InDesign using Fontin and Calibri fonts.

# Cambridge Semitic Languages and Cultures

## General Editor Geoffrey Khan

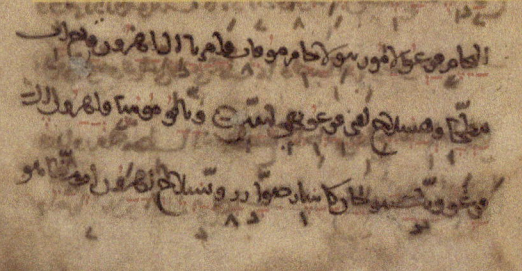
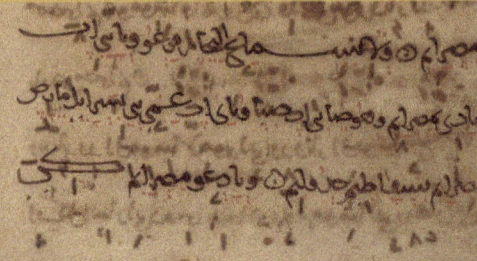
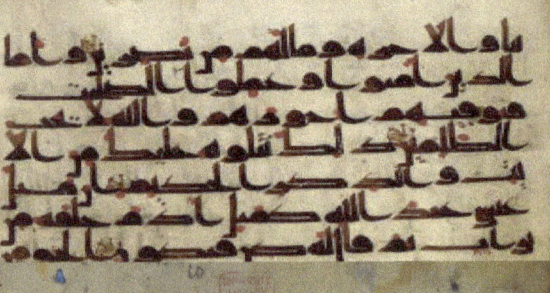

www.ingramcontent.com/pod-product-compliance
Lightning Source LLC
Chambersburg PA
CBHW062025290426
44108CB00025B/2782